MILTON AND THE PAULINE TRADITION

A Study of Theme and Symbolism

Timothy J. O'Keeffe
Southern Connecticut State College

UNIVERSITY
PRESS OF
AMERICA

LANHAM • NEW YORK • LONDON

Copyright © 1982 by

University Press of America,™ Inc.

4720 Boston Way
Lanham, MD 20706

3 Henrietta Street
London WC2E 8LU England

Library of Congress Cataloging in Publication Data

O'Keeffe, Timothy J.
    Milton and the Pauline tradition.

    Bibliography: p.
    Includes index.
    1. Milton, John, 1608–1674–Religion and ethics. 2.
Paul, the Apostle, Saint. 3. Bible. N.T. Epistles of Paul–
Criticism, interpretation, etc. I. Title.
PR3592.R4038   821'.4   80–5892
ISBN 0–8191–2453–2   AACR2
ISBN 0–8191–2454–0 (pbk.)

To All Those In My Family Who Have Passed On
"To Fresh Woods, and Pastures New"

ACKNOWLEDGEMENTS

I would like to acknowledge permission by the following publishers to quote from the following works:

Abingdon Press for Interpreters Dictionary of the Bible, 1962.

Bobbs-Merrill Educational Publishing for John R. Mulder, The Temple of the Mind, 1969.

The Catholic University of America Press for Apologetical Works and Minucius Felix, trans. Rudolph Arbersmann et al., 1950.

Funeral Orations by St. Gregory Nazianzen and St. Ambrose, trans. Leo P. McCawley, S.J. et al., 1953.

St. Basil, Ascetical Works, trans. Sister M. Monica Wagner, C.S.C., 1950.

Saint Cyprian: Treatises, trans. & ed. Roy J. Defarrari, 1958.

Columbia University Press for John Diekhoff, Paradise Lost: A Commentary on the Argument, 1958.

Concordia Publishing House for Luther's Works, Vol. 26, 1963; Vol. 27, 1964, Vol. 29, 1968.

Cornell University Press for Irene Samuel, Plato and Milton, 1965.

Duquesne University Press for Th'Upright Heart and Pure: Essays on John Milton, ed. Amadeus P. Fiore, O.P., 1967.

Frederick Ungar Publishing Co. for Michel de Montaigne, In Defense of Raymond Sebond, 1959.

Houghton Mifflin & Co. for The Complete Poetical Works of John Milton, ed. Douglas Bush for the Cambridge Editions, Copyright (c) 1965 by Douglas Bush.

The Huntington Library for Joseph Wittreich, Visionary Poetics, 1979.

John Knox Press for Rudolph Bultmann, _The Old and the New Man in the Letters of St. Paul_, trans. Keith R. Crim, 1967.

Magi Books for St. Thomas Aquinas, _Commentary on St. Paul's Epistle to the Galatians_, trans. F.R. Larcher, 1966.

Mouton & Co. for Thomas Kranidas, _The Fierce Equation_, 1965.

Northwestern University Press for Michael Fixler, _Milton and the Kingdoms of God_, 1964.

The Society for Promoting Christian Knowledge for _Tertullian's Treatise on the Resurrection_, trans. Ernest Evans, 1960.

University of Toronto Press for Northrop Frye, _The Return of Eden_, 1965 and _Essays in English Literature from the Renaissance to the Victorian Age_, 1964.

William B. Eerdmans Publishing Co. for E. Earle Ellis, _Paul and His Recent Interpreters_, 1961.

Yale University Press for _The Complete Prose Works_, ed. Don M. Wolfe et al. 8 Vols. 1953--.

TABLE OF CONTENTS

PREFACE

The following study arose from a dissertation that focused on patterns of imagery in John Milton's prose. In this effort it became apparent that the exploration of the historical development of the images from various sources, such as classical, biblical, folkloric, or encyclopedic was more interesting than merely describing the patterns. Biblical imagery per se was too large a topic, and James Sims had earlier explored the biblical influence on Milton. The Epistles of St. Paul alone provided sufficient material for a serious study.

The choice of St. Paul's letters was appropriate because basic motifs emanating from them cropped up everywhere in Milton's prose and poetry. Then, too, no part of the Bible seemed to determine the meaning of Christianity more than did Paul's letters, with their critical interpretation of the crucifixion and death of Jesus of Nazareth, and its impact on Judaism and the Hellenic world of ideas. At the same time, the Columbia index to the Complete Works revealed a staggering number of citations to the Epistles. Working from innumerable and haphazard references seemed fitter for a computer than the mind of this writer, and so an effort was made to reread the works of Paul, genuine or questionable, and the Acts of the Apostles (although of dubious accuracy) from the perspective of a seventeenth-century humanist.

The obvious symbolic motifs in the Epistles are discussed in the ensuing pages not as poetic ornaments as depicted in Renaissance-poetics handbooks but as symbolic strands providing a basis for interpreting the meaning of Christianity as Milton understood it. Symbolism in this profound sense also includes ideas that interweave with imagery both to envision religious notions and rationalize theological subtleties of vital interest to the Reformation and Milton. As an example, symbolic parallels appeared between Paul's view of the Mosaic law and the Reformers' view of canon law, and the claims of the Pharisees and Sadducees to understand the will of God through the Law and canon lawyers were based on the same intoxication with self sixteen-hundred years apart--as Luther and others saw it.

However, no leap of faith or theological intuition was necessary to cover the historical gap, for the Church Fathers, especially Augustine and Chrysostom, had established a tradition of commentary that was to continue through Aquinas and into the Reformation. The major Reformers, such as Luther and Calvin, produced an extensive set of commentaries on the scriptures, providing a defense of their positions. Examining just these two provided sufficient background for Milton's use of what had become the Pauline tradition. A perusal of other, sometimes more conservative, figures such as Colet and Hooker shed other light on Milton's reading of the letters of St. Paul. It soon became difficult to know at what point to stop reading the many thinkers in the sixteenth and seventeenth centuries who exploited Paul to buttress both political and religious arguments.

In his prose Milton used the Epistles consciously to reenforce contentions on church government, divorce, and political theory from the 1640's to the 1660's. Pauline symbolism offered structural, dramatic, and thematic pattern and texture for Milton's poetry, especially the major epic, symbolism which no doubt came to him naturally and immediately. His major themes in _Paradise Lost_ almost indivisible from those of the Epistles, are written in some cases in the very language of the Apostle.

I am indebted to the work of modern theologians like Cerfaux, Bultmann, and Bornkamm and to the excellent scholarship on Milton's prose and poetry. Specific indebtedness is of course cited, but there is a larger debt to these workers in the academic vineyard and to the various fine editions and explanations of both Milton's prose and poetry. I have usually cited the prose in the Columbia edition for the sake of consistency but have taken advantage of the introductions and notes in the continuing Yale edition. All references to the poems are to the helpful edition of Douglas Bush, and all biblical quotations are from the King James version.

Finally, I would like to thank all those who directly or indirectly assisted me in a project that has taken several years to complete and several more to get published. J. Max Patrick and John T. Shawcross both read the manuscript in its basic form and offered constructive suggestions. Southern Connecticut State College granted me a sabbatical to prepare the final copy, and I am indebted to all those responsible for that precious time, so necessary to finish the text. My wife not only typed but helped edit the final copy while tolerating the anxieties of a spouse looking over her shoulder. Ultimately the responsibility for any and all defects must be mine.

The need to support a family both economically and emotionally and to make a slight contribution to our understanding of John Milton, a great poet and thinker, has pulled me to and fro. The former responsibility is both demanding and rewarding but also immediate while the latter is equally demanding and rewarding but less immediate. I trust, nevertheless, that the pages that follow will demonstrate the task was worth it after all, to parody myself more than Prufrock.

INTRODUCTION

What direction Christianity would have taken if
Saul of Tarsus had not experienced a violent reversal
of his persecution of the early Jewish Christians and
had not written his letters to his various congregations is a matter for conjecture. Outside of the
possibility that the new sect would have remained confined to those Jews who felt that Jesus of Nazareth
was the Messiah, it is likely that the teachings and
actions of the carpenter's son would have been the
only foci of Christianity. Paul's role was to focus
on the signal event in Jesus' life, his death and
resurrection, and to amplify the impact of this
miraculous sequence for those who listened to his
preaching and had his Epistles read to them. Thus
Paul became an apologist and propagandist for the new
religion, "the Chosen Vessel," as St. Jerome called
him.[1] Albert Schweitzer noticed that the Acts of the
Apostles contains no references to any literature of
Paul's, and only later were there any allusions to
his Epistles by Clement of Rome, Ignatius, and the
Gnostics.[2] Paul's letters reflect controversy in
most cases because he was steering Christianity into
a direction which others found shocking or unpleasant.
For example, St. Peter regarded the Mosaic rites as
essential for new Christians, but Paul was adamant
about the freedom from these obligations that Christ
had brought to his followers. Centuries later, in
the Reformation, Paul again became the center of controversy, and, as shall be shown, in ways strikingly
similar to the manner in which he had been controversial during his lifetime.

Paul decided that he had to make a final and
irreversible break from the past, that he had to
oppose Christ to the Torah, and that he had to condemn
those Jews who refused to see Jesus as the Christ.
In doing so, he may have been guilty of setting in
motion the cancer of anti-Semitism by rejecting the
beliefs of Judaism and, to less tutored minds, rejecting the Jews as a people. However, the early
Jewish Christians did not all assume that they had

1

to choose one fork in the road over another. Jacob
S. Raisin, from the Judaic standpoint, has remarked
that

> The Judeo-Christians also on their side at
> first regarded themselves as part and par-
> cel of the House of Israel and were all
> zealous for the Torah . . . . the Judeo-
> Christians, even after they organized a
> congregation of their own, did not sever
> their relation with Catholic Israel. Ex-
> cept for their belief that Jesus was the
> promised Messiah, they clung to the fun-
> damental doctrines and ceremonies of Juda-
> ism. They observed the Abrahamic rite,
> rested on the Sabbath, celebrated the fes-
> tivals, and like strict Pharisees fasted
> on Mondays and Thursdays. . . . They ne-
> ver faltered in their loyalty to the "Law,
> the Prophets, and the Lord."[3]

Nevertheless, Paul's rejection of the core of beliefs of a nation and his view of the Jews as a stubborn people to whom Christ became "a stumbling
block" set the pattern for attacks on Jews as a
"stiff-necked people" who had rejected the truth
and executed the Son of God.

Interestingly enough, the traditional portrait
of the Pharisees for Christians, first painted by
Paul, and then copied for generations without question, that they were legalistic drones, may be entirely without foundation. The term Pharisee has
come to mean someone who glorifies the letter of
the law over its spirit and who insists on rigidity
of belief and observance. The Pharisees intended
not to solidify but to make the Torah more flexible,
to provide a guideline for the Jews for every conceivable moral situation in which a man could find
himself. No doubt, some Pharisees were carried a-
way with the details of the Law, but Jeremiah had
earlier warned about this external concept of the
Law, which represented the way of God, the Creator
of the universe. The Lord would, he said, make a
new covenant: "I will put my law in their inward
parts, and write it in their hearts"(Jer. 31.33).

2

S. S. Cohon has also pointed out how the Rabbis censured those who would make the study of and obedience
to the Torah not an end in itself but a means of
self-aggrandizement.[4] St. Paul, after his dramatic
conversion on the road to Damascus, exhibited a familiar human trait, of inverting his position 180
degrees and switching from the role of persecutor
of Christians to enemy of the exaltation of the Torah above Christ.

Paul admitted his problem to the Galatians but
nonetheless interpreted its solution as glorifying
God:

> For ye have heard of my conversation in
> time past in the Jews' religion, how that
> beyond measure I persecuted the church of
> God, and wasted it.
> And profited in the Jews' religion above
> my equals in mine own nation, being more
> exceedingly zealous of the traditions of
> my fathers.
> . . . .
> Neither went I up to Jerusalem to them
> which were apostles before me; but I went
> into Arabia, and returned again unto Damas-
> cus.
> Then after three years I went up to Je-
> rusalem to see Peter, and abode with him
> fifteen days. (2. 13-14, 17-18)

The Acts of the Apostles records this meeting with
Peter, which took place because Paul and Barnabas
were having difficulties with the gospel message.
At the council a group of Pharisees raised the
question of circumcision, which becomes for Paul
and for his commentators through the Reformation
the symbol of the ceremonial law. Peter and the
Pharisees wished to require circumcision of the Gentile converts (Acts 15). Paul and Barnabas won
their point, and it was not required of the new converts, but from a purely utilitarian missionary
point of view, it is hard to blame Paul and Barnabas for their stand. How many adult male Gentiles
would have been willing to succumb to a painful
operation in order to become Christians? On the
other hand, the Jews more than likely took the position that the ceremonial law was designed to

increase piety, to make man more aware of his responsibilities to his Maker. There was no compromise
in any case except that the missionary field was divided up, and Jewish Christians evidently continued
the practice of circumcision and other rites of the
Torah.

From the above it might seem that Paul entirely rejected Judaism, but this is not the case at all.
As shall be seen in Chapter One, Paul's attitude toward the nature of man and of the flesh is distinctly Hebraic and not at all Hellenic or Platonic. Briefly, the Greeks observed a very sharp distinction between the soul and body, with clear and emphatic approval of the former and equally clear and emphatic
disapproval of the latter--at least those Greeks
following the teachings of Socrates and Plato. The
Homeric Greeks accepted no such disapproval of the
bodily side of man. This distinction passed into
Christianity not from Judaism but from the Platonic
and Aristotelian influences which penetrated Christianity from St. Paul himself but especially from Augustine and later Aquinas. Nevertheless, a careful
investigation reveals that St. Paul's concept of
what is translated into English as "the flesh" reveals that his censures of the flesh are not what
one would expect. He is not condemning matter, as
the Manicheans did, nor the flesh as an obstructive
shell, as the Platonists did, but applying a correc-
tive to man in his hostility toward God. The self
of man and not his body of flesh, his self-confid-
ence (really arrogance), causes sin and evil, not
the fact that his soul is hampered by existence in
the body, as for example, Andrew Marvell's dialogue
poems between the soul and body or pleasure drama-
tize the conflict. The attitude of Paul is the attitude of Judaism, that "No unbridgeable gap exists
between the body and spirit, nor is the flesh vile
and corrupt."5 Paul, then, does not regard the fleshly appetites as evil anymore than did Milton centuries later, for the poet, in his maturity, reflects the Pauline stance.

Paul has been called "the elusive Apostle," and
it is no easy task to ascertain precisely what he
means all the time. In fact, Albert Schweitzer makes

4

the entertaining comment that "the Apostle always becomes unintelligible just at the moment when he begins to explain something."[6] Part of the problem resides in the fact that, unlike St. Thomas Aquinas,
who summarized medieval belief, or Milton, who wrote
Of Christian Doctrine as a systematic exposition of
Protestant belief, Paul was writing letters to various congregations who had assorted moral or spiritual difficulties. He was addressing himself to specific dilemmas as they arose, as a kind of epistola-
ry troubleshooter, whether it was a question of the
"super" or "pseudo" apostles challenging his authority, allegiance to the Torah, or the question of re-
turning a slave to his owner. Adolph Deissman notes
that Paul had no developed system of ethics or escha-
tology.[7] A second area of confusion is based on
Paul's assertion that he was "all things to all men,"
and he felt he had to be to tailor his appeal to multifarious cultural groups. As different people read
the Epistles, they seem to read into Paul what they
wish to see or what their age seems to see. Luther
could conclude that Paul was "the most stubborn foe
of free choice,"[8] while Milton could imbibe much
from Paul and yet maintain that man's reason and
will exercised themselves in matters of moral choice.
Further, to read about Christ from Paul without reference to the story of Jesus' life in the Gospels
is to miss his human dimension. One finds little
warmth and humanity in much of the theological polemics of the major writers of the Reformation since
they are more interested in the relationship between
Christ's sacrifice and righteousness or justification, as was Paul.

Paul's main themes of love or charity, the unity
of the church through the body of Christ, the rejection of the Mosaic law (partial or complete) and the
substitution of the Gospel, the need for justification through faith in Christ, the rejection of the
wisdom of the Greek world, the parallel between the
old man and the new, the eschatological hope of man-
kind--these are presented in a style that is sometimes polemical, sometimes ironic, sometimes rhap-
sodic, but always fascinating. Very early Augustine
had pointed out Paul's use of antithesis in the context of God's creating "the beauty of the universe

5

. . . out of contraries."[9] More than likely this rhetorical habit was part of the classical training he had received at Tarsus, for throughout the Epistles Paul, like Milton, is fond of setting up antithetical themes and images: new man-old man, light-dark, freedom-slavery, harmony-disharmony, etc. Paul's imagery finds sustenance in frequently homely and everyday situations, just as had Jesus' parables. Paul's audiences were largely composed of average citizens and not the aristocracy or the sophisticated. The story of his failure in Athens to proselytize the cosmopolitans, as told in the Acts of the Apostles, provides us with a basis for seeing a degree of tension in the style of the Apostle to the Gentiles. Although he was obviously trained as a rhetorician and often employed prosopopœia and antithesis, for example, he harbored a strong resentment against the "jangling" of the schools, a disharmony of mind which constituted noise without the addition of charity to temper the elevation of the ego through knowledge and rhetorical training. Adolph Deissman has characterized Paul's Greek as unliterary but without vulgarism,[10] a style designed to reach as many as possible while offending as few as possible.

It is the thesis of Wayne Meeks that Paul can be read intelligently if one attempts to ascertain the arguments of Paul's opponents through his responses. In this light the issues become clear under the pressure of controversy, and it may be that Christianity has been shaped to a degree by these arguments and by Paul's fondness for dialectical debate. This view of the Epistles may also explain the apparent self-contradictions in Paul, such as his emphasis to the Galatians on the freedom that Christ brings while his instructions to the Corinthians emphasize rules and control.[11] Evidently someone among the Galatians was insisting on the Mosaic law while Corinth, known as a city of sin in the first century, from Paul's perspective, needed some control. One of his foes among the Corinthians may have argued that Christ's sacrifice had eliminated all sanctions against the sins of the body, and therefore the day could be seized with impunity. In the midst of such controversy Paul could write

6

glowing, memorable descriptions of charity or dis-
arm his readers by the casual remark about himself
that at one point he did not know whether he was in
the body or out of it--a mystic's unself-conscious-
ness.

As a person, St. Paul has not often been regarded as warm and kind anymore than could Milton on
the basis of his controversial prose. When an individual is involved in dialectical combat, he cannot
appear as the epitome of sweet reasonableness, even
though this image befit the mild-mannered Richard
Hooker, who came as close as one could to such perfection. As W. Wrede remarked, "The more humane
virtues of reasonableness and fairness, magnanimity,
tolerance, and respect for every personal right . .
. . did not constitute the strength of Paul. But
it is due to him to remember that they did not constitute the strength of Christianity in that age."[12]
St. Jerome, something of a polemicist himself, contrasted the sternness of Paul with the gentleness of
Barnabas.[13] Milton's term for Paul, the "transcendent Apostle," suggests more admiration for than love
of the man who influenced him, the Reformation, and
Christianity.

The major impact on his life was his sudden,
dramatic awareness of Christ, but this dynamic assault happened to a man who was a Jew, supposedly a
student of Gamaliel, and who was trained in the classical tradition. Acts 9 describes Saul's experience:

> AND Saul, yet breathing out threatenings and
> slaughter against the disciples of the Lord,
> went unto the high priest.

> And desired of him letters to Damascus to the
> synagogues, that if he found any of this way,
> whether they were men or women, he might
> bring them bound unto Jerusalem.

> And as he journeyed, he came near Damascus:
> and suddenly there shined round about him a
> light from heaven:

> And he fell to the earth, and heard a voice
> saying unto him, Saul, Saul, why persecutest

thou me?

And he said, Who art thou, Lord? And the
Lord said, I am Jesus whom thou persecu-
test: it is hard for thee to kick against
the pricks.

And he trembling and astonished said, Lord
what wilt thou have me to do? And the Lord
said unto him, Arise and go into the city,
and it shall be told thee what thou must do.

And the men which journeyed with him stood
speechless, hearing a voice, but seeing no
man.

And Saul arose from the earth; and when his
eyes were opened, he saw no man: but they led
him by the hand, and brought him into Damascus.

Analysis fails before such an account, and without
doubt, the experience inverted Paul's psyche completely. Nevertheless, as has been said above, Paul
maintained much of his Jewish heritage, and his
thinking in major and minor ways remained Judaic or
at least found source in the Old Testament. The ty-
pological importance of Adam and Abraham as figures
in the Epistles, for example, cannot be forgotten.
The former (depending upon the translation of Romans 5.12) is responsible for Original Sin, which
must be overturned by the new Adam, Christ. The latter becomes representative to Paul of a covenant of
faith and not of works of the Mosaic law. Consequently, even though Paul rebels against fundamental Judaism, he does so on the basis of what he conceives the role of Judaism to be in the scales of
divine providence. Even in small ways, Paul reflects
Jewish lore, such as his demand that women cover
their heads in worship because the angels above would
get impure thoughts by seeing the glory of women,
their hair. Even while repudiating his heritage, he
cannot ignore it.

Paul's hellenism also appears in various guises
besides his literary style. He evidently favored the
Septuagint over the Hebrew texts of the Bible, a

8

surprising choice since it was a translation and not
the original text. His reactions against the claims
of the Greek world to wisdom have already been mentioned, but one of the thematic elements in the Epistles, particularly those to the Galatians (regarded
by Luther as a declaration of independence from the
Mosaic law and therefore the canon as well) was the
concept of freedom. This notion was not at all Hebraic but hellenic, as the development of democracy
testifies. The phrasing of this idea of Christ's
freeing man, as Adolph Deissman says, is based on
the idea of a slave buying back his freedom by get-
ting enough money and arranging for one of the gods
in the temples to sponsor his manumission. In this
way, Christ buys the Christian his freedom from the
slavery of sin by his sacrifice on the cross.[14]
Paul, his commentators, and the Reformers, including Milton, never seemed to question the validity of
slavery but were content to employ the metaphor to
typify the condition of remaining in sin. Later ages
came to see the evils of slavery and to distinguish
between Paul's cultural bent and his witness to eternal truth. Thus, those who would insist that women
should never enter the ordained ministry do so on
the basis that Paul placed women in a secondary position in the church. Others would insist that on
this question, as on the issue of slavery, Paul was
simply a man of his time and limited by that time's
perspective.

Throughout this study, that a most definitive
tradition of commentaries on the Pauline epistles appeared becomes obvious. If St. Paul developed certain themes and symbolic patterns in his letters,
these were carefully explored and explained by commentators, from the early church, through the Middle
Ages, and into the Reformation. The first and perhaps best of all of them, who is quoted and cited
by his successors repeatedly, is St. John Chrysostom, who was deeply influenced by Paul. As a recent
translator asserted about Chrysostom's work, he "has
left us as many as 250 homilies on the Epistles of
St. Paul . . . which are generally considered to be
the finest commentary ever written on the Epistles
of the Apostle of the Gentiles."[15] Part of the reason for Chrysostom's success as an interpreter of

9

Paul was the fact that he was quite fluent in Greek
and explained vexed passages with sensitivity and
understanding and that the early world of the church
had not changed very much since Paul had lived. To
indicate how highly Chrysostom was held in esteem,
the first Greek book printed in England was De
Joannis Chrysostomi Homiliae duo in 1543 in St.
Paul's Churchyard, London.[16] Indeed, Luther developed his lectures on the Epistle to the Hebrews
partially on the basis of quotations from Chrysostom.[17]

St. Thomas Aquinas wrote commentaries on Paul's
letters between 1259 and 1265, and 1272 and 1273.
Section One, from Romans 1.1 to I Corinthians 7.9,
constitutes his work, but the remainder was written
from his notes by Peter of Tarentasia and Reginald
of Pyperino. Unfortunately Thomas was commenting
only on the Vulgate and did not understand Hebrew or
Greek as far as is known.[18]

This study has searched outside strictly Pauline
commentaries when a particular author, whether in the
early church or during the Reformation, built much of
his theological stance on the basis of what he saw in
the Pauline epistles or when Milton made a habit of
referring to these particular matters in contexts
related to the Pauline themes and symbolic patterns
examined here. Therefore, St. Augustine could hardly
be ignored, and indeed the title and thrust of one of
his shorter works, On the Spirit and the Letter,
reflects his careful reading of St. Paul. Further,
one editor has remarked that the Pauline Epistles
were the dominant influence on Augustine Christianity.
Another gives equal proportion to both "Platonic
thought and Pauline motives."[19]

By the time of the Reformation the stage was
set for the Reformers to write voluminous commentaries
on all the epistles, including the pastorals, which
some scholars found of debatable authorship. Luther
and Calvin wrote more than anyone else on Paul, an
indication that the epistles were centrally fixed to
the Reformation's development. Albert Schweitzer has
argued that "The Reformation fought and conquered in
the name of Paul. Consequently the teaching of the

10

Apostle of the Gentiles took a prominent place in
Protestant study."[20] The Reformation had a habit
of citing Paul in defense of its positions, such as
the doctrine of election, of theological deter-
minism, that is, a denial of the efficacy of free
will, or the stress on faith, and of the repudiation
of works in the scheme of salvation. For the Reformers the medieval emphasis on works was attacked
as a violation of the immensity of Christ's sacrifice
and an indication of the arrogance of canon lawyers
who assumed, like Pelagius, that man basically could
save himself by his own works. For a theologian like
John Colet, who was deeply influenced by Marsilio
Ficino, Paul's occasional Platonic coloring, his
desire to be freed from the body of flesh, attracted
him most. But whatever the appeal, Colet's effusive
comment on Paul's richness is not atypical: "Yet I
think that no one can explain it all. For so great
is the treasure, and so abundant the store, of wisdom
and divineness hidden in the Apostle's language,
that, whatever any one may have quarried and brought
forth from the mine, there will still ever be an
inexhaustible remainder, to be brought to light by
some wise man."[21]

    John Milton shares with the Reformers this
admiration for St. Paul, and although _Of Christian_
Doctrine is not a commentary on the Pauline epistles,
throughout this work and Milton's polemical prose
there appear innumerable allusions to St. Paul, direct
and indirect. His poetry, especially _Paradise Lost_,
also manifests the influence that the "transcendent
Apostle" had on the mature Milton. He and the Reformers found of supreme importance the fact of the
Redemption and not the humanity of Christ in the sense
of the recollection of a warm human being (albeit
possessed of divinity) who suffered little children
to come unto him. St. Paul, as has been perceived by
W. Wrede, presents a Jesus whose humanity is that of
an "impalpable phantom," and the Reformers followed
this portrayal. Milton's early "Nativity Ode" and
"Upon the Circumcision" demonstrate in differing ways
how the poet found it easier to come to terms with
the theological abstractions of the incarnation and
redemption than to sense the experiential selfhood

11

of Christ. In the mature _Paradise_ _Regain'd_ there
is a noble attempt to portray the Son of God as a
man approaching the epiphany of his divinity, even
though, as _Of_ _Christian_ _Doctrine_ testifies, this
divinity does not equal the Father's. Nevertheless,
most readers find the hero of the poem somewhat
cerebral, cold, and forbidding.

Luther, Calvin, Melanchthon, and the rest of
the Reformers also view the Pauline parallel between
the first Adam and the second Adam of Romans in a
similar vein. The Christ becomes the "one greater
Man" who overturns the balance of guilt and rescues
mankind both by sacrifice and by example, evincing
for man the virtues of faith, patience, trust, and
obedience, and offering himself as a voluntary sacrifice for the seduced couple in the Garden of Eden.
In this sense, the true hero of _Paradise_ _Lost_ is
Adam-Christ, neither precisely one nor the other
since they are united together thematically as
unwilling and willing victim. Both must suffer for
their manhood, the first for the sin of sentimentalism or uxoriousness and the second because he
must expiate the sin of the first, and the only way
that he can is as true man. Through the proto-
evangelium and her love of Adam, Eve becomes the
heroine of the poem after her betrayal of her husband.

Milton's treatment of the Redemption by Christ
reveals his emphasis on the act of love by the Son
which restores man to a point where he is not as
depraved as Calvin imagines him to be. C. A. Patrides
has provided a convenient summary of four theories of
the act of divine atonement:

(1) Recapitulation--in terms of the Adam parallel;
(2) Ransom--God is forced to pay the devil his
due;
(3) Satisfaction to God--God's honor must be
assuaged; and,
(4) Legal-Penal Substitution--according to
Luther and Calvin, God's wrath must be
satisfied by punishment.[22]

The language of Book Three of _Paradise Lost_ contains
some ambiguities as to which theory Milton embraces,
but it is patently evident that the most suitable
explanation in the poem encompasses the notion of
Redemption as an act of love, that the Son offers
himself with that selfless impulse to save mankind.
Elias Andrewes has cited Romans 5.8 and Second Corinthians as demonstrating that the act of the Cross
represented the supreme performance of love for Paul
and not a divine demand for rigid justice by the
Father.[23]   In his epic Milton equates the two:
justice is fulfilled by love; and intertwined with
the equation of the Adam-Christ and the love act of
Christ is Milton's humanism which elevates man above
the level of the opinions of Luther and Calvin, who
consistently denigrate the nature and condition of
man. Even when stating precisely that the _flesh_ of
man is not evil since created by God, Calvin falls
back to his position that the nature of man is evil
or prone hopelessly to evil. Perhaps a distinction
should be made between what Calvin consciously concluded from Scripture and what he felt about man as
a result of his own psyche shaped by his experiences
and heritage. Ruth Mohl emphasizes in Milton the
value of man as opposed to the medieval and Reformist
view, which suggests disdain, and reminds us that
there could have been no second Adam unless there
was a first one.[24]

     Milton differs from the Reformers precisely on
the relative importance of love or charity in the
scheme of justification. Luther, obsessed by a sense
of his own guilt and by the temptations of the devil,
found security and a feeling of righteousness only
in the belief that Christ would completely save him
on the basis of faith alone. There was no necessity
for works to insure righteousness before the Lord.
Luther had given up on himself as an instrument,
even partial, of his justification and sanctification
because of his profound sense of unworthiness, and so
the only hope lay in the absoluteness of Christ's
Redemption. Thus faith was the absolute virtue, as
it was for Calvin. Both men and the other Reformers
had a cultural and historical reason as well for
thinking this way.

The medieval church had insisted that love expressed itself through works, and all the legalisms of canon law were set in motion to insure that each Christian performed certain works to guarantee his salvation. In this way Paul's lofty concept of charity or love became equated with rather meaningless actions like having innumerable masses said, repeating stereotyped prayers, and contributing money to the church. Milton agreed with Luther and Calvin that this almost Pelagian emphasis on self-justification through works was legalistically equivalent to the stress of the Pharisees in fulfilling the Mosaic law in order to get oneself right in the eyes of God.[25] Nevertheless, Milton drew the line on the question of whether man could or could not cooperate with the grace that the Redemption bestowed upon him. Once again, Milton's humanistic world-view produced a synergistic compromise, as seen in Paradise Lost. One of the means of salvation that Michael reveals at the end of the poem to Adam is "faith and faithful works," a phrase that most of the Reformers would have found impossible to accept. Milton could accept and even embrace it for he could not tolerate the idea that man was a helpless creature with no ability whatsoever to do good. The Judaic tradition included reason as one of man's ethical attributes, the ability to know the good in order to perform it, and with this view Milton stood in agreement. Finally, to return to complete the circle, as it were, love or charity was for Milton as for Paul, the greatest of the three virtues, faith, hope, and charity as the Protestant poet said in Of Education. Love of God, for Melanchthon and for Milton, was equivalent to obedience, and the upsurge of tone in Book Ten of Paradise Lost results from the theme of love, first expressed by Eve. Luther and Calvin, in their commentaries on Corinthians, had a difficult time with the thirteenth chapter of the first letter, in which St. Paul writes his celebrated hymn or paean on this virtue in memorable imagery. As shall be shown, the Reformers by and large refused to allow this Pauline hierarchy to stand, even though their mentor, Paul, had clearly listed it in the supreme position, but this argument is not settled even today.

Milton did agree with the Reformers on two other

themes that pervade his anti-episcopal tracts and
his mature poetry, particularly _Paradise_ _Lost_ and
Paradise _Regain'd_. The first is the equation of
the Pauline view of the wisdom of the Greeks, of
the world, with the alleged wisdom of Scholastic
thinking and the theology of the high church. The
second is the equation of the liturgy of the churches
of Rome and of England with idolatry, the idolatry
that St. Paul had fulminated against in unmistakable
terms. Paul had seen in the pagan rites of the
Greek world an utter hostility to the worship of
the true God, as he had seen in their philosophy a
contempt for the truth of Christ's _liebestod_. Both
he and the other Church Fathers like Augustine
ridiculed the learning of the Greeks, which constituted the only learning of the world as far as they
were concerned. For Paul and the tradition that
followed him, the learning of the classical world
was meaningless in the light of its completely
ignoring the essential truth of Christ's redeeming
all men, and this tradition is the rationale for the
Son's rejection of the sophistication of Athens in
Paradise _Regain'd_. Secondly, the learning of the
Greek could hardly be considered worthy of respect
since these allegedly sophisticated people still
worshipped bestial and absurd idols. Albert
Schweitzer points out how the powers of evil, for
Paul, still dominate those who offer sacrifice to
idols despite the freedom from the Powers effected
by the resurrection of Christ.[26] And so in _Para-
dise_ _Lost_ Milton correlates the waywardness of the
Israelites in their worship of idols to the fallen
angels and their idolatry against God by setting
themselves up as gods. Milton also sees in episcopal theology and liturgy the same correlation that
Paul saw in the Greek philosophy and worship of
idols--both are hostile to Christ.

To be more specific, these twin themes symbolize the evil nature of both the churches of the pope
and of William Laud in the 1640's. Both ecclesiastical institutions wish to bring down the spiritual to
the level of worshipping idols, that is, statues,
crucifixes, stained glass windows, holy water, _etc_.,
and this degeneration for the Reformers and Milton
constitutes idolatry. It is the worship of objects

15

and not God, and it also is the product of the arrogance of those who set up the idols. In some sense,
they are substituting themselves for God. In the
same way the theologians of Rome and Canterbury
pretend to a learning which stands in opposition to
the simple truth of the Cross, a basic complaint of
Paul's Epistles with regard to both Greeks and Jews.
All the spinning of cobwebs, as Bacon described
scholasticism, produces nothing despite all the energy
expended in its production, but from the religious
aspect of the argument, it evidences an arrogance of
the self. Man establishes his truth in opposition
to God's; the Aristotelian attempt to intellectualize
the mystery of the cross is engendered by intellectual pride, the worst of sins. Paul had condemned
the Greeks for this sin, and the Reformers and
Milton condemned their opponents for the same offense.

The subsequent chapters will endeavor to define
and illustrate these very important themes in the
Reformation as they were found in the Epistles of
St. Paul and explain where Milton stands as a man of
his time facing religious questions and expressing
his interpretation of the Pauline tradition--explic-
itly in his prose and symbolically in his poetry.

Joseph Wittreich has shown how the tradition of
prophecy based largely on the Book of Revelation
plays an important role in how Milton "sees" his
vision in Lycidas and the major poems.[27] So too,
here, it is important to remember that Milton sees
the problems of the Christian believer and poet
through the language and imagery of the Scriptures.
These don't simply influence his thinking--they are
the conceptualizing and picturing embedded in his
mind, for language, as the venerable Whorfian
hypothesis long ago argued, determines in substantial measure, how we view reality. For Milton and
the serious thinkers of his day, St. Paul's Epistles
were a glass through which they saw, not darkly but
profoundly.

[1]*Against the Pelagians* in *Saint Jerome: Dogmatic and Polemical Works*, trans. John N. Hritzu (Washington, D.C., 1965), p. 261.

[2]*Paul and His Interpreters: A Critical History*, trans. W. Montgomery (London, 1912), p. 119.

[3]*Gentile Reaction to Jewish Ideals*, ed. Herman Hailperin (New York, 1953), p. 333.

[4]*Judaism: A Way of Life* (New York, 1948), p. 129.

[5]*Judaism*, p. 160.

[6]Schweitzer, *Interpreters*, p. 37.

[7]*Paul: A Study in Social and Religious History*, trans. William E. Wilson (London, 1926), p. 50.

[8]*On the Bondage of the Will* in *Luther and Erasmus: Free Will and Salvation*, trans. & ed. Philip S. Watson et al. (Philadelphia, 1969), p. 218.

[9]*City of God*, trans. John Healey, ed. R.V.G. Trasker (London, 1967), I, 327.

[10]Deissmann, *Paul*, p. 50.

[11]"Paul as Heretic," course at Yale Divinity School, spring, 1970.

[12]*Paul*, trans. Edward Lummis (London, 1907), p. 38.

[13]*Against the Pelagians*, p. 323.

[14]*Light From the Ancient East*, trans. Lionel R.M. Strachan (New York, 1910), pp. 322-328.

[15]Rev. Thomas Halton, trans., *In Praise of Saint Paul* by St. John Chrysostom (Washington, D.C., 1963), p. 9.

[16] J.H. Lupton, trans., _An Exposition of St. Paul's First Epistle to the Corinthians_ by John Colet (Ridgewood, N.J., 1965), p. 36, n. 1.

[17] _Lectures on Titus, Philemon, and Hebrews_ in Luther's Works, trans. & ed. Jaroslav Pelikan and Walter A. Hansen (St. Louis, 1968), XXIX,xii.

[18] Richard A. Murphy, O.P., trans. & ed. _Commentary on Saint Paul's Epistle to the Galatians_ by St. Thomas Aquinas (Albany, 1966), pp. viii, ix.

[19] Whitney J. Oates, ed., _Basic Writings of Saint Augustine_ (New York, 1948), I, xxi; George G. Leckie, trans., _Concerning the Teacher and On the Immortality of the Soul_ (New York, 1938), pp. ix-x.

[20] Schweitzer, _Interpreters_, p. 2.

[21] _An Exposition of St. Paul's Epistle to the Romans_, trans. J.H. Lupton (Ridgewood, N.J., 1965), pp. 56-57.

[22] _Milton and the Christian Tradition_ (Oxford, 1966), pp. 130-142.

[23] _The Meaning of Christ For Paul_ (New York, 1949), pp. 50, 52-55.

[24] _Studies in Spenser, Milton, and the Theory of Monarchy_ (New York, 1962), pp. 82-86.

[25] See Luther, _Lectures on Galatians, 1535, Chapters 5-6; Lectures on Galatians, 1519, Chapters 1-6_, ed. Jaroslav Pelikan & Walter Hansen, in Luther's Works (St. Louis, 1963), esp. XXVI, 152.

[26] Schweitzer, _Interpreters_, p. 56.

[27] _Visionary Poetics: Milton's Tradition and His Legacy_ (San Marino, 1979).

CHAPTER ONE

THE FLESH: A NEED FOR DEFINITION

Various attempts have been made to classify
Milton as a thinker following this tradition or that:
thus he is seen as a Puritan, a Christian Humanist,
an Independent, a Protestant, and a Christian Platonist.[1] Irene Samuel and Herbert Agar have classified
him as a Christian Platonist in the mold of Augustine
and later of Edmund Spenser.[2] However, there are
different ways that philosophers and poets can be
humanists, and John Donne, Lancelot Andrewes, or
Richard Hooker partake of humanism differently than
John Milton did. There are different ways of being
Platonists, and John Colet or Edmund Spenser join the
ranks of Platonism differently than John Milton did.
For many years now there have been fewer and fewer
scholars using the word "Puritan" to apply to Milton,
and he must in some sense be a Protestant like the
Reformers, Luther, Calvin, Melanchthon, and others.
The object of this chapter is not to claim a final
categorization of Milton as any one of the above
kinds of thinkers or as fitting any special combination but to focus on one facet of Milton's
theological and philosophical orientation which
can clarify our thinking on the entire subject.

All too often a tendency arises to assume that
Milton developed and maintained a negative attitude
toward the flesh, a tendency only mitigated in the
description in Book Four of _Paradise Lost_ of the
connubial relationship of Adam and Eve before the
Fall. The concept of the flesh is extremely compli-
cated in Western thought, especially considering
the triple confluence in the Renaissance of Judaic,
Christian, and Platonic and Neoplatonic viewpoints.
An examination of some of the key philosophic figures
from Plato to the Protestant Reformers reveals that
Milton's reaction to the concept of the flesh is
based significantly on St. Paul's Epistles, where
the flesh or _sarx_ is not identical with the desires
of the body or glands but is more closely identified
with the _soma_ or human self which opposes the absolute

divinity. The sins of the flesh cover a multitude, and they are not the result of the husk or shell or prison house of the body or flesh (Platonic concepts). The flesh or glandular body is not evil or negative but must be subsumed as a part of man's nature, which will eventually, in a glorified state (according to Paul), join the soul so that the whole entity of man will achieve justification in the eyes of God. This brief summary represents Milton's mature thought on the subject and not the stagey or pseudo-platonism of A Mask.[3] In this position Milton is supported by St. Paul, Tertullian, Aquinas, and the major Reformers.

Negative statements about the flesh will be found in Milton's prose, but these represent a negative feeling, in general, toward "carnal" or "fleshly" minded men, who suffer from a distorted sense of values and who put their self above Christ's sacrifice in the process of justification and salvation. In the divorce tracts, by and large, the term "flesh" refers specifically to the physical side of marriage, as might be expected, but the general use of the word has not been properly highlighted in the past.

But first to some basic historical definition. Tertullian offers a graphic synopsis of the Greek view of the body in his treatise on the resurrection:

Is there not, forthwith and throughout [the Gentile world], reviling of the flesh, attacks upon its origin, its material, its fate, its whole destiny, as being from its first beginning foul from the excrement of the earth, more foul thereafter because of the slime of its own seed, paltry, unstable, reproachable, troublesome, burdensome, and (following on the whole indictment of its baseness) fated to fall back into the earth from whence it came and to be described as a corpse, and destined to perish from that description too into no description at all from thenceforth, into a death of any and every designation?[4]

Plato, of course, provides the foundation for negative attitudes toward the human flesh as the cause of evil.

In the _Timaeus_ the creation of the flesh indicates
its inferiority, for the Creator is thought to make
the souls, but "the created gods" fashion the bodies
of men. They, imitating the Creator, designed a
body as a "vehicle of the soul" and then in turn
created within the body another soul of a different
nature which was susceptible to the passions. This
elaborate and indirect process was conceived in
order not "to pollute the divine any more than was
absolutely unavoidable."[5]

In the _Symposium_ Diotama related to Socrates the
journey to absolute beauty as a ladder which must be
ascended, from those concrete, physical beings which
are beautiful to beauty absolute. This pure beauty
stands in contrast to beauty on earth. Diotama
poses the question, "But what if man had eyes to see
the true beauty--the divine beauty, I mean, pure
and clear and unalloyed, not clogged with the pol-
lutions of mortality and all the colours and vanities
of human life--thither looking, and holding converse
with the true beauty simply and divine?"[6] The negative tone and attitude toward the flesh is clear,
but at least, in the early stages of the progress
of the true Platonic lover, the lower elements can
be employed as stepping stones to the higher. In
the same dialogue Pausanias, however, says that the
lover who loves the body is vulgar and even evil.[7]
Thus there appears an ambiguous and ambivalent attitude toward the flesh; although essentially negative,
there is a grudging permission granted to regard the
body of flesh as a means to love that which is higher,
despite the fact that this leads ultimately to a
rejection of the flesh.

In the _Phaedrus_ Socrates presents the famous
image of the winged horses and charioteer in which
the "human charioteer" drives two horses, one "the
soul in her totality" and the other "the imperfect
soul." The former soars upward in order, but the
latter loses her wings and droops to the ground,
where she receives "an earthly frame," and this
combination of imperfect soul and earthly frame is
"a living and mortal creature." The reason that the
imperfect soul falls is that the wing, the "corporeal
element," becomes enmeshed in evil and wastes away,

21

losing the blessed sights of the inner heaven
which the gods and the demi-gods enjoy.[8] The body
itself, in the same dialogue, is depicted metaphorically in an unpleasant light in the context of the
pre-existence of the human soul which looks back
toward its rarified past: "we were admitted to the
sight of apparitions innocent and simple and calm
and happy, which we beheld shining in pure light,
pure ourselves and not yet enshrined in that living
tomb which we carry about, now that we are imprisoned
in the body, like an oyster in his shell."[9]

The Phaedo presents the most extensive account
of "The bodily nature" that appears in the dialogues.
Socrates explains to Simmias that death is the release
of the soul from the body and that the body cannot
perceive the reality of absolute beauty or absolute
good. The soul, in fact, perceives pure knowledge
only when it is freed from the elements which "infect
the soul." Not only does the body hinder knowledge,
but it also provides the source for most evils in
this classic relation of the blame placed on the
body:

For the body is a source of endless trouble to
us by reason of the mere requirement of food;
and is liable also to diseases which overtake
and impede us in the search after true being:
it fills us full of loves, and lusts, and
fears, and fancies of all kinds, and endless
foolery, and in fact, as men say, takes away
from us the power of thinking at all. Whence
come wars and fightings, and factions? whence
but from the body? Wars are occasioned by the
love of money, and money has to be acquired
for the sake and in the service of the body;
and by reason of all these impediments we have
no time to give to philosophy; and, last and
worst of all, even if we are at leisure and
betake ourselves to some speculation, the
body is always breaking in upon us, causing
turmoil and confusion in our enquiries, and
so amazing us that we are prevented from
seeing the truth. It has been proved to us
by experience that if we would have pure
knowledge of anything we must be quit of the
body . . . .[10]

22

The body is thus responsible for distracting the soul
from its proper concerns through its demands and
through its evil activities. As we shall see, St.
Paul emphasizes the evils of the flesh, but these
include a variety of evils which are evil because
they oppose the spirit (Gal. 5.19-21). The evil of
the body in Platonic doctrine consists in restraining
the soul from its true intent through "the chains of
the body." The philosopher must look upon death with
joy since it will free the soul, unlike the stoic who
extols temperance because he is afraid of death and
would like to maintain the ability to enjoy pleasure.
He is no lover of wisdom.[11] After death the soul
who loves the body cannot bear to leave the body and
so remains close to it despite its decay, "prowling
about tombs and sepulchres, near which, as they
tell us, are seen certain ghostly apparitions of
souls which have not departed pure, but are cloyed
with right and therefore visible."[12] The proper
attitude is to "be of good cheer" about relinquishing
the body, which during life has pursued pleasure
instead of knowledge, because the soul will be happy
in its natural state without the soul after death.[13]
It is no surprise, then, that the official position,
if one can use such a phrase, of Platonism is that
the body inhibits the soul, distracts it from true
wisdom, and generally is to blame for the evils of
the world.

    Philo Judaeus, in the first century after
Christ, attempted to combine the Talmud and the Torah
with Platonism:

    God is for Philo a non-fleshly, non-corporeal
    being. Hence He may be known only by the
    friends of the soul who can set aside the
    husk of the flesh; for the soul, too, is
    non-fleshly and non-corporeal. Thus the
    body or the flesh is for the soul a burden,
    bondage, coffin, or urn. It is a corpse
    which it lags around with it. Hence it
    must come out of Egypt, the body, this is
    possible for man in ecstasy, ... Here
    the flesh is simply the physical part of
    man which hampers the flight of the soul and
    the growth of wisdom. . . . Freeing from the

flesh in ecstasy is essential, not because
the flesh leads to sin, but because it pre-
vents the non-material soul from soaring up
to the heavenly heights of God. If, then,
the flesh is opposed to all piety, and carnal
desire to all knowledge of God, the physical
antithesis is in view. Flesh is not the
total man who is condemned by God, as in the
OT, but the physical constitution of man
which acts as a drag on the flight of the
soul. Only when remaining in the physical
state and refusing the flight of the soul
is regarded as guilty, does the antithesis
become ethically significant.[14]

This tendency of Philo attempts to tailor the concept of the flesh of the Old Testament to the Platonic bias, at the expense of the former.

Plotinus, the third-century Neoplatonist,
perceives this Platonic aversion to the flesh in his
reading of the Dialogues: "Everywhere, no doubt, he
[Plato] expresses contempt for all that is of sense,
blames the commerce of soul with body as an enchain-
ment, an entombment, and upholds as a great truth
the saying of the Mysteries that the Soul is here a
prisoner. In the Cavern of Plato and in the Cave
of Empedocles, I discern this universe, where the
breaking of the fetters and the ascent from the
depths are figures of the wayfaring towards the
Intellectual Realm. . . . In all these explanations
he finds guilt in the arrival of the Soul at body."[15]
Plotinus remarks that the thought is abroad that
life in the body is most unhappy, with the human
"body its prison or tomb, the Cosmos its cave or
cavern."[16] Plotinus' own position is somewhat different.

He attributes the difficulties of the soul in
the human body to its severance from the "Soul of
the All," not from any intrinsic evil in the body or
flesh itself. Speaking of human souls, he observes
their self-centeredness and alienation:

they descend from the universal to become
partial and self-centered; in a weary desire
of standing apart they find their ways, each

to a place of _its very_ own. This state long
maintained, the Soul is a deserter from the
totality; its differentiation has severed it;
its vision is no longer set in the Intellectual;
it is a partial thing, isolated, weakened, full
of care, intent upon the fragment; severed from
the whole, it nestles in one form of being; for
this, it abandons all else, entering into and
caring for only the one, for a thing buffeted
about a worldful of things: thus it has
drifted away from the universal and, by an
actual presence, it administers the particular;
it is caught into contact now, and tends to
the outer to which it has become present and
into whose inner depths it henceforth sinks
far.

With this comes what is known as the casting
of thewings, the enchaining in body: the Soul
has lost that innocency of conducting the
higher which it knew when it stood with the
All-Soul, that earlier state to which all its
interest would bid it hasten back.

It has fallen: it is at the chain: debarred
from expressing itself now through its intellectual phase, it operates through sense; it
is a captive; this is the burial, the encave-
ment, of the Soul.[17]

Plotinus refuses to go so far as to condemn the flesh
as did the Gnostics and the Manicheans; for him anything can partake of the nature of good. Assuming
that matter has always existed, then existence by
itself is sufficient to guarantee a sharing in goodness. If matter came into being, it would still
share goodness because of the nature of the maker.
"In sum: the loveliness that is in the sense-realm
is an index of the nobleness of the Intellectual
sphere, displaying its power and its goodness alike:
and all things are for ever linked; the one order
Intellectual in its being, the other of sense; one
self-existent, the other eternally taking its being
by participation in that first, and to the full of
its power reproducing the Intellectual nature."[18]
This position on the goodness of created matter

25

adheres to the traditions of Judaism and Christianity on the basis of the Creation story in Genesis and to the judgement of the mature John Milton. But also symmetrical with Judaism, Christianity, and Milton is the observation of Plotinus that the souls which have divided off from the Soul of the All become distracted from their true concern and become troubled and distressed by what is transient and irrelevant.[19]

The Theological Dictionary offers an excellent summary of the various philosophical opinions on and theological attitudes about the nature of man. Plato had declared the distinction between the soma and the psyche; the Stoics regarded the soul as corporeal and attempted to establish a balance between the two; and Epicurus also attempted such a balance while distinguishing the "non-spiritual parts of the body," sarx, from the dianoia. Sarx thus "describes the nature or substance which determines the nature of man." The term soma had originally meant corpse in Homer.[20] According to Ernest Evans, in English the word "flesh" sounds very "materialistic," but in Greek and Latin this was not the case. "In those languages 'body' (σῶμα, corpus) originally meant a dead body, and hardly ever succeeded in losing all sense of inertness and lifelessness: whereas 'flesh' (σαρς, caro) envisages the presence, actual or potential, of an animating soul."[21] In Plato it became a "single whole which is self-contained," the shell which holds man down. For Aristotle it means the human body, but in Hebrew there was no consistent equivalent for the word.[22]

Despite the fact that Aristotle was originally a student of Plato, his attitude toward the body was not negative at all. He declared that the soul needs the body for its "affections," saying, "If we consider the majority of them, there seems to be no case in which the soul can act or be acted upon without involving the body; e.g., anger, courage, appetite, and sensation generally. Thinking seems the most probable exception; but if this too proves to be a form of imagination, it too requires a body as a condition of its existence."[23] Throughout the De Anima there appears almost no negative reaction to the flesh of the body.

In the Old Testament, a very different conception becomes apparent, one which does not emphasize the distinction between spirit and flesh, as had the Greeks, but that between God and man:

Here man is seen from the very first in his relation to God. As creature of God he is flesh, always exposed to death. God's breath is his life, his soul. The will of his heart is Yes or No to God's commandment. Man is understood in terms of his relationship, not his nature. He is what he is in relation. Thus flesh is his situation before God. When he is viewed in this way, he can no longer be split up into a divine part and an earthly part. If there is to be a distinction, it can only be between God and man, heaven and earth. That is, only cosmic dualism is conceivable.[24]

In Hebrew the word bāsār commonly refers to the "muscular tissue of a person's living body." The Israelites did not see the soul as hostile to the flesh but perceived man as both soul and flesh. There is no fundamental connection between the flesh and sin.[25]

This Old Testament concept of man as a "totality" pervades the New Testament, including the Epistles of St. Paul.[26]

Lucien Cerfaux reveals how neither Jesus, Paul, nor the Jewish world in the first century A.D. believed that the flesh was evil but that evil occurs only "when man yields to its temptations."[27] S.S. Cohon explains the traditional Judaic view of the flesh in the glandular sense: "Our instinctual responses are neither moral nor immoral, neither sinful nor virtuous, but neutral and may be turned into good or evil. They became evil, when, in disregard of moral and religious standards, they are permitted to run unbridled and to grow into wild lusts."[28] He notes how sin is essentially a callousness toward God which sets up the self in the place of God. Glorifying the self, asserting that one makes

oneself righteous, and all the petty arrogance that
is associated with this self-righteousness constitute
sin.[29] Cohon also shows that like medieval Christians
some Jewish believers underwent an ascetic, even
morbid trend in the denigration of the flesh, but
this tendency represented more an aberration than the
true line of Judaism.

St. Paul observes the wholeness of man, in opposition to the Platonic theory of man as divided into
psyche and soma, mind and body. The soul animates
the body and forms a unity with the body while living,[30]
and the Apostle employs the term pneuma to characterize
the spirit of man or the Holy Spirit, suggesting the
unity between the two. The flesh and the mind are
not separated but are a part of the conflicting
entity called man.[31] Rudolph Bultmann synopsizes
this attitude:

> Rather, man is a living unity . . . . He is a
> person having a relationship to himself (soma).
> He is a person who lives in his intentionality,
> his pursuit of some purpose, his willing and
> knowing (psyche, pneuma). This state of living
> toward some goal, having some attitude, willing
> something and knowing something, belongs to
> man's very nature and in itself is neither
> good nor bad . . . this structure (which for
> Paul is, of course, the gift of the life-
> giving creation) offers the possibility of
> choosing one's goal, of deciding for good or
> evil, for or against God.[32]

This set of distinctions and emphases is found
repeatedly in Erasmus' and Milton's approach to
Christian morality and theology--the Christian has
moral options which he can and does exercise, and
the sarx or flesh does not refer to that which is
ipso facto evil. In Paul's Epistles (and later for
some of the chief Reformers and Milton) the term
sarx "can mean the whole sphere of that which is
earthly or 'natural'." The soma is not just the body
but the self, then, and the body is not distinct from
the spirit in Hellenistic dualism. The sarx can
indicate the passions or glandular flesh, as it does
when Paul is berating the Corinthians for sexual
immorality, but in a larger sense it denotes the

28

hostility of the human self to the divine absolute.[33]

In the early church Tertullian offered an interesting compromise with his synthetic view of the soul and the body. Rather than perceiving, in Platonic fashion, the body as a house for the soul, he sees body and soul as joined and intertwined together in concrete form. He concludes that it is difficult to determine whether the soul is the "vehicle" of the flesh or whether the reverse is true, whether the former serves the latter or the latter serves the former. The soul enjoys nature and the elements of the world through the flesh, and so the flesh is not evil or degenerate. He insists that the flesh will share "things eternal" with the soul and that God, who breathed life into flesh in the Genesis story, would never abandon it. Further, the soul, because it shares the suffering of the body in a mutual manner, proves that the soul is corporeal. Edwin Quain observes that Tertullian "insists that the soul is a body, but a body of a peculiar kind, and one that will, of its very nature, lack many of the attributes of a material body. Thus, in spite of its invisibility, it is still corporeal."[34]

St. Augustine stressed the importance of the will in human activity in opposition to the Manichaean emphasis on natural evil and to the Platonic preoccupation with the evil of the fleshly body. It is "a bad will, rooted in a bad love" which causes sin and which results from pride, the desire to exercise the will's power by putting the material over the spiritual.[35] And so Paul's concept of evil leads to Augustine's.

In sum, as far as St. Paul and the early church were concerned, the concept of the flesh, whether the Greek sarx or the Latin caro or carnis, very often refers to man as a being in contrast and often conflict with God, and when the concept flesh is alluded to, it does not necessarily suggest essential evil. The mind and the will play a role in determining the basic goodness or evil of an action.[36] In English most of the meanings of the word flesh in the OED are dominated by the glandular and sexual connotations of the word, but among the "Extended and figurative uses

(chiefly of Biblical origin)" we find several fitting
in with the Pauline conceptualization of interest
here:

(1) That which has corporeal life. <u>All flesh</u>.
    <u>each flesh</u> (<u>omnis caro</u>, Vulg. . . .
(2) The animal or physical nature of man;
    human nature as subject of corporeal
    necessities and limitations. . . .
(3) The sensual appetites and inclinations as
    antagonistic to the nobler elements of
    human nature. In theological language
    (after St. Paul's use of σαρξ) applied
    more widely to the depraved nature of man
    in conflict with the promptings of the
    Spirit . . . .

In English bibles by and large, the term <u>soma</u> is
translated by <u>body</u> while <u>sarx</u> is rendered as <u>flesh</u>,
with all its negative connotations, as the defini-
tion in the <u>OED</u> of "depraved nature of man" suggests.
Since preachers of an ascetic bent have been obsessed
with sexual sin, the Pauline meaning of the word has
been distorted in theological discussions and controversy, and that was precisely the problem that the
Reformers and Milton recognized.

The Reformers understood that the concept of the
flesh which Paul deprecates is not just the passions
but his entire nature, that which in the Old-Testament
tradition was opposed to the divine. However, for
Luther, the will possessed no freedom or capability of
doing good because man's nature or self was totally
depraved and helpless without the overwhelming impact
of Christ's sacrifice on the cross. Luther was angry
that the Roman Catholic Church had taught that the
term <u>flesh</u> in the Pauline Epistles meant sexual desire.
St. Paul had made clear the inclusiveness of the term
in Galatians 5.19-21:

> Now the works of the flesh are
> manifest, which are these; Adultery,
> fornication, uncleanness, lasciviousness.
>
> Idolatry, witchcraft, hatred, variance,
> emulations, wrath, strife, seditions,
> heresies,
> Envying, murders, drunkenness, revellings,
> and such like . . . .

Luther clarifies the implications of the problem of definition:

> Here most plainly of all it is evident that flesh is understood, not only in the sense of lustful desires but as absolutely everything that is contrary to the spirit of grace. For heresies, or party spirit and dissensions, are faults of the keenest minds and of such as shine with an exceedingly saintly outward appearance. I am saying this in order to establish what I said above: that by flesh the whole man is meant and that in like manner the whole man is meant by spirit, likewise that the inward and the outward man, or the new man and the old, are not distinguished according to the difference between soul and body but according to their disposition.[37]

The flesh as the living body escapes condemnation only to be included under, ironically, a blanket censure of man in general, a conclusion favored by Calvin as well. Luther does note that Paul will occasionally use the term flesh to mean "wicked desires" but insists that most of the time Paul denotes "the weakness of our nature which is prone to sin." In his On Romans he appears to contradict himself by saying that "The nature (in itself) is good, but the corruption of it is evil. A person is said to be an 'old man' not merely inasmuch as he does the works of the flesh, but also, and that with far greater right, inasmuch as (outwardly) he acts righteously, seeks after wisdom, exercise himself in all manner of spiritual gifts, and even loves and honors God."[38]

Luther seeks support from St. Jerome's Hebrew Questions to prove that the "flesh" refers to "our created weakness which is prone to evil."[39] Standing accused are the three powers of the soul: the desires, the will, and the intellect, and not just the desires of the flesh, which is what the "Papists condemn."[40] Arrayed against the obsessions of Origen and Jerome with the lowness of sexual desire, he is opposed to medieval Christianity's preoccupation with sexual purity and abstinence as an ideal upon which to mold one's life, despite Paul's precedent in the

twelfth chapter of First Corinthians for iterating
the control and not negation of sexual desire.[41] In
his debate with Erasmus on the freedom of the will,
Luther broadened his concept of the flesh to include
all mankind--on the basis of his reading of Scripture:
"not just one portion, or the most excellent thing,
or the governing part of man is flesh, but . . . the
whole man is flesh; and not only that, but the whole
people is flesh, and as if that were not enough, the
whole human race is flesh." This flesh, however,
exists in the kingdom of Satan.[42] Opposed to this
overpowering evil of the flesh is the goodness of
the Spirit (a Pauline antithesis), which brooks no
compromise.

As a biblical scholar, Luther is to be given
credit for noting that the Hebrew has one word for
flesh or body while modern languages have two, and he
regrets that the translators of the Scriptures have
not consistently observed the distinction.[43]

When Philip Melanchthon, the friend and colleague
of Luther, speaks of Original Sin, he does not dwell on
the faults of the flesh but mainly on the soul and
heart of man, and he ever highlights the role of obedience in the plan of salvation.[44]

Throughout his various commentaries on the
Epistles of St. Paul, John Calvin maintains a position similar to that of Martin Luther: an enormous
distinction is posited between Christ and everything
else in which man could possibly believe. The
distinction is similar to the Hebraic dichotomy in
the Old Testament with the notable exception that
Christ and not God, for the Reformers, is the antithesis of the flesh. Nevertheless, Calvin fits into
the central biblical and Pauline tradition which does
not oppose psyche to sarx but God to self or soma.
He comments on Philippians 3.4, "Though I might also
have confidence in the flesh. If any other man
thinketh that he hath whereof he might trust in the
flesh, I more." In the context Paul is clearly
speaking of the Christian's reaction to the Hebraic
insistence upon circumcision, a special field of
reference for the term flesh. Nevertheless, Calvin
expands the meaning to cover, literally, a multitude

of sins: "For under the term _flesh_ he includes
everything of an external kind in which an individual
is prepared to glory . . . he gives the name of _flesh_
to everything that is apart from Christ."[45]

Paralleling Luther's views almost precisely,
Calvin opposes the spirit to the flesh and deni-
grates those who would argue that the latter applies
only to sensuality:

> The term _flesh_ is not restricted to the lower
> appetites merely, as the Sophists ⌊Roman
> Catholic theologians and canon lawyers⌋ pretend,
> the seat of which they call sensuality, but is
> employed to describe man's whole nature. For
> those that follow the guidance of nature, are
> not governed by the Spirit of God.[46]

Like Luther he equates the flesh with the "old man,"
the new man being that which is regenerated by the
Spirit.[47]

Calvin has a great deal of difficulty correlating
his belief in man's total depravity and his creation
in the image of God as sketched twice in the first
chapter of Genesis. However, the Fall, for Calvin,
has almost thoroughly destroyed what had been divine
in man. In the _Institutes_ he is forced into a reluctant admission that something divine remains in mankind, and that is, as the Humanists were fond of
pointing out, man's ability and tendency to look
upward toward the heavens. Both Ovid and Cicero had
remarked on this capability of the human animal.
Calvin even admits there is something of God reflected
in the body of man. And yet, on the very same page,
he says, "we journey away from God so long as we
dwell in the flesh, but . . . we enjoy his presence
outside the flesh." Notably Calvin, in speaking of
the faculties of the soul, prefers the term "will"
over "appetite" as that which impels man toward evil.[48]
The Fall, in any case, has done ultimate damage to
man so that only the elect, who are reborn in the
Spirit, can undo some of the harm, and even then, they
can achieve fulfillment only in heaven: "Now God's
image is the perfect excellence of human nature which
shone in Adam before his defection, but was subsequently
so vitiated and almost blotted out that nothing remains

after the ruin except what is confused, mutilated, and disease-ridden. Therefore in some part it now is manifest in the elect, in so far as they have been reborn in the spirit but it will attain its full splendor in heaven."[49] The passage is remarkably full of qualifiers when dealing with man while still in the body, but the qualifiers vanish when man reaches heaven.

The fact that St. Paul mentions heresies in Galatians 5.20 proves that the flesh includes much more than just sensual appetite.[50] Glossing II Corinthians 12.7, Paul's famous statement of a goad or prick or spur in his flesh, Calvin regards this flesh as not the body at all but the unregenerated part of the soul. Ultimately Calvin agrees with Luther that man's entire nature is depraved and that to distinguish elements in that nature as more or less evil is a mistake.[51] "For under the term _flesh_ he ⌊Paul⌋ includes everything of an external kind in which an individual is prepared to glory . . . he gives the name of _flesh_ to everything that is apart from Christ."[52]

For Calvin, because of Original Sin even infants possess a nature which is the "seed of sin," a nature despicable in the sight of God before Baptism. Although alleging that this sacrament can remove the stigma in some way, he elsewhere speaks about "the depraved natures of man, in whom nothing can be seen but materials for destruction."[53] At other times he sounds Platonic despite himself when he characterizes man as living "cooped up in this prison of our body," which produces sin, or when he mixes Platonic and Pauline metaphors, "But no one in this earthly prison of the body has sufficient strength to press on with due eagerness."[54]

This view of total depravity was so widespread among the Reformers that men who might seem as far apart as Martin Bucer and John Colet agree on this issue. The former argues that man's nature is so corrupt and so inclined toward evil that it has to be coerced into virtue and away from vice.[55] Even Colet, who was profoundly influenced by Marsilio Ficino and the Neoplatonism of the Renaissance, with its fervent desire to be freed from the body, pronounces, when

commenting on I Corinthians 12, that "By _flesh_, St.
Paul almost always means the whole human nature;
whose knowledge is death, and whose wisdom is enmity
with God."[56]   As we shall see in a later context,
the flesh's wisdom is censured by the Reformers, but
in this chapter it is important to remember that
Colet's typical response to the flesh is to desire
a release from the confines of the tabernacle in
which his soul resides--the despicable body of the
flesh.

Thomas Jacomb, in his sermons on the Epistle to
the Romans published in 1672 (about the time of
Paradise Lost and _Paradise Regain'd_), offers his
definition of the flesh in the tradition of Luther
and Calvin but initially provides several meanings
from the term. In a general sense, in what he calls
"a double synecdoche," it means either the whole
body or the whole man, the whole nature of man. In
a strict sense it is part of the body and the body in
turn a part of man.[57] In the Scriptures, according
to Jacomb, the flesh refers to "that corrupt, sinful,
depraved, vitiated nature that is in man as he comes
into the world." He cites St. Paul primarily in
support of his position, as well as John and James.
Later he continues his definitive comments and agrees
that the most common interpretation is the "nature"
of man which is degenerate in man after the Fall,
citing in his notes Piscator, Anselm, and Peter Martyr,
all three of whom use the terms "vitiatam" or "viti-
orum" to designate man's nature when he is in the
flesh.[58] However, in another place he sees the flesh
as the tendency of the soul toward evil and away
from good, the "sensitive soul" which is hostile to
the reason. Jacomb also lists the sins of the flesh
and the virtues of the Spirit respectively: "pride,
covetousness, uncleanness, &., all centre in the
flesh; so, be it humility, heavenly-mindedness, holy
love, &c., all centre in the Spirit." Therefore he
concludes that the flesh is synonymous with evil and
the Spirit with good. He distinguishes between the
obvious sins of the flesh, gluttony, drunkenness,
adultery, and secret sins like pride, envy, and covetousness and claims that the Stoics, while adjuring
the former, cultivated the latter."[59] Whatever the
term _flesh_ delimits, it possesses negative values.

Jacomb identifies the old Adam as representing those who walk after the flesh and Christ as those who walk after the Spirit, on the basis of Galatians 5.16, 17, 24, and Romans 6.12. He is consistent in affirming that the flesh includes both physical desire and the evil desires of the soul, but he demands that proper attention be paid more to the physical than to the spiritual. The tensions within his mind become evident when we read elsewhere that both Adam's and Christ's bodies, though created differently, were both "holy and spotless," but nevertheless he cannot accept Christ's taking a normal body since it had to be tainted by the Fall.[60] Unlike Hebraic interpretations the Christian tradition, following St. Jerome's translation of the Bible, felt compelled to read the story of the Fall in Romans and conclude that not only death but sin entered the world with Adam's disobedience (Rom. 5.12), and then to dwell upon and even become obsessed with the idea of sin, particularly sexual sin.

Thomas Cartwright, a contemporary of Jacomb's and Milton's, commenting on Colossians 2.8-10, refuses to believe that the "creature itself is this filthiness" but that it is "the spiritual corruption and infection in the body and soul joined together."[61] So once again, with the expansion of the term flesh from the glandular or instinctive or concupiscible appetites to the whole nature of man, the concept of man's depravity becomes inclusive. The reverse conclusion might have been that since the glandular flesh is not essentially evil, then man has an opportunity to save himself, and this was the conclusion to which John Milton came. He remained within the Hebraic and Pauline tradition that the self, when hostile to God, was the guilty party in the provenance of sin--and not created matter, matter created after the image of God, despite the Fall.

Milton does not accept the absoluteness of the Hellenistic and Platonic separation of soul from body but argues for the unity of man in the tradition of the Old and New Testaments. Following his humanistic inclinations, he significantly departs from the Reformers in his insistence that man's nature is not totally depraved and that matter itself is not

evil by any means, thus opposing the Manichean
belief in the control over the flesh by a god of
evil. In Of Christian Doctrine, he opposes the
notion of Creation ex nihilo on the basis that Creation out of matter is highly logical: "Neither is
it more incredible that a bodily power should issue
from a spiritual substance, than that what is spiritual should arise from body: which nevertheless we
believe will be the case with our own bodies at the
resurrection."[62] He could hardly then have regarded
the flesh with a jaundiced eye.

In Paradise Lost the unity of the spiritual and
the material is clear before the Fall. God the
Father, in order to counterbalance the evil done by
the War in Heaven, speaks of creating a new race
called men who will populate the earth but who will
be able to ascend eventually and join Heaven to earth:

. . . men innumerable, there to dwell,
Not here, til by degrees of merit raised
They open to themselves at length the way
Up hither, under long obedience tried,
And earth be changed to heav'n and heav'n to earth,
One kingdom, joy and union without end. (VII. 156-
161)[63]

Raphael, explaining the mystery of Creation and the
chain of being in traditional terms, specifies a
gradation, a hierarchy of matter ascending to the
pure spirit of the angels, a pattern which should be
observed in the behavior of man:

All things proceed, and up to him return,
If not depraved from good, created all
Such to perfection, one first matter all,
Endued with various forms, various degrees
Of substance, and in things that live, of life;
But more refined, more spiritous, and pure,
As nearer to him placed or nearer tending,
Each in their several active spheres assigned,
Till body up to spirit work, in bounds
Proportioned to each kind, So from the root
Springs lighter the green stalk, from thence the
leaves
More airy, last the bright consummate flow'r
Spirits odorous breathes: flow'rs and their
fruit,
Man's nourishment, by gradual scale sublimed,

To vital spirits aspire, to animal,
To intellectual; give both life and sense,
Fancy and understanding, whence the soul
Reason receives . . . ,
. . . . .Time may come when men
With angels may participate, and find
No inconvenient diet, nor too light fare;
And from these corporal nutriments perhaps
Your bodies may at last turn all to spirit,
Improved by tract of time, and winged ascend
Ethereal, as we, or may at choice
Here or in heav'nly paradises dwell;
If ye be found obedient, ... (V. 470-501)

This lovely picture of the providential plan which
glorifies the unity of all nature reenforces Milton's
opposition to the strict duality of matter and spirit.

When Milton comments on man in Of Christian
Doctrine, the same unity obtains in that just as
matter and spirit are not utterly hostile, the
microcosm of man is one entity. It is noteworthy
to see Milton defending this position on the basis
of Genesis and First Corinthians:

man is a living being, intrinsically and
properly one and individual, not compound or
separable, not, according to common opinion,
made up and framed of two distinct and different
natures, as of soul and body, but that the whole
man is soul, and the soul man, that is to say,
a body, or substance individual, animated, sensitive, and rational; . . . for man himself,
the whole man, when finally created, is called
in express terms 'a living soul.' Hence the
word used in Genesis to signify 'soul,' is
interpreted by the apostle, I Cor. xv. 45.
'animal.' Again, all the attributes of the
body are assigned in common to the soul.'64

The passage in Corinthians refers to both Adam and
Christ: "The first man Adam was made a living soul;
the last Adam was made a quickening spirit." There
is no question but that Milton insists upon the
unity of soul and body on exegetical grounds, particularly on the basis of the Pauline Epistles, for he

makes a sweeping generalization about the meaning
of the word _flesh_ in this gloss on Hebrews 12.9:
"for 'flesh' is taken neither in this passage nor
probably any where else, for the body without the
soul."[65] Indeed in the same discussion in _Of
Christian Doctrine_ he insists that sin proceeds from
the soul.

Milton's position in his maturity remains
constant: he pays allegiance on this philosophical
and theological problem to neither the strict Reformers nor the Platonists nor Neoplatonists. He
is antagonistic toward what he and the Reformers saw
as the medieval preoccupation with evil as primarily
sensual and toward the escapism, if one can call it
that, of the Neoplatonists from the body. Nevertheless, although he stands together with Calvin and
Luther on the unity of man on scriptural grounds, he
radically and significantly departs from them in
rejecting the total depravity of man. Luther's thesis
in his argument with Erasmus, that the human will is
unable to move toward the good, is rejected by Milton.
He dissociates himself from all three attitudes and
takes a more Hebraic and Pauline view of human nature.
His youthful Neoplatonism, as seen in _A Mask_ and the
Italian sonnets, represents a stage through which he
passed. In fact, a primary thrust of _A Mask_, according to George F. Sensabaugh, is the repudiation of
the false Neoplatonism at the court of Charles I,
which concealed some flagrant sexual promiscuity, all
in the name of Platonic love, a far cry from that
expressed in Spenser's hymns on the subject.[66]

To return to _Paradise Lost_, the description of
Adam's and Eve's wedded love in Paradise before the
Fall reflects Milton's positive orientation toward
the physical and sexual side of man's nature. Pruri-
ence and false modesty have no place in this prelap-
sarian state, in which Eve's curls "implied"

Subjection, but required with gentle sway,
And by her yielded, by him best received,
Yielded with coy submission, modest pride,
And sweet reluctant amorous delay.
Nor those mysterious parts were then concealed;
Then was not guilty shame; dishonest shame
Of Nature's works, honor dishonorable,

Sin-bred, how have ye troubled all mankind
With shows instead, mere shows of seeming pure,
And banished from man's life his happiest life,
Simplicity and spotless innocence. (IV. 308-318)

Some readers, enlightened by Women's Liberation,
might object both to the subjection and the "amorous
delay" as being unworthy of a woman, but nevertheless
Milton rejects the rigors of a Calvin or Luther by
pointing out the speciousness of shame and courtly
honor in sexual behavior.

On the other hand, an argument could be made for
a Platonic vision of sexual morality and human love
on the basis of a remark by Raphael to Adam when he
expresses a weakness for Eve:

In loving thou dost well, in passion not,
Wherein true love consists not; love refines
The thoughts, and heart enlarges, hath his seat
In reason, and is judicious, is the scale
By which to heav'nly love thou may'st ascend
Not sunk in carnal pleasure, for which cause
Among the beasts no mate for thee was found.
                                    (VIII. 588-594)

But the context and the speaker must be kept in mind
here, for Raphael is warning Adam against the suprem-
acy of passion over reason, which is in keeping with
Milton's perspective. Secondly, this is Raphael
speaking, not the "epic voice," and Raphael, only
moments later, blushes "Celestial rosy red" when he
is asked by Adam about angelic copulation, suggesting
that he has not come to terms with his own nature,
which in the poem includes sexual relations, a distinct Miltonic addition to angelic activities.

Sexual love in marriage, for Milton, represents
a command of God and is good, just as matter is
good, the creation of God out of himself. Thus only
hypocrites condemn what is not only desirable in
marriage but what is commanded by God for the con-
tinuance of the species, despite the fulminations of
a St. Jerome against the human body. Notably, Adam
and Eve enjoy sexual relations just after paying
homage to God in prayer; is it blasphemous to presume
that, in fact, Adam and Eve are paying homage to God

through their sexual activities in marriage?

> This said unanimous, and other rites
> Observing none, but adoration pure
> Which God likes best, into their bow'r
> Handed they went; and eased the putting off
> These troublesome disguises which we wear,
> Straight side by side were laid, nor turned,
>   I ween,
> Adam from his fair spouse, nor Eve the rites
> Mysterious of connubial love refused;
> Whatever hypocrites austerely talk
> Of purity and place and innocence,
> Defaming as impure what God declares
> Pure, and commands to some, leaves free to all.
> Our Maker bids increase; who bids abstain
> But our destroyer, foe to God and man?
> Hail, wedded Love, mysterious law, true source
> Of human offspring, sole propriety
> In Paradise of all things common else.
> By thee adulterous lust was driv'n from men
> Among the bestial herds to range . . . . (IV. 736-
>   754)

Following this passage is a brief depiction of dalliance, harlotry, "Casual fruition," and "court amours,"
the target of Milton in A Mask. The absurdities and
pretensions of courtly love distort the intention of
God in providing mankind with a noble and beautiful
means of expressing marital love and propagating the
species (PL. IV. 758-775).

Before the Fall, neither Adam nor Eve suffers
from lust or the burning that St. Paul cures by marriage, but afterwards they are tortured by the itch
of lust. This burning is anticipated by Satan's
suffering when he sees the couple in the Garden before
the Fall: he writhes in sexual torment as one of his
punishments for rebelling against God:

> "Sight hateful, sight tormenting! thus these two
> Imparadised in one another's arms,
> The happier Eden, shall enjoy their fill
> Of bliss on bliss, while I to hell am thrust,
> Where neither joy nor love, but fierce desire,
> Among our other torments not the least,
> Still unfulfilled, with pain of longing pines."
>   (IV. 505-511)

41

Unfulfilled sexual desire becomes the objective
correlative for the state of man or angel after their
rebellion against God's wishes. After Eve, to use
Adam's words, is "Defaced, deflow'red, and now to
death devote," and Adam eats the apple,

> They swim in mirth and fancy that they feel
> Divinity within them breeding wings
> Wherewith to scorn the earth. But that false fruit
> Far other operation first displayed,
> Carnal desire inflaming: he on Eve
> Began to cast lascivious eyes, she him
> As wantonly repaid; in lust they burn,
> Till Adam thus 'gan Eve to dalliance move. (IX.
> 1009-1016)

The irony here is splendid; the unfortunate couple
seek "Divinity" in the apple and then mistake sexual
arousal for the lift of penetrating insight into the
mysteries of the universe. The litotes of "Far other
operations first displayed" (the couple is still naked)
crushingly exhibits sexual hunger as a poor substitute
for sapience. It might seem here that Milton is slip-
ping into a rejection of the flesh, despite the distinction he makes between wedded love and "dalliance,"
but the evil here lies not in the glandular flesh
itself but in the almost masochistic enjoyment of the
desire for sexual satisfaction and not the satisfaction
itself. Sex before the Fall evidently did not include
lust or "burning" but love for each other. Frustra-
tion or death follow sin, and it seems supremely
logical that Eve suggest to Adam that they end the
human race by discontinuing the act of married love.
The origin of the Fall, then, lay not in the flesh or
the glands but in the desires of the soma or self to
attain knowledge and power which was not ordained for
the human condition. That sexual lust is produced
by this intellectual fault is clear, and readers should
not confuse the cause and effect relationship. The
flesh is not the villain.

John Mulder states precisely the central belief
about the holistic nature of man:

> If the Christian estimation of man's place in the
> universe is dualistic, the view of the composition
> of his body and soul is no less so. However, we

42

ought to avoid confusing the Christian distinction
between body and soul with the neo-Platonic view,
which opposes soul to body. The neo-Platonist
holds that the body imprisons the soul, and he
emphasizes the strife between these two parts of
man. Augustine again defines the orthodox view:
'the life of the soul is not one thing, and that
of the body another: but both are one and the
same, i.e., the life of man as man.' The Christian contrast is not between a carnal body and
a spiritual soul, but between a man who is carnal
in soul and in body, and a man spiritual in soul
and body.[67]

In other words, the Christian tradition's central position has been to accept the Aristotelian distinction
between the soul and body in conjunction with the
Hebraic and Pauline emphasis on the self which chooses
to oppose the will of God.

For St. Paul the impact of Christ changes man's
situation with respect to his <u>soma</u> and his <u>sarx</u>:
"And they that are Christ's have crucified the flesh
with the affections and lusts" (Gal. 5.24). As the
<u>Theological</u> <u>Dictionary</u> points out, the change does
not arise from a retreat from the flesh or physical
desires or into mysticism: "For though we walk in
the flesh, we do not war after the flesh" (II Cor.
10.3), that is, "the believer always lives physi-
cally εv $\sigma\alpha\rho\kappa\iota$" Thomas Jacomb, commenting on this
passage, explains that to walk in the flesh means
living a natural life full of mortal frailty, but to
war after the flesh (<u>kata sarka</u>), according to the
flesh means functioning actively, with the glandular
flesh as the principle of human life.[68] In some
sense, the <u>sarx</u> is man, and he cannot simply escape
from it, as Plato and his followers would have man
do. For Paul the <u>sarx</u> and the <u>pneuma</u> must function
together as a totality, not fight against each
other. On the other hand, the man who lives by the
<u>sarx</u> or who walks "according to the flesh" opposes
God.[69] In summary, then,

Man is not essentially determined by his nature,
whether by his bodily constitution or by the
material world which is about him. He is
finally qualified by his relation to God and

43

> hence to his fellow-man. . . . Salvation does
> not lie in a retreat from corporality (e.g.
> sexuality) to the spiritual (e.g. study of the
> Law or asceticism). Bodily and mental functions
> are viewed in comprehensive unity as a common
> expression of human life. Both can separate man
> from God and both can be put in the service of
> God. . . . Hence the flesh is not a sphere which
> is to be differentiated from other earthly things
> and which is intrinsically bad or especially
> dangerous. It becomes bad only when man builds
> his life on it.[70]

The act of faith in Christ must be put into effect
not only through the intellectual or emotional facets
of man but in terms of his whole "bodily life." The
translation of Paul's soma into "person," "personal-
ity," is partially acceptable as long as it refers
specifically to the whole man and not some part of
him.[71]

In the early church and through St. Augustine,
many of the Fathers were aware of the distinctions
that Paul made in this area and maintained that the
flesh was not intrinsically evil; St. Augustine held
to this position against the Manichean heresies. St.
Irenaeus, remarking on Paul's view of the flesh,
notes that "he did not surely condemn the substance
of flesh in that passage [Col. 3.10] where he said,
'Put ye off the old man with his works'." Indeed,
Irenaeus devotes a whole chapter of Against Heresies
to the theme, "Unless The Flesh Were To Be Saved,
The Word Would Not Have Taken Upon Him Flesh."[72]
Tertullian also holds this position, supporting the
"carnis dignitatem" and the "aeque caro," the dignity of the flesh and the nobility of the flesh. He
etymologically notes that "'man' in the strict sense
means the flesh, for this was the first possessor of
the designation 'man'."[73]

St. John Chrysostom, in various commentaries on
the Epistles, evinces a certain degree of impatience
with those who denigrate the body of flesh and regard
it as a whipping boy. He ridicules rites of purification and the public baths: "I would not myself
cease to frequent the baths, if it made us pure, and

cleansed us from our sins! But these things are
trifling and ridiculous, the toys of children. It
is not the filth of the body, but the impurity of
the soul, to which God is averse."[74] Even more
strongly he condemns those who, like Origen, go to
the extreme length of mutilation of their bodies in
order to avoid lust (Milton too censured, though
ironically, Origen's extreme act). From Chrysostom's
perspective such actions are wrong for two reasons:
the sins of the flesh are caused by the soul and
mutilation assumes that God's handiwork is defective:
"they draw down the Apostolic curse and accuse the
workmanship of God, and take part with the Manichees
⌊who⌋ . . . call the body a treacherous thing."[75] On
the positive side, he defends marriage and procreation
because, again, it is God's work, and he brings to his
defense Paul's statement in Hebrews 13.4: "Marriage
is honourable in all, and the bed undefiled: but
whoremongers and adulterers God will judge."[76] Chrysostom exploits some of Paul's metaphoric language to
urge control of the body: "'For it is a race, and a
manifold struggle and a tyrannical nature continually
rising up against me, and seeking to free itself.
But I bear now with it, keep it down, and bring it
into subjection with many struggles.' . . . He said
not, 'I kill:' for the flesh is not to be hated,
but, I keep under subjection; which is the part of a
master not an enemy, of a teacher not of a foe, of a
schoolmaster not of an adversary."[77] Chrysostom,
explicating Romans 8.12, 13, distinguishes between
the evil of the deeds of the body and the body, the
glandular flesh, which is not responsible for evil.[78]

St. Augustine's position basically supports the
concept of the goodness of God's Creation, but he
does emphasize the deleterious effects of the Fall on
man's nature. As Charles Norris Cochrane, citing the
Confessions, observes, "as, against the Manicheans,
he held tenaciously to the doctrine that there was no
intrinsic evil in what is called 'matter.' And,
with equal vigour, he denied the idealist contention
that material existence is involved in necessary
ambiguities and contradictions, from which escape
becomes possible only in the life of pure 'form'."[79]
Augustine himself had been influenced by the Manicheans, and he confesses that the conception of

matter and flesh as evil held him back from embracing Christianity. In speaking of the birth of Christ as man, he felt, "Such a nature, then, I thought could not be born of the Virgin Mary without being mingled with the flesh; and how that which I had thus figured to myself could be mingled without being contaminated, I saw not. I was afraid, therefore, to believe Him contaminated by the flesh. Now will Thy [God's] spiritual ones blandly and lovingly smile at me if they shall read these my confessions, yet such was I."[80] In the City of God Augustine affirms the goodness of the flesh: "evil could no longer be ascribed to the 'substance or nature of the flesh'," and "it is not the body but the corruptibility of the body which is the soul's burden."[81] Finally in "The Enchiridion," chapters 13, 14, and 15 regard being as good, and evil as needing something good in which to inhere, rejecting the concept of the total depravity of man.[82]

One of the basic arguments for the essential goodness of the human body and its normal wants rests upon Christ's taking the form of human flesh in which to save mankind. St. Paul had asserted that Christ

thought it not robbery to be equal with God:

But made himself of no reputation,
and took upon him the form of a servant,
and was made in the likeness of men. (Phil. 2.6-7)

As already pointed out, Irenaeus had written a chapter in Against Heresies entitled "Unless the Flesh Were To Be Saved, The Word Would Not Have Taken Upon Him Flesh. . . ." Tertullian argued that the body of Christ was truly flesh and not a phantasm. He bases his contention on the passage in Philippians quoted above and comments on it: "Thus that clay, already putting on the image of Christ who was to be in the flesh, was not only a work of God but also a token of him. What is the use now, with intent to sully the origin of the flesh, of flinging about the name of earth, as of a dirty ignoble element." Tertullian also points out that the Scriptures, including Paul's Epistles, insist that the bodies of men are members in Christ, and that Paul himself distinguished between condemnation of the "activity of the flesh" and the

46

fundamental goodness of the flesh itself.[83]

Chrysostom also devotes his energy to the defense of the flesh on the basis of Christ's assuming human flesh, rising from the dead, and ascending into heaven in the flesh. Glossing I Thessalonians 4.14, he challenges the Docetae and the Marcionites who challenge the validity of the flesh: "Where are they who deny the Flesh? For if He did not assume Flesh, neither did He die. And if He did not die, neither did He rise again."[84]

In the Reformation Calvin accepts the notion of Colossians 1.22 that Christ took on man's body despite the theologian's attitude toward what he conceived as its baseness. Paul, he asserts, "meant, therefore, to intimate, that the Son of God had put on the same nature with us, that he took upon him this vile earthly body, subject to many infirmities, that he might be our Mediator."[85] Although he accepts Paul's important point about Christ's behavior, he cannot shake the feeling that the flesh is yet corrupt, although he says elsewhere that the flesh is really the whole self and not just "this vile earthly body." Combatting the Platonic and ascetic tendencies of some Christian theorists, Thomas Jacomb argued that Christ truly took on flesh in vigorous fashion, implying clearly that there was nothing untoward in his doing so.[86]

Thus far it has been urged that the <u>sarx</u> embraces much more than just the purely physical or glandular facets of man, that it properly designates the individual in his opposition to his maker, that the body or flesh of man is not inherently evil, and that one argument for this last assertion is Christ's assuming human flesh. In the context of the self's hostility toward its maker, St. Paul makes an absolute distinction between those who would depend upon themselves for salvation or who would pride themselves on their achievements or wisdom and those who understand that Christ is the source of salvation, wisdom, and power. In his Epistle to the Romans, Paul makes a distinction between Christ's being born of David's house "according to the flesh" (the earthly sphere) and his power "according to the spirit of holiness" (1.3-4). The

47

Apostle expands upon this theme in the seventh
chapter when he characterizes the power of the flesh:

> For when we were in the flesh,
> the motions of sin, which were by the law,
> did work in our members
> to bring forth fruit unto death.
>
> . . . But I see another law in my
> members, warring against the law
> of my mind, and bringing me into
> captivity to the law of sin which is in my
> members. (7.5,23)

He continues in Chapter Eight to expand upon the
theme. While in particular censuring dependence upon
the Mosaic law for righteousness, he amplifies the
hostility of the self-flesh to Christ's redemption:

> For they that are after the flesh
> do mind the things of the flesh; but
> they that are after the Spirit the things of the
> Spirit.
>
> For to be carnally minded is
> death; but to be spiritually minded is life and
> peace.
>
> Because the carnal mind is en-
> mity against God: for it is not sub-
> ject to the law of God, neither indeed
> can be.
>
> So then they that are in the flesh
> cannot please God. (8.5-8)

Paul continues in this vein to distinguish radically
all of Creation and God.

In his Epistles to the Corinthians, Paul condemns the flesh in its function as boaster of wisdom,
the wisdom of the flesh as opposed to the wisdom of
the Spirit. (See Chapter Four for further discussion
of this idea.) In essence, Paul says, "no flesh
should glory in his presence" (I Cor. 1.29). Paul
scolds the Corinthians because they have allowed
themselves to become "carnal," in terms of their
fighting among themselves. Chapter Ten of Second
Corinthians finds Paul defending himself against
accusations of falling victim to pride in his own

flesh, of "boasting." "For though we walk in the
flesh, we do not war after the flesh" (v. 3), that
is, although man must live in the condition of the
flesh, he does not have to employ the elements of the
flesh. God does not work his will in that fashion.

The Theological Dictionary demonstrates that in
the Pauline Epistles the sarx is set in contrast to
the pneumata or pneuma, the former representing "the
Earthly Sphere" as well as just the physical or
muscular body. Men can then be divided in terms of
those who live according to the flesh and those who
live according to the spirit--the carnal or fleshly
and the spiritual.[87] The Church Fathers noted this
distinction, with Tertullian defending the flesh or
carnis but attacking the "mind of the flesh," the
mindset of the individual who is carnal. This person
commits "carnalia." Thus, "those who could not please
God were not such as were in the flesh but such as
lived in fleshly fashion," reminiscent of Paul's
defense of himself in Second Corinthians. When the
"operation of the flesh" is stopped at death, then
the flesh itself can be saved.[88] Origen believes in
the existence of an inferior soul, a "corporal soul";
when it agrees with the will of the spirit, it produces men following the flesh.[89] Clement of Alexandria, quoting a great deal of Romans 8, stresses
Paul's dichotomy between the flesh and the "carnal
mind," that is, between the flesh of the body and
the self's mentality, and comments that Paul makes
the assertion "that no one may, like Marcion, regard
the creature as evil."[90]

Paul uses another set of terms to define the
antipathy between the two kinds of men: the familiar
"old man" vs. "new man." Writing to the Colossians,
he urges them to relinquish the habits of their
"members," including not only the glandular sins but
also "anger, wrath, malice, blasphemy, filthy commu-
nication out of your mouth." He concludes,

Lie not one to another, seeing
that ye have put off the old man
with his deeds;

And have put on the new man,
which is renewed in knowledge

after the image of him that created
him. (Col. 3.9-10)

St. John Chrysostom provides a penetrating analysis
of these lines which maintains the distinctions and
categories established by Paul:

It is worth inquiring here, what can be the
reason why he calls the corrupt life, <u>members</u>,
and <u>man</u>, and <u>body</u>, and again the virtuous
life, the same. And if <u>the</u> <u>man</u> means 'sins,'
how is it that he saith, with his deeds? For
he said once, <u>the</u> <u>old</u> <u>man</u>, shewing that this
is not man, but the other. For the moral
choice doth rather determine one than the substance, and is rather <u>man</u> than the other.
For his substance casteth him not into hell
nor leadeth him into the kingdom, but his
same choice: and we neither love nor hate any
one so far as he is man, but so far as he is
such or such a man. If then the substance be
the body, and in either sort cannot be account-
able, how doth he say that it is evil? But
what is that he saith, <u>with</u> <u>his</u> <u>deeds</u>? He
means the choice, with the acts. And he call-
eth him <u>old</u>, on purpose, to shew his deformity,
and hideousness, and imbecility . . . .[91]

Thus the old man lives according to the flesh, <u>kata</u>
<u>sarka</u>, and must be renewed by Christ, live according
to the spirit, and become the new man. Depending
upon the flesh and its selfhood and not living in the
flesh is evil. Thomas Aquinas remarks upon the distinction between living "in the flesh" and "by the
flesh," with the latter constituting an evil way of
life.[92] Luther sees the individual as a "carnal man"
when the soul and the flesh agree, and he interprets
Paul's depiction of the Corinthians as carnal (I Cor.
313) because of their refusal to change their attitudes to absorb the significance of Christ.[93] Calvin
defines "according to the flesh" without any reference whatsoever to sexuality or lusts and depends upon
Chrysostom for part of his definition. For Calvin
the phrase means "acting unfaithfully, or conducting
one's self improperly in his office."[94] Philip Airay,
a seventeenth-century commentator, makes a distinction
between living "in the flesh" and "after" the flesh

and concludes that to live in the flesh means simply
to live in the body, but he adheres to a Platonic
line in stating that to live after the flesh means
following "the filthy lusts of the flesh."[95]

The term _flesh_, as we have seen, can refer to a
particular kind of mentality which takes pride in
itself; and a special kind of self-pride for St. Paul,
the Reformers, and Milton was pride in the alleged
ability of man to save himself either through the
Mosaic law, the laws and rites of Roman Catholicism,
or those of English episcopacy. St. Paul warns the
Philippians about having confidence in the flesh,
particularly in the practice of circumcision as a
means of achieving righteousness:

> Beware of dogs, beware of evil
> workers, beware of the concision.
>
> For we are the circumcision,
> which worship God in the spirit,
> and rejoice in Christ Jesus, and have
> no confidence in the flesh.
>
> Though I might also have confidence
> in the flesh. If any other man
> thinketh that he hath whereof he
> might trust in the flesh, I more. (3.2-4)

Paul goes on to relate his own accomplishments in the
flesh, his knowledge of the law, his status as a
Pharisee. Commenting on this passage, the _Theological
Dictionary_ singles out the hostility to Christ of
this kind of flesh. "Here again . . . σάρξ
embraces in the first instance the natural descent of
the Israelites, but also Pharisaism, zeal for the
Law, legal righteousness, and hence the intellectual
and religious functions of men in particular. Hence
the direct revelation of the righteousness which is
of God in Christ makes all other things ζημία. . . .
They are not bad, but they can no longer be considered
as objects of confidence, as the foundation of life."
In Romans the sin of those who abide by legalism is
manifested. This legalism produces a bondage for man
on a par with the immorality of those in the pagan
world.[96] Rudolph Bultmann, explicating Galatians 3.3,
notes that observing the letter of the Torah is the
same as living "according to the flesh" since "the

51

flesh" means putting trust and faith in the self over God.[97] Chrysostom interprets Philippians 3.1-3, Paul's warning against "boasting" in the flesh, as referring to pride in the rite of circumcision as a means of self-justification, and Augustine pursues this approach with reproval for the "carnal Israelites . . . for their own righteousness" as a substitute for God's.[98] In his commentary on Galatians, Aquinas understands the term _flesh_ in this manner: in a general sense referring to what is human but in a particular sense alluding to what is subsumed under the Mosaic law. Needless to say, he does not include canon law under this rubric, as the Reformers were later to do.[99]

Luther, equating the Mosaic law and the doctrine of salvation by works, isolates the "flesh" as the reason for their undesirable existence. He concludes that "Thus 'flesh' is the very righteousness of wisdom of the flesh and the judgment of reason, which wants to be justified through the Law. Therefore whatever is best and most outstanding in man Paul calls 'flesh,' namely, the highest wisdom of reason and the very righteousness of the Law."[100] Calvin agrees with Luther in asserting that, in many cases, (such as I Cor. 1.30 and Gal. 5.18) St. Paul employs the term _flesh_ to mean all that is human, but Calvin also cites the antithesis between Christ and the flesh in its denotation of the Law or externals in which the individual "is prepared to glory."[101]

Michael Servetus reduces the range of the term _flesh_ from all mankind to paganism and the Mosaic law: "Worship was formerly carnal and earthly, in groves, high places, images, and tabernacles of wood and houses of stone. But now God is spiritually worshipped in the living Christ alone. Again, he now destroys all sins, to which we were kept exposed by the law. Indeed, in the law no other forgiveness of sins was known than a carnal and earthly one." The Jews, he claimed, were afraid of "the carnal vengeance of the law" and offered "carnal expiation" as described in Leviticus (like "those shadowy expiations weak,/ The blood of bulls and goats" of _Paradise Lost_ XII. 291-292).[102] The Jews and the pagans were both wrong in thinking that their sacrifices, both "carnal" and

"shadowy," as Milton and Servetus note, could offer
them salvation. As Servetus puts it, "All, even
the most holy, who were under the law, were carnal . .
. . All were born under a shadow of spiritual ones. .
. . Again notice the carnal priesthood of Aaron, and
the carnal commandment." It is interesting that
Servetus, while using the word _flesh_ in this sense,
still uses Pauline language which suggests the glandular meaning of the flesh: "but the flesh lusteth
against the spirit." And yet the work "lusteth" can
be construed to mean "oppose."[103]

Milton's contemporaries saw this specialized
meaning of "flesh " as referring to the strict observance of the letter of the law (usually ceremonial)
and Scripture, on the presumption that this observance
was sufficient for righteousness. Philip Airay,
discussing Philippians, uses the phrase, "carnal sense
and reason," to apply to a literal reading of Scripture.[104] Thomas Jacomb defines the concept as "the
Jewish ceremonial law, with the several rites, ceremonies, appurtenances thereof. . . . the fleshly observation of the ceremonies of the law," and he doubts
that anyone can observe these in a spiritual manner.[105]
He contrasts the Manichean belief in the evil of the
glandular flesh, "rejected by all," with Origen's associating the flesh with the ceremonial law, "with
respect to the gross and literal sense and meaning of
that law." He notes that Beza rejects Origen's view
but that Grotius asserted that the flesh was "the
state of men under the law." It is significant that
this definition does not apply, in Grotius' view, to
man after the Fall, but much later, after the covenant
of Moses with the Lord.[106] Paul Bayne distinguishes
the spiritual substance of God's worship and the carnal "manner" of worship designed for a church in its
childhood.[107] Thomas Cartwright also fastens upon
the ceremonial law as the villain in that "these were,
for the filling of the flesh, viz., they were but
belly-matters appertaining to the flesh, and therefore
perishable with the flesh, which hath been spoken of
before; or for the pleasing of man's fleshly mind,
therefore to be avoided."[108]

Milton's antiprelatical tracts, in tune with
Servetus and his contemporaries, see the flesh as the

representation of the attempt to bring religion down
from the spirit to the level of laws and ceremonies
(in this case episcopal but derived from the Mosaic)
which claim to provide righteousness. Milton's
negative imagery in the opening of Of Reformation
envisions the dragging down of spiritual worship to
the level of stale robes and ceremonies passed down
from Aaron's priesthood, the true worship of the
flesh:

> that such a Doctrine should through the grossnesse,
> and blindnesse, of her Professors, and the fraud of
> deceivable traditions, drag so downwards, as to
> backslide one way into the Jewish beggery, of old
> cast rudiments, and stumble forward another way
> into the new-vomited Paganisme of sensuall Idol-
> atry, attributing purity, or impurity, to things
> indifferent, that they might bring the inward
> acts of the Spirit to the outward, and customary
> ey-Service of the body, as if they could make
> God earthly, and fleshly, because they could not
> make themselves heavenly, and Spirituall: . . .
> Worship circumscrib'd, they hallow'd it, they
> fum'd it, they sprincl'd it, they be deck't it, not
> in robes of pure innocency, but of pure Linnen,
> with other deformed, and fantastick dresses in
> Palls, and Miters, gold, and guegaw's fetcht
> from Arons old wardrope, or the Flamins vestry:
> ⌊Note the Servetian association⌋ then was the
> Priest set to con his motions, and his Postures
> his Liturgies, and his Lurries, till the Soule
> by this meanes of overbodying her selfe, given
> up justly to fleshly delights, bated her wing
> apace downeward: and finding the ease she had
> from her visible, and sensuous collegue the body
> in performance of Religious duties, her pineons
> now broken, and flagging, shifted off from her
> selfe, the labour of high soaring any more, for-
> got her heavenly flight, and left the dull, and
> droyling carcas to plod on in the old rode, and
> drudging Trade of outward conformity.[109]

Although the image of the bird sounds as if it came
from the Phaedo, the proper definition of flesh here,
although conflated slightly with the Platonic, still
conforms to the Pharisaic meaning condemned by St.
Paul. In Animadversions Milton fears that England

will not continue the Reformation begun by Wicklyf
in the fourteenth century which challenged "humane
Principles, and carnall sense, the pride of flesh
that still cry'd up Antiquity, Custome, Canons,
Councels, and Laws."110

Basing his judgements on St. Paul's definition
of the Mosaic law, Milton repeats the censure of
episcopacy's preoccupation with fleshly ceremony and
ritual and with the legalisms of the code: "For the
ministration of the law consisting of carnall things,
drew to it such a ministery as consisted of carnall
respects, dignity, precedence, and the like." The
former simplicity of apostolic Christianity has been
corrupted by infatuation with materialistic and legalistic detail.111

The Reason of Church-Government hammers on the
conflict between the Gospel and the fleshliness of
episcopacy's dependence upon traditions and man's
pride in his knowledge of religion. The Gospel
opposes "the pride and wisdom of the flesh."

> And wherin consists this fleshly wisdom and
> pride? in being altogether ignorant of God
> and his worship? no surely, for men are
> naturally asham'd of that. Where then? it
> consists in a bold presumption of ordering
> the worship and service of God after mans own
> will in traditions and ceremonies. Now if the
> pride and wisdom of the flesh were to be
> defeated and confounded, no doubt, but in
> that very spirit wherin it was proudest and
> thought it self wisest, that so the victory
> of the Gospel might be the more illustrious.
> But our Prelats instead of expressing the
> spiritual power of their ministery by warring
> against this chief bulwark and strong hold of
> the flesh, have enter'd into fast league with
> the principall enemy against whom they were
> sent, and turn'd the strength of fleshly pride,
> and wisdom against the pure simplicity of
> saving truth.112

The argument in this pamphlet fits in neatly with the
basic points advanced earlier in this chapter: that
the flesh can be defined as man's pride in his self,

55

whether his wisdom or his alleged power to save his
own soul. For Milton this presumption and arrogance,
as it was for Paul and the Reformers, deserved the
most insistent reprimand. That for both Milton and
the Reformers St. Paul provided the groundwork for
their arguments can be proved by even a casual reading of the relevant texts, especially Milton's Reason.
For example, taking certain liberties with the text,
Milton cites II Corinthians 10.4-5 to substantiate
his arguments: "This is the approved way which the
Gospel prescribes, these are the spirituall weapons
of holy censure, and ministeriall warfare, not
carnal, but mighty through God to the pulling downe
of strong holds, casting down imaginations, and every
high thing that exalteth it selfe against the knowledge of God, and bringing into captivity every
thought to the obedience of Christ.[113]

        In An Apology this warfare assaults "the proud
resistance of carnall, and false Doctors,"[114] the
theologians of canon law who seek to impose the
restrictions of man on Christians in the name of God.
In Paradise Lost Michael's warning to Adam about the
future corruption of the church, with its "grievous
wolves" (like the wolf in Lycidas), depicts how these
predators will turn the church to their own selfish
ends and how they will attempt to violate Christian
liberty through canon law:

        Spiritual laws by carnal power shall force
        On every conscience; laws which none shall find
        Left them enrolled, or what the Spirit within
        Shall on the heart engrave. (XII. 521-524)

The logical extension of Milton's thinking on the
imposition of laws of the flesh on the spiritual
realm becomes his antipathy to the use of civil force
in church matters in A Treatise of Civil Power in
Ecclesiastical Causes. Quoting Romans 14.4 in support of his position, he argues that the only one
with power to proclaim laws in churchly matters is
Christ. As he did in the antiprelatical tracts, he
quotes the tenth chapter of Second Corinthians,
insisting that "we do not warre after the flesh" and
condemning churchmen who want the civil magistrate
to impose "fleshlie force" on Christians.[115] We can
see that Milton's use of the term flesh has a special

meaning when he discusses man's attempt to impose his
own will on others in matters of ecclesiastical import.
Notably, in the divorce tracts the terms _carnal_ and
fleshly almost inevitably mean the physical or sexual
aspect of marriage, but both meanings have their
proper and useful function for Milton in their respective contexts.

To return to the more general meaning of flesh--
the self of man in his hostility to his maker--if the
flesh itself is not the guilty element in the compo-
sition of man, then something else must be responsible
in a view of man which focuses on his morality and his
relationship to God. Depending upon the particular
commentator on Paul's Epistles or on the Scriptures in
general, either the will or the soul is guilty.
Ernest Evans, in his introduction to Tertullian's
Treatise _on_ _the_ _Resurrection_, asserts that the censures
of the flesh found in the Bible "are really directed
against the soul which has misused the flesh for lower
purposes."[116] Irenaeus notes that Paul's statement
that "Those who are in the flesh cannot please God"
has a moral and not a physical basis.[117] The attitude
of Philo Judaeus, although complex, states that the
νοῦς is somehow enslaved by the σαρξ, but that the
will has the ability to choose the good.[118] St. John
Chrysostom, glossing Galatians 5.17, remarks that the
flesh is good but that the "apostate will" is not.
In his remarks on Paul's letter to the Galatians,
Chrysostom explains, "his discourse does not relate
to the substance of the flesh, but to the moral
choice, which is or is not vicious."[119] St. Augustine observes Paul's long list of sins of the flesh
in Galatians 4 and concludes that the flesh refers to
desires other than purely "carnal" in the glandular
sense, saying that Paul "takes flesh for man, as the
part for the whole." For Augustine the soul is the
cause of sin and the reason that the body is corrupted in the first place, as Augustine perceives the
relationship in the _City_ _of_ _God_. In the _Confessions_
he defines evil as "a perversion of the will."[120]

Calling Augustine as a witness, Aquinas comes to
a dual, and perhaps ambiguous, conclusion in that, he
asserts, the self is responsible for evil but that
the soul is hindered by the flesh, in Platonic fashion.

It is worth quoting extensively the conflation of
the two views of responsibility for evil in this
ostensibly Aristotelian philosopher:

> First, as to the Apostle's mentioning things that
> do not pertain to the flesh, but which he says
> are works of the flesh, such as idolatry, sects,
> emulations, and the like. I answer that, accord-
> ing to Augustine in The City of God, (Bk. 14),
> he lives according to the flesh who lives accord-
> ing to himself. Hence flesh is taken here as
> referring to the whole man. Accordingly, what-
> ever springs from disordered self-love is called
> a work of the flesh. Or, one should say that a
> sin can be called 'of the flesh' in two ways;
> Namely, with respect to fulfillment, and in this
> sense only these are sins of the flesh that are
> fulfilled in the pleasure of the flesh, namely,
> lust and gluttony; or with respect to their root,
> and in this sense all sins are called sins of the
> flesh, inasmuch as the soul is so weighed down
> by the weakness of the flesh . . . that the
> enfeebled intellect can be easily misled and
> hindered from operating perfectly. As a conse-
> quence, certain vices follow therefrom, namely,
> heresies, sects and the like. In this way it
> is said that the 'fomes' ⌊tinder⌋ is the source
> of all sins.121

Aquinas is aware of the confusion inherent in a care-
less interpretation or translation of the term flesh.

In the Reformation John Calvin and the lesser
known Juan Valdez do not place the blame for evil on
the glandular flesh but on the mind or soul. Calvin
advises, "Only let my readers observe that Φιλαυτια,
self-love, which is put first, may be regarded as the
source from which flow all the vices that follow
afterwards. He who loveth himself claims a superiority in everything, despises all others, is cruel,
indulges in covetousness, treachery, anger, rebellion
against parents, neglect of what is good, and such
like.122 Juan Valdez, basing his position on St.
Paul's listing of the sins of the flesh, joins glandular sins to "those that are of the mind, such as
ambition, and self-esteem, with curiosity, as those
that are of the body, and which are peculiarly

connected with the five bodily senses." For him
the factionalism of the Corinthians, which upset
St. Paul, is fundamentally carnal. He distinguishes
between self-love and the love of God. "They, who
love themselves, do everything in a carnal manner,
acting from self-love and self-interest. Whilst
they, who love God, do everything in love."[123] Paul
Bayne, a preacher who died in 1617, makes a distinction between having concupiscence and acting according to concupiscence, to walk after it, affirming
that all men possess concupiscence. The man who is
in Christ, however, does not walk after it. The
"seat of corruption," for Bayne, is "not only the
sensual part, but the mind of man."[124] Bayne thus
distributes the responsibility for evil between the
instinctive flesh and the mind of man.

In Of Christian Doctrine Milton places the blame
variously on the will, the mind, or simply the individual or self, and he opposes the concept of total
depravity and the placing of the blame on the body,
even after the fall of Adam:

> I answer, that to create pure souls destitute
> of original righteousness--to send them into
> contaminated and corrupt bodies--to deliver
> them up in their innocence and helplessness to
> the prison house of the body, as to an enemy,
> with understanding blinded and will enslaved--
> in other words, wholly deprived of sufficient
> strength for resisting the vicious propensities
> of the body--to create souls thus circumstanced,
> would argue as much injustice, as to have created
> them impure would have argued impurity; it would
> have argued as much injustice, as to have created
> the first man Adam himself impaired in his nature,
> and destitute of original righteousness.[125]

From his humanistic perspective, he wishes to give
man the opportunity to have some role in saving himself, even though he knows that Christ is the fundamental basis of righteousness. For Luther and Calvin
Christ is only the basis of salvation, and man is so
corrupted that he cannot cooperate in any way with
God's grace. The will, as Luther insists, throughout On the Bondage of the Will, cannot perform good
acts. Erasmus, Luther's opponent, maintains the

59

opposite, as does Milton, who concludes, "the will is clearly not altogether inefficient in respect of good works, or at any rate of good endeavors; at least after the grace of God has called us: but its power is so small and insignificant, as merely to deprive us of all excuse for inaction without affording any subject for boasting."[126] The will, however limited, can do good or evil; it makes a choice.

A distinction must be drawn in terms of the will's and/or the mind's or reason's responsibility for doing good or evil, whether it is man's nature before or after the Fall that falls under examination. In Paradise Lost, the Father, speaking defensively of his justice, declares that man is created free to choose although he will choose evil:

He and his faithless Progeny, whose fault?
Whose but his own? Ingrate, he had of me
All he could have; I made him just and right,
Sufficient to have stood, though free to fall. . .
What pleasure I from such obedience paid,
When will and reason (reason also is choice)
Useless and vain, of freedom both despoiled,
Made passive both, had served necessity,
Not me. (III. 96-111)

After Adam and Eve succumb, there arises "Evil concupiscence . . . in the shape of an innate propensity to sin." Milton further defines responsibility for evil in terms of Genesis 6.5, which blames not the glandular flesh but the psychic elements of man: "every imagination of the thoughts of his heart was only evil continually," and Milton's term in this context is mind. Elsewhere in Of Christian Doctrine he admits the will is "already in a state of perversion."[127] Whichever word is used, mind, will, reason, nevertheless for Milton evil remains a psychic phenomenon and not one that can be attributed to the flesh or to all of man's nature--a rejection of total depravity.

Chapter Five of Galatians has been basic in this chapter as a source for a definition of the flesh, but Paul, in writing to the Galatians in the same chapter, also sets in hostile stance the flesh to the Spirit:

60

> This I say then, Walk in the
> Spirit, and ye shall not fulfil the lust
> of the flesh.
>
> For the flesh lusteth against the
> Spirit, and the Spirit against the
> flesh: and these are contrary the one
> to the other: so that ye cannot do the
> things that ye would. (16-17)

Paul speaks about the antithesis between the Spirit
and the law and lists the various sins, already discussed above, which fall under the category of the
flesh. The Spirit is not seen as the antithesis of
the lower appetites or the glandular flesh but of the
self or apostate will which arrogantly defies the
Spirit. Aquinas also reads the passage in this light:

> He says therefore: It is necessary that by the
> spirit you overcome the desire of the flesh,
> for the flesh lusteth against the spirit. But
> one might have a doubt here, because, since
> lusting is an act of the soul alone, it does
> not seem to come from the flesh. I answer that,
> according to Augustine, the flesh is said to
> lust inasmuch as the soul lusts by means of the
> flesh, just as the eye is said to see, when as
> a matter of fact, it is the soul that sees by
> means of the eye. Consequently, the soul lusts
> by means of the flesh, when it seeks according
> to the flesh, things which are pleasurable. But
> the soul lusts by means of itself, when it takes
> pleasure in things that are according to the
> spirit, as virtuous works, contemplation of di-
> vine things, and mediation of wisdom: 'The de-
> sire of wisdom bringeth to the everlasting king-
> dom' . . . the lusting of the flesh hinders the
> desires of the spirit . . . when the soul is
> occupied with the lower things of the flesh, it
> is withdrawn from the higher things of the spi-
> rit.[128]

Aquinas further rejects "the Manichean error" of
believing that the flesh which the Spirit rejects is
evil: "For in things necessary the spirit does not
contradict the flesh, as we are told in Ephesians
(5:29): 'No man hateth his own flesh'."[129] In the
Reformation Luther takes the stance of assuming that

the Fall has caused man to desist living in the Spirit and to adopt a life in the flesh.[130]

A very clear and obvious contrast to the Pauline view of the flesh is offered by the Neoplatonists of the Renaissance. Marsilio Ficino's commentaries on and translations of the Socratic dialogues, the Theologica Platonica and the Opera Platonica, provide the cornerstone of this popular and fashionable view of the relationship between the soul and the body. In the context of interpreters of St. Paul, it is valuable to examine the attitudes of John Colet (1467-1519) who was the dean of St. Paul's and a major Christian humanist of the fifteenth century. He wrote several commentaries on St. Paul's Epistles, in particular on Romans and Corinthians. In his commentary on Romans, he demonstrates a significant debt to Ficino, quoting him at length for several passages, and notably in these passages, Ficino quotes St. Paul on the qualities of God's love.[131] Colet had travelled to Florence and may have heard some of Ficino's lectures on the Pauline epistles in the Cathedral Church.[132]

Colet's description of the trials of living in the body echoes familiarly to readers of Plato and Ficino: "so long as we are here and abiding in this vain and shadowy life, shrouded in this poor and murky body, ⌊we must⌋ patiently endure all things, and stand fast in the highest hope." Colet's characterization of the human condition sounds very much like Ficino's depiction of the descent of the soul into the body, "tenebrosum longeque dissimilem,"[133] but Colet's wording reverberates to the language of St. Paul in terms of patiently enduring and standing fast. It is no wonder then that Colet would interpret Paul's epistles, particularly his comments on the flesh, in Neoplatonic fashion. According to the dean, "This miserable and forlorn condition of man, and lamentable bondage of the soul, is here bewailed by St. Paul; and bitterly does he complain of the injustice and tyranny of the sensual body." Colet follows the familiar pattern, seen in the Phaedo, of the soul's sinking downward in its pursuit of the interests of the body, which is blind and self-indulgent, to its inevitable destination--its "everlasting destruction." The other alternative is for the body to be "transformed" and made like the soul, its natural leaden weight notwithstanding, so that the soul, through love of God, can be made "like to the nature of God."[134] The paradigm represents simplicity: the body can be made like the soul, and then the soul can be made like God, but the fate of the soul depends upon the course of the body. Love is the elixir which allows the transformation, a Christianized Neoplatonic love based, from both Colet's and Ficino's point of view, not just on the Platonic love of the good and the beautiful but on the love of God as rendered in Paul's letters to the Corinthians. This eclectic viewpoint manifests dramatically the ability of the reader of the Bible and of the classics in the Renaissance to fuse ideas from theoretically hostile camps.[135] Even John Calvin echoes the language, if not occasionally the thought, of the Neoplatonists: "we are joined to holy souls, which have put off their bodies, and left behind all the filth of the world" and "so long as we are confined in the prison house of the flesh, 'we are away from the Lord' (II Cor. 5:6)."[136] In the last sentence, the two attitudes toward man are combined.

Philip Airay provides specific Platonic reasons why the Christian desires to escape from the body:

(1) "heaven is our home."
(2) The soul is better with Christ than with the body.
(3) "the body is as a prison of the soul."
(4) "We know only in part in the body, not in full."
(5) "And what else is this sinful body, but as a prison of the soul, wherein it is so shut, that it hath no liberty till it return unto him that gave it."

Airay also adds a sixth reason, which is distinctly Pauline, that the members of the mystical body desire to be with the Head, but even the obviously Platonic reasons possess Pauline overtones.[137]

The younger Milton's prose and poetry reflect a tendency toward the popular Neoplatonic conception of the relationship between soul and flesh, although

Irene Samuel grants the Bible first place and Platonism second in Milton's thought, a priority accurate
throughout Milton's life.[138] Nevertheless in the
early 1630's Milton seemed captivated by Platonism
as a vehicle for expressing his ideas on both the
religious or ecclesiastical problems of the day and
the personal problem of death. The concept of the
soul as soaring upward toward the good and plummeting
downward toward evil depicts for Milton the conflict
between the individual Christian or the members of
the church and the infatuation with earthly or carnal
pomp of episcopacy. According to Milton in the early
1640's, episcopacy's exaltation of ceremony represents
a form of spiritual degeneracy, a wrongheaded notion
of what is holy. Thus in Of Reformation he berates
this pseudo-religion: "the Soule by this meanes of
overbodying her selfe, given up justly to fleshly
delights, bated her wing space downeward . . . her
pineons now broken, and flagging, shifted off from her
selfe, the labour of high soaring any more, forgot her
heavenly flight."[139]

     The early poetry evinces the common synthesis of
the Augustinian attitude toward the city of earth and
the correlative of the Platonic ascent away and up
toward a heaven of pure Idea. "On the Death of a
Fair Infant" emphasizes the grisly aspects of death,
common enough in the poetry and drama of the day, in
the picture of the infant's body dissolving in the
grave:

     Yet can I not persuade me thou art dead,
     Or that thy corse corrupts in earth's dark womb,
     Or that thy beauties lie in wormy bed,
     Hid from the world in a low-delved tomb;
     Could Heav'n for pity thee so strictly doom?
         Oh no! for something in thy face did shine
     Above mortality that showed thou wast divine.
                                        (ll. 29-35)

The thought of dissolution is evidently too much for
the poet, or perhaps more accurately, would have been
too much for the parents of the child, and so the
young Milton presents another possibility reflecting
the Platonic notion of the soul as being wrapped
inside some enclosure, here "human weed":

     Or wert thou of the golden-winged host,

Who having clad thyself in human weed
To earth from thy prefixed seat didst post,
And after short abode fly back with speed,
As if to show what creatures heav'n doth breed,
    Thereby to set the hearts of men on fire
To scorn the sordid world, and unto heav'n aspire?
                                        (ll. 57-63)

The same pattern appears in "On Time," where the poet
plays on the paradox, inverting the carpe diem motif,
that the faster time moves or "devours," the faster
it will destroy itself and fulfill eternity (later
Andrew Marvell had his lovers devour time). Milton,
adopting the first-person plural, represents mankind
awaiting the chance to shed the body and be united
with the Beatific Vision:

When once our heavenly-guided soul shall climb,
Then all this earthly grossness quit,
Attired with stars, we shall for ever sit,
    Triumphing over Death, and Chance, and thee, O
    Time. (ll. 19-22)

    A Mask has been read by A.S.P. Woodhouse in terms
of the Christian orders of nature and grace and by
Sears Jayne as an allegory of the Platonic ascent of
the soul based on Milton's reading of Ficino.[140] One
may read the poem as a Christian or a Renaissance
Platonic allegory approximating the kinds of alterna-
tives of "L'Allegro" and "Il Penseroso" in that the
reader may prefer to make some absolute choice of the
one reading or the other in the case of the masque or
state a preference for one way of life over the other
in the case of the twin poems (although there are
other options). Sears Jayne takes the right tack by
citing Milton's remark in the Apology for Smectymnuus,
where he summarizes his progress from reading romances
to Plato and Xenophon, and then to Christian materials
of edification. The youthful thinker and poet characterizes his intellectual progress from philosophy to
theology.[141] By the time Milton reached his philosophical and poetic maturity, he examined more deeply
the Platonic concept of the soul chained inside the
flesh on the basis of his having absorbed the Hebraic,
Pauline, and Reformation distinction, not between soul
and body (although that is still maintained) but
between the self and God, which is hostile to Him

unless it recognizes its proper nature and ends.
However, A Mask accepts the faults of the flesh as
responsible for the inability of the soul to reach
God, whether in the Christian or Platonic sense.
Ficino characterizes the relationship between the soul
and the body or glandular flesh in this manner:

> The soul originally lived contentedly in the
> presence of God; then, because of its desire for
> love of the body, it fell into the body and
> joined with the body, where it was swamped with
> forgetfulness and with the ignorance whence all
> springs. This physical world reflects the
> nature of that divine world, presenting to us
> visibilia by which we may surmise the nature of
> the invisible world. The soul is easily excited
> to a desire for heaven because it is naturally
> inclined in that direction. But even sunk as
> it is in a gross body, the soul can still escape
> the effects of the body.[142]

As Sears Jayne puts it, "The alternative which is put
before the Lady is not a choice between two equally
natural courses; the other victims of Comus have all
chosen the fleshly alternative, but the Lady chooses
the course which preserves more fully her freedom,
her capacity ultimately to throw off the chains of
the body and return to God."[143] The Lady's choice
can be regarded as a Platonic one or as a Christian
one but in the latter case in what can be conceived
as a historical distortion of Christianity. The
celibate attitudes of some of the early Church
Fathers, or the reformed-drunk attitude toward the
glandular flesh of St. Augustine in his Confessions,
or the negative reactions of a St. Jerome toward
enjoying sexual relations led medieval Christianity
away from the emphasis of Judaism and Pauline Christianity on the unity of soul and body and on other
moral neutrality or even the goodness (as typified in
Genesis) of the glandular flesh of man. St. Thomas
defined sensuality as "the appetite of things pertaining to the body . . . the name of the sensitive
appetite," and insisted that these appetites should
obey reason. They are natural, but nevertheless
these "concupiscible appetites" do constitute one
source of sin.[144] Thomas thus appears reasonably
balanced in his conception of the appetites, but

66

nevertheless the glandular flesh is singled out for criticism.

As supportive evidence for a proper definition of the flesh, one of the basic proofs that belief in the goodness of the flesh stands as basic and central to Christianity is the doctrine of the Resurrection of the body, or flesh in this context. If the flesh is truly and irrevocably evil, then it could hardly be assumed into heaven by resurrection. When Christ was asked by the chief priests and scribes "in the resurrection" which husband of the woman who had had seven husbands, he replied:

But they which shall be accounted worthy to obtain that world, and the resurrection from the dead, neither marry, nor are given in marriage:

Neither can they die any more: for they are equal unto the angels; and are the children of God, being the children of the resurrection.
(Luke 20.35-36)

Paul addressed himself to the concept of the resurrection of man and had to clarify whether this process involved only a spiritual or a complete resurrection of the whole man. His basic statement in First Corinthians relates the resurrection of Christ to the resurrection of the dead, but at first he does not specify whether he is speaking about the soul or the whole man:

Now if Christ be preached that he rose from the dead, how say some among you that there is no resurrection of the dead?

But if there be no resurrection of the dead, then is Christ not risen:

And if Christ be not risen, then is our preaching vain, and your faith is also vain.

. . . .

For if the dead rise not, then is not Christ raised. (15.12-14, 16)

Then he explicitly states that he is talking of the "flesh," that there are various kinds of flesh, that the body "is sown in dishonour; it is raised in glory: it is sown in weakness; it is raised in power," and

that "what is corruptible and mortal will put on
what is incorruptible and immortal"(15.35-54). Supporting the basis of this chapter, Corinthians distinguishes between the Hellenic and Platonic acceptance
of a soul housed in a body, which should be removed,
and the body as that which receives immortality: "not
for that we would be unclothed, but clothed upon, that
mortality might be swallowed up in life" (5.4). In
II Timothy 2.18 Paul insists that the resurrection of
the body is yet to be.

Charles Cochrane remarks on the vital importance
of the doctrine of the resurrection of the body
because it "is a belief of supreme importance, for
it means that there is nothing inherently 'fatal' in
matter, whether the matter of the individual human
body or of what we call 'material' civilization."[145]

E.E. Ellis notes that despite the fact that some
modern Christians regard resurrection as spiritual,
for Paul the resurrection was indeed physical. Albert
Schweitzer affirms that Paul's belief in the value and
resurrection of the body proves that he was not a
Platonist.[146] Among the Corinthians Paul had to
counter the opposition and ridicule of Platonists to
the horrible idea of having the soul once again
encased in a body after death or the attitudes of
those Christians who felt that they had already risen
and were fully spiritual while yet alive.[147]

For the Church Fathers the resurrection included
the body. Irenaeus devoted several chapters of
Against Heresies to this conclusion, including one
with the following lengthy title:

The Power And Glory of God Shine Forth In The
Weakness of Human Flesh, As He Will Render Our
Body A Participator Of The Resurrection And Of
Immortality, Although He Has Formed It From The
Dust Of The Earth; He Will Also Bestow Upon It
The Enjoyment Of Immortality, Just As He Grants
It This Short Life In Common With The Soul.

He defends the worthiness of the flesh to receive
eternal life.[148] Irenaeus employs Paul's argument
that man will be raised because Christ was. Even
Origen, who obviously had some enormous problems

coming to terms with his own flesh and who practiced
self-mutilation, commenting on I Corinthians 15.44,
agrees that there is a true resurrection of the body.[149]
Justin Martyr also supported the body's resurrection.[150]

One of the arguments of Tertullian asserts that
the resurrection of the flesh is analogous to the
operation of nature, an argument which Paul himself
uses in I Corinthians 15 in terms of the sowing of seed
(to be taken up later in this chapter): "Moreover the
earth also learns from heaven: to clothe the trees
after their stripping, to colour the flowers and, to
dress itself in grass again, to bring to light the
same seeds as have perished. A marvelous exchange . .
. . . the whole creation is resurrect." Thus the process does not constitute a "mystery," as Paul called
it, or a miracle but a natural part of the divine
plan. Echoing Paul, Tertullian points out that both
Adam, the author of sin, and Christ, the author of
resurrection, both rise in body from the dead.[151]

St. John Chrysostom's commentaries on the various
Pauline Epistles iterate this basic belief and relate
it to Paul's Christocentric emphases. Chrysostom
avers that man had to learn that the body is to be
raised, that it loses its corruption, that it will
rise to heaven, that it becomes immortal, and that
it exists on a par with angels. He regards the resurrection of Christ as a proof that Christ truly
assumed flesh. Chrysostom urges that there is no
reason to mourn death because of the resurrection of
the body. The "sting" of death is defeated only if
the body rises. Commenting on Philippians 3.21, he
contrasts the suffering of the body with its change
in heaven.[152] Augustine, while repeating the accepted notion of the resurrected body, made two interesting observations. In one version of the story of
Abraham's sacrifice of Isaac in Genesis, he notes,
Isaac was actually executed and then resurrected,
thus becoming a type or prototype of resurrection.
Secondly, citing Plato's _Phaedrus_ and Vergil's _Aenead_,
Augustine defends the theory that man would have been
made immortal if he had not sinned, a point that is
indirectly evidenced in Milton's _Paradise Lost_ (VIII.
150-161).[153]

One might expect that in the Reformation John Calvin, with his basic unhappiness about the human body or flesh, would find it impossible to accept the resurrection of the body after death. However, the reverse is explicitly true: Calvin makes his position quite definite on the basis of Christ's resurrection, especially with reference to the need of making the members of Christ's mystical body conform to the head (see Chapter Four below). Calvin's correlation of the created goodness of man's soul and body before the Fall and the doctrine of the resurrection of the body deserve complete reproduction for they present a fairly balanced picture of man:

> The Manichaeans gave a worthless reason for this notion, holding it utterly inappropriate that the flesh, being unclean, should rise again. As if there were no uncleanness in souls, which they nevertheless did not debar from hope of heavenly life! It was as if they were to say: 'What is infected with the taint of sin cannot be divinely cleansed.' I say nothing here of that delusion that the flesh was by nature unclean since it was created by the devil. I am only showing that whatever now exists in us that is unworthy of heaven does not hinder the resurrection. Yet first, since Paul enjoins believers to cleanse themselves of all defilement of flesh and spirit (II Cor. 7.1), the judgement he elsewhere pronounces is a consequence of this: that 'everyone may receive back . . . through his body whether good or ill' (II Cor. 5.10). With this agrees what he writes to the Corinthians: 'So that the life of Jesus Christ may be manifested in our mortal flesh' (II Cor. 4.11). For this reason, in another passage he prays that God may keep their bodies as well as their souls and spirits sound 'until the day of Christ' (I Thess. 5.23). And no wonder! For it would be utterly absurd that the bodies which God has dedicated to himself as temples (I Cor. 3.16) should fall away into filth without hope of resurrection! What of the fact that they are also members of Christ? (I Cor. 6.15) Or that God commands all their parts to be sanctified to him? . . . Similarly, Paul, when he exhorts us to obey the Lord both

70

in body and in soul, for both are of God (I Cor.
6.20), surely does not allow that what he has,
so to speak, claimed as sacred to God should be
condemned to eternal corruption![154]

Other Reformers expressed the same confidence in
the Resurrection of the flesh, some relating this doctrine to that of the mystical body of Christ, as had
Calvin. Melanchthon had cited St. Paul in support of
his contention that both the soul and the body would
be renewed.[155] Philip Airay insisted that the second
resurrection, of the body, depends on a first, inner
resurrection of the individual soul.[156] Juan Valdes
emphasizes the same point as Calvin, that the members
of Christ must be liberated through the resurrection
of the mystical body.[157] Tying in a third strand,
Thomas Jacomb relates the rising of the body to both
Christ as Head of the Body and as Second Adam.[158]

Milton's ideas on the subject conform almost
precisely to Calvin's except for the latter's emphasis on the vitiated condition of the flesh after the
Fall. In Of Christian Doctrine Milton repeats the
argument that if there were no resurrection at the
end of the world for both soul and body, "we should
not be conformed to Christ, who entered into glory
with that identical body of flesh and blood, wherewith he had died and risen again."[159] Thus the
belief in the goodness of the flesh, whether before
or after the Fall, remained a constant in Milton's
theology. Opposing the Platonists of the Renaissance,
he claims that God resurrects man "not for the
separation of the soul from the body, but for the
perfecting of both." Milton regards the doctrine as
a means of consolation for the people of Paul's time.
He also believed that the soul died or slept along
with the body ("slept," a word that St. Paul favored),
and Calvin agreed that the soul slept until the General Judgement. For the former the soul and the body
would "conjointly" be received into heaven.[160]

In the poetry of Milton, we have seen how until
at least A Mask (1634) Milton had accepted, perhaps
uncritically, the Platonic dichotomy between soul and
body, with all the negative overtones reserved for the

71

body. It is possible that <u>Lycidas</u> (1637) marks a turning point because in the synthesis of the poem (11.165-185), the doctrine of the resurrection plays a pronounced role, especially since the context indicates that it is the body that is being resurrected. Earlier in the poem the speaker had dallied "with false surmise" in thinking that he could strew flowers on the bier of Lycidas but was shocked by the realization the body would be destroyed in horrible fashion on "the bottom of the monstrous world." And so there is no distinction whatsoever between soul and body with reference to Edward King or Lycidas, the dead shepherds. With the injunction to cease weeping, the tone of the poem ascends on the basis of the resurrection of the body through Christ, the Good Shepherd, a theme pronounced repeatedly by Milton and his contemporaries. The symbolism establishes the sacramental effects of grace or purification through water, but beneath this motif emerges the resurrection of the shepherd--as a natural phenomenon, as Tertullian had pointed out:

> Weep no more, woeful shepherds, weep no more,
> For Lycidas, your sorrow, is not dead,
> Sunk though he be beneath the wat'ry floor;
> So sinks the day-star in the ocean bed,
> And yet anon repairs his drooping head,
> And tricks his beams, and with new-spangled ore
> Flames in the forehead of the morning sky:
> So Lycidas sunk low, but mounted high,
> Through the dear might of him that walked the waves.
>   (11. 165-173)

To return to the Pauline Epistles and another element in the traditional belief about the resurrection of the body, St. Paul had defended the doctrine on the basis of its being a natural phenomenon, as had Tertullian later, but the special metaphor chosen was that of the sowing of seed, which dies, or appears to die, and then is raised. This metaphor of seed fits in symmetrically with the tradition of the seed of Eve (the proto-evangelium) and of Abraham referred to in Genesis, from which the Christ was descended. Paul defends the notion of resurrection against the detractors among the Corinthians:

But some man will say, How are the dead raised up?

and with what body do they come?

Thou fool, that which thou sowest is not quickened, except it die:

And that which thou sowest, thou sowest not
that body that shall be, but bare grain, it may
chance of wheat, or of some other grain:

But God giveth it a body as it hath pleased him,
and to every seed his own body.

. . . .

So also is the resurrection of the dead. It is
sown in corruption; it is raised in incorruption.

It is sown in dishonour; it is raised in glory:
it is sown in weakness; it is raised in power:

It is sown a natural body; it is raised a
spiritual body. There is a natural body, and there
is a spiritual body. (II Cor. 15.35-38, 42-44)

Tertullian's analogy between the resurrection of
the flesh and the operation of nature has already been
cited, but especially significant in this context is
his phrase, "to bring to light the same seeds as have
perished, and not to bring them to light until they
have perished." The seed image thus catches the attention of commentators on the resurrection of man's body.
Origen, quoting I Corinthians 15 extensively to justify
and explain the doctrine, stresses the basic goodness
of the created flesh to receive such a blessing from
God: "That the matter which underlies bodies is capa-
ble of receiving those qualities which the Creator
pleases to bestow, is a point which all of us who
accept the doctrine of providence firmly hold." Origen
establishes a distinction between the terms, "sown"
and "raised," implying that sowing is of the earth,
raising is of Heaven, and then classifying the resurrection of the body as a mystery. This separates him
from Paul and Tertullian, whose assumption is that the
process of resurrection is natural and not supernatural.[161] However, the belief in God's direct intervention is supported later by John Chrysostom.[162] St.
Basil concludes that if we are buried with Christ,
then the body does not experience a true corruption
but "only in semblance, as a planting of seed."[163]

It is profitable to examine St. Ambrose's
analysis of the subject because Milton commented in
his marginalia that Ambrose based his doctrine on
the Bible but especially on St. Paul.[164] Noting that
Paul called the human body a seed, Ambrose asserts
that the pattern of resurrection is found in nature,
in the cycle of dew, heat, "the fruits of the earth,"
and "the setting and rising of constellations." He
argues that since grain and fruit come up, why not
the body? The earth can put the body back together
again, just as seeds can produce plants. Ambrose
adds to the analogical support for the doctrine by
citing the phoenix as an example of rising from the
dead: "That bird in the country of Arabia, which is
called the Phoenix, restored by the renovating juices
of its flesh, after being dead come to life again:
shall we believe that men alone are not raised up
again?"[165] He goes on to describe the bird as having
a life of five hundred years and that at death the
bird enters his casket with perfumes and incense and
then a worm comes from its juices. He states that
some believe that the bird resurrects from its own
ashes, later a notion that was to become commonplace.
Herodotus, Tacitus, and Pliny also refer to the fabu-
lous phoenix, as well as St. Cyril of Jerusalem, and
St. Basil, these fathers with reference to the resurrection of the body.[166] Interestingly enough, as
Cruden's Concordance points out, the eagle in some
books of the bible was believed to have the same
capacity as the phoenix for rejuvenation. Accordingly Ambrose says that the eagle is "born again from
its ashes."[167]

E.Ernest Evans, discussing Tertullian's ideas on
the subject, perceives the phoenix as symbolic of
nature's ability to renew itself.[168] Tertullian,
providing an example of the confusion between the
phoenix and the eagle, argues for the resurrection on
the basis of Psalms 103.5: "God also says, in his
own scriptures, And thou shalt flourish like the
phoenix, that is, out of death, out of burial, so
that you may believe that the substance of the body
can be exacted of the flames as well. Our Lord has
declared that we are of more value than many sparrows:
if not also phoenix, there is not much in it. But
shall men die once for all while birds of Arabia are

74

assured of their resurrection?"[169] Milton's image
of the eagle in _Areopagitica_ perhaps contains such
resurrectional overtones.

In the Reformation Calvin supported the rising
of the body in accord with both reason and nature,
insisting that the same body man is born with is the
one that rises in a glorified state. He notes that
Paul, although admitting that the concept is a mystery, "goes to work, however, in another way. For he
shows, that the resurrection is so far from being
against nature, that we have every day a clear illustration of it in the course of nature itself--in the
growth of the fruits of the earth. For when the seed
has sown, unless the grains die, there will be no
increase. Corruption, then being the commencement
and cause of production, we have in this a sort of
picture of the resurrection." He urges that the concept that rotten bodies rise up is "not at variance
with reason, that our bodies should be restored in
another condition, since, from bare grain, God brings
forth so many ears of corn, clothed with admirable
contrivance, and stored with grains of superior quality." The present life is the seed time and the resurrection is the harvest of souls.[170]

Richard Hooker also relates the resurrection of
the flesh to "the school of Nature."[171] Juan Valdes
expresses the same analogy graphically: "As it
happens with a grain of wheat sown, which will not
spring up unless it mortify and rot, so man's body
will not rise again unless he first die; and just as
the grain of wheat is sown bare, and springs up clad;
so our bodies are buried corruptible and rise incorruptible: they are buried passible and rise impas-
sible; and it appears that these are two things that
St. Paul had in view."[172]

We have already seen Milton's orthodox belief
in the resurrection of the body expressed both in
his prose and poetry, but we have not seen how the
defense of the doctrine finds symbolic outlet in the
poetry. One controversial example is the fate of
Samson at the end of _Samson Agonistes_; in terms of
the decorum necessitated by the Judaic background of
the poem, the hero could not be resurrected from the

dead or look forward to a Christian heaven. And so
he, as the Chorus says, "now li'st victorious / Among
thy slain self-killed (11.1663-1664). After the
Semichorus gloats over the death of the pagan and
decadent Philistines in the theater, it depicts Samson in positive and dynamic terms through various
images from nature, the source or analogy of the
resurrection:

> And as an ev'ning dragon came,
> Assailant on the perched roosts
> And nests in order ranged
> Of tame villatic fowl; but as an eagle
> His cloudless thunder bolted on their heads.
> So virtue, giv'n for lost,
> Depressed, and overthrown, as seemed,
> Like that self-begotten bird
> In the Arabian woods embost,
> That no second knows nor third,
> And erewhile a holocaust,
> From out her ashy womb now teemed,
> Revives, reflourishes, then vigorous most
> When most unactively deemed,
> And though her body die, her fame survives,
> A secular bird, ages of lives. (11. 1692-1707)

Douglas Bush states that the image of the phoenix is
not symbolic of the Christian resurrection but refers
"to human regeneration and earthly fame."[173] Milton
could not assert that Samson was resurrected and has
to be content to depict him explicitly, after death,
as a famous hero of the tribe of Dan. However, since
the eagle in the Old Testament was regarded as possessing powers of rejuvenation similar to the phoenix
and since the phoenix was a commonplace symbol for
the resurrection, Milton came as close as he could to
asserting a resurrection for Samson by instilling in
his contemporary readers' minds the affective connotations of rising from the dead, which they would
sense if they had at all read the Church Fathers or
John Calvin, for example.

The second vital image from nature first used
by St. Paul to represent and explain the resurrection
of the body is that of seed. However, the Book of
Genesis contains another basic reference to seed
which is vital for seeing how Milton combines the

motif of the seed of Eve, thence of Abraham, and thence of Mary with the seed of the resurrection in Paradise Lost. In Genesis, the Lord says to the serpent that "I will put enmity between thee and the woman, and between thy seed, and her seed; it shall bruise thy head, and thou shalt bruise his heel" (3. 15). He also says to Abraham, after he has voluntarily agreed to sacrifice his son:

> That in blessing I will bless thee, and in multiplying I will multiply thy seed as the stars of the heaven, and as the sand which is upon the sea shore; and thy seed shall possess the gate of his enemies;
>
> And in thy seed shall all the nations of the earth be blessed; because thou hast obeyed my voice. (22. 17-18)

In Paradise Lost Milton maintains the upward movements of Books Ten, Eleven, and Twelve partially by the motif of the seed which will allow the eventual resurrection of Adam and Eve and so of all mankind, if they will follow the dictates of their Creator. The divine economy of the proto-evangelium provides for the woman initially responsible for the Fall to become the vehicle by which mankind is restored. When the Son descends to pronounce the sentence on the fallen pair, he judges the serpent precisely in the words of the Book of Genesis. The narrator relates the prophecy by the Son to its eventual fulfillment by him incarnated. The ambiguity of the sentencing of the serpent in the Bible and in the poem confuses Satan, who assumes that the serpent only, and not he, will be punished, and that a simple bruise is worth his victory:

> True me also he hath judged, or rather
> Me not, but the brute serpent in whose shape
> Man I deceived; that which to me belongs
> Is enmity, which he will put between
> Me and mankind; I am to bruise his heel;
> His seed, when is not set, shall bruise my head.
> A world who would not purchase with a bruise,
> Or much more grievous pain? . . . . (X. 494-501)

In the poem Eve initiates the reconciliation with Adam, and so begins the effectuation of the plan

77

of Redemption through her seed. In deciding to avoid
the terrors of death she advises:

>   Then let use seek
> Some safer resolution, which methinks
> I have in view, calling to mind with heed
> Part of our sentence, that thy seed shall bruise
> The Serpent's head; piteous amends, unless
> Be meant, whom I conjecture, our grand foe
> Satan, who in the serpent hath contrived
> Against us this deceit. To crush his head
> Would be revenge indeed; . . . (X. 1028-1036)

Thus, by considering the significance of the redemptive plan according to her seed, Eve puts into effect
the seminal redemption. Immediately, in Book Eleven,
the Son speaks to the Father and offers himself as a
sacrifice for mankind so that man will be united with
him, as he is to the Father (XI.22-44). The Father
reacts by ordering Michael down to Paradise to drive
the couple out of the garden but also, and more importantly, to provide the message of Redemption, the
good word, in the language of seed and covenant:

> Dismiss them not disconsolate; reveal
> To Adam what shall come in future days,
> As I shall thee enlighten; intermix
> My cov'nant in the woman's seed renewed. (XI.
>   113-116)

In the meantime Adam has prayed and received the
impression that the Father has been placated, pointing to "His promise, that thy seed shall bruise our
foe" (XI.155). With this statement to Eve, he
praises her as the mother of mankind and thereby
represents their reconciliation and Eve's new role,
not as seductress or tool of destruction. This
motif combines with that of the "one just man" who
will point the way for the rest of mankind; one of
the just men, like Abdiel the just angel, is Abraham.
Michael tells Adam of Abraham and refers to the bene-
diction of his seed in Genesis: "in his seed / All
nations shall be blest" (XII.125-126). Michael then
relates Eve's seed to the Christ, whose resurrection
will allow the resurrection of man:

> This ponder, that all nations of the earth
> Shall in his seed be blessed; by that seed
> Is meant thy great Deliverer, who shall bruise

The Serpent's head; . . . . (XII. 147-150)

The poem has now moved into history, and the
thrust of this history advances from the covenant of
the Jews with God to the event of the Incarnation by
means of typology. Moses will teach the Jewish people,

> informing them, by types
> And shadows, of that destined Seed to bruise
> The Serpent, by what means he shall achieve
> Mankind's deliverance. (XII. 232-235)

Adam thanks Michael for these revelations, "those
chiefly which concern / Just Abraham and his seed. .
. ." (XII.272-273). Michael, however, is not finished,
for he identifies the man who will come from the royal
line of David, originally from Eve's seed (XII.325-328)
and sketches the birth of Christ. Next Michael depicts
the death of Christ and his resurrection, which shall
defeat not only Satan but Sin and Death as well. Satan's head shall be bruised, and death shall not prevent man from ascending in resurrection to glory:

> This Godlike act
> Annuls thy doom, the death thou shouldst have died,
> In sin for ever lost from life; this act
> Shall bruise the head of Satan, crush his strength,
> Defeating Sin and Death, his two main arms,
> And fix far deeper in his head their stings
> Than temporal death shall bruise the victor's heel.
> Or theirs whom he redeems, a death like sleep,
> A gentle wafting to immortal life. (XII. 427-435)

Eve has been sleeping all the while, but she dreams a
good dream to counterbalance her earlier, bad dream,
and she understands the plan of salvation and her role
in it as the provider of the seed which will produce
the savior. The poem then symbolizes the divine process in which the seed of man, like the seeds of
nature, will be planted, apparently die in the cold
ground, and then grow to be harvested. In prophecy,

> "What is created, then, is a transcendental form
> whose objective is transcendental vision. Prophecy
> is, these poets would say with Blake, 'Ideal Form,
> The Universal Mold.' A perfect literary microcosm,
> prophecy is a new creation revealing the secret of
> all creation, whereby order is brought out of chaos
> and unity wrested from division."174

79

Such a symbol fulfills the definition of prophecy.
Any consideration or suggestion that the seed of man
or of matter in general is evil or somehow unworthy
is completely absent from Paradise Lost. The seed and
its flesh possess innate goodness.

Furthermore, if the Fall has in some way degen-
erated the flesh in any way, then St. Paul offers the
opportunity for the flesh, or body, to ascend to heaven
in what is now commonly known as a "glorified condition":

All flesh is not the same flesh: but there is
one kind of flesh of men, another flesh of beasts,
another of fishes, and another of birds.

There are also celestial bodies, and bodies
terrestrial: but the glory of the celestial is
one, and the glory of the terrestrial is another.

. . . .

So also is the resurrection of the dead. It is
sown in corruption; it is raised in incorruption:

It is sown in dishonour; it is raised in glory:
it is sown in weakness; it is raised in power:

It is sown a natural body; it is raised a spiritual body. There is a natural body, and there is
a spiritual body. (I Cor. 15.39-40, 42-44)

Paul maintains the cause-and-effect relationship
between the resurrection of the first Adam and the
second Adam in that Christ's resurrection is a "quickening spirit," a lifegiving agency which provides life
for the soul of man, and also, in the process of raising and glorifying man's body, for that too (I Cor. 15.
45-50). Paul realizes the immensity of what he is
saying and so comments: "Behold, I shew you a mystery;
We shall not all sleep, but we shall all be changed"
(I Cor. 15.51).

The Church Fathers fastened on this doctrine
almost immediately and proclaimed it as a source of
consolation to believers. Justin Martyr related the
concept of the glorified body to Chapter Thirty-Seven
of Ezekiel, in which Ezekiel goes out into the valley
of the dry bones (a favorite image of T.S. Eliot) and
the Lord clothes the bodies with flesh and they stand.

The Lord then tells Ezekiel that he will open the
graves of the house of Israel so that they can enter
into the land of Israel. Justin Martyr concludes
that Ezekiel is speaking in eschatological terms of
the future of bodies already in the grave.[175] Sulpicius Severus, commenting on the demise of St. Martin,
characterizes his appearance in terms of the transformation of the resurrected body: "they saw his
face as if it had been the face of an angel. His
limbs too appeared white as snow, ... as if he
had been manifested in the glory of the future resurrection, and with the nature of a body which had
been changed."[176] Origen, once again a surprising
person to cite in defense of glorified flesh, seems
eager to accept this notion as he speaks in the
clothing metaphor of which St. Paul was so fond:
"This matter of the body, then, which is now corruptible shall put on incorruption when a perfect
soul, and one furnished with the marks of incorruption, shall have begun to inhabit it. And do not be
surprised if we speak of a perfect soul as the clothing of the body . . . . when Jesus Christ . . . is
said to be clothing of the saints, according to the
language of the apostle, 'Put ye on the Lord Jesus
Christ.' As Christ, then, is the clothing of the
soul, so for a kind of reason sufficiently intelli-
gible is the soul said to be the clothing of the
body, seeing it as an ornament to it, covering and
concealing its mental nature,"[177] a reversal of the
usual metaphor. Origen speaks in language which
represents a fusion of Platonic ideas of the body as
a covering or shell for the soul, but he gladly
embraces the thought of this shell being transformed
into something heavenly. From an esthetic perspective, Origen views the analogy between the heavenly
bodies of the solar system and the glorified bodies
of men who are resurrected, according to I Cor. 2.9):
"it may be conceived how great are the comeliness,
and the splendour, and brilliancy of a spiritual
body." He further notes how the same body man had
on earth will clothe him in heaven, but it will pass,
with the will of God, into a new condition.[178]

Tertullian distinguishes between the Platonic
and Pauline perceptions in terms of the metaphors
used by both sides: "In the Platonic view, the body

is a prison, in that of St. Paul, it is the temple of God because it is in Christ."[179] After pointing out Paul's emphasis on both Adam's and Christ's resurrecting from the dead, he explains the process whereby the old body is glorified. For him "an additional body" is constructed over the old body, but the original body is not destroyed but "increased" and preserved. Fusing the metaphor of the planted seed as the basis for resurrection and the theme of the glorified body, he comments on the old body, "for when sown it is merely grain, without the clothing of its husk or the foundation of its ear or the defences of its beard or the pride of its stalk: but when it rises up it has made interest by multiplication, is built up in compactness, is drawn up in rank, fortified with apparel, and clothed in every sense."[180] St. John Chrysostom, commenting on Philippians 3.21, where Paul depicts the bodies of men as being "fashioned like unto His glorious body," observes that Paul could be speaking figuratively and not with doctrinal literalness. Chrysostom relates Paul's statement on the question in Corinthians to John 12.24 and insists that God and not the ground causes the body to rise: that it is not a natural process but a divine one (in opposition to Tertullian). The substance of the body remains the same, but its beauty becomes greater, all of this because, as St. Paul stated, of Christ's pledge "of the life to come."[181]

Augustine, with his emphasis on the subjection of the body to the will, characterizes the state of the body in the celestial city as "no more an encumbrance to the soul, by corruptibility, but is now become spiritual, perfected, and entirely subject unto the sovereignty of the will." Citing Romans 8. 10, 11 on Christ's "quickening" of the mortal bodies of men, he interprets Paul's distinction between "a living soul" and the "quickening spirit" (I Cor. 15. 45) as referring respectively to "a natural body" and "a spiritual body."[182]

St. Thomas Aquinas presents a question, "Of the Integrity of the Bodies in the Resurrection," in the Summa Theologica and in Scholastic fashion offers an incredible set of details on the nature of the

glorified body. He does not provide any defense of
the doctrine but is fascinated by speculations on the
resurrected condition, reflecting the Aristotelianiz-
ing of Christianity in the Middle Ages. Where Paul
was content to typify the whole question as a mystery,
Thomas insists on hypothesizing on the qualities of
the body, even though he is not disturbed by the lack
of any data, Biblical or otherwise, to support his
conclusions.[183]

The Reformation maintained the tradition of
belief in the resurrected body, but Luther and Calvin
differed somewhat in their definition of the glorified
body. For Luther "a new (glorified) body is raised
up which is free from passion and sin,"[184] and Melanchthon agrees with him.[185] Calvin, however, maintains
that men will be given new bodies in the resurrection,
citing Tertullian's On the Resurrection of the Flesh
in support of his contention. For Calvin the present
body is animated by the anima or soul, but the risen
body will be inspired by the Spirit and so will be
"more excellent." Man, he maintains, has his animal
nature from Adam but will have his heavenly nature
from Christ.[186] Valdes agrees precisely with Calvin
on these points.[187] Calvin's attitude toward the
present body of flesh regards it as "a house of tabernacle," in St. Paul's phrase, and posits that it is
therefore temporary and without foundation "as a
frail hut, to be inhabited by them for a few days."
Calvin, ever mindful of the distinction between sheep
and goats, iterates that the wicked will present to
God nothing but "a disgraceful nakedness," but believers will appear before God clothed in Christ with
a glorified body.[188] Like Origen he seems to greet
the doctrine of the resurrection of the body with a
sigh of relief because of his jaundiced view of man's
condition in this life. He finds it difficult to
maintain a distinction between the flesh as divinely
created and therefore good (the Hebraic and Pauline
conceptions) and the glandular flesh as the insti-
gator of evil.

Milton and his contemporaries in England had no
quarrels with the doctrine as Calvin presented it on
the basis of Paul's Epistles. For Milton the body is
spiritualized at the Resurrection, and there is no need

for a new body since all is subsumed under the action of glorification.[189] Samuel Bolton, accepting this tradition, rhapsodizes. in Pauline metaphor: "They shall arise perfect bodies, freed from sickness and all imperfections; spiritual bodies (I Cor. 15.44), not in regard to substance but in regard to qualities; immortal bodies, never to die more; glorious bodies, every one filled with brightness and splendour, shining as the sun in the firmament."[190] Thomas Jacomb quotes Philippians 3.21 and associates the doctrine of the risen body with that of the mystical body of Christ: "The head is risen, and the members shall rise also, by virtue of the union that is betwixt them. Quod praecessit in capite, sequitur in corpore, as Augustine speaks."[191] Philip Airay finds encouragement in the doctrine that Christ will transform "the vile body" into one "like unto his glorious body."[192] He waxes eloquent on the contrast between the present condition of our bodies and their future state:

> Now they are vile, and rotten, and naught, but then they shall be changed, and be made like unto Christ his glorious body: . . . How many aches, infirmities, diseases are we troubled withal in our bodies! What wounds, and swellings, and sores, full of all manner of corruption, are our bodies subject unto! What labours, what perils, what watchings, fastings, cold, nakedness, imprisonments, how many kinds of deaths are they subject unto! How soon are they cut down like grain! . . . our bodies which were weak, shall be raised up in power; our bodies, which were natural, needing food, raiment, rest, sleep, physic, and the like, shall be raised up spiritual, needing none of these things, but being, as the angels of God, exempt from all wants and infirmities of this life.[193]

One of the most surprising things about the doctrine of the glorified body is, as Josephine L. Burroughs observes, that for Marsilio Ficino, the architect of Renaissance Neoplatonism, the final end of the soul, its happiness in heaven, can only be complete when it is reunited with the body, which has been "made everlasting," as Ficino put it.[194] This represents the degree to which Platonism was Christianized in the Renaissance.

To return full circle, our perception of Milton
as a man steeped in the Hellenic, Judaic, and Christian traditions should be guided by the knowledge
that Milton's attitude toward the flesh of man, in
his maturity, depended heavily on a dual conception
of the glandular flesh. The flesh is not responsible
for all the sins of man, but the self, often translated by the word <u>flesh</u>, is that which, in its hostility to its Maker, produces evil. Milton's Christian
humanism, not his Platonism, dominates his thinking
and his poetry.

NOTES: CHAPTER ONE

[1]See C.S. Lewis, _A Preface to Paradise Lost_ (London, 1942) and Douglas Bush, _Paradise Lost in Our Time_ (Ithaca, 1945) for Milton as humanist, a position central to an appraisal of Milton.

[2]For example, see _Plato and Milton_ (Ithaca, 1965), p. viii.

[3]Irene Samuel, _Plato and Milton_, pp. 10-11, sees the poem as essentially Platonic but in a "conventional" sense.

[4]_Tertullian's Treatise on the Resurrection_, trans. E. Ernest Evans (London, 1960), p. 13.

[5]_The Dialogues of Plato_, trans. Benjamin Jowett (New York, 1892), I, 460-462, 491.

[6]_The Dialogues_, I, 582.

[7]_The Dialogues_, I, 553.

[8]_The Dialogues_, I, 452-453; see also pp. 460-461 for Socrates' detailed description of the horses.

[9]_The Dialogues_, I, 456-457.

[10]_The Dialogues_, II, 205.

[11]_The Dialogues_, II, 206-208.

[12]_The Dialogues_, II, 224-225. See also p. 255 on the soul's attachments to the body. Jowett long ago pointed out how Milton follows this notion precisely in _A Mask_, 11.463-475.

[13]_The Dialogues_, II, 262.

[14]_Theological Dictionary of the New Testament_, ed. Gerhard Friedrich, trans. Geoffrey W. Bromeley, 1971, pp. 122-123, hereafter cited as _Theological Dictionary_.

[15]_Enneads_, trans. Stephen MacKenna, rev. B.S. Page, 2nd ed. (New York, n.d.), pp. 357-358.

[16]_Enneads_, p. 359. Irene Samuel, _Plato_, p. 37, states that the _Enneads_ in the seventeenth century were regarded as "the very echo of Plato."

[17]_Enneads_, pp. 360-361.

[18]_Enneads_, p. 363.

[19]_Enneads_, p. 364.

[20]_Theological Dictionary_, pp. 123, 1025-1057.

[21]_Tertullian's Treatise_, p. 188.

[22]_Theological Dictionary_, pp. 1025-1057.

[23]_De Anima_ in _The Works of Aristotle_, trans. and ed. W.D. Ross et al. (Oxford, 1931), III, 402b.

[24]_Theological Dictionary_, p. 123.

[25]_Encyclopedic Dictionary of the Bible_, 2nd rev. ed., (New York, 1963), pp. 782-783.

[26]_Theological Dictionary_, p. 124.

[27]_The Christian in the Theology of St. Paul_ (London, 1967), p. 57.

[28]_Judaism: A Way of Life, An Introduction to the Basic Ideas of Judaism_ (New York, 1948), p. 284; see also pp. 35 and 95f.

[29]_Judaism_, p. 302.

[30]Cerfaux, _Christian_, pp. 308, 310.

[31]Rudolf Bultmann, _The Old and New Man in the Letters of Paul_, trans. Keith R. Crim (Richmond, 1967), p. 38.

[32]_Theology of the New Testament_, trans. Kendrick Grobel (New York, 1951), I, 209. See also Ernest DeWitt Burton, _Spirit, Soul and Flesh_ (Chicago, 1918), pp. 193-198. Burton argues that the word _sarx_ of St. Paul possesses hereditary associations, the special heredity of the Jewish people, and ethical associations not dependent upon the fact that man is composed of material flesh. Thus the totality of man, his pride in himself, is denoted by _sarx_, not the Platonic shell which man is well rid of if he is to obtain the good. By implication the _sarx_ then suggests the Mosaic law.

[33]Bultmann, _Theology_, I, 234, 194-197, 199.

[34]_Treatise on the Resurrection_, pp. 23, 27, and _On the Soul_ by Tertullian in _Apologetical Works and Minucius Felix Octavius_, trans. Rudolph Arbersmann et al. (New York, 1950); _Treatise_, p. 166.

[35]Charles Norris Cochrane, _Christianity and Classical Culture: A Study of Thought and Action from Augustus to Augustine_ (London, 1957), pp. 447-448.

[36]See the _Dictionary of the Bible_, rev. ed. (1963); _Interpreters' Dictionary of the Bible_, 4 vols, 1962, and the _Encyclopedic Dictionary of the Bible_.

[37]_Lectures on Galatians_, 1535, Chapters 5-6; _Lectures on Galatians_, 1519, Chapters 1-6 in _Luther's Works_, ed. Jaroslav Pelikan and Walter A. Hansen (St. Louis, 1964), XXVII (1519), p. 367. See also XXVI, 139-140.

[38]_Commentary on the Epistle to the Romans_, trans. J. Theodore Mueller (Grand Rapids, 1954), p. 86.

[39]_Luther and Erasmus: Free Will and Salvation_--Erasmus, _De Libero Arbitrio_, trans. and ed. E. Gordon Rupp and A.N. Marlow and Luther, _De Servo Arbitrio_ (_On the Bondage of the Will_), trans. and ed. Philip S. Watson and B. Drewery (Philadelphia, 1969), pp. 74-75.

[40]_On Galatians_, XXVII, 89.

[41]_On the Bondage of the Will_, p. 265.

[42]On the Bondage, pp. 273-275. See also On Galatians, XXVI, 125 and On Romans, p. 102, where Luther denies any light to human nature. He entitles one chapter in On the Bondage "The Whole Man--Body, Soul, and 'Spirit'--Is 'Flesh'." In this sense, because of his acceptance of the doctrine of Original Sin, which Judaism does not accept, and which, exegetically, rests on a question of the translation of Romans 5.12, the glandular flesh is not singled out as evil.

[43]On the Bondage, p. 265.

[44]Melanchthon on Christian Doctrine: Loci Communes 1555, trans. and ed. Clyde L. Manschreck (New York, 1965), p. 79.

[45]Commentaries on the Epistles of Paul the Apostle to the Philippians, Colossians, and Thessalonians, trans. John Pringle (Grand Rapids, 1948), p. 89.

[46]Commentary on the Epistles of Paul the Apostle to the Corinthians, trans. Rev. John Pringle (Grand Rapids, 1948), I, 124. See also Institutes of the Christian Religion, ed. John T. McNeill and trans. Ford Lewis Battles (Philadelphia, 1960), 2 vols. in The Library of Christian Classics, XX and XXX, I, 289-290.

[47]Commentaries on the Epistles of Paul to the Galatians and Ephesians, trans. Rev. William Pringle (Grand Rapids, 1948), p. 163.

[48]Institutes, I, 186, n. 7, 188, 195; cf. 696-697.

[49]Institutes, I, 190.

[50]Calvin, On Galatians, p. 166.

[51]Institutes, I, 252-253.

[52]On Philippians, p. 89.

[53]Institutes, II, 1311, and On Philippians, p. 198.

[54]Institutes, I, 777; II, 1312; I, 689.

[55]De Regno Christi in Melanchthon and Bucer in The Library of Christian Classics, ed. Wilhelm Pauch (Philadelphia, 1969), p. 383.

[56]An Exposition of St. Paul's First Epistle to the Corinthians, trans. J.H. Lupton (Ridgewood, N.J., 1965), p. 118.

[57]Sermons on the Eighth Chapter of the Epistle to the Romans (Verses 1-4) in Nichols Series of Commentaries (Edinburgh, 1868), VIII, 230.

[58]Sermons, pp. 68, 69, 167.

[59]Sermons, pp. 80-81.

[60]Sermons, pp. 69, 252-253. See also p. 73.

[61]A Commentary Upon The Epistles of St. Paul Written To The Colossians (Edinburgh, 1864), p. 36/446.

[62]The Works of John Milton, ed. Frank A. Patterson (New York, 1933), XV, 25, hereafter cited as Works. I will be using this edition for all quotations from the prose but consulting the Yale edition, especially the excellent notes cited below.

[63]The Complete Poetical Works of John Milton, ed. Douglas Bush (Boston, 1965), p. 344. All subsequent references to Milton's poetry are to this edition.

[64]Works, XV, 41.

[65]Of Christian Doctrine in Works, XV, 51.

[66]"The Milieu of Comus," SP, 41 (1944), 238-249.

[67]The Temple of the Mind: Education and Literary Taste in Seventeenth-Century England (New York, 1969), p. 104. Ruth Mohl concludes that the mature Milton fits into the tradition of Catholicism, Arminius, the Cambridge Platonists, and the Quakers in accepting the possibility of sinlessness of man. (Studies in Spenser, Milton and the Theory of Monarchy (New York, 1949), pp. 129-130.

[68] Sermons, p. 67.

[69] Theological Dictionary, pp. 134-135.

[70] "sarx," Theological Dictionary, p. 135.

[71] Theological Dictionary, pp. 1065, 1066, 1060.

[72] The Apostolic Fathers with Justin Martyr and Irenaeus, American Edition, ed. A. Cleveland Cox (New York, 1885), Bk. V, pp. 538, 541, Chapter XIV.

[73] Treatise on the Resurrection, pp. 15, 17.

[74] The Homilies of S. John Chrysostom, Archbishop of Constantinople, on the Epistles of St. Paul the Apostle to Timothy, Titus, and Philemon, trans. C.M. (Oxford, 1843), p. 224.

[75] Commentary on the Epistle to the Galatians, and Homilies on the Epistle to the Ephesians, of S. John Chrysostom, Archbishop of Constantinople, trans. J.H.N. (Oxford, 1840), pp. 79-80.

[76] The Homilies of S. John Chrysostom, Archbishop of Constantinople, on the Epistles of St. Paul the Apostle to the Philippians, Colossians, and Thessalonians, trans. C.M. (Oxford, 1843), pp. 330-331.

[77] The Homilies of S. John Chrysostom, Archbishop of Constantinople, on the First Epistle of St. Paul the Apostle to the Corinthians, trans. J.K., Part I (Oxford, 1839), pp. 310-311.

[78] The Homilies of S. John Chrysostom, Archbishop of Constantinople, on the Epistle of St. Paul the Apostle to the Romans, trans. C.M. (Oxford, 1841), p. 236.

[79] Christianity and Classical Culture, p. 390; see also p. 417.

[80] Basic Writings of Saint Augustine, ed. Whitney J. Oates (New York, 1948), I, 69.

[81] Cochrane, p. 417 and City of God, Bk. XIII, Ch. 16.

[82] *Basic Writings of Saint Augustine*, I, 658-730.

[83] *Treatise on the Resurrection*, pp. 7, 19, 29.

[84] *On Philippians, Colossians, and Thessalonians*, p. 407.

[85] *On Philippians and Colossians*, p. 159.

[86] *Sermons*, pp. 232-236.

[87] *Theological Dictionary*, pp. 125, 146-147. Wayne Meeks, "Paul as Heretic."

[88] *Treatise on the Resurrection*, pp. 127, 129, 131.

[89] *De Principiis* in *The Writings of Origen*, trans. Rev. Frederick Crombie (Edinburgh, 1869), I, 246, 247, 248.

[90] *Stromata*, in *Ante-Nicene Christian Library: Translations of the Fathers*, ed. Rev. Alexander Roberts and James Donaldson, Vol. IV (Edinburgh, 1868), p. 417.

[91] *On Philippians and Colossians*, pp. 271-272.

[92] *Commentary on Saint Paul's Epistle to the Galatians*, trans. F.R. Larcher (Albany, 1966), p. 63.

[93] *Commentary on the Epistle to the Romans*, trans. J. Theodore Mueller (Grand Rapids, 1954), p. 97, and *On the Bondage*, p. 263.

[94] *On Corinthians*, II, 132, 320.

[95] *Lectures Upon the Whole Epistle of St. Paul to the Philippians* (Edinburgh, 1864), p. 77.

[96] *Theological Dictionary*, pp. 130, 133.

[97] *Theology*, I, 240.

[98] *On Philippians*, p. 119 and *City of God*, II, 149.

[99] *On Galatians*, pp. 55, 79, 80.

[100] On Galatians, XXVI, 55, 216.

[101] On Corinthians I, 92; On Galatians and Ephesians, p. 163; On Philippians, p. 89. The flesh for Calvin also refers to externalities like ceremony or dead doctrines which have no future, e.g., On Galatians, p. 82.

[102] Michael Servetus, On the Righteousness of God's Kingdom in The Two Treatises of Servetus on the Trinity, trans. Earl Morse Wilbur in Harvard Theological Studies, XVI (Cambridge, Ma., 1932), p. 240.

[103] Servetus, pp. 242, 251.

[104] On Philippians, p. 399.

[105] Sermons, p. 67, n. 1.

[106] Sermons, p. 167.

[107] An Entire Commentary Upon the Whole Epistle of St. Paul to the Ephesians . . . , gen. ed. Rev. Thomas Smith (Edinburgh, 1866), p. 161.

[108] Commentary . . . Colossians, p. 43 / 453.

[109] Works, III, 2-3.

[110] Works, III, 145-146.

[111] Works, III, 198-199.

[112] Works, III, 245.

[113] Works, III, 267.

[114] Works, III, 313.

[115] Works, VI, 8, 22-23.

[116] Treatise on the Resurrection, p. xviii.

[117] Cited by Evans, Treatise, p. xxxiv.

[118] *Theological Dictionary*, pp. 122-123.

[119] *On Galatians*, pp, 82-84, 86.

[120] *City of God* in *Basic Writings*, II, 27, 28; *Confessions* in *Basic Writings*, I, 104.

[121] *Commentary on Saint Paul's Epistle to the Galatians*, pp. 173-174.

[122] *Commentaries on the Epistles to Timothy, Titus, and Philemon*, trans. William Pringle (Grand Rapids, 1948), p. 238.

[123] *Commentary Upon St. Paul's First Epistle to the Church at Corinth*, trans. John T. Betts (London, 1883), pp. 48, 50, 51, 306.

[124] *An Entire Commentary*, p. 117.

[125] *Works*, XV, 47.

[126] *Works*, XV, 211.

[127] *Works*, XV, 193, 195, 73.

[128] *On Galatians*, p. 169.

[129] *On Galatians*, p. 170.

[130] Philip S. Watson, Introduction to *Luther and Erasmus*, p. 16.

[131] John Colet, *An Exposition of St. Paul's Epistle to the Romans*, trans. J.H. Lupton (Ridgewood, N.J., 1965), pp. 29-32.

[132] J.H. Lupton, trans., *An Exposition of St. Paul's Epistles to the Corinthians*, p. 26, n. 1.

[133] Colet, *On Romans*, p. 26, 26 n. 1.

[134] Colet, *On Romans*, pp. 22, 60.

[135] Irene Samuel remarks on the difficulty of fixing the boundary between Platonism and Christianity. See *Plato and Milton*, p. 69.

[136]Commentaries on the Epistle of Paul the Apostle to the Hebrews, trans. and ed. Rev. John Owen (Grand Rapids, 1948), p. 334; Institutes, II, 987.

[137]Lectures Upon the Whole Epistle of St. Paul to the Philippians, . . . , p. 80.

[138]Plato, p. 16.

[139]Works, III, pp. 2-3.

[140]"The Argument in Milton's Comus," UTQ, II (1941), 47-71; "Comus Once More," UTQ, 19 (1950), 218-223; and "The Subject of Milton's Ludlow Mask," in Milton: Modern Essays in Criticism, ed. Arthur Barker (New York, 1965), pp. 88-111.

[141]Jayne, p. 90.

[142]Quoted in Jayne, p. 95.

[143]Jayne, pp. 93-94.

[144]The Summa Theologiae of Saint Thomas Aquinas, trans. Fathers of the Dominican Province, rev. Daniel J. Sullivan (Chicago, 1952), I, 429; II, 180.

[145]Christianity, p. 485.

[146]Paul and His Recent Interpreters (Grand Rapids, 1961), pp. 47, 97.

[147]Martin R.P. McGuire, Funeral Orations by Saint Gregory Nazianzen and Saint Ambrose, trans. Leo P. McCawley, S.J., et al. (New York, 1953), p. xiv.

[148]Against Heresies in The Apostolic Fathers, pp. 529, 531, 532; 560-561 and chapters 3, 31, and 32.

[149]De Principiis, p. 137.

[150]Ernest Evans, trans., Tertullian's Treatise, pp. xxvi-xxvii.

[151]Treatise, pp. 33, 139.

[152] On Philippians and Colossians, pp. 237, 407, 150; On Corinthians, Part One, p. 591.

[153] City of God, II, 131, 15-16.

[154] On Philippians, p. 44; On Timothy, p. 225; Institutes, II, 989, 990, 998-999.

[155] Loci Communes, p. 283.

[156] On Philippians, p. 126.

[157] Juan Valdes, Commentary Upon St. Paul's First Epistle to the Church at Corinth, p. 265. See also pp. 272, 278.

[158] Sermons, p. 272.

[159] Works, XVI, 353.

[160] Works, XV, 247, 231-233, 223, 229; Calvin, On Corinthians, II, 21-22.

[161] Contra Celsum in The Writings of Origen, trans. Rev. Frederick Crombie (Edinburgh, 1864), I, 224, 287.

[162] On Corinthians, Part Two, p. 583.

[163] Concerning Baptism in Ascetical Works, trans. Sister M. Monica Wagner C.S.C. (New York, 1950), pp. 366-367.

[164] Works, I, 47.

[165] On the Belief in the Resurrection in Some of The Principal Works of St. Ambrose, trans. Rev. H. De Romestin (New York, 1896), pp. 182, 183, 184.

[166] On the Belief, p. 183, 183 n. 1.

[167] Two Books Concerning Repentance in Principal Works, p. 346.

[168] Treatise on the Resurrection, p. xviii.

[169] Treatise, p. 35.

[170]On Corinthians I, II, 47, 50. See also Institutes, II, 993.

[171]Of The Laws of Ecclesiastical Polity, intro. Christopher Morris (London, 1963), I, 211.

[172]Valdes, p. 287.

[173]Complete Poetical Works, p. 556, n. 1699.

[174]Joseph Wittreich, Visionary Poetics, p. 25.

[175]The First Apology in Writings of Saint Justin Martyr, ed. Thomas B. Fall (New York, 1948), p. 89.

[176]Letters of Sulpicius Severus in A Select Library of Nicene and Post-Nicene Fathers of the Christian Church, 2nd series, trans. Philip Schaff and Henry Wace, Vol. XI (New York, 1894), p. 23.

[177]De Principiis, p. 80.

[178]De Principiis, pp. 267, 270.

[179]On the Soul, p. 296.

[180]Treatise on the Resurrection, pp. 139, 153-155.

[181]On Philippians, p. 150, and On Corinthians, Part Two, pp. 583-590.

[182]City of God, II, 255, 20-21.

[183]The Summa Theologiae of Saint Thomas Aquinas, Summa II, Ques. LXXX, pp. 956-992.

[184]On Romans, p. 84.

[185]Loci Communes, p. 289.

[186]Institutes, II, 999; On Corinthians I, Vol. II, pp. 50-51, 56.

[187]Valdes, pp. 290, 291, 292-293.

[188] On Corinthians II, pp. 217, 218.

[189] See Milton's Of Christian Doctrine in Works XV, 25; XVI, 377.

[190] The True Bounds of Christian Freedom (London, 1964), p. 47.

[191] Sermons, p. 58.

[192] On Philippians, p. 210.

[193] On Philippians, pp. 316, 318.

[194] "Five Questions Concerning the Mind" in The Renaissance Philosophy of Man, ed. Ernst Cassirer et al. (Chicago, 1948), p. 192.

CHAPTER TWO

THE LAW AND THE LETTER

In Galatia St. Paul faced the problem of a group
of what were called false or pseudo- or super apostles
who had proselytized among the Galatians, preaching
a n adherence to the Jewish Law. Paul had been away,
but his letter to the Galatians expresses his rejection
of the Law in the face of the Crucifixion and Resurrection of Christ. The Torah, as recognized by the
Pharisees, was composed of the written Pentateuch and
the legal writings, which were originally oral. The
Pharisees attempted to keep the Torah alive by making
it relevant to all occasions, to cover all conceivable
situations where God's will had to be done.[1] Others
saw the Torah as a repository of wisdom. The false
apostles had been teaching adherence to the Law as
necessary for salvation, and the first two chapters
of the Epistle to the Galatians establish Paul's authority as an apostle and his rebuke of Peter on the question of circumcision, the symbol of the Law:

But neither Titus, who was with me, being a
Greek, was compelled to be circumcised:
And that because of false brethren unawares
brought in, who came in privily to spy out our
liberty which we have in Christ Jesus, that they
might bring us into bondage. . . . (2.3-4)

But when Peter was come to Antioch, I withstood
him to the face, because he was to be blamed.
For before that certain came from James, he
did eat with the Gentiles: but when they were
come, he withdrew and separated himself, fear-
ing them which were of the circumcision.
And the other Jews dissembled likewise with
him; insomuch that Barnabas also was carried away
with their dissimulation.
But when I saw that they walked not uprightly
according to the truth of the gospel, I said unto
Peter before them all, If thou, being a Jew,
livest after the manner of Gentiles, and not as
do the Jews, why compellest thou the Gentiles to
live as do the Jews?
We who are Jews by nature, and not sinners of

the Gentiles,

> Knowing that a man is not justified by the
> works of the law, but by the faith of Jesus Christ,
> even we have believed in Jesus Christ, that we
> might be justified by the faith of Christ, and
> not by the works of the law: for by the works of
> the law shall no flesh be justified. . . .
> For I through the law am dead to the law, that
> I might live unto God. (2.11-16, 19)

Paul, as the Apostle to the Gentiles, determined to
stand fast on the issue of full justification by
Christ's sacrifice and insisted that the Law did not
apply to the Gentiles. The question of whether Gentile Christians could be circumcised or not became
the test case; Peter had taken a conservative position
and wished the Gentiles to observe the ceremonial law,
and Paul soundly rebuked him for it. The tenth chapter of Acts records Peter's dream which allegorically,
through abrogation of the dietary laws, advised Peter
to extend the Gospel to the Gentiles, who were also
blessed by the Holy Spirit. On the one side are
faith in Christ, grace, and freedom; on the other
are the Law, man's own deeds, and the bondage of sin.

During the Reformation an interesting parallel
was drawn between the false apostles and the Roman
church in that both were insisting on adherence to
the law, the one Mosaic, the other Canon. Luther
correlates the "false apostles" and the papists, who
"stubbornly insist that human traditions cannot be
dropped without putting salvation in jeopardy."
Luther was concerned about statements like Boniface
VIII's bull, <u>Unam Sanctam</u> of November 18, 1302, which
pontificated that "We declare, say, define, and proclaim to every human creature that they by necessity
for salvation are entirely subject to the Roman pontiff."[2] Calvin estimates both the Mosaic and Canon
laws similarly: "The Papists must therefore be held
equally censurable with the false apostles; and with
this additional aggravation, that, while the former
proposed to keep those days which had been appointed
by the law of God, the latter enjoins days, rashly
stamped with their own seal, to be observed as most
holy."[3] He further equates both groups in terms of
their insistence on actions as opposed to faith in
Christ, and on their opposing the flesh to the

Spirit.[4] He accuses the false apostles of hypocrisy
and pride in their "unreasonable zeal for the law."
Ultimately Calvin envisions the issue as a conflict
between "Christian liberty" as did Paul, and he condemns the false apostles for insisting on externals
and not comprehending the meaning of Christ's death.[5]
Michael Servetus, who incidentally was put to death
in Calvin's Geneva, made the same association between
the law of God, or the Mosaic law, and "monastic
laws," both of which put men under a curse; and even,
worse, the latter are manmade.[6] This is almost precisely the position that Milton took in the anti-
prelatical and divorce tracts: that his opponents
are merely interested in legalistic externals and not
at all in the liberty which Christ bestowed upon all
men.[7]

Since the concept of the Mosaic law became em-
broiled in the polemics of the Reformation, it is
helpful to define the Law from the point of view of
those reformers who had rejected it, partially or
totally, as a means of justification. S.S. Cohon
notes how in post-Talmudic commentary the Torah's
injunctions are classified as either "rational or
ethical" or "traditional or ceremonial."[8] Early in
the history of the church, St. Ambrose had offered a
brief symbolic definition which said that "according
to the Law there are these three: the shadow, the
image and the reality. The shadow is in the Law; the
image is in the Gospel; the reality shall be in the
Judgement."[9] This kind of eschatological representation vaguely anticipated the analytics expended in
the sixteenth and seventeenth centuries. Depending
upon the context, the word _law_ can include the external law of God, the judicial law, the natural law,
ceremonial or moral sides of the Mosaic law, or canon
law. For example, in the _Reason of Church-Government_
Milton defines the Mosaic law as either political or
moral, and if moral it contains what is "perpetually
true and good, either in religion, or course of
life"; the natural law within; and the authentic
gospel. In a _Treatise_ . . . _Civil Power_ he cites St.
Paul as including both the ceremonial and the ecclesiastical facets of the Law as "_weak and beggarly
rudiments_."[10]

Commenting on Hebrews 7.12, Martin Luther offers the following distinctions:

> In the first place, according to the lower under-
> standing, by which he ⌊Paul⌋ means only the
> ceremonials, namely, the vestments and external
> adornments of the priests, likewise the offering
> and sacrifices of the flesh of beasts, likewise
> the judgments and teachings pertaining to leprosy
> and the uncleanness resulting from touching the
> dead, and the like. Thus the meaning is that
> the law has been changed; that is, ceremonies of
> this kind prescribed by the law have been abro-
> gated, and the things that were signified by
> these have themselves been instituted, that is,
> the spiritual and inner garment and adornment
> of the priests. . . .[11]

Here obviously Luther is talking about and illustrating the ceremonial law of the Old Testament, but a
second definition of his, based on Romans and Galatians, is "whatever is commanded by God and by man,
whether it is ceremonial or judicial or moral."[12]
Thus, there stands a distinction between judicial,
moral, and ceremonial facets of the Law, but it is
not clarified.

Luther's friend and colleague, Philip Melanchthon, is more precise in his definitions:

> The law in Moses has three parts. The First part
> is called <u>lex</u> <u>moralis</u>, that is, laws about vir-
> tues; . . . <u>eternal</u> <u>law</u>, or the law about the
> 'judgment of God against sin.' The second part
> is <u>lex</u> <u>ceremonialis</u>, that is, laws about the
> Church, which are concerned with external works,
> like sacrifices, and prohibited eating of the
> flesh of swine, all of which were established
> for a certain time, as in ancient Judaism. The
> third part is <u>lex</u> <u>judicialis</u>, that is, laws about
> civil government, about justice, inheritance, and
> peace. There is a great difference between the
> first part, which pertains to the eternal, and
> the other two, which pertain to the temporal.[13]

Melanchthon, with his sharp analytical mind, further
defines "the eternal, unchangeable wisdom and principle of righteousness in God himself," and indicates
that this law did not begin or end with Judaism.[14]

Within the Law then there is the moral, ceremonial, and judicial, but the first, the moral or eternal, transcends Moses and Judaism. Calvin accepts these distinctions and further adds that "the law of God which we call the moral law is nothing else than "a testimony of natural law and of that conscience which God has engraved upon the minds of men." He further asserts that the law to St. Paul meant not only ceremonies but also the moral law in opposition to the Papists who think the reverse because of Origen and Jerome.[15] Michael Servetus adds that the ceremonial law claimed the power to sanctify while the moral law asserted the ability to justify, although Christ now does both.[16]

Allied with Augustine and Aquinas, Richard Hooker offers some definitions of the word law, which fit in neatly with the thinking of Calvin and other theologians of the Reformation. Hooker distinguishes between two eternal laws of God, the "first law eternal" of God which covers his actions, and "the second law eternal," which applies to natural creatures such as men. This second law is the model to which the laws of men should correspond, and this law is easy for men to discover. The connection between the eternal natural law and those laws of Scripture involves no contradiction for Hooker: "laws human must be made according to the general laws of nature, and without contradiction unto any positive law in Scripture."[17] God left the Jews three laws, the moral, ceremonial, and judicial, and those laws whose "end" continues, such as the moral law. He further distinguishes between laws of doctrine and laws of "regiment," the former presumably the moral law which is immutable and the latter pertaining to the discipline and order of the church. These latter are not immutable. Hooker also explains such distinctions with the terms "ceremonies" and "Covenant," the former temporary but the latter, based on the Decalogue as permanent. Laws of discipline and ceremony are generally left in the care of the church, but not all are necessarily so, according to Hooker's reading of Calvin's Institutes.[18] Hooker's emphasis resides on distinctions made between those laws which have been abrogated by Christ's sacrifice and those which have not.

Samuel Bolton, a seventeenth-century commentator, focuses on those laws which are found in the Old and New Testaments, "any doctrine, instruction, law, ordinance, or statute, divine or human, which teaches, directs, commands, or binds men to any duty which they owe to God or man."[19] (Bolton claims that the etymology of the word Torah is based on another word meaning to throw darts.) Thus, the term may refer to the moral, ceremonial, or judicial Law. He states explicitly "SEVEN PURPOSES FOR WHICH THE LAW WAS GIVEN," under the direction of the two great ends of the Law, the "political" or "divine":

(1) "To restrain transgression" by revealing sin and God's wrath with it. Presumably without the Law, the evil, depraved state of man would lead to moral anarchy.
(2) "the law was given to uncover and reveal transgression" in the sense that the conscience had to be convinced of sin and so look for help.
(3) "the law was given to humble men for sin."
(4) "for a direction of life, a rule of walking to believers."
(5) "to reveal the imperfections in our performance of duties."
(6) "as a reprover and corrector for sin."
(7) "to be a spur to quicken us to duties."[20]

The repetition inherent in the above suggests the strong emphasis of Bolton on the depravity of man. Paul Bayne accepts the distinctions made by Hooker and others between the moral law, the ecclesiastical or ceremonial law, and political laws governing the state of the Jews.[21] Hooker and those on the conservative side in the English church tended to correlate contemporary ceremonial law with Mosaic ceremonial law, while those on the left regarded this latter as having no effect on church discipline or ritual. Thomas Jacomb points out that it is not always easy to comprehend which law St. Paul is talking about when he is censuring it (e.g. Romans 8.3,4), whether the Law given to Adam, the natural, or that given to the Israelites, the Decalogue.[22]

For Judaism, as S.S. Cohon remarks, the importance of the moral and ceremonial law is paramount:

"The essence of Judaism is revealed not only in its
creedal affirmations and rational conceptions but also
in the ethical and ceremonial law. Six hundred thir-
teen commandments, say the rabbis, were given unto
Moses at Sinai: two hundred forty-eight mandatory,
corresponding to the number of parts in the human
body, and three hundred sixty-five prohibitory, corresponding to the days of the year. The whole body
of Halachah is derived from the Heaven-revealed Torah,
and is coextensive with life. It represents the means
whereby men express their faith."23

        Most vital to any discussion of the law during
the Reformation is the concept of the natural law
engraven on the heart as opposed to the Mosaic law
engraven on stone tablets, a favorite symbolic and
philosophical distinction of Milton's. Calvin was
faced with interpreting II Corinthians 3.6-7:

        Who also hath made us able ministers of the
        new testament; not of the letter, but of the
        spirit: for the letter killeth, but the spirit
        giveth life.
        But if the ministration of death, written and
        engraven in stones, was glorious, so that the
        children of Israel could not stedfastly behold
        the face of Moses for the glory of his counten-
        ance; which glory was to be done away.

Lucien Cerfaux regards lines 1-18, including the passage above, as "a rabbinical commentary on Exodus 34.
29-35, the account of Moses receiving the Decalogue
from God on Mt. Sinai"; Rudolph Bultmann correlates
the term fleshly (II Cor. 3.2) with Ezekiel 11.19;
36.26, in which the Lord promises to replace stony
with fleshly ones for the Israelites, and notes that
the heart, kardia, refers to the ability to love
rather than think.24 Calvin refers to Jeremiah 31.34
(correctly 31.33) with its promise that God "will put
my law in their inward parts, and write in their
hearts" and allies it with Paul's similar conception
in Corinthians. The contrast with the Mosaic law
becomes clear; "the former literal, the latter spiritual doctrine; the former he [Paul] speaks of as
carved on tablets of stone, the latter as written
upon men's hearts."25

105

Michael Servetus associates the distinction
between the two kinds of law, the stony and the
fleshly, with Jeremiah. 31.33, who prophesies a new
covenant: "But this shall be the covenant that I
will make with the house of Israel; After those days,
saith the LORD, I will put my law in their inward
parts, and write it in their hearts; and will be
their God, and they shall be my people." The distinction is between death and life, bondage and
freedom, the letter and the Spirit.[26] Richard Hooker
goes so far as to assume that some ceremonial laws
fit into this category of being "written in men's
hearts."[27]

Milton agrees with the distinctions made by
Melanchthon and Calvin and the contrast between the
Mosaic law as externally written on stone and the
natural law embedded in the hearts of men. In western civilization the concept of the natural law was
not a Judaic or Christian concept originally but
stemmed from the thinking of Greek philosophers even
before the time of Plato.[28] St. Paul presumably had
absorbed this concept as his statement in Romans
implies: "For when the Gentiles, which have not the
law, do by nature the things contained in the law,
these, having not the law, are a law unto themselves"
(2.14, cited by Milton in Works XVI, 101). Milton
attributes to the idea a Christian history when he
claims that "The unwritten law is no other than that
law of nature given originally to Adam, and of which
a certain remnant, or imperfect illumination, still
dwells in the hearts of mankind; which, in the regenerate, under the influence of the Holy Spirit, is
daily tending towards a renewal of its primitive
brightness." However, he bases Paul's dichotomy on
the prophets Jeremiah, Isaiah, and Joel.[29] The term
law, according to Milton is also applied to "heavenly doctrine in the abstract, or the will of God,
as declared under both covenants."[30] Milton thus
envisions the natural law as the eternal will of God
imprinted in the heart of man, which, although it is
obscured by the Fall, is revitalized by the Holy
Spirit. This law existed before Moses ever came
down from the mountain. As Milton explains in Of
Christian Doctrine, the law comprises two elements:
(1) "that rule of conscience which is innate, and

engraven upon the mind of man" and (2) "the special
command which proceeded out of the mouth of God (for
the law written by Moses was long subsequent) . . .
Hence it is said, Romans ii. 12 'as many as have
sinned without law, shall also perish without law'."[31]
This was a central problem for St. Paul: how could
he, as a missionary, treat Gentiles on the same basis
as Jews, who had had the orientation of and sometimes
training in the Mosaic law.

Arthur Barker has most thoroughly discussed the
climate of ideas in the Puritan revolution in the
middle of the seventeenth century, and he points out
the role that appeals to natural law played in the
theo-politics of the day. Referring to Thomas Goodwin's Right and Might, he observes how difficult it
was to distinguish between the natural law and the
impact of the Holy Spirit, especially in matters of
politics:

> Goodwin's law written in the fleshly tables
> of men's hearts is of course simply the law of
> nature; and it must be distinguished from the
> law written only in the hearts of true believers
> by the Holy Spirit. It is the law of reason not
> of faith. But that theoretical distinction was
> difficult to preserve, especially when reason
> and faith, natural and spiritual law, were
> together involved in the dispute over the rights
> of conscience. The phrases appropriate to the
> one were readily transferable to the other; and
> their transference, either by analogy or identi-
> fication, is especially the mark of radical
> Puritan thought.[32]

In the political arena or from the scholarly perspective, there is absolutely no way of confirming such
distinctions if a "radical Puritan" claimed that his
thinking reflected the impression left in his heart
by the Holy Spirit. It was much easier with primi-
tives, who had no knowledge of Christianity, to conclude that their behavior was governed by the natural
law engraven in their hearts by God. Barker also notes
that Goodwin took almost precisely the same position
as Milton in Of Christian Doctrine and Paul in Romans--
that the pagan is saved or condemned on the basis of
the law of God planted within.[33]

The concept of the natural law had a long history in Christianity, going back as far as St. Augustine's On the Spirit and the Letter, where he remarked that the Gentiles have the law written within them since as humans they retain "the image of God in them."[34] He further argued, using the image of the branches grafted onto the olive tree in Romans 11, that the Gentiles can join the main trunk of Judaic Christianity through faith and love in Christ.[35] Barker notes that Goodwin agreed with this position, but this dispensation for the Gentiles is not the same as the natural law; it is the granting of righteousness through Christ and the Gospel. St. Paul sternly warns the Romans in allegorical terms that the Jews have felt the wrath of God and so will they if they do not believe: "For if God spared not the natural branches, take heed lest he also spare not thee" (Romans 11.21).

Even early in the sixteenth century, support had crystallized for the concept of salvation for those living outside the pale of formal Christian belief on the basis of the natural law. Just as the Gentiles lived outside the milieu of Judaic Christianity in the early years of the church, some Protestants viewed themselves in the same position with regard to Roman Catholicism, with its traditions and canon law. John Colet, for example, emphasizes the irrelevancy of the Mosaic law: "And if the Gentiles, without having the Law given them, lived well, it harmed them not to have not the Law. So likewise if the Jews lived ill under the Law, then for them to have the Law profited nothing."[36] Calvin agrees that there is a natural law of God in the hearts of all men, and he includes even the "reprobate" who would properly worship God except for their stubbornness.[37] With his preoccupation with the worse elements in man, however, he contradicts himself in his commentary on Hebrews, lamenting that the natural law in man seems to be a perverse one and that it can be neutralized only by the Spirit of God. "In short, the word of God never penetrates into our hearts, for they are iron and stone until they are softened by him; nay, they have engraven on them a contrary law, for perverse passions rule within, which lead us to rebellion. In vain then does God proclaim his Law by the voice of man, unless he writes it by his Spirit on our hearts, that is, unless he forms and prepares us for obedience."[38] Calvin is here commenting on Hebrews 8.10, the delineation of the New Covenant: "I will put my laws into their mind, and write them in their hearts: and I will be to them a God, and they shall be to me a people," an echo of Ezekiel 27.26, 27. Calvin is maintaining, with his own particular emphasis, the distinction between the natural law instilled by God in all men and the new law of the Spirit which is given to man by the sacrifice of Christ.

Milton consistently maintains the distinction between the natural law and the law of the Spirit and does not assume that the law of the Spirit is necessary for any good acts, negating any natural perverseness. Thus there is no ultimate conflict between man's depravity and the Spirit. Milton, in the Second Defence, looking back on his writings on divorce, says, "My explanation was in accordance with divine law, which Christ did not revoke; much less did He give approval in civil life to any other law more weighty than the law of Moses."[39] In Tetrachordon he states that the Mosaic law cannot violate "the free dictates of nature and morall law" or "charity also and religion in our hearts."[40] And so the natural law is never abrogated, certainly not by the Mosaic law, and charity and religion remain superior to the code of Moses.

The relationship between the judicial facet of the Mosaic law and civil or worldly authority and law is somewhat ambiguous in the Reformation. Luther believes that the Mosaic law is necessary in some respects, but his explanation of the connections between worldly and religious law is not at all clear. His argument may be summarized in this way; he says that "conscience has no relation to the Law [Mosaic] or to works or to earthly righteousness. . . . In society, on the other hand, obedience to the Law must be strictly required." He goes on to depict life on earth as "the dirt and filth of this physical life" and to conclude that the Law (presumably Mosaic) belongs here, although true righteousness (a spiritual condition) belongs above. It is not at all clear what the connection between the judicial aspect of the Mosaic law, apparently applicable on earth, and

righteousness is supposed to be. He further muddies
the picture by arguing that there is a time for the
Law and for the Gospel and that sometimes the Gospel
is irrelevant: "There is a time to hear the Gospel
and a time to know nothing about the Gospel." He
further characterizes the Mosaic law as a "spiritual
prison" which keeps men from some sins punishable by
civil law."[41] Philip Melanchthon, whose primary
ethical emphasis focuses ever on obedience, concludes
that worldly authority is "the voice of the Ten Commandments" and that it punishes violations of the
commandments.[42] Martin Bucer, however, stated that
Christ nullified the "civil laws of Moses."[43]

Milton's basic position is to separate the civil
from the Mosaic law (in this case the Decalogue) and
to insist that the civil magistrate does not have the
authority to compel men in matters of religion. He
does not dwell on the possible function of the Mosaic
law to deter men from violating civil law, as in the
case of homicide, which is punishable by both laws.
In the divorce tracts, he removes the issue of divorce
from the law entirely and perceives it as a question
of conscience and insists that the judicial law cannot regulate sin. He further separates the civil law
of the early days of the church, which he says "is
the honour of every true Civilian to stand for," from
the later "pontificall Canon" law which puts Christians into bondage.[44] His clearest statements on the
subject appear in Of Civil Power, where he insists
that the civil law should not interfere with the freedom of the Christian in matters which are religious
and should not attempt to use outward, corporal force
in this area:

> Christian magistrates . . . ⌊should⌋ meddle not
> rashly with Christian libertie, the birthright
> and outward testimonie of our adoption: least
> while they little think it, may think they do
> God service, they themselves like the sons of
> that bondwoman ⌊Hagar, Abraham's wife⌋ be found
> persecuting them who are freeborne of the spirit;
> and by a sacrilege of not the least aggravation
> bereaving them of that sacred libertie which our
> Saviour with his own blood purchas'd for them.[45]

110

Arthur Barker's discussion of this problem cannot be improved upon in its development in the Whitehall debates. Ireton had introduced Israel as a model and argued that the Christian magistrate could restrain those nonbelievers from performing acts of irreligion. This position was similar to that of the twenty-third chapter of the <u>Westminster Confession</u>, but John Goodwin contradicted the analogy between the Jewish and the Christian magistrate by asserting that the Jewish magistrate in the Old Testament had his power from God, but since the Gospel abrogated the Jewish law that the Christian magistrate had no such power. <u>The Leveller</u> of 1659 alleged that the magistrate could only be concerned with "outward acts of morality" but not with inner religion or worship. This position corresponds to Milton's conclusions on the subject.[46] The important point to keep in mind is the vital role which thinking men in the seventeenth century assigned to the question of the Mosaic law in the light of the redemption of Christ.

The ceremonial laws of the Mosaic code were concerned with dietary laws, purification, the keeping of the feast days, and other matters that were primarily external and distinct from either the moral or judicial elements of the Law in the Old Testament. Although we are concerned here with the attitude of the Reformation and Milton toward ceremonial injunctions, it is salutory to refer to the situation as it existed back into the time of the Old Testament. "Thus the priests of ancient Israel identified piety with scrupulous regard for the requirements of the national cult. The way of securing God's favor was through the punctilious fulfillment of the prescriptions of ritual in minutest detail. The prophets, on the other hand, with their deeper sense of the holiness of God, repudiated the sacrificial cult as well as the stated festivities as the all-effective means of gaining God's favor, and called for a piety that expresses itself in the self-consecration of the individual and nation to God."[47]

There is not a great deal of concern with the ceremonial law on the part of the early Church Fathers or in the Middle Ages, but they became of paramount importance in the Reformation because this law was

111

analogous to the ceremonies of the Roman church and
formed the basis for a rejection of the latter. Just
as St. Paul had rejected Jewish ceremony and ritual
and St. Peter had had the vision of the unclean ani-
nals in his dream in Acts, the Protestant reformers
and theologians immediately before them came to the
same conclusion. The chief symbol of these rituals
was circumcision because this rite became the basis
for the contention between Peter and Paul already
alluded to. It was St. Paul's attitude that circumcision was unnecessary for justification under the
New Covenant and that more important than external
circumcision was inner circumcision--of the heart.
In the broad view of the ceremonial law, Milton
includes all of Jewish history before Christ as under
the ceremonial law, even before Abraham.[48]

One of the vexed theological problems of the
Reformation consisted in whether the coming of Christ
entirely abrogated or perhaps totally fulfilled the
Mosaic law in all its ramifications, but most thinkers
seemed to agree that, most certainly, the ceremonial
law was extinct. One of the earliest commentators to
reach this conclusion was John Colet. "For that system," he affirmed, "of rites and ceremonies neither
purifies the soul nor justifies any one; nor, indeed,
without grace could those commands and prohibitions
have been observed."[49] Martin Bucer agreed fully:
"We have no need to observe circumcision, sacrifices,
multiple purifications of the body and of outward
practices which the Lord especially commanded to the
Jews through Moses."[50]

The fourteenth chapter of Romans provided Martin
Luther with his position on ceremonies, that essentially they were matters of indifference and that they
did not concern salvation. St. Paul was upset with
the Romans for being over-concerned with the question
of dietary laws and the observation of feast days.
He was primarily concerned that this issue not prove
a detriment to a man's receiving righteousness: "Let
us not therefore judge one another any more: but
judge this rather, that no man put a stumbling-block
or an occasion to fall in his brother's way" (14.13).
Luther agrees and applies Paul's argument to the
controversy over the retention of Roman Catholic

112

ceremonies in Protestant churches. In commenting on
Galatians, he remarks that St. Jerome had blamed Paul
for "quibbling" over nothing in his argument with
Peter over circumcision, but the question of eating
with Gentiles Luther regarded as important precisely
in its not being relevant to salvation.[51] Melanchthon follows the same line of thinking, urging that
St. Paul was anxious about ceremonies because the
false apostles were insisting that they were necessary
for salvation. He admits that these rules in the Old
Testament served a valid function in that they, "when
used rightly, are extolled by St. Paul in Galatians
3:24, 'The law was our custodian to instruct and to
lead us to Christ'; that is, ceremonies and other
disciplines were given to us for remembrance and restraint until we should come to the true knowledge
of Christ."[52]

Calvin, interpreting Romans 9 to 12, asserts the
connection between the ceremonial law of the Old Testament and the ceremonies of Rome, both of which are
rejected by the Gospel.[53] He censures the Roman tendency toward imitation: "For they have partly taken
their pattern from the ravings of the Gentiles, [the
foolish wisdom theme], partly, like apes, have rashly
imitated the ancient rites of the Mosaic law, which
apply to us no more than do animal sacrifices and
other like things . . . . Hence, some sort of Judaism
comes to light in ceremonies, and other observances
bring cruel treatment upon pious minds."[54] On the
basis of St. Paul's statements in Colossians 2.13, 14,
to the effect that Christ has metaphorically nailed
the ceremonies of the Mosaic law on his cross, Calvin
concludes that ceremonies "are shadows whose substance
exists for us in Christ." Elsewhere he avers on the
same passage that Christ has freed us from the "hand-
writing ordinnances" [sic] in Colossians.[55] He
insists that it was the intention of St. Paul to
obliterate the ceremonial law until the eschatological coming of Christ because Christ is the only basis
for its effectiveness.[56] Calvin's position on ceremonies is clear; he asks rhetorically, "What, then,
was the purpose of ceremonies? Were they useless?
Were the Fathers [of the Old Testament] idly employed
in observing them? He [Paul] illustrates briefly two
statements, that in their own time they were not

113

superfluous, and that they have now been abolished
by the coming of Christ," and so now are only
"ancient shadows."[57]

Calvin also argues that, with the abolition of
the ceremonies, the priesthood is also null and void.
St. Paul, according to Calvin, teaches that not only
are ceremonies obsolete and dead but that the "Levitical priests" function only in a shadowy way much
below the exemplar of Christ. Calvin maintains that
the Roman priesthood has become obsolete because
Christ fulfilled the priesthood of the Old Testament
and that no need exists for imitating Christ's sacrifice in the Mass. The Reformer employs St. Paul's
image of the shadow from Hebrews 10.1: "For the law
having a shadow of good things to come, and not the
very image of the things, can never with those sacrifices which they offered year by year continually
make the comers therunto perfect." He interprets
the ceremonial law as an image taken from painting,
that is, the preliminary sketch with which a painter
begins a painting. "The Greeks," he says, called
"this indistinct representation σκιαγραφια ; in
Latin perhaps umbratilem" is "the full likeness."[58]
Milton is fond of the "shadowy expiation of bulls
and goats" as an image to represent the same concept.

Calvin graphically summarizes the abrogation of
the ceremonial law for the Christian:

Thus the law that consisted in judgments and in
teachings concerning the justification of the flesh
has certainly been changed; for the cleanness or
the uncleanness which the Priest of grace judges
and teaches do not pertain to leprosy, the flesh,
hair, attire, house, etc., but to sins of uncleanness of the spirit and the conscience. For in
the new law there is no difference between a
leprous Christian and one who is not leprous, or
a menstrous woman and a young woman in childbed,
or a filthy garment and a garment that is clean.
In short, the only thing that makes a difference
among Christians is sin, which pollutes the conscience. Although everything else, so far as
it is outside in the flesh, formerly made a distinction between Jew and Jew, yet now it makes no
distinction whatever between Christian and

114

Christian.⁵⁹

Richard Hooker takes a contradictory (for the
Reformers) and complex approach to the abrogation
of the ceremonial law, distinguishing between the
ceremonies of the Mosaic law during Paul's time and
ceremonies of the traditional churches of his time,
a distinction Calvin and Milton could not accept.
Citing the fourth chapter of Galatians, he quotes
(evidently incorrectly according to the editor) Martin Bucer, who finds sympathy and understanding for
those Jews in Paul's time believing that God had
indeed ordained the ceremonial laws on fasting and
dieting and the calendar. They faced the dilemma
of accepting or rejecting Paul's teaching, which set
aside the ceremonial law as opposed to the Redemption
of Christ."⁶⁰ On the other hand, Hooker himself condemns the pseudo-apostles for insisting that ceremonial observance was essential for salvation: "They
acknowledged Christ to be their only and perfect
Saviour, but saw not how repugnant their believing
the necessity of Mosaical ceremonies was to their
faith in Jesus Christ."⁶¹ Referring to the Mosaic
law of ceremonies, he insists at one point that they
are "clean abrogated" despite their "solemnity" since
God ordained them temporarily. Nevertheless, later
in The Laws he is appalled that ceremonies in his
own time are derided since they perform a valuable
function in providing "edification" for the sense of
sight in the worshipper. Indeed, in an even later
passage, he states that Christ's sacrifice did not
repeal the law of ceremonies because Christian Jews
continued these legalities and sacrifices until the
destruction of the Temple. At least, he argues, the
names, such as priest, etc., were continued, and now
the terms can be used metaphorically. They are not
compelled to be used, but they are not forbidden
either.⁶² He maintains that the sacraments are not
subsumed under the notion of ceremonies since he did
not wish their validity to be questioned. We see
here the difficulties of a man who dearly loved the
sights and sounds of pomp, pageantry, and traditional
ritual, and although he would like to maintain them
in worship as a source of edification, he has to find
some way to interpret Paul's judgements on the Mosaic
law. Most Reformers at the very least argued for the

elimination of ceremonies on the basis of the Epistle
to the Galatians, but Hooker finds it difficult to
accept their abrogation and so finally compromises
and finds an Anglican middle way in the assertion
that although the Christian church is not compelled
to follow them, yet it is not forbidden their use.

Milton opposed the ceremonial code in three
arenas: the religious, the domestic, and the political, but this antipathy is especially apparent in his
contempt for the attempts of the Anglican church to
impose, from his viewpoint, the ceremonies associated
with Rome. These, as Calvin had said, are neutralized
by the sacrifice of Christ; hence in Of Reformation
Milton complains that the episcopal party has caused
the English church "to backslide one way into the
Jewish beggery, of old cast rudiments." The Epistles
of St. Paul further form the basis for this argument
in the same pamphlet when Milton portrays the ceremonies of Baptism and the Mass as "preferring a foolish Sacrifice and the rudiments of the world [Col. 2.8],
as Saint Paul to the Colossians explaineth, before a
savory obedience to Christs example."63

In The Reason of Church-Government Milton condemns the ceremonial demands of the Roman and the
Anglican churches. He regards these ceremonies as
standing in direct opposition to Christ and the Gospel, and the term flesh or fleshly designates a
belief in the ordinances of the ceremonial law. Milton regards the entire ceremonial law as being directed,
originally, toward Christ's priesthood and therefore
as now being defunct. Episcopacy makes the mistake
of embracing hostility toward Christ insofar as it
refuses to forego ceremony: "And thus Prelaty both
in her fleshly supportments, in her carnall doctrine
of ceremonie and tradition, in her violent and secular
power [is] going quite counter to the prime end of
Christs comming in the flesh."64 Milton scorns the
use of altar linens and the altar railing as "dead
judaisms," and he sees the pursuit of empty ceremony
as leading into the "dangerous and deadly apostacy"
of the Roman church which insists wrongfully on this
external nonsense as necessary to salvation. He
charges that the prelates have forsworn "the heavenly
teaching of S. Paul for the hellish Sophistry of

Paganism," citing various sacramental gestures as the sign of the cross on the infant's forehead during Baptism and the washings (the Lavabo) during the eucharistic ceremony which were too much like both Roman Catholicism and the washings in the Mosaic law. He sets in antipathy "tradition and fleshly ceremony to confound the purity of doctrin which is the wisdom of God." In An Apology's censure of ceremony, he associates "those ceremonies, those purifyings and offrings at the Altar" of contemporary episcopacy with the beliefs and customs of "the foolish Galatians."[65] Milton is afraid that the externals of ceremony will make ugly the simple appearance of the inner worship of God, "Which to dresse up and garnish with a devis'd bravery abolisht in the law, and disclam'd by the Gospell addes nothing but a deformed uglinesse." He even correlates the specious trappings of the English church with the attire of the Whore of Babylon, the Roman church.[66]

Just as St. Paul had inveighed against the false apostles for centering righteousness and justification on the Mosaic rites, Milton and the reformers rebuked the English church for moving in the same direction as the Roman church which had elevated ritual, tradition, and ceremony to the status of the Gospel, a violation of the clear intent of Christ's coming. As Arthur Barker observed, Milton regarded the Levitical priesthood as abrogated for Christianity.[67] Alluding to St. Paul's Epistles, Milton sums up his own position in Civil Power many years later:

It will be sufficient in this place to say no more of Christian libertie, then that it sets us free not only from the bondage of those ceremonies, but also from the forcible imposition of those circumstances, place and time in the worship of God: which though by him commanded in the old law, yet in respect of that veritie and freedom which is evangelical, S. Paul comprehends both kindes alike, that is to say, both ceremonie and circumstances, under one and the same contentiousness name of weak and beggarly rudiments, Gal. 4.3.9, 10. Col. 2.8 with 16.[68]

It is a commonplace among theologians that St.
Paul regarded circumcision as symbolic of the con-
finement of the Mosaic law (not just the ceremonial
aspect) and that he sets at odds the fleshly obses-
sion with circumcision and the Spirit and freedom
of the Gospel. Paul is more interested in an inward
circumcision than an outward.[69] To read between the
lines of Paul's hostility to circumcision presents
difficulties; he regards it primarily in its symbolic
aspect, but one wonders how the Gentiles in Paul's
missionary world reacted to it. From a purely human
point of view, what adult male Gentile would be
anxious to undergo a rather painful surgical operation, especially Greeks, who more than likely
regarded it as evidence of the barbarism they
attributed to all other cultures besides their own?
In any event, Paul had two very sound reasons for
opposing the demand of the Judaic Christians that
the Gentiles be circumcised--the theological and the
human.

St. Paul consistently rejects circumcision
throughout his Epistles, although he considers it as
having had a place when the Old Testament was in
effect. He tells the Romans that the Jews profited
from it because they were the keepers of the word of
God. Nevertheless, no man is "righteous," whether
Jew or Gentile, and the "deed of the law" justify no
one (Rom. 3.1, 2, 10, 20). In speaking to the Corinthians about purity and marriage, he uses circumcision
as an illustration, citing its neutrality and indifference per se and as symbolic of keeping the commandments, so that the various vocations are equally
indifferent to righteousness (I Cor. 7.18-20). Paul's
conflict with Peter, delineated in Galatians 2, has
already been recounted, and Paul continues his argument in the fifth chapter. He encourages the Galatians to abide by the freedom of Christ and to ignore
circumcision, which has no effect and will even nul-
lify the sacrifice of Christ. Here Paul is taking
a more extreme position than before in response to
his opponents who were making an issue out of the
need for circumcision. He even establishes a direct
antithesis between circumcision and Christ, indicating
that those who still wish circumcision put themselves
under obligation to the entire law and fall from

grace. In contradiction to circumcision, Paul advises "faith which worketh by love" (Gal. 5.1-6). Those who clamor for circumcision are motivated only by a desire to glory in the flesh and can't themselves keep the Mosaic law (Gal. 6.8, 12, 15). In writing to the Philippians, he warns them against those demanding circumcision and, in rhetorical terms, turns the word circumcision against his opponents by asserting that those who believe in the worship of God in spirit and of Christ are now the true "circumcision." Jeremiah 9.26 had perhaps suggested the image of inner circumcision in his castigation of the Israelites: "all the house of Israel are uncircumcised in the heart." To the Philippians Paul portrays his own zeal for the law and ridicules it as "dung" (Phil. 3.2-8). In Colossians he crystallizes the doctrine of the inner circumcision:

> And ye are complete in him, which is the head of all principality and power:
> In whom also ye are circumcised with the circumcision made without hands, in putting off the body of the sins of the flesh by the circumcision of Christ. (2.10, 11)

Thus Paul declares himself most explicitly in his view of circumcision's hostility to the sacrifice of Christ, which is the only means of justification. The editor of Chrysostom's homilies on Romans, indicating the importance attached to circumcision, notes that "The younger Buxtorf, in his preface to his father's Synagoga Judaica, gives specimens of their language [of the Jews on circumcision], as from Cad Hakkemach, 'Such is the power of Circumcision, that none who is circumsised goeth down into Hell'."[70] No more, according to Paul.

Very early in the history of the Church the Fathers accepted Paul's philosophy on circumcision, including the concept of inner and outer circumcision. Justin Martyr in The First Apology quoted Jeremiah 9.26 (thinking it was Isaiah) on inner circumcision, and in his Dialogue with Trypho, he urged that Trypho "be circumcised rather in your heart." He also quotes Deuteronomy 10.16: "Circumcise therefore the foreskin of your heart, and be no more stiffnecked," and concludes that circumcision was given to the Jews only

119

that they might suffer. He further maintains that
Christians will be saved without circumcision. Justin
uses a rather strange metaphor when combating Trypho,
his Jewish adversary:

> We who have received the second circumcision
> with stone knives are indeed happy. For your
> first circumcision was and still is administered
> by iron instruments, in keeping with your hard-
> ness of heart. But our circumcision, which is
> the second, for it was instituted after yours,
> circumcises us from idolatry and every other
> sin by means of sharp stones, namely, by the
> words uttered by the Apostles of Him who was
> the Cornerstone and the Stone not cut with
> human hands.[71]

One of the arguments against circumcision stipu-
lated that Abraham, who lived before the Mosaic law,
was never cicumcised but was saved by faith. Irenaeus
presents this assertion and regrets that the "circumcision and the law of works occupied the intervening
period." Part of one of his long chapter headings in
Against Heresies reads as follows: "Perfect Righteousness Was Conferred Neither By Circumcision Nor By Any
Other Legal Ceremonies."[72] Ignatius of Antioch also
rejected "mere carnal circumcision" and tells his
readers to live in Christ, not in the law of circumcision.[73] Origen, glossing I Cor. 7.18 on circumcision, noted that "it was the design of the Holy Spirit
. . . to show that we were not to be edified by the
letter alone," and in Contra Celsum he observes that,
on the basis of Galatians 5.2, Paul's disciples were
not allowed to circumcise themselves.[74] Clement of
Alexandria argues that Paul circumcised Timothy not
because of any belief in its effectiveness but because the apostle was afraid of alienating Jews
trained in the Law.[75]

St. John Chrysostom makes some very interesting
comments on the question of circumcision, but he
defines circumcision as an inward state and then
develops a fascinating paradox. External circumcision
of itself has no force, but Chrysostom avers that the
Gentiles have circumcision when they keep the Law
through adherence to the natural law. Those Jews,
however, who through insistence upon external

circumcision, do not. He concludes that neither the
Mosaic law nor circumcision are bad themselves.[76]
He redefines the man who truly keeps the law of God
as the Jew who observes circumcision in an analogical
sense. Those who become circumcised out of fear of
the Mosaic law and those who cannot believe in the
power of grace receive no good from what they do. He
notes the irony of Paul's circumcising Timothy in
order to abolish circumcision. Timothy thus gained
the confidence of the Galatians by being circumcised
and then taught them the new dispensation from the
Mosaic law. Naturally the Galatians were unaware of
this unusual strategy, according to Chrysostom. He
accuses St. Peter of duplicity in his relationship
with Gentiles. For Chrysostom the Mosaic law is
simply "superfluous." There may be circumcision
among the true members of the church, but it makes
no difference as long as they worship God in spirit.[77]

Augustine carries on the tradition of Chrysostom's
that the law is observed out of fear and not out of
the goodness of the will. He notes, "But what the
Apostle calls the circumcision of the Heart, represents
a will free from all unlawful desire. And this is not
created by the letter which teaches and threatens, but
by the Spirit who helps and heals."[78]

Three of the above points reappear in the Reformation: first, that circumcision and more importantly
what it symbolizes has nothing to do with justification; second, that the law of ceremony, Mosaic or
Roman Catholic, is based on fear and should be rejected; and third, that, as John Colet put it, "Circumcision of the heart and purification of the mind; [is
that] in which alone man's justification consists."[79]

Luther maintains these basic positions, first
defining circumcision as "the Jews with all their
powers and all their glory" and "uncircumcision" as
the accomplishments of the Gentiles, "all their wisdom,
righteousness, laws, powers, kingdoms, and empires."
He explicitly associates the upholders of the Mosaic
with the advocates of canon law in that both are
willing to shed blood over such details as "eating
meat, celibacy, feriae, etc." excommunicating those
who disagree with them. Establishing an important

parallel, he observes how the Jews gloried in circumcision while the Greeks glory in wisdom.[80] Agreeing with Chrysostom that St. Paul does not condemn circumcision per se but only as it claims the ability to justify, he sets up a rigid choice of depending either on the Law or Christ: "If you keep the Law, Christ is of no avail to you." Just as the Gentiles should not have been compelled to be circumcised since it was not necessary for righteousness, contemporary Christians should not have to observe the laws of fasting and other indifferent acts. All should be as free as the patriarchs and the saints of the Old Testament who, according to Luther, "were free in their conscience and were justified by faith, not by circumcision or the Law."[81] He quotes Augustine to the effect that "The circumcision of the heart, is according to Paul, the cleansed will," and he condemns the "false apostles" of Paul for their hypocrisy and arrogance in demanding circumcision of others while not obeying the Law themselves, associating them with present-day bishops and princes, "sycophants of the pope," and "our fanatics" who teach circumcision.[82]

Calvin, quite sensitive to the symbolic meanings of circumcision, distinguishes its two roles as a vehicle of meaning: as representative of the death-giving Mosaic law and as anticipating the Gospel of Christ. He makes a distinction between Paul's dual attitude toward circumcision: "a seal of the righteousness of the faith," and "a token of condemnation, because men bind themselves by it to keep the whole law." He basically defines circumcision as a "figure" of Christ's redemption, comparing it to Baptism, a sign but not the real thing, whose effectiveness entirely depends upon Christ.[83] Commenting on St. Paul's statement that "Circumcision is nothing, and uncircumcision is nothing" (I Cor. 7.19), he agrees that both are matters of indifference. The abolition of circumcision eliminates the mystery which was originally conveyed by it; today it is not only not a sign, it is useless since Baptism has replaced it as a signal of Christ's coming. Nevertheless circumcision by the Spirit of Christ is the only necessity for the Christian.[84]

The problem with circumcision for Calvin is that

it represents forces opposed to Christ, in Paul's
time the Mosaic law and in Calvin's time the rites
of the Roman church, and therefore it is absolutely
abolished. Those who teach circumcision but don't
obey the Law and those who preach the Roman system
prove the same underneath; they merely protect their
own welfare. In glossing Ephesians 2.11, Calvin
states that uncircumcision was no obstruction to the
Ephesians' "being spiritually circumcised by Christ."[85]
Ultimately he iterates the superiority of the inward
circumcision of Christ over the external circumcision
of both the Mosaic code and the Roman rites:

> For we are the circumcision--[Phil. 3.3] that is,
> we are the true seed of Abraham, and heirs of the
> testament which was confirmed by the sign of the
> circumcision. For the true circumcision is of
> the spirit and not of the letter, inward, and
> situated in the heart, not visible according to
> the flesh. (Rom. ii. 29)

> He [Paul] proves that the circumcision of Moses
> is not merely unnecessary, but is opposed to
> Christ, because it destroys the spiritual
> circumcision of Christ. For circumcision was
> given to the Fathers that it might be the figure
> of a thing that was absent: those, therefore,
> who retain that figure after Christ's advent,
> deny the accomplishment of what it prefigures.[86]

The other Reformers and theologians of the sixteenth and seventeenth centuries agreed essentially
with Calvin's and Luther's positions. They maintained
the inadequacy of circumcision for justification and
the need for a circumcision of the heart, an inward
manifestation of the desire to know and to love God.
Juan Valdes dismisses both circumcision and uncircumcision and thinks that the keeping of the commandments
is more important than either.[87] Richard Hooker
sounds like Calvin when he maintains that circumcision
contradicts faith, whether in the case of the Galatians or Renaissance Christians.[88] Paul's rebuke of
the Philippians on the subject occasioned this remark
by Philip Airay: "by urging circumcision, they
shewed themselves to be only cut in the foreskins of
the flesh, but not to be circumcised in the heart, by
putting off the sinful body of the flesh through the

circumcision of Christ." Those who are of the
"concision" "cut themselves from the unity of the
church" through their insistence upon circumcision;
here Airay associates the cutting of circumcision
with the etymological meaning of schism, a cutting or
tearing.[89] Like Airay Thomas Cartwright emphasizes
the pejorative connection between circumcision as
carnal and the Platonic assumption that the body is
a mass of corruption. The true inward circumcision
"is made by the finger of God, which entereth into
the heart, whereof one fruit is the putting off of
the whole body and mass of sin, which riseth and bud-
deth from the carnal corruption of sin." Paul Bayne
takes a similar jaundiced view of man's nature and
assumes that until man is recreated in Christ he is
unable to perform good works.[90]

Milton was thoroughly imbued with these attitudes
throughout his adult life, especially in his thorough
and profound distaste for meaningless superficialities
in the worship of God. In the proper sense of the
word, Milton was indeed a _Puritan_--opposed to externals
in religion and suspicious of mysterious rituals and
sacramentals. Before we examine the prose and the
poetry for these attitudes as manifested in his explicit statements and in his poetic symbolism, a synopsis
of them and their relation to Paul's Epistles by
Michael Fixler may be helpful:

Paul, who was at pains to define Christianity
as a new covenant and as a way of salvation
offered to the 'spiritual seed' of Abraham,
insistently asserted the true spiritual communion of the Kingdom of Christ as independent
of the rigorous marks of obedience to the
Mosaic ritual and ceremonial law, principally
designating the practice of circumcision and
the observance of the Jewish dietary laws.
It is for this reason that we find the enun-
ciation of the freedom from the old law, the
Pauline conception of Christian liberty (as in
the Epistle to the Galatians) so intertwined
with the imagery of the table and the metaphor
of spiritual circumcision.[91]

Milton agrees with Calvin on the correlation between

circumcision and Baptism and quotes Martin Bucer's interdict against circumcision, sacrifices, and rituals of purification enunciated in the Old Testament. Bucer contends that the only use these have is to help the Christian receive the sacraments of Baptism and the Eucharist.[92] In The Doctrine and Discipline of Divorce Milton exploits the arguments about circumcision to prove that divorce was not just a dispensation from the Mosaic law but a true part of the law. He quotes Romans 2.25 on St. Paul's assertion that if a man becomes circumcised, then he must be in debt to the whole law, or else circumcision is a waste of effort. Divorce was an essential part of the Mosaic law and was thus appropriate for the Jews to accept. With the abrogation of the ceremonial law, both circumcision and the law on divorce are obsolete.[93] In Considerations . . . Hirelings Milton expresses contempt for a literalistic reading of Scripture and relates it to the absurd belief that Paul's wish that the Galatians who brought circumcision to the flock be cut off--which some interpreted as a physical "cutting off."[94]

In Of Christian Doctrine Milton, emphasizing the connection between circumcision and Baptism that Calvin had perceived, describes circumcision as "the seal of the righteousness of faith" but only for Abraham and believing adults and not for infants who can't believe or disbelieve. He contrasts circumcision and the passover with Baptism and the Lord's Supper as respective "representations" of the two convenants, quoting Galatians 5.3 and Romans 4.12 and 1.25 to establish that later "circumcision seems to have typified the covenant of works." We will turn to the question of the relationship between circumcision and the doctrine of salvation by works later (See below, pp. 172-178). Milton is not happy with the analogy between Baptism and circumcision because the latter was established during the time of the Mosaic law and sacrifices and thus totally confined the worshipper to complete observance of the entire law (Gal. 5.3). Baptism, on the other hand, initiates Christians into the Gospel "which is a reasonable, manly, and in the highest sense free service."[95]

It appears somewhat curious that after all that

has been said about circumcision attention is now
directed toward Milton's early poem, "Upon the Circumcision." However, although Milton looked negatively
upon the general concept of circumcision as a requirement for justification and salvation, he viewed the
circumcision of the Christ child in a totally different
light, a light which proves, paradoxically, to be
quite consistent with his broad negativism. There is
a submerged paradox in the poem in that circumcision,
normally in the Reformation associated with legalistic requirements, becomes symbolic of the promise of
Christ to redeem man by his suffering. Calvin had
noticed this particular symbolism in the ritual of
circumcision, but Milton develops the paradoxical
symbol in detail. Because of the sin in the world,
the child must suffer the shedding of his blood, a
proleptic representation of the eventual suffering and
death on the cross:

> He who with all heav'n's heraldry whilere
> Entered the world, now bleed to give us ease;
> Alas, how soon our sin
> > Sore doth begin
> > His infancy to seize! (11.10-14)

The poet's emphases focus on the simultaneous
fulfilling of the law and of love: "O more exceeding
love, or law more just?" (1.15), a major theme of
Paradise Lost. The austere Son in Paradise Regain'd
has nothing but short shrift for Satan's concern for
the Israelites in his temptation of arms and worldly
power since they are "distinguishable scarce / From
Gentiles but by circumcision vain" (III. 424-425).
Considering the fact that the Son himself is a Jew,
this proves to be a remarkable statement. Perhaps
this contempt for circumcision measures how Milton's
feelings for poetic subjects had changed over the
years. Nevertheless the speaker and his situation
must be kept in mind; the character is fulfilling a
dramatic role in rejecting Satan's temptations. In
the earlier lyric the young poet indulged in a subject and a style in the baroque tradition of bleeding
wounds, popular in the Counter-Reformation, but later
his approach is more intellectual and, to use a modern
phrase, issue oriented.

126

One of the most well known of St. Paul's themes
was his insistence that too close an adherence to the
Mosaic law both moral and ceremonial produced legalism
and excessive devotion to the letter of the Law as
opposed to the Spirit. A careful distinction must be
made between the two sets of ideas involved within
this antithesis: those who adhere to the Mosaic law
produce a legalistic attitude hostile to the Spirit
of God in the Gospel, and these same Pharisaic minds
also produce a minute attention to the details of the
law, forgetting its general intention or spirit. Semantic confusion may ensue if the two antitheses are not
kept distinct, although they are intimately related.
In the second chapter of Paul's letter to the Romans,
he censures those who judge others according to the
Mosaic law because they themselves are guilty of the
very sins they condemn in others. One is not saved
by hearing or listening to the Law but by doing it,
and the Gentiles are saved by performing the inward
natural law. According to Elias Andrewes, Paul owes
his emphasis "upon the inwardness of religion to the
Sermon on the Mount."[96] Paul notes the danger of
trying to live according to the letter as opposed to
living according to the inner law (circumcision vs.
uncircumcision): "And shall not uncircumcision which
is by nature, if it fulfill the law, judge thee, who
by the letter and circumcision dost transgress the
law?" (2.27). Ironically those who live by uncircumcision are put in a position to judge those who live
by circumcision, a reversal of the original problem
to which Paul was addressing himself. Later Paul
tells the Romans that "we should serve in newness of
spirit, and not in the oldness of the letter" (7.6).
To the Corinthians Paul makes his famous statement,
"for the letter killeth, but the spirit giveth life"
(II Cor. 316). This is the ultimate danger of the
Mosaic law--it leads to death and not life, the death
of the soul in failing justification before God.
Judaism has been aware of the dangers of excessive
literalism. As S.S. Cohon reminds his readers, "Men
should not insist on the letter of the law, for on
account of this sin Jerusalem was destroyed. Instead
they should ever follow the law of goodness."[97]

If the concept of the letter of the law appears
easy enough to define, the concept of "Spirit" or

"spirit" in the Epistles is not so conducive to simple
definition. In Hebrew the word is <u>Ruach</u> and in Greek
<u>Pneuma</u>, wind or air. When referring to God, the word
may designate the third person of the Trinity or the
spirit of God or the spiritual part of man (<u>Cruden's
Concordance</u>). In Romans 8 the term is first contrasted with <u>flesh</u>, but the latter concept has
already been explored in this connection in Chapter
One. Some verses later it is delineated by Paul as
the "Spirit of God" or "Spirit of Christ," contrasting
with the flesh and bondage, which appear to designate
the Law. The Spirit also defines a life-giving and
healing power, a sanctifying agency, and a power
behind miracles (Rom. 8.26-27; 15.16, 19). When
writing to the Corinthians, Paul characterizes the
spirit as providing knowledge of things spiritual to
mankind (I Cor. 2.10-14; 12.8), as granting justification (6.11) along with Jesus, and as providing
faith. Essentially the Spirit grants spiritual powers
of various kinds to man (I Cor. 12.4-13). In Galatians 4.23-29, Paul refers to the Old Testament as
a body and the New Testament as a spirit to match
letter, <u>gramma</u>, with spirit, <u>pneuma</u>.[98] One of the
major problems for Christianity, not precisely germane here, is whether the Spirit is either a separate
person of a trinity, a manifestation of God, or as
some divine quality. Milton denied that the Spirit
referred to a distinct person.

In the Reformation an excellent if subjective
definition from the Protestant perspective is offered
by Philip Melanchthon:

> The "Spirit" means the <u>Holy Spirit of God</u> him-
> <u>self in us</u>, effecting life, light, and joy in
> us, so that the heart truly experiences fear
> of God, comfort, faith, prayer, and strength
> in tribulation. Origen spoke of the "letter"
> as a knowledge of history, and of the "spirit"
> as a knowing of the meaning, as when one under-
> stands that the paschal lamb signifies the
> Messiah. But even this knowing is also a
> "Letter," if the Holy Spirit is not in the
> heart.[99]

Luther also notes that the Spirit opposes both the

Law and the flesh, and Calvin emphasizes the former's life-giving qualities when it is received into the heart.[100] Michael Servetus follows this pattern of symbolic reasoning about the lifegiving qualities of the Spirit by quoting Romans 8, "the law of the Spirit of life made us free from the law of sin and of death."[101] John Colet takes his customary approach of stressing the contrast between the physical body and the Spirit in that those led by the Spirit "have rendered the body a light burden, and obedient to reason."[102]

Thomas Jacomb, going into some detail on the question, equates the law of the Spirit and that of sin and death with the law of faith and that of works, that is, "the evangelical and the Mosaical law." He cites in support of his equation Ambrose, Chrysostom, and Paraeus. The Spirit comes through Christ and gives life to sinners. As Jacomb phrases it:

> The Holy Spirit of God, which is a living Spirit
> in himself, and which also as a regenerating
> Spirit works the divine and spiritual life in
> the soul; and the law of the Spirit of life is
> the power and commanding efficacy of the sancti-
> fying Spirit in his gracious operations upon the
> hearts of such and such persons, by which they
> are made free from the law of sin and death;
> that is, from the absolute domination, tyranny,
> and full power of sin and death.[103]

As we shall see, one of the major complaints against the Mosaic law is the charge that it brings both sin and death to man.

Milton, in traditional terms, defines the Spirit and its workings. He points to the "quickning power of the Spirit" in opposition to externals in religion. The Spirit also dwells in men's hearts and, for the regenerate, helps renew the law of nature within. It descended fifty days after the Crucifixion and thus began the kingdom of the Spirit antithetical to the spirit of the Law. As was mentioned, Milton did not regard the Spirit as necessarily constituting a sep- arate person in God but as the spirit of God himself or one of his various divine qualities but not essentially distinct.[104]

In the early Church the problems of Jewish Christianity and its emphasis on the details of the Law bothered the Fathers. Origen called these Christians "EBIONITES" because they held to the poverty of the Mosaic law and did not desert it.[105] St. Ambrose applied the concept of legalism to anyone who adheres to the letter or literal meaning of the text: "misbelievers make out the written word to mean that it means not, set forth only what this letter bears on the face of it, instead of the underlying sense. This way went the Jews to destruction, despising the deep-hidden meaning, and following only after the bare form of the word, for 'the letter killeth, but the Spirit maketh alive'."[106] Thus the Fathers interpreted the letter-spirit antithesis with reference not only to the divine Spirit but also to the manner of investigating and explaining the meaning of Scripture.

Augustine took such careful note of Paul's concern over the letter of the law versus its spirit that he wrote his work, On the Spirit and the Letter, and Charles Norris Cochrane remarks that Augustine invoked St. Paul to reject literalism.[107] Augustine perceives that the letter-spirit formula can apply to both readings of the Law and of the Scriptures, and he establishes the point that the antithesis refers not only to figurative expressions and their deciphering but also to the need for the soul to be nourished by spiritual and not literal comprehension. However, a strict reading of the Law, as Paul had argued, leads to death if it is not countered by an infusion of the Holy Spirit.[108]

The Reformation accepted the contrast between the letter and the spirit without extraordinary analysis. Calvin's Institutes teaches that the letter conveys death and the spirit life. In his commentary on Corinthians, he expressed the distinction between the letter and the spirit neatly; in speaking against Origen's equation of a spiritual with an allegorical reading of the text, he says, "For by the term letter he [Paul] means outward preaching, of such a kind as does not reach the heart; and, on the other hand, by spirit he means living doctrine . . .

through the grace of the Spirit." He further expands his definitions: By the term _letter_, therefore, is meant literal preaching--that is, _dead_ and _ineffectual_, perceived only by the ear. By the term _spirit_, on the other hand, is meant _spiritual_ doctrine, that is what is not merely uttered with the mouth, but effectually makes its way to the souls of men with a lively feeling." Calvin identifies the Spirit as Christ, who gives life in opposition to the death-giving nature of the Law.[109] Philip Melanchthon defines the letter as "any command, teaching, or work without the Holy Spirit" which provides only a superficial understanding of history, and Michael Servetus complains that the monks "judaize" as literally as the Pharisees.[110]

Milton, however, became fascinated by this distinction as early as his jottings in his _Commonplace Book_, which refer to Savanarola's injunction "that one should obey the spirit rather than the letter of the law." In _Of Reformation_ he laments the habit of reading Scriptures by the letter without "the quickning power of the Spirit," thus fusing the two facets of the formula, the divine and lifegiving powers of the Spirit and the generous explication and reading of Scriptures.[111]

The most vital use of the contrast between the letter and spirit appears in the divorce tracts where one of Milton's greatest difficulties was explaining Christ's statement in Matthew 19.6 that "What therefore God hath joined together, let not man put asunder." A quite literal reading of the text leaves the case for divorce difficult if not impossible if Scripture is to be the authority for deciding questions of marriage and divorce, particularly the words of Christ himself. Milton describes this kind of literal reading as "alphabetical servility," and one of Milton's tactics for advancing his case on divorce is to argue by analogy or _reductio ad absurdum_ that since what the Scripture said about the Sabbath cannot be taken literally, then what Christ said about divorce cannot be taken literally either. Christ interpreted the injunction against work on the Sabbath tenderly, and arguments about divorce based on his words should reflect the same kind of compassion, especially since Christ was treating a question of the Law and not the

Gospel, the latter should be interpreted more chari-
tably. Quoting Martin Bucer, Milton urges that the
law of Moses should be interpreted in "the Spirit of
Christ."112

Milton consistently opposes literalistic readings
with the guidance of charity. Contradicting the joining together of an unhappy couple in wedlock, he
pleads against the traditional attitude sanctifying
marriage absolutely, "All which we can referre justly
to no other author then the Canon Law and her adherents, not consulting with charitie, the interpreter
and guide of our faith, but resting in the meere element of the Text." Later he associates "the extrem
literalist" with canon law again. One of his most
eloquent statements on the subject is found in The
Doctrine and Discipline of Divorce, where he berates
strict theological readings of the Scriptures and
laments that they have caused so much trouble already
in the church:

And if it be thus, let those who are still bent
to hold this obstinate literality, so prepare
themselves as to share in the account for all
these transgressions; when it shall be demanded
at the last day by one who will scanne and sift
things with more then a literal wisdom of en-
quiry, for if these reasons be duely ponder'd,
and that the Gospel is more jealous of laying
on excessive burdens then ever the Law was,
lest the soul of a Christian which is inesti-
mable, should be overtempted and cast away.113

By definition Tetrachordon's approach to the
question of divorce had to deal with the four key
texts in Scripture pertaining to divorce. Milton
liberally reads the texts in support of his conclusions, insisting upon the "intention of a precept"
and not its misleading superficial readings. He
continues the pattern of rhetorical dialectic by
employing the epithets, "crabbed masorites of the
Letter," to characterize his foes and then by associating them with "cruelty and enthralment" and with
"the foppish canonist," all of which is posed anti-
thetically to "the lawgiving mouth of charity."114
As Arnold Williams points out, the "masorites" were
Jewish scholars who interpreted the text of Scripture

on the basis of spelling, vowel points, and obscure words and etymologies."[115]

In _Paradise Lost_, Michael summarizes the effects of literalism on the development of the Church; the legalists will

> . . . though feigning still to act
> By spiritual, to themselves appropriating
> The Spirit of God, promised alike and giv'n
> To all believers; and from that pretense,
> Spiritual laws by carnal power shall force
> On every conscience; laws which none shall find
> Left them enrolled, or what the Spirit within
> Shall on the heart engrave. (XII.517-524)

The crushing impact of the legalistic mode will be to force conscience through carnal power, in opposition to the Spirit of God's natural law engraved on the heart.[116]

Thus far we have defined the Mosaic law in its various manifestations and in its conflict with the inner natural law, the emphasis on circumcision as necessary for salvation, and the antagonism between fulfillment of the letter of the law and of the spirit (in two senses). It is now necessary to explore the functions and rationale of the Mosaic code as envisaged by St. Paul, the Church Fathers, the Reformers, and Milton.

One of the most notable purposes of the Law, according to St. Paul, was the fact that it revealed sin, "for by the law is the knowledge of sin" (Rom. 3.20). Paul's audience of Romans must have been curious about his denunciation of observation of the code and no doubt asked, what then was the function of the Mosaic law? His reply was "that offence might abound" (Rom 5.20), and he stresses the point repeatedly--that sin is clearly identified as sin through a knowledge of the Law (Rom 7.13). In his first letter to the Corinthians, Paul makes his case even stronger: "the strength of sin is the law," (15.56) implying a causal relationship between the two. To the Galatians and the Hebrews he indicates that the scriptures have "concluded all under sin" in order that Christ could come to those who had

133

faith (Gal. 4.22; Heb. 9.15). There is then a logic to the relationship between the Mosaic law and the coming of Christ, the former creating a realization of sin and the latter removing it.

One of the problems with this relationship remains the dilemma of determining whether the Mosaic code caused sin or simply made it known, a question attended to by the Fathers. Irenaeus merely says that the Law "made sin to stand out in relief."[117] Clement of Alexandria, focusing on epiphany more than causality as had Irenaeus, comments on Romans 3.20: "The law did not cause, but showed sin. For, enjoining what is to be done, it reprehended what ought not to be done."[118] Chrysostom, glossing Galatians 3.22, observes that evil would have destroyed everyone in the Old Testament except for the Law, which encouraged them to seek the Redeemer. He sees the Law as a result and not a cause of sin. Chrysostom berates the Jews because they have ignored the warnings of the Law to flee from sin and so have caused the Law to condemn them.[119] Augustine went so far as to urge that the Law excited sin since it made it more enticing, as a forbidden fruit of sorts. He also takes the traditional position of viewing the manifestation of sin as a motivating force for the Jews to seek Christ. Nevertheless he returns to the point that sin is made more fascinating because of the Mosaic restrictions against it: "When therefore the Law, which is the strength of sin, so that sin, taking occasion by the Commandment works all manner of desire; from whom are we to seek for self-control, unless for Him Who knows how to give good gifts to His sons? The Law may simply manifest sin or render it desirable because of strictures against it."[120] As Charles Norris Cochrane perceives, Augustine "shrewdly observes, to stop short with a body of prohibitions [without a plan for salvation] is not to destroy but merely to intensify the desire to sin."[121] Augustine, however, establishes a cycle of salvation: the Law leads to "knowledge of sin"; faith leads to "grace against sin"; grace leads to "healing of the soul; which leads to "freedom of the will," which leads to "the love of righteousness," which leads again to "obedience of the law."[122]

Aquinas followed the Augustinian tradition of regarding the Law, as given to the Jews, as manifesting human weakness, in particular, "wickedness, weakness, passion, and ignorance," as cited by Bede. Although the Law made an effort to control sinfulness, it had to fail and then direct men toward grace, toward Christ and the Gospel. To reverse the priorities, as it were, and set the Law above the Gospel and grace, like the Galatians, would constitute perversion:

they would pervert the gospel of Christ, i.e., the truth of the Gospel teaching, into the figure of the Law--which is absurd and the greatest of troubles. For a thing ought to be converted into that to which it is ordained. But the New Testament and the Gospel of Christ are not ordained to the Old, but contrariwise, the Old Law is ordained to the New Law, as a figure to the truth. Consequently the figure ought to be converted into the truth, and the Old Law to the Gospel of Christ, not the truth into the figure, or the Gospel of Christ into the Old Law.[123]

The emphasis in the Reformation focuses not only on the epiphany of sin, but also on the revelation of the inability of man to do anything about sin once he knows he is a sinner. There is thus a grim realization, according to the Reformers, that man is totally limited in his efforts to do anything to save himself even when he comprehends his sinfulness under the Mosaic code, usually the Decalogue. Even John Colet, who anticipated many of the Reformers by some years, averred that the Law did two things in this respect: it indirectly occasioned the sinning of men more than they had sinned before, and it created the awareness that men would have been better off if the moral law of Moses had never been given. "Therefore," he says, "the true function and the chief and proper use of the Law is to reveal to man his sin, blindness, misery, wickedness, ignorance, hate and contempt of God, death, hell judgment, and the well-deserved wrath of God."[124]

Luther agreed with Paul on the Law's manifestation

135

of sin when he entered into the controversy over free
will with Erasmus. He also claimed the Original Sin
was unknown until Moses' Covenant when the Law was
made known. This interesting conclusion qualifies
the definition of Original Sin in that those who lived
prior to the promulgation of the Law may not then be
guilty of Original Sin. Luther makes a distinction
between the Decalogue and the ceremonial law, stating
that the former "is the power of sin through knowledge
of oneself" but that the latter made things sinful
which were not unless so designated.[125] In other
words, sins against the moral law existed absolutely
but were manifested by the promulgation of that law,
but those under the ceremonial law existed only upon
the announcement of that law.

Philip Melanchthon expanded upon the theme of
the Law's evincing sin in terms of the Law also
demonstrating God's nature. One is obliged to learn
about sin because of its characteristic of being
hostile to "divine wisdom and order." He supports
this contention by Christ's statement that he came
"not to destroy the law, but to fulfill it." Conversely one may learn about God from what pleases
him and also learn from human weakness and punishments
resulting from such weakness. In isolating the uses
of the Mosaic law, Melanchthon specifies that "law
teaches and with fear and punishments forces one to
keep his external members under discipline, according
to all the commandments about external works."[126]

Calvin's emphasis fixes on the revelation of the
weakness and depravity of man's nature, a far cry
from the position of the Church Fathers. In commenting on Galatians 3.19, he says of Paul, "He means
that the law was published in order to make known
transgressions, and in this way to compel men to
acknowledge their guilt."[127] In the _Institutes_,
assuming an even stronger position, he concludes that
the Mosaic law was supposed to have "convicted ⌊us⌋
of our depravity" in order that man might admit his
"weakness and misery." This posture, however, applies
to man even regenerated, whereas Arminius concluded
that this revelation of evil applied to man under the
Law. Calvin finds it difficult to distinguish the
educational role of the Law from its function as judge

136

and convictor of guilt. Thus he urges that "it warns,
informs, convicts, and lastly condemns, every man of
his own unrighteousness."[128] Significantly Calvin
takes the tradition of the Law as manifesting sin to
its adherents and applies it to all men, thus making
more desperate the hope of man without some overpowering divine intervention in the history of mankind
or in his individual and personal spiritual journey.

Others in the Reformation agreed that the Law
was designed to reveal sin although not necessarily
to uncover the total corruption of man's nature.
Michael Servetus emphasizes the distinction between
the negative aspects of the Law and the positive ones
of Christ's grace. "The law of Moses is a law of
death, and the strength of sin; but the grace of Christ
is pure mercy. And it says χάρις, that is, favor
freely given, or a kind of goodwill of one conferring
kindnesses, and giving many gifts, and befriending
and directing us in every respect."[129] Juan Valdes
establishes the logical sequence of the Law, sin, and
death in terms of the preceding producing the subsequent: "just as death is mighty through sin, so
likewise sin is mighty through the Law: for where
there is no sin there is no death. Had God not
imposed Law upon the first man, he never could have
broken it; and had he not broken it, he had not sinned; and had he not sinned, he would not have been
condemned to death with all his descendants."[130]
Thomas Jacomb agreed with Calvin that the Law failed
because man's nature failed since "the law strength-
ens sin, and sin weakens the law," that is, the Law
gives to sin the power of condemnation and death.
Further, since man's condition is corrupt, sin
becomes "more active, impetuous, and boisterous."
The Law therefore becomes truly impotent.[131]

In the _Doctrine_ _and_ _Discipline_ _of_ _Divorce_ Milton
is faced with the difficult task of answering the
charge that the Mosaic law apparently allowed sin
because Moses permitted the Jews to put away their
wives (Matt. 19.7, 8). Milton claims that the Mosaic
law could not "license a sin" and proceeds to support
his contention by a quotation of Romans 5.20: "_The_
Law _enter'd_ _that_ _the_ _offence_ _might_ _abound_." Next he

agrees with the assertion that sin had to be made
obvious because of its violation of God's will, which
could only be satisfied by the offering of grace in
the new covenant. The Law, he insists, cannot deliberately mislead men, a contradiction in terms, and
sin and the Law are ever at odds. The Law must
announce sin for, "If the Law be silent to declare
sin, the people must needs generally goe astray,
for the Apostle himself saith, he had not known lust
by the Law."[132] Therefore, if Moses allowed divorce
under the Law, it could not have been a sin against
that very same Law.

In Of Christian Doctrine Milton, although acknowl-
edging an implied promise in the prophets that the Law
could provide eternal life, cites numerous passages in
Romans that demonstrate the Law manifests sin.[133]

St. Paul had used the schoolmaster personifi-
cation to represent the Law's role as guide to the
Redemption of Christ:

> Wherefore the law was our schoolmaster to bring
> us to Christ, that we might be justified by
> faith. But after faith is come, we are no
> longer under a schoolmaster. (Gal. 3.24-25)

The term schoolmaster is misleading since the
paidogoges was a slave employed more as a discipli-
narian than as a teacher of any stature (Cruden's Concordance). Thus the term contains derogatory implications. Clement of Alexandria, who lived in the
early part of the third century and who was fluent in
Greek, after distinguishing between the Law's causing
sin and making it known, speaks approvingly of the
prosopopoeia :   "And how can the law be not good,
which trains, which is given as the instructor
(παιδαγωγός) to Christ, that being corrected by
fear, in the way of discipline, in order to the
attainment of the perfection which is by Christ?"[134]
It may be that Clement, in writing and speaking to
Greeks, was anxious to create the best image possible
for the Old Testament and its traditions out of which
Christianity was born. Chrysostom concludes that the
Law has educated the Jews in virtue and the knowledge
of sin and encouraged them to seek Christ; but now
that Christ has come, the Law is like a schoolmaster

confining a mature student.[135] Augustine, following suit, remarks how the term _pedagogue_ implies one watching or guiding a child until maturity, until the time for inheritance has arrived, associating the Law with fear and the new covenant with love.[136]

The Reformation accepted the necessity of the Mosaic code in its role as pedagogue until such time as man matured in Christ. Luther admits this need although conceding the unpleasantness of the Law.[137] Melanchthon sees the Law's function as providing "external morality" and "worldly authority" to help men maintain morality.[138] Calvin grants the need for the Law but only for a short time until the day when Christ would mature man's understanding since he is the repository of "all the treasures of wisdom and understanding." He notes the image of the _paedogoges_ and the association of the Jews with children.[139] Milton also envisions the Law in this sense but rhetorically reverses the role of the Jews and the Law in contrast to the Gospel: "For the imperfect and obscure institution of the Law, while the Apostles themselves doubt not oft-times to vilifie, cannot give rules to the compleat and glorious ministration of the Gospell, which lookes on the Law, as on a childe, not as on a tutor."[140]

If the Law had been a _paedogoges_, then it was also a source of slavery or bondage to St. Paul in that it confined the Jews under its restrictions and under sin itself. Paul warned the Romans against this facet of the Law because it controlled man for his entire life. As long as the Law, which is of the flesh, holds its power, "the motions of sins" functioned in the human body. As Augustine had warned (See above, p.134), the Law intensifies desire, in St. Paul's words, "all manner of concupiscence." The Law conflicts with the inward law of God and brings man unto "captivity" because of the emphasis on sin (Rom 7). Only the law of the Spirit can free man (Rom 8.2). This explains precisely why Paul is disturbed by the false apostles' attempt to substitute the Law for the Gospel and thus slavery or bondage for freedom (Gal. 2.4). Paul admits to the Galatians that man was under subjection to all the elements of the world, not just the Law, but the Son of God has

139

been sent in order to make men adopted sons, no
longer servants. The Apostle is angered and so asks
the Galatians, "But now, after that ye have known
God, or rather are known of God, how turn ye again
to the weak and beggarly elements, whereunto ye desire
again to be in bondage?" Paul then employs the allegory of the two sons of Abraham, Isaac and Ishmael,
the son of Agar (or Hagar), representing respectively
the freedom of the Gospel and the bondage of the Law.
Paul urges the Galatians to cast out the bondwoman
and embrace the free woman and her son (Gal. 4). In
this way Paul establishes an absolute antithesis
between the slavery of the Law and the freedom of the
Gospel.

The Church Fathers immediately absorbed this concept because very early in the Church the problem
remained very much alive. Sulpicius Severus describes
Adrian's forbidding Jews from entering Jerusalem as
a good thing because it would separate the "slavery
of the law" from the freedom of faith.[141] Athanasius
insists that, although Christ came as a servant, he
maintained his superiority over the "slavery of corruption and the curse of the Law."[142] Augustine cites
the second stage of the Christian's life as slavery
under the law because the knowledge of sin merely
makes man guilty and does not liberate him from sin.
The Law begets man in bondage but anticipates the
coming of Christ.[143] There stands, therefore, a close
connection between the knowledge of sin through the
Mosaic law and its slavery, the one perhaps causing
the other.

Martin Luther, very sensitive to the consciousness
of sin, equates sin with "the servitude of the Law,"
and he resents the power of the Law over conscience
as well as the flesh. The conscience becomes more
"disquieted" as it attempts to fulfill the Law, and
it thus remains subject to "the slavery of the Law."
Luther equates the slavery of the Mosaic law with the
"miserable slavery of the pope," and he insists that
the Law may rule the body and its members but not the
conscience.[144]

Slavery and bondage typified the Law for other
reformers as well. Michael Servetus depicts the

140

"ministration" of the Law as one of both "death" and "bondage."[145] Samuel Bolton distinguishes between "Legal" and "Evangelical" obedience in that the former is performed reluctantly while the latter is exercised to find Christ. The Law demands obedience which is humanly impossible and so produces servitude. And thus "Universal bondage . . . is a bondage to the law, both to the rigour and curse of the law."[146]

Milton applies the doctrine of the slavery of the Law to many areas: the ecclesiastical, the domestic, and the redemptive. In Reason he rejects the imposition of legalistic conceptions from canon law on the same basis as he rejects those of the old law. Echoing Paul closely, he opposes the "weake and beggarly elements" and condemns the practice of putting "the heirs of liberty and grace" under the bondage of Agar, a practice which almost cancels "that birthright and immunity which Christ hath purchas'd for us with his blood."[147]

In the divorce pamphlets Milton complains that canon law puts the heirs of the Gospel in a worse yoke than they had experienced under the Mosaic law. In Doctrine and Discipline of Divorce, he adapts a statement of Peter at the Council of Jerusalem, "Why tempt ye God to put a yoke upon the necks of Christian men, which neither the Jews, Gods ancient people, nor we are able to bear: and nothing but unwary expounding hath brought upon us." Making the same point in Tetrachordon, he alludes to I Corinthians 7 and exhorts that it would be a "mockery" to bind a heathen with a Christian. If this were to be done, then Christian liberty is not based on Christ but "in the pleasure of a miscreant."[148] Milton's dialectic on this subject closely follows Paul's thinking:

The Law is, if it stirre up sin any way, to stirre it up by forbidding, as one contrary excites another, Rom. 7. but if it once come to provoke sin, by granting license to sin, according to Laws that have no other honest end, but only to permit the fulfilling of obstinat lust, how is God not made the contradiction of himself? . . . . That the whole Law is no furder usefull, then as man

141

uses it lawfully, St. Paul teaches I. Tim. 1.
And that Christian liberty may bee us'd for
an occasion to the flesh, the same Apostle
confesses, Galat. 5. yet thinks not of removing it for that, but bidds us rather stand
fast in the liberty wherewith Christ hath
freed us, and not bee held again in the yoke
of bondage.[149]

In Of Christian Doctrine Milton paraphrases several key
passages in Galatians and Romans in his statement of
the doctrine of Christian liberty opposing the slavery
of the Law.[150]

Just as the Law makes the knowledge of sin
available to man and binds him under sin, so too it
is unable to free man because it is impossible of
fulfillment, thereby revealing the weakness of man
and producing a spiritual death. St. Paul asserts this
explicitly in his letter to the Romans: "Therefore
by the deeds of the law shall no flesh be justified in
his sight: for by the law is the knowledge of sin"
(Rom. 3.20). Adam's sin caused the entrance of sin
and death to enter the world, and the law "imputed"
sin to man; the Law "worketh wrath" (Rom. 4.15; 5.
passim). The Law is weak because it depends upon the
flesh, this law "of sin and death," and only Christ
in the Gospel can repair the work of sin and the Law
(Rom 8 passim). The Law paradoxically produces death
to the Law (Gal. 2.19) since it cannot be fulfilled
and can only anticipate Christ. It also produces a
curse because of its basic defect; St. Paul quotes
Deuteronomy 27.26 to prove his point: "Cursed is
every one that continueth not in all things which are
written in the book of the law to do them" (Gal. 3.10).
Since nobody can fulfill the whole law, then all are
cursed and condemned by it, and only the new law of
Christ can save all men (Gal. 3 passim). The Law
thus is condemned to futility because it can save no
one since no man can fulfill the entire Law.

Both Augustine and Aquinas were aware of the
negative impact of the Law in this regard. Commenting on Romans 2.17-29, the former points out that the
Jews, rather than fulfilling the Law, were violating
it as Paul stated, and so the Law generated "wrath
against them, for sin abounded, being committed by men

142

who know the Law."[151] Aquinas, speaking of Galatians 2.17-18, announced that Christ was not a
"minister of sin" because he provided grace, unlike
the Law "which was an occasion of sin." Echoing St.
Jerome, he asserted that the Law could legally justify Christ, but that after him it is not only dead,
it is "deadly, so that whoever observed them [parti-
cular restrictions] after the passion of Christ sinned mortally."[152]

In the Reformation the inability of men to
satisfy the moral facet of the Mosaic law formed the
cornerstone of Protestant thought since, if they
indeed could not, then righteousness could be achieved
only by Christ himself. John Colet, though no Reformer, saw that the Law did no good for man since he
could not fulfill it.[153] Luther assumes a rather grim
view of the Law when he thinks that both the "spiritual" and the "natural endowments" have been corrupted
and that the Law frightens, humbles, and wears down
the sinner, and reveals death to him. He refers to
epithets of Paul's for the Law like "the elements of
the world," "traditions that kill," and "the power of
sin," but he offers hope in that, from his viewpoint,
the Law binds only the wicked, not the good, who are
in Christ.[154] He delineates "the works of the Law as
a mere pittance" because they cannot prevent people
from committing sin. Equating the law of the Old
Testament with the doctrine of salvation by works, he
notes how the law of works "doubles sin and engenders
death, not that it is evil, but because it commands
actions which we cannot perform without grace."[155]
Luther's colleague, Philip Melanchthon, agreed that
"No man can fulfill the law; that is, no man can
really be conformed to God's will as he in the Law
has indicated that we should be." He cites Romans 4.15
that "the law brings wrath" as one of its uses. Man
simply cannot be obedient to God by himself.[156] This
pronouncedly anti-Pelagian approach found many echoes
in the Reformation.

It is no surprise that Calvin's views accord
with Luther's on this subject. The Law brings death,
causes despair and destroys trust in the Law, curses
us, and nobody is justified through it. The Law can
only justify when man fulfills it completely, and this

condition, if it were possible, could not coexist with
faith. In any case, the Law condemns man because of
man's lack of strength, and therefore only faith can
provide righteousness; and that is why St. Paul iterates his insistence on faith as necessary for salvation.[157] These arguments from Calvin's commentaries
are corroborated in the Institutes, where he says that
"we cast off law righteousness, not because it is
defective and mutilated of itself, but because, due to
the weakness of our flesh, it is nowhere visible.
Everyone is condemned by the Law, since from a practical position, nobody can obey the entire Law and so
all are cursed. Calvin finds support for his conclusion in both Augustine and Ambrose. Man can find a
foundation only in Christ.[158]

Samuel Bolton does not disagree with Calvin on
the Law's harshness and impossibility of fulfillment:
"The law requires hard and impossible things, yea,
and that in such severity that it will not accept of
the most eminent endeavours without perfect performance. Nor will it accept obedience in much, if a
man fails in a little. Neither will it admit of
repentance after failure. . . . Such is the rigour
of the law."[159]

This failure of the Law to justify and thereby
condemn mankind was applied to Roman Catholic canon
law, which also fails and condemns the believer.
Michael Servetus is adamant on this point. He censures these canon laws as the work of man and not
God, and thus they make men transgressors, destroying the freedom of Christ's Redemption. Servetus is
worth quoting extensively on this issue, for even in
translation, he is quite eloquent:

   From this reasoning we can infer that men can
   not be justified under the monastic laws, just
   as they could not be even under the law of God,
   but are cursed. For it is a most pernicious
   thing to accept the decrees of the Pope, and
   the monastic laws, as if they necessarily bound
   us to salvation, and to put oneself under oath
   to keep them. In the first place, because their
   need of salvation would prove that Christ's salvation is defective it does not suffice without

them. In the second place, because the freedom
from the bond of the law made through Christ is
there brought back into bondage to the law. In
the third place, because the laws make us guilty
of transgression; and we, building up again the
things which we had destroyed, make ourselves
transgressors. Indeed, what is worse, we build
up human laws in place of divine. The laws of
Moses even if they were Divine, even had they
the power of justifying, have been done away;
but we endure human laws, which neither save nor
justify, but lead to more sinning.[160]

Milton, while recognizing the supreme importance
of the Redemption, ever believed that man could play
some role in his own salvation, and he opposed uncon-
ditional election or reprobation, but we can pursue
this question later under the rubric of the fulfillment of the Law (see below, pp. 170-2).

One of the central theological problems with
regard to St. Paul's Epistles and indeed Christianity
is whether the Mosaic law is abrogated by the coming
of Christ or whether it is fulfilled by him. One
solution to the problem lies in concluding, as did
Catholic Christianity, that only the ceremonial law
was abrogated or destroyed, and that the moral law is
still in effect and fulfilled by Christ. For some of
the Reformers, the entire Law was abrogated, but, as
shall be shown, Milton accepts the moral law by
Christ's law of love or charity.

In the nineteenth century, Edward Grafe showed
that the Law for Paul meant "the whole legal code,
and never varies from the conviction that this has
been set aside by the death and resurrection of
Christ."[161] Rudolph Bultmann distinguishes between
the ceremonial and the moral facets of the Law and
concludes that the moral codes of the Law are still
valid, although the ceremonial is not.[162] Paul's
lucidity on the subject is not that apparent, and he
seems to contradict himself at times. In Romans he
contrasts faith and the Law and says, "a man is justified by faith without the deeds of the law" (3.28).
In speaking to the Corinthians, Paul employs the image
of a veil which represents the Law that Moses put over

145

the face of the Israelites and "which vail is done away in Christ" (II Corinthians 3.13-17). The letter to the Galatians states that Paul is dead to the Law in order for him to "live unto God" and that "if righteousness come by the law, then Christ is dead in vain" (Gal. 2.19, 21). Similarly in the next chapter he repeats the assertion that faith and not the Law justifies, but the question of whether this means that the Law is entirely eliminated and of no use at all remains unclear. Certainly it cannot provide righteousness. Chapter Four criticizes the Law, but here only the ceremonial version. In Philippians 3.9 Paul again asserts that the Law does not confer righteousness and implies that it and the other elements of the world are "dying." In I Timothy 1 he specifies that the Law is "not made for a righteous man, but for the lawless and disobedient," and so suggests that it has some function and is abrogated only for those who are righteous in Christ. In Hebrews 7 he argues that the priesthood of Levi granted no "perfection." There appear then various possibilities of interpretation that may be held regarding the impact of Christ's death and resurrection on the Law.

Early in the history of the Church differences of opinion arose. Irenaeus, arguing against the followers of Simon Magus and Marcion, denied that the Mosaic law was hopelessly hostile to the Gospel.[163] Lactantius, citing Jeremiah 4.3, 4 and Joshua 5.2 on the anticipation of the abolition of circumcision, nevertheless states that "he would send His Son, that is, the present law and life, and that He would destroy the old law that had been given through a mortal, so that at last through Him who was eternal He might sanction the eternal law."[164] St. Basil approvingly quotes the key passage in the gospels which appears to answer the question once and for all; Christ said, "Think not that I am come to destroy the law, or the prophets: I am not come to destroy, but to fulfill" (Matt. 5.17). Basil distinguishes between the condemnation of the Law by Paul and his censure of their benefits insofar as these obstruct the "knowledge of Christ and that justice which is in Him."[165] And so each commentator adds his own variations.

St. John Chrysostom further complicates the
problem in that first he acknowledges that the Law
has performed a valid function in pointing the way
toward Christ, but he affirms that to continue observing the Law constitutes a transgression. He admits
that St. Paul praises the Decalogue but that he dis-
cards the rest of the Law; nevertheless the Decalogue,
according to Chrysostom, has "become useless to us."[166]
St. Augustine urges that the Law which Paul sees as
dead is not the ceremonial only but also the moral
because Paul says that "knowledge of sin" is produced
by the Law.[167]

Aquinas regards the New Law as fulfilling the Old
by adding what was lacking to the latter. He compares
the Old to a seed and the New to a tree, and he insists
that "The New Law does not void observance of the Old
Law except in the point of ceremonial precepts."[168]

In the Reformation Protestant theologians tended
toward regarding the entire Law as abolished and the
conscience freed from anxiety, but they did see reasons
for still observing the Decalogue. Before the Reformation John Colet took the position that both Christ's
law and the Decalogue should be observed.[169] For
Luther the moral law absolutely does not bring justification, and he opposes those who argue that Christ
justifies only if the Decalogue is obeyed, insisting
that "to die to the Law" means "to be free from the
Law and not to know the Law." He states that Origen,
Jerome, and Erasmus originated the error that Paul
is speaking of the ceremonial law as abrogated and
argues that if the Law justifies, Christ died for no
purpose. Even the political laws of Moses have been
abrogated, not just the moral and ceremonial.[170] The
only possible reasons for obeying the Law are for
"the peace of the world, gratitude toward God, and a
good example by which others are invited to believe
the Gospel." Luther makes a distinction between
what he calls "passive" and "active righteousness,"
the former being granted by God to ease the conscience
of man which is troubled by his inability to fulfill
the Law, and the latter being the presumptuous attempts
of literalistic man to obey the law.[171] Calvin, taking
somewhat different a tack, concludes that the Papists
argue, incorrectly, that Christ died to save us from

the ceremonial and not the moral law. In the _Insti-tutes_ he admits to a partial abrogation of the moral law: "The law is abrogated to the extent that it no longer condemns us," and "Its so-called 'abrogation' has reference to the liberation of the conscience, and the discontinuance of the ancient ceremonies. . . . Through Christ the teaching of the law remains inviolable."[172]

Throughout the Reformation most of the other Reformers almost without exception, regarded the ceremonial law as totally abrogated, but for the most part, expressed uncertainty about the moral law. Some believed that the moral law remained totally in effect, while others felt that the moral law was abrogated in some small degree, insofar as it was unable to condemn as a result of the Redemption. On the far right, as it were, stood Richard Hooker who, in one place, although asserting that the ceremonial law was indeed abrogated, especially with reference to feast days, nevertheless urged that feast days are desirable because they encourage holiness. Elsewhere he remarks that the ceremonial law is abrogated because its end is no more.[173]

Thomas Jacomb took the position that the moral law can do nothing except point to Christ and that there has been "a total negation of the ceremonial law," and so both laws are impotent. He admits that it is not always clear which law Paul regards as abrogated, and in one place he assumes that Paul is speaking of the moral law (Rom. 8.3, 4). Jacomb, however, still maintains that Christians must obey the Law, whether it is defective or not, in a cornucopia of imagery. Although the Law cannot justify, it is valuable "as a monitor to excite to duty, as a rule to direct and guide you in your course, as a glass to discover sin, as a bridle to restrain sin, as a hatchet to break the hard heart, as a schoolmaster to whip you to Christ." Yet the Gospel represents the only true way of life for a Christian to lead him to salvation. God gives, according to Jacomb, the power of the Spirit to assist man in overcoming the sins identified by the Law.[174] Paul Bayne argues that the ceremonial law is totally nullified, with a few ceremonies left to the discretion of the church and

that the moral law is abolished in that "the order
of it in us is changed." Man is freed from its
"justification," "curse," and "rigour." In general
terms the moral law is still binding but not in terms
of its "particularities"; that which binds conforms
to "the law of nature." Those laws abrogated are so
because (1) the reason for them is no longer in
effect; (2) they were limited in time; and (3) metaphorically, they were shadows and were valid only in
the state of man's "minority." Bayne strikes out at
"pharisaical spirits" who lust inwardly while tending
to ceremonial externals--these are exposed by the
abrogation of the Law.[175]

Although he admits confusion in Paul's texts
about which law is dead as a covenant, the nullifica-
tion of which frees men from its negative effects,
for Bolton the ceremonial law is clearly defunct.
Obedience to the moral law is still necessary as a
rule for Christians. The Law's covenant possesses
restrictions: "Hence it is called a subservient
covenant. It was given by way of subserviency to
the Gospel and a fuller revelation of the covenant of
grace; it was temporary, and had respect to Canaan
and God's blessing there, if and as Israel obeyed.
It had no relation to heaven, for that was promis'd
by another covenant which God made before He entered
upon the subservient covenant." This covenant,
however, is not a covenant of works which would be
opposed to grace. Believers are freed from the covenant of the Law and so from its curse; commenting on
Colossians 2.14, Bolton says, "By 'the handwriting
of ordinances' I conceive is not meant the ceremonial
law alone, but the moral law also, so far as it was
against us and bound us over to the curse." The Law
cannot condemn us under the curse because Christ
took it upon his own shoulders. The ceremonial law
is regarded by Bolton as only "an appendix" to the
moral law and so was abrogated, and that part of the
judicial law which is "common and natural" is still
in effect.[176]

Nevertheless, Bolton insists that obedience to
the moral law is still necessary, confirming this
demand by reference to Beza, Zanchius, and Calvin.

Beza, according to Bolton, asserted that "Christ fulfilled the law for us, but not in order to render it of no value to us.". Others claim that we are obliged to the moral law as revised by Christ's injunction to love one another (John 13.34), and Bolton accepts either approach as long as it is grounded on the premise that Christians are still obligated to obey the moral law, although it cannot condemn them.[177] Zanchius concluded that it is not possible to separate observance of the moral law from faith, and Calvin, as cited by Bolton, viewed the moral law as changeless. Finally, in support of his posture Bolton brings to bear the Wittenburg Confession, the Scottish Confession, the Swiss Confession, and one, Daniel Chamier, who perceived the New Testament as both a gospel of grace and "a confirmation of the law." The Law even provides "sanctification" since it tells men how to love.[178] Bolton's reaction to the Law sounds strange in a book which purports to advance Christian liberty since he declares the central abrogation of the Law but then feels compelled to qualify that abrogation until it is nearly meaningless.

There is no question but that Milton viewed the ceremonial law as abrogated; in fact a great deal of his antipathy toward episcopacy is based on this belief. Nevertheless Milton constantly maintained his belief in the efficacy of the moral law, although not the formal Law. He castigates the Papists for imposing not only ceremonies but also imaginary sins on the people, but he avers that the "Statute of Moses" is "most charitable" and not repealed by Christ, although in the context he appears to be referring only to the law on divorce.[179] He later contends that, according to most theologians, only those parts of the judicial law of Moses that were strictly "judaicall" were abrogated, thus removing the burden but not the liberty of the Law. He quotes Paraeus' Commentary on Matthew to the effect that Christ corrected only the Pharisees' reading of the Law and not the Law itself, which was perfect, and he agrees with Paraeus, claiming that those who insist that Christ was correcting the Mosaic divorce law were mistaken. Milton makes the point that the

150

moral law was not abolished--only the ceremonial--
in <u>Colasterion</u>.[180] A liberalizing tendency appears
in <u>Martin Bucer</u>, where the civil law of Moses simply
becomes the best law for Christians to obey, "<u>how
fit they be for Christians to imitate rather then
any other</u>." Because of the freedom of Christ, Christians are not compelled by the civil Mosaic law "in
every circumstance," yet since the statutes were
given to man by God, they ought to be followed more
than any other. Milton separates the ceremonial law
from his admonition.[181] He is obviously moving from
an absolute to a relative position.

Milton's considered judgement on the question of
the Law's abrogation is found in <u>Of Christian Doc-
trine</u>, and it is quite clear that the liberalizing
tendency noted in <u>Martin Bucer</u> continues to the stage
at which he believes the entire Mosaic law is abrogated. "The Spirit and freedom" "supersede" the old
law "of bondage and of the flesh." The Gospel, which
is the new covenant based on faith in Christ, abol-
ishes the entire law of Moses, and on the basis of
Romans 5.7, he concludes that "we are therfore absolved
from subjection to the decalogue as fully as to the
rest of the law." He cites other passages in Paul's
Epistles and from the theologian Zanchius to support
his asseveration that the Law is indeed entirely
abolished. The reasons he supplies are as follows:
Christ made the Law obsolete because the reasons for
its existence were made obsolete. There was no longer
any need to manifest "our natural depravity," or to
make us fear God's wrath, or to lead us to Christ.[182]
He further pleads that 2 Corinthians 3.7 did away with
the Decalogue, the tablets of stone, and that if the
Law is not abolished, then "the promise, the inheritance and adoption are abolished." However, "the
sum and essence of the law is not hereby abrogated;
its purpose being attained in that love of God and
our neighbor, which is born of the Spirit through
faith." Milton depends upon Christ's definition of
the Law in Matthew 22.37-40 as essentially love.
Maurice Kelley notices that, for Milton, the law of
works must give way to a law of grace.[183] And so,
although the operations and functions and consequences
are abolished, its fundamental nature and intention

151

are fulfilled in Christ.

Milton objects to Polanus' contention that we are
freed from the curse of the Law but are still under
obligation to it. The obligation and the curse are
inseparable. He further objects to the argument that
it is morally wise to observe the Law anyway to force
man to realize his sin on the grounds that believers
don't need this "impulse toward Christ." Man may
know the Law, but its practice leads him away from
Christ.[184]

NOTES: CHAPTER TWO

[1] Wayne Meeks, "Paul as Heretic."

[2] On _Galatians_, XXVI, 86, n. 6.

[3] On _Galatians_ _and_ _Ephesians_, p. 125.

[4] On _Galatians_, pp. 68-69, 142.

[5] On _Corinthians_, pp. 86-87. See also On _Corinthians_, II, p. 190; On _Titus_, p. 305.

[6] On _the_ _Trinity_ in _Harvard_ _Theological_ _Studies_, p. 250.

[7] For example, see _Animadversions_ in _Works_, III, 110-113. See Aquinas, _Summa_ _Theologiae_, pp. 1-11, Q. 103, Art. 4.

[8] _Judaism_, p. 101.

[9] On _His_ _Brother_ _Satyrus_ in _Some_ _of_ _the_ _Principal_ _Works_ _of_ _St._ _Ambrose_, n.p.

[10] _Works_, III, 197; _Works_, VI, 29.

[11] On _Hebrews_, p. 191.

[12] On _Hebrews_, p. 193.

[13] _Loci_ _Communes_, p. 83.

[14] _Loci_ _Communes_, pp. 84, 85.

[15] _Institutes_, II, 1504; On _Galatians_ & _Ephesians_, p. 67.

[16] _Righteousness_, pp. 231-232.

[17] _Of_ _the_ _Laws_ _of_ _Ecclesiastical_ _Polity_, intro. Christopher Morris (London, 1963 , 1964), I, 154-155, 210, 236.

[18]*Laws*, I, 332-333, 338, 347-348.

[19]Bolton, pp. 54, 55.

[20]Bolton, pp. 80-81.

[21]*Commentary*, p. 161.

[22]*Sermons*, p. 165.

[23]*Judaism*, p. 11. See also p. 101 where the term "ethical" is equated with "rational."

[24]Cerfaux, *Christian*, pp. 265-266; Bultmann, *Theology*, I, 222-223.

[25]*Institutes*, p. 456.

[26]*Righteousness*, p. 241.

[27]*Laws*, p. 307.

[28]See "Natural Law," *New Catholic Encyclopedia: An International Work of Reference*, 1967.

[29]*Of Christian Doctrine* in *Works*, XVI, 117, 119.

[30]*Ibid*.

[31]*Works*, XV, 179.

[32]*Milton and the Puritan Dilemma 1641-1660* (Toronto, 1942), pp. 148-149.

[33]*Dilemma*, pp. 311-312.

[34]*On the Spirit*, p. 97.

[35]*On the Spirit*, p. 92.

[36]*An Exposition . . . Romans*, p. 2.

[37]*Institutes*, I, 51.

[38]*On Hebrews*, p. 189.

[39] YP. IV, 624.

[40] Works, IV, 135.

[41] On Galatians, XXVI, 112, 116, 117, 336-337.

[42] Loci Communes, p. 131.

[43] De Regno Christi, p. 319.

[44] Works, IV, 214.

[45] Works, VI, 32-33.

[46] Dilemma, pp. 238-239. See Christopher Hill's extensive work on the leveller argument, such as Intellectual Origins of the English Revolution (Oxford, 1965), and Milton and the English Revolution (New York, 1978).

[47] S.S. Cohon, Judaism, p. 16.

[48] Considerations . . . in Works, VI, 54.

[49] On Romans, p. 7.

[50] De Regno Christi, p. 319.

[51] On Romans, pp. 179-180; On Galatians, XXVI, 111.

[52] Loci Communes, pp. 308, 313.

[53] Institutes, II, 1044; On Hebrews, p. xxviii.

[54] Institutes, II, 1190, 1191.

[55] Institutes, I, 364; On Philippians & Colossians, pp. 188-190.

[56] Institutes, II, 1299-1300.

[57] Calvin, ed. William Pringle, On Galatians, p. 19.

[58] On Hebrews, pp. 182, 221, 222.

[59] On Hebrews, p. 192.

[60] "Learned Discourse" in Laws, pp. 52, 53.

[61] "Learned Discourse," p. 53.

[62] Laws, pp. 222, 348, 360, 361, 401-402.

[63] Works, III, 4.

[64] Works, III, 268. I have underlined those adjectives which designate dependence upon the efforts of man to save himself by his own power alone--they have nothing to do with the physical sins of the body in this context, as Chapter One indicates.

[65] Works, III, 355.

[66] Works, III, 355.

[67] Dilemma, p. 296.

[68] Works, VI, 28-29. See also Considerations, Works, VI, 50-51, where Milton asserts that both ceremonies and tithes are abolished.

[69] Sencourt, Paul, p. 141; Cerfaux, Christ in the Theology, p. 494; Christian, p. 378.

[70] C.M., ed., Homilies on Romans by Chrysostom, p. 74.

[71] Writings of Saint Justin Martyr, pp. 91, 171, 172, 190, 212, 325.

[72] Against Heresies, p. 496; Bk. IV, Ch. XVI, p. 480.

[73] On Romans, p. 82.

[74] De Principiis, p. 322; Contra Celsum, p. 319.

[75] Stromata, p. 509.

[76] On Romans, pp. 75, 76, 77.

[77] On Galatians, pp. 74, 32, 36-40; On Philippians, p. 118.

[78] On the Spirit, p. 49.

[79] On Romans, p. 5.

[80] On Galatians, pp. 139, 138; Freedom of the Will, p. 76.

[81] On Galatians, pp. 16, 17, 83.

[82] On Romans, p. 48; On Galatians, XXVII (1535), pp. 130, 131-132; On Titus, p. 36.

[83] On Corinthians, pp. 315-316; Institutes, II, 1300.

[84] On Philippians & Colossians, p. 247. See also On Galatians and Ephesians, p. 149.

[85] On Galatians and Ephesians, pp. 151, 182-183, 233.

[86] On Philippians & Colossians, pp. 88, 184.

[87] Valdes, p. 126.

[88] "Learned Discourse," pp. 34, 58-59.

[89] On Philippians, p. 213; see also pp. 218, 217.

[90] Commentary, p. 147.

[91] Milton and the Kingdoms of God (Evanston, 1964), p. 236.

[92] Martin Bucer in Works, IV, 23.

[93] Works, III, 450.

[94] Works, VI, 17-18.

[95] Works, XVI, 181, 165, 179.

[96] Meaning, p. 61.

[97]Judaism, p. 220.

[98]Cerfaux, Christian, p. 270, n. 1.

[99]Loci Communes, p. 201.

[100]Bondage, p. 304; Calvin, On Corinthians II, pp. 175, 176.

[101]Righteousness, p. 227.

[102]On Romans, p. 25.

[103]Sermons, pp. 101, 103.

[104]Of Reformation in Works, III, 3. Of Christian Doctrine in Works, XVI, 101; XV, 299; XIV, 379, 381, 393, 395, 399 ff. See also Maurice Kelley, This Great Argument: A Study of Milton's De Doctrina Christiana as a Gloss upon Paradise Lost (Gloucester, Mass., 1962), pp. 106-118.

[105]Origen Against Celsus, The Writings, II, 1.

[106]Exposition of the Christian Faith in Principal Works, p. 248. See also Basil, "Concerning Faith," p. 57, and "Concerning Baptism," pp. 365-366.

[107]Christianity, p. 475.

[108]On the Spirit, pp. 39, 40, 42.

[109]Institutes, p. 495; On Corinthians II, pp. 72, 184.

[110]Loci Communes, p. 201; Servetus, p. 251.

[111]Works, III, 3.

[112]Works, III, 24.

[113]Works, III, 382; III, 427.

[114]Works, IV, 174.

[115]Tetrachordon in Complete Prose Works, ed.
Don M. Wolfe et al., (New Haven, 1953), II, 668, afterwards
cited as YP.

[116]Arthur Barker, Dilemma, pp. 149-150, demonstrates
the popularity of this argument in the Leveller pamphlets
in the 1640's.

[117]Against Heresies, p. 448.

[118]Stromata, p. 355.

[119]On Galatians, p. 59; On Romans, pp. 155, 91.

[120]City of God in Basic Writings, II, 4; On the
Spirit, p. 43. See also Bultmann, Theology, I, 264-265.

[121]Christianity, p. 451.

[122]Spirit, p. 103.

[123]On Galatians, pp. 95, 13.

[124]On Romans, pp. 11, 17; On Galatians, XXVI, 308-309.

[125]Bondage, pp. 190, 303-306; On Romans, p. 79; On
Hebrews, p. 212.

[126]Loci Communes, pp. 125, 127, 123.

[127]On Galatians and Ephesians, p. 100.

[128]Institutes, II, 1313, 1312, n. 20; I, 354.

[129]Righteousness, p. 239.

[130]Valdes, p. 297.

[131]Sermons, pp. 168, 169-170, 165.

[132]Works, III, 438.

[133]Works, XVI, 107.

[134]Stromata, p. 355.

135On Galatians, pp. 59, 60.

136On the Spirit, p. 73.

137On Galatians, XXVI, 345-346.

138Loci Communes, pp. 55-56.

139Institutes, pp. 106-107, 108, 454-455.

140Reason in Works, III, 195.

141A Select Library of Nicene and Post-Nicene Fathers of the Christian Church, 2nd series, trans. Philip Schaff and Henry Wace, Vol. XI (New York, 1894), p. 112.

142Discourse, II, p. 355.

143"Enchiridion," pp. 727-728; On the Spirit, p. 69; City of God, II, 158.

144On Romans, p. 92; On Galatians, XXVI, 11, 4-5, 7; XXVII, 49.

145Righteousness, p. 241.

146Bounds, pp. 140-144, 145-146.

147Works, III, 198.

148Works, IV, 202.

149Works, IV, 130.

150Works, XVI, 125-163 passim.

151On the Spirit, p. 48.

152On Galatians, pp. 56-58, 49-50.

153On Romans, pp. 11, 17.

154On Galatians, XXVI, 174, 324, 325, 327, 334, 365, 159.

[155] On Titus, p. 85; Bondage, pp. 49-50.

[156] Loci Communes, pp. 123, 66-69.

[157] On Galatians & Ephesians, pp. 70, 72-73, 76-77, 88-89, 90.

[158] Institutes, pp. 810, 353, 354; see also pp. 351-352, 323, 356.

[159] Bounds, p. 149.

[160] On the Trinity, p. 250.

[161] Interpreters, p. 44.

[162] The Old and the New Man in the Letters of Paul, pp. 26-27.

[163] Against Heresies, p. 434.

[164] The Divine Institutes, trans. Mary Francis McDonald (Washington, D.C., 1964), p. 288.

[165] "The Morals" in Ascetical Works, trans. Sister M. Monica Wagner, C.S.C. (New York, 1950), p. 119; "The Long Rules" in Ascetical Works, pp. 254-255.

[166] On Galatians, pp. 42, 59; On I Timothy, pp. 15, 17.

[167] On the Spirit, pp. 49-50, 65.

[168] Summa Theologiae, II, 327, 328, 329.

[169] On Romans, pp. 51-52.

[170] On Galatians, XXVI, 150, 155-157, 180-181. See also Bondage, pp. 320-304; On Galatians, pp. 447, 448, 373.

[171] On Galatians, XXVI, 4-6.

[172] On Galatians, pp. 76-77; Institutes, pp. 362-363.

[173]The Laws, II, 355, Bk. V; I, 329, 331, Bk. III.

[174]Sermons, pp. 164, 166, 173, 174, 176, 130.

[175]Commentary, pp. 162, 130.

[176]Bounds, pp. 28-29, 55, 99, 30, 32-33, 56.

[177]Bounds, pp. 56, 57, 58.

[178]Bounds, pp. 58, 59-60, 64, 70.

[179]Reason in Works, III, 369.

[180]Tetrachordon, IV, 138-141; 260-261.

[181]Works, IV, 23-24.

[182]Works, XV, 299; XVI, 125, 129, 131, 147.

[183]Works, XVI, 143, 145; Kelley, p. 176.

[184]Works, XVI, 147-149, 149-151.

CHAPTER THREE

THE GOSPEL, LOVE, AND LIBERTY

We have seen the negative aspects of the Law and
its failure to perform what the Reformers and Milton
felt was the task of religion, and throughout the discussion it became manifest that there is a multiple
antithesis operating in opposition to the Law. This
antithesis is composed of the Gospel, Christ, the
Spirit, grace, faith, and charity; in varying measures
these spiritual basics supply what the Law could not.

St. Paul's theme was always the preaching of the
Gospel, the message or news about Christ, which offered
the only means of salvation. Introducing himself to
the Romans as a bearer of the good news to both Jew
and Gentile, barbarian and Greek,on the basis of the
salvific power of the Gospel, he cites the Gospel's
"mighty signs and wonders" to impress his audience.
God will judge all men according to the Gospel and not
the Law, and this specifically is Paul's role according to God's will--to spread the Word to all. Paul
occasionally speaks in gnostic terms, describing the
Gospel as "secret," since the beginning of the world
but now revealed to those who will listen. He tells
the Corinthians that they are reborn in the Gospel
but that all must live by the Gospel as well as preach
and understand it. He is anxious about the Galatians
because the false apostles have perverted the Gospel
by basing salvation on the Law as well as the Gospel.
Abraham received a message from God long before the
Gospel was preached to all men, but this dispensation
was due to his faith and not to the power of the Law.

In his commentary on Corinthians II, Calvin provides a thorough and precise contrast between the
Gospel and the Law on the basis of Piscator (Pisca-
toris Scholia in Epist. II ad Corinth.). These are
the radical differences:

1.	Novi Testamenti (New Testament)	1.	Veteris Testamenti (Old Testament)
2.	Spiritus (Spirit)	2.	Literae (Letter)
3.	Vitae (Life)	3.	Mortis (Death)

163

4. Inscriptum cordibus (Written on men's hearts)	4. Inscriptum lapidibus (Written on stones)
5. Semper durans (Everlasting)	5. Abolendum (To be done away)
6. Justitiae (Righteousness)	6. Damnationis (Condemnation)
7. Excellenter gloriosum (Eminently glorious)	7. Illius Respectu ἄδοξον (Comparatively devoid of glory)
8. Perspicuum (Clear)	8. Obscurum (Obscure)

The Gospel is "the doctrine of life, because it is the instrument of regeneration," but the Law can only "condemn" because it only prescribes the role of a good life "without renewing man's soul."[1]

The major focus in the Institutes with regard to the Gospel centers on the Gospel's promise to mankind in that the Gospel "confirmed and satisfied whatever the Law had promised, and gave substance to the shadows." The prophets of the Old Testament manifested Christ but in secret, as Paul says in Romans (1.15; 3.31; 16.25). Calvin points to Augustine's having distinguished between the promises of the Old Testament and those of the New, especially the obscurity of the former and the clarity of the latter.[2]

Samuel Bolton speaks clearly on the superiority of the Gospel to the Law: "The law is subservient to the Gospel. Its purpose is to convince and humble us, and the Gospel is to enable us to fulfil the obedience of the law. The law sends us to the Gospel for our justification; the Gospel sends us to the law to frame our way of life." However, obedience to the Gospel is based on love and not legalism.[3]

Milton held that the Gospel stood unqualifiedly superior to the Old Law and its promise and testament because the Gospel terminates the Old Law. In The Reason of Church-Government he contradicts the claim that episcopacy was founded on the authority of the Old Testament on this basis: "for that the Gospell is the end and fulfilling of the Law, our liberty also from the bondage of the Law I plainly reade." The natural law and the Gospel form the basis of morality: "That which is thus morall, besides what we fetch from those unwritten lawes and Ideas which nature hath

ingraven in us, the Gospell, as stands with her
dignity most, lectures to us from her own authentick
hand-writing, and command, not copies out from the
borrow'd manuscript of a subservient scrowl, by way
of imitating." The Gospel in no way imitates the Law
but perfects it, although the Law provides the concept of a ministry, teaching, and discipline, which
is given over to presbyters; but bishops are not
derived from the moral law, which to Milton was not
abrogated. Samuel Stollman argues unpersuasively
that the Law is internalized and somehow "Hebraic" in
a positive sense but that the external aspects of the
Law, the "Judaic" are rejected. I see nowhere that
this dichotomy holds up in Milton's thinking because
it ignores the monumental role of the Gospel, as
described here.[4]

He consistently admired and hailed the simplicity of the Gospel in opposition to what he conceived
as episcopacy and Roman Catholicism, which "hath made
it self high in the world and the flesh to vanquish
things by the world accounted low, and made it self
wise in tradition and fleshly ceremony to confound the
purity of doctrin which is the wisdom of God." The
law of the Gospel is inner, sincere, and simple:

Certainly Readers, the worship of God singly in
it selfe, the very act of prayer and thanksgiving
with those free and unimpos'd expressions which
form a sincere heart unbidden come into the outward gesture, is the greatest decency that can be
imagin'd. Which to dresse up and garnish with a
devis'd bravery abolisht in the law, and disclam'd by the Gospell addes nothing but a deformed
uglinesse. And hath ever afforded a colourable
pretense to bring in all those traditions and
carnalities that are so killing to the power and
vertue of the Gospell.[5]

The act of dressing up the Gospel suggests treating it
as a whore; the Gospel, however, proves that neither
the hierarchy nor the glitter are necessary in the
reason of Christian religion.

The Doctrine and Discipline of Divorce cites the
Gospel as a liberating force away from strict obedience because the "prime end of the Gospel" is to

provide grace and to satisfy the demand for obedience.
The Law still exacts obedience but should not, according to Milton, be more extreme than it was before the
Gospel. He still maintains the validity of the moral
law and must argue for divorce on this basis; later
he concluded that the moral as well as the ceremonial
law of Moses was also abrogated, and so could argue
for liberation on a different basis.[6] Thus he must
debate on uncomfortable terms with his opponents as
long as he grants the validity of the Mosaic law on
divorce along with Christ's statement about divorce
in Matthew. He seems to get himself involved in
contradictions. The Gospel, he claims, constitutes
a covenant which reveals grace and justifies by faith
only, but then he qualifies this statement with the
proviso, "if we endeavour to square our moral duty by
those wise and equal Mosaic rules, which were as
perfect as strict and as unpardonable to the Jews as
to us."[7] Milton is being pulled in precisely different directions and has not yet shed the notion that
the Law not only does not justify but does not demand
obedience.

        In both the tracts on civil government and
religion and Of Christian Doctrine, the theme of
maturity and voluntary compliance dominates. In Civil
Power he sets the "special privilege and excellence
of the free gospel over the servile law." Milton
attacks the argument that civil power and force are
necessary in the religious arena because the kings in
the Old Testament used sanctions to enforce religion.
His argument is based on the superiority of the Gospel
over the Law:

    But to this besides I return a threefold answer:
    first, that the state of religion under the
    gospel is far differing from what it was under
    the law: then was the state of rigor, childhood,
    bondage and works, to all which force was not
    unbefitting; now is the state of grace, manhood,
    freedom and faith; to all which belongs willing-
    ness and reason, not force: the law was then
    written on tablets of stone, and to be performed
    according to the letter, willingly or unwillingly;
    the gospel, our new covenant, upon the heart of
    every beleever, to be interpreted only by the

sense of charitic and inward persuasion.[8]

In *Of Christian Doctrine* Milton emphasizes the voluntary aspect of the Gospel over the slavishness of the
Mosaic law and regards the former as a "new dispensation" of grace which is superior to the old covenant
because of its clear announcement of Christ himself.
He cites many passages in St. Paul's Epistles to
demonstrate the perfection of the Gospel over the Law.[9]

Arthur Barker provides an excellent summary of
several of the arguments discussed here with at least
one qualification. He asserts correctly that for the
Calvinist the moral law in the decalogue maintained
its force externally for Christians. He claims, however, that in *Tetrachordon* Milton urges the inner law
of the heart as a substitute for all external morality.
This is true, as Barker indicates, in the later pamphlets on legal-ecclesiastical matters and in *Of
Christian Doctrine*,[10] but it is not in *Tetrachordon*.
The conceptual framework of this pamphlet argues
against a rejection of external rules since the
passages in scripture which Milton highlights themselves deal with external morality. As summarized
above (pp. 106-107) Milton explicitly says that the
"*judaicall*" elements in the moral law were abrogated,
and he refers to Paraeus' commentary on Matthew that
contends that Christ corrected not the Law but Pharisaical interpretations of the Law. And so, during the
arguments on divorce, for Milton, the moral facets of
the Law still possess cogency for Christians.

The center of the Epistles of St. Paul is, of
course, Christ, the Son of God, made man, "according
to the flesh," who has power through his resurrection
from the dead, who extends grace to the obedient and
faithful of all nations (Rom. 1.1-5). Christ makes
men "dead to the law," "is the end of the law," and
brings righteousness (Rom. 7.4, 10.4, 10.10). He will
judge all men, the living and the dead (Rom. 14).
Paul explains to the Corinthians that "of him are ye
in Christ Jesus, who of God is made unto us wisdom,
and righteousness, and sanctification, and redemption"
(I Cor. 1.30). He reminds them that they are of the
body of Christ (see Chapter Four below) and that

167

Christ should be "made manifest in our body" (II
Cor. 4.10). When speaking to the Galatians, Paul
regards Christ as the authority for his preaching,
unlike the Law which was delivered by angels (Gal. 1.1).
In the second and fifth chapters to the Galatians is
found, in essence, the antithesis between Christ and
the Law, and the focal point of the antithesis is that
Christ justifies and the Law does not, and that if one
believes in the Law, he cannot believe in Christ.
Paul tells the Hebrews that Christ has offered himself
as a ransom to free men from death and bondage (presumably of the Law, which offers only death) (Heb. 2).
He also is the ultimate sacrifice made to "purge your
conscience from dead works to serve the living God"
(9.14). Christ's mission provides righteousness to
all men, and in doing so, marks the end of the power
of the Mosaic law. As we have seen already, the
nature and extent of this dispossession of the Law is
interpreted in various ways.

As far as our discussion is concerned, the important question is to ascertain Christ's role with reference to the Law as it was interpreted by the Fathers
and the Reformers. Athanasius, emphasizing the vivify-
ing qualities of the resurrection of Christ, believes
that Christ has conquered death and "put an end to
the law," citing the second chapter of Hebrews to support his assertion.11 St. Jerome quotes Romans, Corinthians, and Galatians extensively to support the
opposition of faith and grace to the works of the old
law.12 Jerome found this belief essential to combat
the Pelagian doctrine that man could save himself on
his own. St. Augustine quotes Romans 3.20-22 and
concludes that Christ fulfills the Law and that righteousness resides in the New Testament although it
receives "confirmation from the Old."13

Aquinas maintains that the spiritual law of Christ
makes Paul dead to the law of the Old Testament, and
the old law merely looked forward to Christ in typo-
logical fashion. He agrees with Paul that Christ is
not "the minister of sin" and asserts that in Galatians "the Apostle plainly is arguing against them
that if the death of Christ is the sufficient cause
of our salvation, and if grace is conferred in the
sacraments of the New Testament, which have their

efficacy from the passion of Christ, then it is
superfluous to observe, along with the New Testament,
the rituals of the old law in which grace is not conferred nor salvation acquired, because the Law has led
no one to perfection, as it had in Hebrews."[14] Aquinas,
however, includes also the sacraments as part of the
New Testament.

Luther makes the antipathy between the Law and
Christ absolute on the basis of Galatians 5.4 and
equates the works of the old law with those of "papists,
monks, nuns, priests, Mohammedans, and sectarians."
Christ's death defeats "the Law, sin, death, hell, the
devil, the world, and the flesh":

> Therefore when Christ took away the fear of death,
> He set us free from slavery to sin and by this
> same act destroyed him to whom we were subject
> only through the fear of death. Yet he did not
> destroy him in such a way that he did not exist;
> but just as we are freed from the devil, not so
> that he does not exist, but so that he is not
> feared, etc.[15]

Calvin waxes poetic in his delineation of Christ's
lucidity in contrast to the obscurity of the Law.
Christ, who took the curse of the Law on his shoulders,
has a "glorious face" which is superior to the veil of
Moses which more "dazzles men's eyes than enlightened
them. He notes Paul's use of the term παρρησια,
confidence, to contrast "with the obscurity of the
law." Echoing Malachi 4.2, he depicts Christ as "the
Sun of righteousness." In the Institutes Calvin adds
two other effects of Christ's redemption: liberation
from death and mortification of the flesh. Christ
gave man what the Law could only offer if man could
fulfill the entire Law by offering himself as a "ransom" or a "price." In sum, "Paul justly calls Christ
the fulfillment or end of the law. For it would be
of no value to know what God demands of us if Christ
did not succor these laboring and oppressed under its
intolerable yoke and burden."[16]

Theologians as far apart as Calvin and Hooker
agreed on the centrality of Christ and his fulfillment
of the demands of the Mosaic law. In this area Hooker

opposes the Roman Catholic position as he conceives it, that is, that man can justify himself through penance and good deeds. It is God through Christ who puts away the sin of man by "not imputing it," and who pardons all punishment because Christ has fulfilled all the demand of the Mosaic code.[17] Thomas Jacomb agrees with both Calvin and Hooker and adds the following paradigm on the role of Christ with respect to the Law:

(1) Christ was made under the law.
(2) That being made under the law he fulfilled it.
(3) That his fulfilling of the law is imputed to believers; so as that in him they fulfilled the law also.

Because Christ fulfilled the Law, Christians do not have to obey it for righteousness sake, but because it is God's love, they must obey it out of "love and gratitude."[18] Once again ambiguity and ambivalence obtain on the degree to which the Law is abrogated because of Christ's redemption. Nevertheless Christ and love remain the undeniable focus of the question.

Milton's view of the question conforms essentially with that of Luther and Calvin in terms of regarding Christ as "the only lawgiver" in religious matters and in terms of regarding the Law as dead, which event nullifies man's contract with the Law. Christ makes us dead to sin and the Law so that "we may bring forth fruit in him from a willing godliness, and not by the compulsion of law." In Of Christian Doctrine Milton says that "Christ fulfilled the law by perfect love to God and his neighbor, until the time when he laid down his life for his brethren, being made obedient unto his Father in all things."[19]

In Paradise Lost, which illuminates the role of Christ in redemption and whose themes are based on Christ's role, places Christ offstage a great deal, and so he loses the center of attention to Satan and Adam and Eve. However, in the providential plan of the Father, it becomes clear that Christ is meant to provide the resolution of the tragedy of the Fall. Later we shall see how his love and grace play a vital role in this process, but it is sufficient now to demonstrate his superior role in the context of the

Mosaic law, whether ceremonial or moral. Michael
describes the sacrifice of Christ in terms of his
ability to justify man, as Paul had explained it in
the Epistle to the Hebrews, iterating that Christ
represents the only effective sacrifice for man's
sins. Adam asks Michael during the latter's summary
of the history of the Jews in the Old Testament why
God remained close to them:

> This yet I apprehend not, why to those
> Among whom God will deign to dwell on earth
> So many and so various laws are giv'n;
> So many laws argue so many sins
> Among them; how can God with such reside? (XII.
> 280-284)

Michael provides the perfect answer:

>   To whom thus Michael: "Doubt not but that sin
> Will reign among them, as of thee begot;
> And therefore was law given them to evince
> Their natural pravity, by stirring up
> Sin against law to fight; that when they see
> Law can discover sin, but not remove,
> Save by those shadowy expiations weak,
> The blood of bulls and goats, they can conclude
> Some blood more precious must be paid for man,
> Just for unjust, that in such righteousness
> To them by faith imputed, they may find
> Justification toward God, and peace
> Of conscience, which the law by ceremonies
> Cannot appease, nor man the moral part
> Perform, and not performing cannot live.
> So law appears imperfect, and but giv'n
> With purpose to resign them in full time
> Up to a better cov'nant, disciplined
> From shadowy types to truth, from flesh to spirit,
> From imposition of strict laws to free
> Acceptance of large grace, from servile fear
> To filial, works of law to works of faith.
> And therefore shall not Moses, though of God
> Highly beloved, being but the minister
> Of law, his people into Canaan lead;
> But Joshua when the Gentiles Jesus call,
> His name and office bearing, who shall quell
> The adversary Serpent, and bring back
> Through the world's wilderness long-wandered man
> Safe to eternal Paradise of rest. (XII.285-314)

Several ideas stand out. Christ supplants Moses, the old law leads as a shadow to Christ, both the ceremonial and moral law are included in the rejection of the Mosaic law, and the ranging in antipathy respectively of shadow to truth, flesh to spirit, law to grace, fear to willingness, works to faith—all are Pauline themes.

With Christ as the matrix of justification and salvation, faith in Christ becomes essential for the believing Christian, and there is little argument on this point in the Reformation. Controversy, however, surrounded the question of whether faith alone saves mankind or whether works and love must be added. Definitions in this area must be precise because some of the Reformers regarded love and works as synonymous. On the other hand, the concept of faith in Christ is not very carefully defined but taken for granted. Rudolph Bultmann perceives Paul as understanding faith "primarily as obedience" but not as a work since the will surrenders itself to an outside authority.[20] The Reformation, however, associated obedience with works and so opposed faith and works as mutually hostile and even contradictory.

According to Paul, the core of faith in Christ depends upon believing that he was crucified, died, and raised from the dead:

> We having the same spirit of faith, according as it is written, I believed, and therefore have I spoken; we also believe, and therefore speak;
> Knowing that he which raised up the Lord Jesus shall raise up us also by Jesus, and shall present us with you. (II Cor. 4.13-14)

His perpetual problem with the Galatians was to impress upon them the necessity of faith in Christ over a belief in the works of the Law: "Received ye the Spirit by the works of the law, or by the healing of faith?" (Gal. 3.2). Christ has redeemed man from the curse of the Law, and faith in him should not be distorted by reliance on the works of the Law (Gal. 3.8, 10, 11, 12). As previously noted, circumcision, the symbol of the Law, is meaningless in the face of "faith which worketh by love" (Gal. 5.6). The Law becomes a curse

172

without faith, which is represented by the inner circumcision of the Spirit.[21]

The conflict between faith and the works of the law occupied the Church Fathers, and they were careful to distinguish between works demanded by the Law and those encouraged by love or charity. Chrysostom links both faith and charity but argues that faith fulfills the Law, implying a relative weight to love and an absolute value to faith.[22] Augustine fixed upon the argument that the Jews made the mistake of thinking that righteousness came from their works and not from faith in Christ, but he includes in faith love and not the fear of the Law. One chapter in "Enchiridion" is entitled "Faith Without Works Is Dead And Cannot Save Man."[23]

Aquinas, commenting on Romans 3.28, "Therefore we conclude that a man is justified by faith without the deeds of the law," distinguishes between the ceremonial and the moral, equates the moral law of Moses with the natural, and concludes that man is justified by observation of the moral law insofar as it emanates from God. He even adds the ceremonial law as it relates to the sacraments and insists that man should obey all these laws.[24] The basic problem for the Reformation was to be the impossibility of accepting what Thomas said about man's obligations, for it implied that Christ neither abrogated nor even fulfilled the Law.

According to Aquinas, the important phrase, "faith formed by love," "fides charitate formata" (Gal. 5.6), meant that faith demanded works to demonstrate love, but Martin Luther denied this dogma because faith depends entirely on Christ's gift, and he relates the concept of works under the Mosaic law to those under the Roman church--both unnecessary for justification. Opposing the pope, he avers that faith will not yield although charity or love may, but matter of conscience are not to be considered matters of charity according to St. Paul, despite what the pope may claim.[25] If "faith formed by love" is essential to salvation, then Christ's sacrifice is nullified. Faith may work by love, but love by itself through works does not justify. It is most interesting that the word love in

173

this context, in effect, is synonymous with the word law. This results undoubtedly from the negative associations arising from the Roman church's allowing the concept of works of charity to degenerate into little more than a mercenary institution. In his commentary on Hebrews, Luther maintains that the only work which can be acceptable for the Christian is faith in Christ, from whom our patience and humanity flow. He rebukes Peter Lombard's view that the "works of the old Law were of no value, even if they were done in faith and love." According to Luther, this faith would have saved them. He sees nothing wrong in ceremonies, tonsures, etc., but they are wrong when used as ends in themselves. He quotes Romans 2.25 on circumcision and asserts that "the keeping of the Law has become a transgression of the Law."[26] The foundation of Luther's position is that the sacrifice of Christ suffices for justification and salvation; anything else, the Decalogue, ceremonies, "love," or sacraments, can under no circumstances be substituted for this overwhelming event. Faith, for Luther, does not equal obedience, which leads to works (done in love according to Aquinas) but knowledge: "Faith is nothing else but the truth of the heart, that is, the right knowledge of the heart about God. But reason cannot think correctly about God; only faith can do so. A man thinks correctly about God when he believes God's word."[27] Faith and reason appear to be mutually exclusive for Luther.

Philip Melanchthon fundamentally agrees with his friend Martin Luther and attacks the issue from a slightly different perspective. The prophets said that the people were saved "through faith in the Messiah, and not through law." He denies that any righteousness can be achieved through external morality and confirmed that it is granted only through the Son of God. "Pelagians, papists, monks," he claims, incorrectly believe that "external morality is a fulfillment of the divine law and that on account of his own works man is justified before God and merits forgiveness of sins."[28] As Luther indicated, adherence to the doctrine of works simply detracts from the glory of Christ.

174

Calvin also believed in the positions outlined above--that faith in Christ alone justifies, without exception, and that Papist emphasis on actions or works is wrong. Faith does work with love and "is invariably accompanied by good works," but it justifies by itself and doesn't need anything else to assist it. Works are entirely excluded, and not just ceremonial works but all, "whatever title may grace them."29

Milton's attitude on faith and works in Of Christian Doctrine appears closer to Aquinas' than it is to the Reformers', and he makes a subtle distinction in his definition of works. He agrees that the works of the Law do not save but "faith which worketh by love" (echoing Aquinas), but he urges that the works of faith are different from the works of the Law. "Hence we are justified by faith without the works of the law, but not without the works of faith; inasmuch as a living and true faith cannot consist without works, though these latter may differ from the works of the written law." Further, God, to Milton, is the "primary efficient cause of good works," and the proximate causes are virtues. Faith, "not agreement with the decalogue," justifies, and only faith can make a work good. Thus no works can be good except by means of faith; faith, from an ontological viewpoint, is the "form" of good works.30 The Son's speech to the Father in Book Eleven in Paradise Lost corresponds to Milton's position in Of Christian Doctrine. The Son summarizes the providential plan for mankind. Man will be

Tried in sharp tribulation, and refined
By faith and faithful works, to second life,
Waked in the renovation of the just. (XI.63-65)

Michael repeats the thematic pattern of "faith formed by love" when he depicts the trials and successes of the Apostles, who will receive

The promise of the Father, who shall dwell,
His Spirit, within them, and the law of faith
Working through love, upon their hearts shall write,
To guide them in all truth . . . . . . (XII.487-490)

Milton thus appears to take an intermediate position through his definition of works according to faith as distinguished from works according to the Law, whether Mosaic or Canon.

Abraham was used by St. Paul as the perfect
example of faith in the Old Testament, and because
he lived before the Law was given to Moses, he was
saved by faith alone, not by works. He even appears
to be regarded by Paul as a Christian, according to
Lucien Cerfaux.[31] Chapter Four of Romans provides
the basics of the Apostle's position. Assuming that
all are condemned, both Jew and Gentile under the Law,
Paul writes that Abraham was justified by his faith,
"not in circumcision, but in uncircumcision," and he
was circumcised in order to be "the father of all who
believe." The promise of God to Abraham about his
seed bearing the Messiah was based entirely on his
faith and not on the Law (Romans 4). The children of
God descend from Isaac, who represents the promise
given to Abraham and not the Law (Rom. 9.7-8). Paul
continues the same dichotomy in speaking to the Galatians: Abraham's seed is blessed, but those under
the Law are cursed. Abraham even blesses the Gentiles
for his seed leads to Jesus Christ four hundred and
thirty years before the Law was promulgated. One can
see why Abraham, in some sense, can be regarded as
the first Christian who makes all men outside the Law
his heirs (Gal. 3.6-17, 29). Paul develops the argument further in the fifth chapter, alluded to previously, in which the two sons of Abraham represent
the two covenants, the son of Agar or Hagar, the
slavish Law, and Isaac, the free promise of Christ,
the former the present Jerusalem and the latter the
"Jerusalem which is above." The Galatians must reject
the bondwoman's son and embrace the son of the free
woman (Gal. 4.21-31). In writing to the Hebrews, Paul
iterates Abraham's genealogy and faith and includes
Enoch and Noah in this tradition of faith in the Old
Testament. However, he concentrates on Abraham and
Sarah, whose faith led to the promise, and on Isaac
who is regarded as a figure of the resurrection to
come because it was believed that God raised him back
from the dead after he was actually slain by Abraham
in Genesis (Heb. 11.1-19).

The Church Fathers also fastened on this argument
to advance the cause of non-Judaic Christianity. Justin Martyr asserted that Adam, Enoch, Abraham, and Lot
were all uncircumcised and so had absolutely nothing

176

to do with the Law, even indirectly. (Genesis 17. 10-14 had indicated that circumcision would be for Abraham and his descendents the sign of the cove- nant.)[32] Irenaeus, devoting an entire chapter to the subject, "Abraham's Faith Was Identical With Ours," insisted that it existed before either the Law or circumcision.[33] Origen, who advanced the theory of allegorical reading of the Bible, cited the fourth chapter of Galatians on Abraham and his wives as an example.[34] Chrysostom regarded Abraham as a great example to emulate because of his justification by faith, and the Jews prided themselves on their descent from Abraham while the Christians are blessed, through Christ, by Abraham's seed. Chrysostom follows Paul's distinction between the sons of Abraham as represent- ing the two covenants, the old and the new: "The bondwoman was called Agar, and 'Agar' is the word for Mount Sinai in the language of that country. So that it is necessary that all who are born of the Old Cove- nant should be bondmen, for that mountain where the Old Covenant was delivered hath a name in common with the bondwoman. And it includes Jerusalem, "The barren, like Sarah, represent those born after the Spirit in the New Covenant. The bondwoman, the Old Covenant, should be rejected because it is not the true heir."[35] St. Augustine cites the fourth chapter of Galatians like Origen but employs the account to symbolize the two cities, the earthly and the heavenly.[36]

During the Middle Ages Thomas Aquinas regarded the circumcision of Abraham as symbolic because the promise was fulfilled in Christ, and to Aquinas the old Jerusalem represents "the bondage of legal obser- vances."[37]

John Colet distinguishes between circumcision as the symbol of Abraham's faith and its later representa- tion of the Law.[38] Luther approvingly returns to the basic argument of Paul that Abraham was saved by faith and not by works, characterizing Abraham and "all de- vout people" as embracing faith and as opposed to reason. The Law did not abrogate the promise given to Abraham, and the allegory of Agar and Sarah is explain- ed in this manner. The covenant under Agar contains conditional promises and leaves the conscience in desperation because no one keeps the Law. The new covenant from Isaac liberates men from the Law and vivifies them. Sarah is regarded by Luther as "the bride of Christ who gives birth to all."[39]

Calvin's view corresponds to what has been said above. He repeats that Abraham was not under the law of works but adds his own allegorical interpretation (although he was suspicious of allegorizing) of Sarah and Agar. In the church they represent the two mothers:

> Doctrine is the mother of whom we are born, and is twofold, Legal and Evangelical. The legal mother, whom Hagar resembles, gendereth to bondage. Sarah, again, represents the second, which gendereth to freedom; though Paul begins higher, and makes our first mother Sinai, and our second, Jerusalem. The two covenants, then, are the mothers, of whom children unlike one another are born; for the legal covenant makes slaves, and the evangelical covenant makes freemen.[40]

Abraham for Calvin represents the pattern of achieving righteousness through faith, which justifies man through belief in Christ as the source of righteousness or justification, which contravenes the works of the Law.[41] Servetus also relates typologically Abraham and Christ together through the proto-evangelium or seed image in Genesis: "Abraham is promised the blessing of seed, multiplying, and an inheritance; and all these Christ has conferred upon us through faith."[42]

Others in the Reformation observed the same distinctions although in their own fashion. Richard Hooker, close to the Roman view of the necessity of works for salvation, sympathetically looked upon the position of the Jews, who could not accept Paul's distinction between Abraham as a type of the faithful man and the father of the Jewish nation which lived by the Law:

> The Jews were persuaded, that God, for the love he bore unto Abraham's integrity and virtue, did, in lieu of his obedience and faithful service,

make him the root of a sanctified generation
of men on earth; and that God bringeth no man
to life, which is not either born, or else
adopted the son of Abraham: circumcised also
as he was, and consequently tied to all the
laws which Abraham's posterity received at the
hands of Moses. For which cause the very
Christian Jews themselves were offended when
they saw that the Apostles did impart the grace
of external vocation to the Gentiles, and never
tie them to any such conditions.[43]

Like Hooker, J.B. Lightfoot in the nineteenth century,
attempted an impartial view of the difficulty faced by
Jewish Christians in Paul's time, Jews who saw themselves as the seed of Abraham and therefore tied to
circumcision and the Law. He makes an interesting
separation between what he calls "double seed; a
natural seed, that of the Jews; and a faithful seed,
that of the believing Gentiles."[44] The Reformers
regarded themselves and all true Christians as the
offspring of the seed of faith and not of circumcision
or works.

Milton's Paradise Lost contains numerous examples
of those who demonstrate, like Abraham, firm faith to
God, including Abdiel in Paradise Lost, who was "Among
the faithless, faithful only he" (V.897), but his
faith has no bearing on the problem of the Mosaic law.
Book Twelve of the poem, however, offers an insight
into Milton's use of the eleventh chapter of Hebrews,
where Abraham, Enoch, and Noah are commended for their
belief in the covenant of faith. Michael tells Adam
that God will select "A nation from one faithful man
to spring," that is, Abraham, who follows God's directions and travels to the land of Canaan without a
quibble. Moses is delineated as the intermediator who
will last until the advent of the true mediator Christ
and establish laws pertaining to "civil justice" and
"religious rites." God is delighted with men as long
as they are obedient, but this covenant anticipates
the covenant of Abraham fulfilled in the Messiah (XXI.
223-269). In Book Eleven Enoch is depicted as the
individual, like Abdiel, who speaks out, in faith,
against evil, and Enoch also dares to speak out and is
saved from death. Noah preaches at assemblies of God's

wrath, but he too is ignored (XI.663-671, 700-711, 719-726).

One symbolic element related to Abraham as representative of Christian faith is the blessing of his seed, already alluded to, which leads to David and then Jesus; but looking backwards, this blessed seed extends to Eve, whose seed begins the whole cycle of redemption. This particular image in the providential economy is treated in Chapter Six below, where Eve's role is set in the context of the Adam-Christ parallel.

In addition to faith, in order for man to be justified, he needs grace, a quality or essence most difficult to define. Etymologically the word means _gift_, and in the Christian context it is a free gift of God which may be described as God's "mercy," "the enjoyment of his favour," or "A Christian virtue." C.A. Patrides points out how the term charis, grace, is not specifically Christian but antedates Christianity, and "during the classical Greek period, it denoted "the sense of beauty, charm, and perfection, or favour, affection, and kindness."[45] It is easier to say, on the basis of the Epistles, what it does rather than what it is; that is, it can be defined more functionally than essentially. As a gift of God, grace provides redemption on the basis of Jesus Christ (Rom. 3.24; Rom. 5.21; Eph. 2.5, 8; Titus 3.7); those who have faith in the promise like Abraham will receive grace (Rom. 4.16; Rom. 5.2); it abounds more than sin does (Rom. 5.20); and it opposes the law of works and substitutes for it (Rom. 6.14-15; Gal. 5.4). Essentially, faith in Jesus Christ brings grace, a gift of God, which offers redemption, and it contradicts both sin and the Law precisely on this basis. In terms of the Reformation's perspective on grace and works, Augustine provided a medial position. On the basis of I Timothy 1.9, he concludes that the Law leads the "unrighteous" to grace. The righteous man may use the Law by urging it on the unrighteous so that it will lead them to grace. Grace is not given as a reward for doing good works but in order to enable man to perform good works, to help man to fulfill the Law. Grace can also heal the wounds of sin.[46] From the vantage point of this century, Rudolph Bultmann

states that "prevenient grace" (coming before) makes
a good decision possible but does not eradicate free
will, and that Paul maintains man's "radical dependence" upon God's grace.[47]

During the Middle Ages Thomas Aquinas follows
Paul and Augustine in terms of Christ's bringing grace
unlike the Law which brings sin; Pelagius was mistaken
in thinking that man could fully obey the Law without
grace. However, Aquinas and the medieval church
insisted that the sacraments of the New Testament conferred grace.[48]

During the Reformation the sacraments were regarded as mere works which were unable to confer grace.
Luther rebuked the contention of Peter Lombard that
the sacraments of the New Testament confer grace because, in his view, "faith is already the grace that
justifies" through Christ. Luther agreed with the
medieval position that "the doctrine of grace simply
cannot stand with the doctrine of the Law. One of
them must be confirmed or substantiated."[49] In the
conflict between Luther and Erasmus on free will,
Erasmus had defined "prevenient grace" as "the free
gift of God to desire those things which lead to
eternal life." He also offered these definitions of
four kinds of grace:

(1) "implanted by nature and vitiated by sin,"
    which grace all men possess, "but some do
    not call this grace at all";
(2) "peculiar grace" or "stimulating grace," that
    awakens the sinner to a sense of his own con-
    dition;
(3) "cooperating grace"--"that makes the will
    effective";
(4) "a grace that carries things to a conclusion."[50]

Presumably "peculiar grace" would correspond to "prevenient grace," which anticipates a good act of man
but would not interfere with his free will. Luther
believed that the operation of grace negates the free
will of man. In terms of the role of the Law and
work-righteousness, which he equated, those depending
upon works for righteousness resist grace, but believers are justified by faith because they accept

181

God's grace.[51] C.A. Patrides reduces the four kinds
of grace to three or two: preventing, co-working,
and working, that is, divided in terms of spiritual
temporality, before a spiritual choice and then afterwards.[52]

As far as the Reformation is concerned, grace
and faith are very closely associated in that both
oppose the Mosaic law and works and that both achieve
a state of righteousness for man. Calvin sums up in
exemplary fashion: "To be Christians under the law
of grace does not mean to wander unbridled outside
the law, but to be engrafted in Christ, by whose grace
we are free from the curse of the law, and by whose
Spirit we are free from the curse of the law, and by
whose Spirit we have the law engraved upon our hearts."[53]

Milton's attitude on the antithesis between the
Law and grace changed as he grew older but in a confusing manner. For example, in Reason he unflaggingly
holds up the covenant of "the heirs of liberty and
grace" under the Law, asserting that the two are
incompatible. Nevertheless, when arguing the divorce
issue, he allows himself to get so involved in the
details of the legal argument that he hedges somewhat
on the question, qualifying the Christian's freedom
from the Law. "The Gospel," he says, "is a covnant
reveling grace, not commanding a new morality, but
assuring justification by faith only, contented only
if we endeavour to square our moral duty by those wise
and equal Mosaick rules, which were as perfect as
strict and as unpardonable to the Jews, as to us;
otherwise the law were unjust, giving grace of pardon
without pardon. . . ."[54] Milton is forced into this
position by maintaining that the Mosaic dispensation
(he would call it law) allowing divorce is the basis
for his conclusion that divorce is permissible for
current Christianity. As long as he argues on the
basis of the Mosaic permission to divorce as law, he
cannot regard the Law in total as totally abrogated,
as he had done in Reason, and as he was to do later.

In Of Christian Doctrine he characterizes the
"covenant of grace" as "far more excellent and perfect

than the law" and maintains that "the law is abolished principally on the ground of its being a law of works; that it might give place to the law of grace. . . . Seeing then that the law worketh wrath, but the gospel grace, and that wrath is incompatible with grace, it is obvious that the law cannot co-exist with the gospel."[55] Here he stands in full agreement with both Calvin and Luther on the issue of grace during the Reformation.

The free and generous operation of grace on man can be seen readily in the close of Paradise Lost, particularly when the poem ascends toward reconciliation on the parts of Adam and Eve and God.

The third element in the Pauline scheme of salvation is love or charity, and the words can be used interchangeably as long as the special meaning of almsgiving is ignored or at least given little importance in comprehension of the terms. In the New Testament Christ had extolled love and regarded it as the fulfillment of the Law, and Paul, especially in the thirteenth chapter of Of First Corinthians, had rhapsodically placed it superior to faith or hope as the greatest of all virtues. The concept is intertwined with the notion of Christian liberty in the sense that St. Augustine had later said, "Love God and do what you like," and this statement has been equated with Paul's view of the subject. To love God is synonymous with freedom.[56] The word agape (αγαπη) incorrectly got into English scripture because of Wyclif, who translated it from the Latin charitas, and so used the word charity, not love. Translators in the Reformation, knowing the Greek, reintroduced the word love.[57]

Paul told the Romans to love one another honestly and that "love is the fulfilling of the law," (12.9, 10; 13.10) and so, along with grace and faith, love is considered as another element opposed to the Mosaic law. Speaking to the Greeks at Corinth, Paul contrasts love with arrogance based on Greek wisdom (I Cor. 8.11), and in his hymn to charity Paul appears to regard faith as nothing without charity, although the Reformers were to disagree with what is apparently Paul's evaluation. Love is patient and not cynical

183

and superior to prophecies and knowledge, and most
important for our discussion: "And now abideth faith,
hope, charity, these three; but the greatest of these
is charity" (I Cor. 13). Another central passage,
this to the Galatians, is that in Christ the only
important thing is "faith which worketh by love" (Gal.
5.6). He warns the Galatians against using the liberty
he has given them for lust and advocates their employing it in love of neighbor (Gal. 5.13) along with
other virtues like "joy, peace, longsuffering, gentleness, goodness, faith, meekness, temperance" (Gal. 5.
22-23). His letter to Timothy explains charity as
"the end of the commandment" (I Tim. 1.5). Paul thus
takes the position of Christ (Matt. 22.37-39) that
love is the greatest commandment, love of both God
and neighbor, but the question eventually arose in the
Reformation, is it necessary to righteousness?

   In the early church the theme of love became
widespread as a strong element of Christianity.
Irenaeus complains that the followers of Simon Magus
and Marcion are "puffed up" with pride and have no
charity.[58] Clement, quoting Paul's statement that
love fulfills the Law, relates love to Christ who loves
mankind.[59] St. Ambrose writes eloquently on the same
subject: "And truly has he loved who fulfilled his
duty diligently, who spared his enemies, who loved his
foes, who pardoned those by whom he was entreated, who
did not even allow those who strove to usurp his power
to perish. That voice is of one not partially, but
fully perfected in the Law, saying: 'I have loved.
For love is the fulfillment of the law'."[60] Augustine,
too, encourages the replacement of the Law by love;
indeed the title of one chapter in his "Enchiridion"
is "Love is the end of all the commandments, and God
himself is love." Augustine associates the law of
love with the law of nature "written in the heart,"
and the man who "becomes a lover of the Law through
the life-giving Spirit," as opposed to the death-
dealing powers of the laws of stone. A consistent pattern of advocacy of the inward power of love over the
external power of the Law, and even over faith, emerges
in Augustine's thought.[61]

   Aquinas focuses the element of love on Christ,

who, he says, gave himself up out of obedience and
love, and he provides three reasons for connecting
love with Christ:

(1) It distinguishes man from the Old Law of fear;
(2) Christ proclaimed law "in terms of charity";
(3) Christ fulfilled the law and showed us how to
     imitate him.

Only pride expresses hostility to the admonition to
love. Aquinas makes the paradoxical point that, although Paul, in speaking to the Galatians, tells them
that they are free and then asks them to "serve one
another," charity is free despite its requirement that
one person serve another through charity.[62] Aquinas
does not explain what he means exactly, but perhaps he
suggests that the motivation to charity should be
spontaneous; but once accepted, if a person is truly
pursuing charity, he is then compelled to serve his
fellow man.

Luther was concerned if not obsessed with the
means by which a man achieved righteousness in the eyes
of God, and his basic conclusion that faith in Christ
alone provided righteousness caused him some difficulty
when faced with the Pauline concept of love. As has
been shown earlier, he associates love with works and
takes the position that love itself, in this sense,
does not justify man. He remarks of the Scholastics,
"where they speak of love, we speak of faith," a
statement accurately measuring the difference in perception and emphasis between them.[63] Once he has
established the point of love's inability to provide
righteousness, then he can approach the question of
the role of love more comfortably. Although theoretically opposing the Roman church's insistence on "faith
formed by love," he does concede that the Law can be
fulfilled entirely by love as long as it is added to
faith, and he praises the commandment to love others
as oneself, perceiving that it comes from one's heart.
He even calls it "the highest virtue." Nevertheless,
when he quotes I Corinthians 13.13 on "faith, hope,
love," he omits, "And the greatest of these is love."
In commenting on Galatians 6.2, "Bear ye one another's
burdens, and so fulfill the law of Christ," he describes
it as a "very considerate commandment," and states that

185

Christ gave man only the law of loving one another
(John 13.34). He further deepens Aquinas' definition
of love in the <u>Summa Theologiae</u>, that love means "to
wish someone else well," to mean that each man should
bear the burdens of someone else, especially those
which he would prefer not to bear.[64] In his quarrel
with Erasmus, Luther also asserts that charity should
be considered in the interpretation of the letter of
the law. Ultimately he agrees with the tradition
that love is the fulfillment of the Law; he quotes
Romans 14.10 and concludes that "love for one's neighbor is the sum and concise statement of the whole Law."
Nevertheless he argues that because love is the fulfilling of the Law, since the Law has been abrogated,
there is no need for love but only faith. This
identification of love with the doctrine of salvation
by works effectively destroys the concept and value
of love for Luther. He qualifies Paul's central emphasis to extinction.[65]

Calvin agrees with Luther that love is the Law's
fulfillment and also insists that love takes a "subordinate position" to faith. He grants that love has
value in "promoting peace and harmony in the Church
. . . . gentleness and lenity . . . . ⌊and it⌋ coun-
teracts emulation."[66]

Michael Servetus' position on love conflicts with
Calvin's and Luther's in that, for him, love is superior to faith, and yet he agrees that faith precedes
love. Both of these virtues are necessary for a complete justification and reward, an attitude similar
to Milton's phrasing, "faith and faithful works,"
the key to justification at the end of <u>Paradise Lost</u>.
The title of the fourth chapter of Servetus' <u>Right-
eousness</u> . . . is "On Love," which virtue performs
the following:

"1. Love fulfills the law, and all excellence is
ascribed to it." 2. Faith justifies. 3. "Yet
love holds the highest place. Faith must be followed up by works of love, which ensure the readier
forgiveness and increase the reward of glory. 4.
Outward acts spring from the inward spirit. Good
deeds react on the character, but also active
effort is required. 5. Faith precedes love, and

186

is the foundation of salvation; but love is
greater and has a wider range, is more difficult to exercize, and more permanent, and is
directed to both man and God. 6. It is
through love that faith leads to eternal life.
Love follows faith and perfects it. 7. Faith
opens the way to all good things. 8. but it
must find its complement in love, which is a
voluntary act, and spreads more widely, and
important as faith is, yet love has its own
reward."[67]

Servetus further iterates, like Augustine, the whole
law consists of love since, if one loves, one does not
violate the commandments. He admits that he disagrees
with Luther on the superior value of love to faith.[68]

Juan Valdes sides with the more radical Reformers
like Luther and Calvin on the issue of the competitive
merits of faith and love. He takes a curious position
on reading the thirteenth chapter of First Corinthians
in that he posits the belief that St. Paul "might have
attributed" to faith what he attributed to love, with
faith as the root and love as the fruit of a tree,
indicating the difficulty the Reformers had with this
passage. Nevertheless, charity is not superior to
faith, according to Valdes.[69]

Those theologians on the more conservative side
in England like Colet and Hooker, remaining with the
established church, maintained Paul's ranking of
charity over faith. As John Colet puts it, "love in
force and power far surpasses faith, and is far more
effectual to raise man on high, and joins him in God.
And hence that saying of St. Paul to the Corinthians:
The greatest of these is Charity."[70] Richard Hooker
reacts to the claims of Calvin and Luther on faith's
unique superiority in negative fashion: "It is a
childish cavil . . . that we tread all Christian virtues under our feet, and require nothing in Christians
but faith; because we teach that faith alone justi-
fieth; or works from being added as necessary duties,
required at the hands of every justified man."[71] Thus,
if faith justifies, works are yet necessary, in some
sense, to complete or substantiate justification.
Semantic ambiguity abounds since the question was often

187

posed as a false dilemma, an either-or proposition,
with the equivocation of love and works-righteousness
doubling the confusion.

The main problem for the Reformers was the fear
of charity's being substituted for faith as the means
of righteousness. If it was given a role lesser than
faith, not too much difficulty ensued in regarding it
as the replacement for the Mosaic law, particularly
its moral aspect.

In the divorce tracts Milton does not adopt the
position that love fulfills the Law and renders it
obsolete. Because he bound himself up with the legal
(in the Mosaic sense) aspects of divorce, he cannot
relinguish the Law as the basis for his argument, and
so he cannot plead absolutely for charity to the elimination of the Law as grounds for permission for divorce.
He thus takes an intermediate stance--that the Law
should be interpreted in a charitable manner and not
in a literalistic sense. He depicts the "Statute of
Moses" (Deut. 24.1) as "most charitable" and not repealed by Christ and cites both Paul and Christ on
charity as the fulfilling of the Law, and yet, paradoxically, Milton still maintains his legalistic
attitude on the issue, not rejecting the Mosaic law
as the basis for his position. However, he needed
that chain in his argument in order to counter Christ's
statement that man could not "put asunder" what God
had put together--the marriage bond.[72] Consistently
he commends the Annotationes in Libres Evangeliorum
(1641) of Hugo Grotius for its charitable and liberal
interpretations of the texts of the Gospels. More
important, the soundest footing for Milton's contention on divorce is the suffering that the couple in a
desperate marriage have to endure, in violation of the
law of charity: "to vexe and wound with a thousand
scandals and burdens above strength to bear . . .
charity commands that the believer be not wearied out
with endles waiting." Milton even regards charity
as the basis of "every act of true faith" and of belief in the Law since St. Paul said that "Charity
beleeveth all things." He censures those who, whether
Papist or Protestant, insist on "ordinances" above
charity as being little better than Pharisees, with

no understanding of the gospel.[73]

In <u>Tetrachordon</u> and <u>Colasterion</u> he becomes a
heretic against the Protestant Reformation in the sense
that he places charity on a level superior to faith,
as he had implied in <u>Divorce</u>. He says in <u>Colasterion</u>,
"Forseeing love includes Faith, what is ther that can
fulfill every commandment but only love?" In <u>Tetra-
chordon</u> he identifies charity with the natural law
within man's heart and then concludes that it is therefore superior to faith also: "Our Savours doctrine
is, that the end, and the fulfilling of every command
is charity; no faith without it, no truth without it,
no worship, no workes pleasing to God but as they partake of charity."[74] All these conclusions, although
based on assumptions with which Calvin and Luther
concurred, are diametrically opposed to the thinking
of both men.

In <u>Of Christian Doctrine</u> Milton designates charity
as "the greatest of all gifts," and claims that the
letter of the law, when it conflicts with the spirit,
should be read according to "the love of God and our
neighbor." He quotes at length both Christ (Matt. 32.
37-40) and Paul (Rom. 13.8; Gal. 5.14) to demonstrate,
as did Luther and Calvin, that love is the fulfillment
of the Law.[75] Later, in <u>Treatise</u> he opposes civil compulsion in matters of conscience on the basis of charity
in that charity as the fulfillment of the law cannot be
forced.[76] Milton had travelled far, at this stage of
his life, from legalism and toward both the spirit and
charity as the basis for an ethic of man's behavior.

The role of charity and its relationship to faith
and obedience and to ethical harmony in <u>Paradise Lost</u>,
particularly with regard to Adam and Eve, will be
shown in a later chapter, "The Pauline Equation in
<u>Paradise Lost</u>," but now it is necessary to examine the
presence in the poem of love or charity as it relates
to law and justice. The term <u>justice</u> in this context
is germane because in Book Three of the poem, where
the Son fulfills the law through love, the law is God
the Father's law long before the Mosaic law was
imposed on the Jews of the Old Testament. After the
Father defensively buttresses his position with respect

189

to the fall of the angels, just past, and the fall of
man, soon to be, the Son is portrayed in the context
of the free will of both creatures:

Beyond compare the Son of God was seen
Most glorious; in him all his Father shone
Substantially expressed, and in his face
Divine compassion visibly appeared,
Love without end, and without measure grace. (III.
138-142)

Two foci need emphasis in this passage: the Son substantially reflects the Father, and he or they radiate
unlimited love. The Father has the unfortunate role
of judge, and the Son seems to sympathize with him
about the difficult decisions he must make. As we
have seen, the Father will offer grace, but divine
justice demands some satisfaction, some ransom for
sin. Man "must die;/Die he or justice must" (III.
209-210). The doom will be executed unless someone
volunteers to fulfill the demands of God's eternal
law. The Son volunteers, "In whom the fulness dwells
of love divine" (III.225), and he prophesies his
victory over Death, after which,

His words here ended, but his meek aspect
Silent yet spake, and breathed immortal love
To immortal men, above which only shone
Filial obedience. (III.266-269)

As St. Augustine said, if you love God, you can do
whatever you like, and the Son does what he does because he loves the Father and because he loves man.
(Since Milton subordinates the Son in Of Christian
Doctrine, it is easier to accept, from the human perspective, the Son's love for the Father, which might
otherwise seem like narcissism on a divine level.)
This love abounds more than glory (III.312). The
narrator praises the love in what appears to be ambiguous, elliptical phrasing, "Love nowhere to be found
less than divine!" (III.411). Although the clause
could mean that such divine love can be found nowhere
else, it could more likely mean that wherever love is
found, it is divine, in keeping with Milton's extolling love as high and sometimes higher than faith in
the divorce tracts. At the end of the poem, Michael,
telling Adam of the Redeemer to come, who will have

190

to die as a matter of obedience but also of love,
which fulfills the Law, admonishes,

> So only can high justice rest appaid
> The law of God exact he shall fulfill
> Both by obedience and by love, though love
> Alone fulfill the law . . . . (XII.401-404)

Perhaps the Son in _Paradise_ _Regain'd_, the Redeemer
himself, would be a more sympathetic figure if he
possessed more love than knowledge since the latter
without the former, as Paul said, "puffeth up."

Within Judaism itself was a place for charity in
the context of the Law. Rabbi Asi contended that
charity held more weight than all the commandments,
and Rabbi Judah praised charity as a means of imitating God's love.[79]

The ultimate effect of Christ's redemption of
man through the gospel, faith, grace, and charity was
to liberate man from the Mosaic law, and this liberation has been characterized as "Christian liberty."
Lucien Cerfaux shows that the concept of liberty was
not at all Semitic but Greek. Despite the fact that
Paul employs the allegory of Sarah and Agar to represent the freedom of the Gospel and the latter to
typify the bondage of the Law, alluded to earlier (see
above, p. 140). "All Paul's arguments, however, are
derived from Greek conceptions, and to the Greeks
freedom was a good in this life, the freedom of cities,
of free men, of wise men and of Philo's mystics."[78]
Man is undoubtedly free from the Law and free before
God. Adolf Deissman makes a fascinating anthropologi-
cal contribution (summarized briefly above) to Paul's
ideas on freedom. St. Paul's concept of "being made
free by Christ," he avers, is based on the practice
of manumission in the ancient world in which a slave
could buy himself free by placing in a temple treasury
the money necessary to free him. The owner and the
slave would come to the treasury, and a rite took
place in front of witnesses in which the slave was
supposedly bought by the god, say Pythian Apollo, and
then given actual freedom. In the same way Christ
buys men's freedom from sin and death.[79]

Paul tells the Romans that they are freed from sin and under the power of grace and that they now live not under fear but under "the Spirit of adoption" (Rom 6.14; 8.15). In writing to the Corinthians, Paul enjoys the use of paradox: someone who is a servant is free in Christ, and someone who is free becomes a servant of Christ. The Spirit of the Lord is the agency which brings freedom (I Cor. 7.22; II Cor. 3.17). The Epistle to the Galatians has been called "the Magna Charta of Christian liberty."[80] Christ has freed men from the Law, and the Galatians are foolish to choose Agar over Sarah, bondage over freedom, and Paul asks the Galatians to maintain the freedom they have received in Christ (Gal. 3.13; 4, 5.1). He advises the Hebrews that they are freed from the old covenant of fleshly sacrifices, and more importantly, from a conscience of dead works: "how much more shall the blood of Christ, who through the eternal Spirit offered himself without spot to God, purge your conscience from dead works to serve the living God?" (Heb. 9.14). Therefore, Christian liberty, as Paul sees it, frees the believer from the Law, sin, and the torments of a conscience based on self-redemption through the works of the Law. However, Paul had a problem with his followers in that they might, as some of the Corinthians did, confuse Christian liberty with license--with sexual license. As Aquinas commented on the dilemma, "But a state is being misused if it declines and if liberty of the spirit is perverted into slavery of the flesh. Now the Galatians were free of the Law; but lest they suppose this to be a license to commit sins forbidden by the Law, the Apostle touches on abuse of liberty, saying, Only make not liberty an occasion to the flesh."[81]

Just as Paul's Epistles to the Galatians was called a Magna Charta, "Luther's Lectures on Galatians of 1531 (1535) deserves to be called a declaration of Christian independence--of independence from the Law and from anything or anyone else except the God and Father of our Lord Jesus Christ."[82] Luther defines liberty on the basis of freedom from torment of conscience, defining the Spirit as freedom from the Law, sin, death, the curse, hell, and God's wrath and judgement, and conversely if the rites of the Law are observed, then liberty is lost. With I Corinthians in

192

mind, Luther envisions Christian liberty as applicable
only to the "spiritual" and not the "unspiritual"
man.[83]

Philip Melanchthon defines Christian liberty as
"the perfect freedom which will come after this mortal
life in eternal blessedness, when God will be in all
the saved, who will have eternal joy in God without
death, without poverty, and without sorrow."[84] John
Colet emphasizes freedom from the slavery of the Law
through the Holy Spirit. He thus takes a dim view of
life in this world and assumes that Christian liberty
will not be possible to even the "spiritual man." He
defines four stages of what he calls "Christian freedom":

(1) Christ's deliverance of man from law to faith.
(2) Next, "the Son of God produces _life in us_"
     and strengthens us.
(3) "The third stage is external: it is freedom
     from two parts of the law of Moses, ceremony
     and civil law,"
(4) "freedom from the precepts of men in church
     regulations."

Christian liberty or freedom thus encompasses inward
liberty and ceremonial, legal, and ecclesiastical
freedom, but not freedom from the moral law.[85] The
Decalogue still maintains power over man, and so on
this point Melanchthon splits with his colleague,
Martin Luther.

In the _Institutes_ Calvin distinguishes three
parts of Christian freedom:

(1) that the consciences of believers, in seek-
     ing assurance of their justification before
     God, should rise above and advance beyond
     the law, forgetting all law righteousness.
(2) "that conscience observe the law, not as
     if constrained by the necessity of the law,
     but that freed from the law's yoke, they
     willingly obey God's will."
(3) regarding outward things that are themselves
     "indifferent," we are not bound before God
     by any religious obligation preventing us
     from sometimes using them and other times

193

not using them, indifferently.[86]

Calvin observes the Pauline metaphor of heirship in which men are free as heirs and not as bondsmen, but his attitude lies somewhere between Melanchthon's and Luther's. The Law does not seem to be abrogated, only the slavish attitude toward the Law. A man can keep the Law willingly and in some sense be subject to it, but if he does not obey it willingly, he must obey it in the old slavish sense. In his commentaries on the Epistles, he attempts to clarify some of the dilemma. The Law is revoked in the power it has over man, in the "tyranny of sin, Satan, and death." Just as the false apostles tried to yoke the Law on the Galatians, the papists are trying to do the same to Christians. Liberty does not mean freedom in an absolute sense but is a question of attitude. As Calvin says, "By the term liberty I do not understand merely emancipation from the servitude of sin [which meant so much to Luther], and of the flesh, but also that confidence, which we acquire from His bearing witness as to our adoption." He iterates his belief in liberty from moral matters of indifference and the consequent relaxation of conscience in this area. He is also, like Paul, afraid that liberty will be confused with sexual license. Nevertheless his basic emphasis falls on the contrast between bondage and fear (elements of the Law) and liberty and confidence.[87]

Calvin emphasized the danger of abusing this new-found freedom, and it had been something of a diffi-culty for Paul in his pastoral work with the Corin-thians, as already noted. Paul had to rebuke his flock for tolerating the incestuous relationship between a man and his father's later wife. Calvin's reservations about the abuses of Christian liberty in this case produced a sense of outrage at such goings on: "the latter would have involved an incestuous connection, abhorrent to all propriety and natural decency."[88] Samuel Bolton also warned against excesses of Christian freedom, starting with the case of Paul's admonition to the Corinthians against eating meat formerly offered to idols (meat sold in butcher shops afterwards). Secondly, Bolton warns against allowing superstitious customs or practices to impose on

Christians, presumably referring to Roman or Anglican ceremonial customs. He distinguishes "four kinds of freedom: natural, political, sensual, and spiritual," condemning the "libertinism" of the third,[89] the kind of freedom that Milton's Comus represents and advocates, the supposed freedom to indulge in nature's bounties without restraint:

> Wherefore did Nature pour her bounties forth
> With such a full and unwithdrawing hand,
> Covering the earth with odors, fruits, and flocks,
> Thronging the seas with spawn innumerable,
> But all to please and sate the curious taste?
> . . . .
> . . . If all the world
> Should in a pet of temperance feed on pulse,
> Drink the clear stream, and nothing wear but frieze,
> Th' All-giver would be unthanked, would be unpraised,
> Not half his riches known, and yet despised,
> And we should serve him as a grudging master.   (ll.
> 710-725)

Comus continues in eloquent fashion to tempt, unsuccessfully, the Lady to this false liberty. In the same context, Sonnet XII decries those who "License they mean when they cry liberty" (l.11).

For Bolton true Christian freedom is "true," "real," and "universal," and man can never again be placed "under the rigour of the law, and its curse." A magistrate, for example, can only compel obedience in that which is the will of God, although Bolton doesn't explain how one is to know when the magistrate is enforcing the latter. The Law does not provide justification; Christ does. Bolton looks to Augustine for a historical perspective on the question: "Augustine describes man under four different conditions. Before the law he fights but is overcome. Under grace he fights and conquers. But in heaven it is all conquest, and there is no combat more to all eternity."[90]

Arthur Barker has effectively discussed the concept of Christian liberty as it pertains to Milton's thought, and a brief summary of some of his conclusions is in order. He demonstrates that Christian liberty generally means a freedom of conscience (although it

does not mean that for Melanchthon or Calvin in
serious matters) for Milton and his contemporaries.
Christian liberty was originally confined to the elect
by God's grace, but eventually it extended to all men,
freeing them from "human ordinances" (Paul's phrase).
Calvin and Luther carefully defined the concept and
restricted this liberty and were afraid it might be
used by "carnal men." Milton specifically takes
Calvin's third part of Christian freedom, "matters
of indifference," and subsumes divorce under this
heading. Barker describes the "received position" as
believing that the gospel had abrogated the ceremonial
and the civil law but not the moral (as Calvin had
said). He goes on to point out that Milton in Of
Christian Doctrine had regarded the entire Law as
nullified. For example, Milton objects to the argument that it is morally wise to observe the Law even
though it is abrogated so that man can realize his sin
on the grounds, so Milton argues, that believers don't
need this "impulse to come to Christ" and that practice of the Law leads away from Christ. He makes an
exception to possessing a knowledge of the Law. Milton also rebukes the contention of Polanus that we
are freed from the curse of the Law but are still under
obligation to it. Both the obligation and the curse
are inseparable, and so Christians are freed from
both.[91] In the divorce tracts, Milton associated the
Law with right reason, according to Barker, although
God's eternal law is a better way of putting the equation. The two are supposed to be synonymous, but, in
some contexts, they may not be. Milton accepts the
Calvinistic notion that one can obey the Law voluntarily and so, in a sense, be freed from it, according to
Barker, which point appears to be contradicted by Milton's statement in Of Christian Doctrine referred to
immediately above. In any case, Milton extends the
liberty to matters beyond those regarded as "indifferent," and to all men, not the special "spiritual"
man, the elect by grace, according to the "secondary
law of nature," which operated after the Fall.

As the discussion here and in Barker's study
demonstrates, Milton progressively expanded the concept of Christian liberty to include all matters of
ethical concern to the Christian, whether ecclesiastical, legal, ceremonial, indifferent, or inward or

spiritual. In the preface to <u>Of Christian Doctrine</u>
Milton views this liberty as releasing man from "divine
law" but also "the law of man." He perceives the Mosaic law as designed only for the Israelites to make
them realize the "depravity of mankind," and formulated so that they would then seek the "promised
Savior." It would also lead other nations away from
its rudiments "to the full strength of the new
creature, and a manly liberty worthy the sons of God."[92]
In <u>Treatise</u> Milton, citing Paul extensively, shows
that Christians are free from the "ordinances of men,"
and argues that it is wrong to bind the conscience.[93]

Milton does not emphasize the dichotomy between
the so-called "natural" or "unspiritual" man and the
"spiritual" man or the elect, which brings his concept of Christian liberty to more men and not to any
elite group. Theologians as far apart as Aquinas and
Luther had distinguished between the two kinds of men.
Luther uses the terms "inner" and "outer" for the spiritual and carnal respectively.[94] The natural man is
bound by law and by conscience, but the spiritual man
is free of both, although Calvin would still insist
that the spiritual man must voluntarily obey the moral
law. Eventually the distinction, as Barker notes, is
impossible to maintain and so disappears in the later
seventeenth century.

NOTES: CHAPTER THREE

[1]On Corinthians II, pp. 177-178.

[2]Institutes, I, 426-427.

[3]Bounds, p. 72.

[4]Works, III, 197. See also Samuel Stollman, "Milton's Dichotomy of 'Judaism' and 'Hebraism'," PMLA, 89 (1974), 105-112.

[5]Works, III, 355.

[6]Works, III, 452.

[7]Works, III, 554.

[8]Works, VI, 30, 25.

[9]Works, XVI, 113, 115, 151.

[10]Dilemma, pp. 319-320.

[11]"The Incarnation of the Word," p. 41.

[12]Against the Pelagians, pp. 306-310.

[13]City of God in Basic Writings, II, 271.

[14]On Galatians, pp. 8, 54-58.

[15]On Thessalonians & Philippians & Hebrews, pp. 137, 141.

[16]On Corinthians II, pp. 180-181, 182-183. See also p. 192. Institutes, I, 512, 532-533, 351.

[17]"Learned Discourse" in Laws, p. 21.

[18]Sermons, pp. 349, 364-365.

[19]Works, VI, 8.

[20] Theology, I, 312, 315-316.

[21] Robert G. Sencourt, Saint Paul: Envoy of Grace (London, 1948), p. 141; Bultmann, Theology, I, 262-263.

[22] On Romans, p. 99.

[23] On the Spirit, pp. 99-100; "Enchiridion," p. 697.

[24] On Galatians, p. 55.

[25] On Galatians, XXVI, 28-29, 88, 91-92, 99, 103, 146-147.

[26] On Hebrews, pp. 123, 219.

[27] On Galatians, XXVI, 238.

[28] Loci Communes, pp. 55-56, 193, 140, 308, 153.

[29] On Galatians, pp. 69, 152-153; Institutes, I, 744, 747, 749.

[30] Works, XVI, 39; XVII, 5, 9, 27.

[31] Christian, p. 272.

[32] Dialogue with Trypho in Writings of Saint Justin Martyr, ed. Thomas B. Falls (New York, 1948), p. 176.

[33] Against Heresies, Bk. IV, Ch. XXI, p. 496.

[34] Centra Celsum, p. 210.

[35] On Romans, pp. 112-126; On Galatians, pp. 52, 69, 70-71.

[36] City of God in Basic Writings, II, 61-62.

[37] On Galatians, pp. 37, 139.

[38] On Romans, p. 7.

[39] On Galatians, XXVI, 226-229, 436-437; On Romans, p. 66.

[40] On Galatians, pp. 135-136, 137-138.

[41] On Galatians, pp. 84-85.

[42] Righteousness, p. 230. See also pp. 231-232.

[43] Laws, Bk. V, II, 532, 533.

[44] Horae, IV, p. 125.

[45] "grace," Cruden's Complete Concordance of the
Old and New Testaments, ed. A.D. Adams et al., (New
York, 1949), and C.A. Patrides, Milton and the Christian
Tradition, p. 198.

[46] On the Spirit, pp. 52-53, 53-54.

[47] Theology, I, 330, 287.

[48] Summa Theologiae I, II, 263.

[49] On Galatians, XXV, 54; On Romans, p. 64; On
Hebrews, pp. 192-193.

[50] Freedom, pp. 52, 62.

[51] On Romans, p. 128.

[52] Milton and the Christian Tradition, p. 203.

[53] Institutes, I, 234. Ernest S. Gohn notes the
importance of grace in ethics for Protestants in the
Reformation like Milton. See "The Christian Ethic
of Paradise Lost and Samson Agonistes," SN, 34 (1962),
243-268.

[54] Works, III, 198; Divorce, Works, III, 554.

[55] Works, XVI, 133.

[56] Andrewes, Meaning, pp. 67, 68.

[57] John Pringle, trans. and ed., Commentary . . .
Corinthians by John Calvin, II, 418, n. 2.

[58]_Against Heresies_, p. 434.

[59]_Stromata_, p. 430.

[60]"Funeral Oration on the Death of Emperor Theodosius," _Some of the Principal Works of St. Ambrose_, trans. Rev. H. DeRomestin (New York, 1896), pp. 314-315.

[61]_On the Spirit_, pp. 79, 87, 76; "Enchiridion," pp. 729, 727.

[62]_On Galatians_, pp. 64, 164, 170, 190.

[63]_On Galatians_, XXVI, 129, 137.

[64]_On Galatians_, XXVI, 279; XXVII (1535), pp. 56, 57, 58, 72, 113.

[65]_Bondage of the Will_, p. 41; _On Hebrews_, p. 197; _On Galatians_, XXVI, 271; see also, XXVII, 114.

[66]_Institutes_, I, 415, 417; _On Corinthians_ I, p. 422.

[67]_Righteousness_, p. 224.

[68]_Righteousness_, pp. 254, 264.

[69]_Valdes_, pp. 231-233.

[70]_On Romans_, p. 28.

[71]"Learned Discourse," in _Laws_, p. 59.

[72]_Divorce_, _Works_, III, 369.

[73]_Divorce_, _Works_, III, 493.

[74]_Works_, IV, 264; IV, 135.

[75]_Works_, XVI, 143, 145, 227.

[76]_Works_, VI, 21.

[77] S.S. Cohon, Judaism, p. 223.

[78] The Christian, pp. 452-453, 456.

[79] Light From the Ancient East, pp. 322-328.

[80] Jaroslav Pelikan and Walter A. Hansen, eds., Luther's Works, XXVI, ix.

[81] On Galatians, p. 163.

[82] Pelikan and Hansen, Luther's Works, XXVI, ix.

[83] On Galatians, XXVI, 293, 410-411, 461.

[84] Loci Communes, p. 194.

[85] Loci Communes, pp. 195, 196, 199-200.

[86] Institutes, I, 834, 836, 837, 838.

[87] Institutes, I, 834, 840-841; On Galatians, p. 147; On Corinthians II, p. 185.

[88] On Corinthians, I, 179.

[89] Bounds, pp. 223-224, 19, 20.

[90] Bounds, pp. 150, 208, 219, 26-27.

[91] Works, XVI, 147-156.

[92] Works, XVI, 13, 103-104.

[93] Works, VI, 31-32.

[94] Aquinas, Summa Theologiae, II, 326.

CHAPTER FOUR

THE BODY OF CHRIST: SACRED SYMBOL

A truly rich and profound symbol of the relationship between Christ and his church developed from
Paul's Epistles, the complex concept and metaphor of
the body of Christ. The body of Christ has been perceived as purely metaphorical, as profoundly symbolic,
and even as a mystical formula. It has been quite
popular with Roman Catholics for centuries, and one
might expect that the Protestant Reformers and Milton
would have nothing to do with such a "fleshly" concept
of Christ, which appears to drag Christ down to man's
level. However, a proper perspective on the body of
Christ makes a very clear distinction between the flesh
of man and the body of Christ, setting up an antithesis
between the fallen condition of man (not his body of
flesh but his self, as Chapter One indicates) and the
desires of man's members and Christ.

Christ is regarded as the head of the body and
the members of the church the members of the body, with
all spiritual life emanating from the head to all the
members. Christ offered his body on the cross for his
church, and the body of the church benefits from this
salvific action; indeed the symbol takes on added dimensions because the impact of Christ's sacrifice on each
man's body is also staggering. Each member of the
church must regard his body as part of the body of
Christ, a temple of the Holy Spirit (an image often
associated with the temple of the body) and keep it
free from sin. On another level not only is the body
of Christ a distributive metaphor, from the head to the
members; but it also describes commutatively the relationship between the members of the church. Each
member of the body has a certain responsibility for the
welfare of its partners, and each one has a particular
place which it should maintain. Trouble arises when
the members do not keep their particular positions and
attempt to usurp over their fellows, thus causing com-
munal suffering. A favorite negative motif of Milton's
is the diseased body, which Kester Svendsen has explored
in detail but without particular reference to the concept of the body of Christ.[1]

The proper functioning of the body leads to a unity, a harmony, and beauty that prompts many commentators on the Epistles like Chrysostom, Calvin, and John Colet to heights of eloquence. A related offshoot of the body of Christ is the representation of the marriage union as a relationship between the head or husband and the wife as collective members under the direction and guidance of the head, just as conversely the Song of Songs and other books in the Bible characterize the connection between God and his people as typical of a love relationship between the bridegroom and the feminine soul. The opportunity of membership in the body of Christ becomes available through Baptism according to most commentators, and the joining looks forward to the eventual total union in the fulness or _pleroma_ of the godhead at the Last Judgement.

That Milton as a radical Protestant (witness _Of Christian Doctrine_) would embrace the doctrine of the body of Christ might seem strange to most readers of his poetry, but Chapter Twenty-Four of _Of Christian Doctrine_ testifies otherwise by its title, "De unione et communione cum Christo eiusque membris, ubi de ecclesia mystica sive invisibili." Secondly, the concept of the mystical or invisible body of the church forms a foundation for Milton's discussion of the reformation of church government in the anti-episcopal tracts of 1641 to 1642. And, thirdly, one of the basic arguments for divorce in _Doctrine_ and _Discipline of Divorce_ is St. Paul's definition of the wife as subject to the head of the body, the husband, in marriage. Milton does avoid some of the more gory representations of the sufferings of Christ's body as presented and exaggerated by the Counter-Reformation in art and literature, but nevertheless the unity of Christ with his church is movingly depicted in his earlier work. As he grew older, there appears to be less and less reference to the conceptual symbol of Christ's body, assuming that _Of Christian Doctrine_ is a product of Milton's middle and not later years.[2]

The earliest appearance of this Christian symbol occurs in the first epistle to the Corinthians. Paul was anxious to wean the Corinthians away from their sexual promiscuity, a habit cultivated zestfully in the seaport town of Corinth, and one of the ways in which he attempted this feat was by injecting the Corinthians with a sense of union with Christ, with a sense of responsibility to Christ as the savior who had released them from the pagan terror of death and of the "powers" who held control over both life and death. John Colet concludes even that wherever the Christological formula, "in Christ," appears Paul is referring to the body of Christ.[3]

There are differences of opinion on the body's nature: does it refer to the cosmos or to the church itself, that is, is the formula cosmic or ecclesiological? Rudolph Bultmann is for the former, but the Theological Dictionary prefers the latter interpretation, at least as far as Paul's Epistle to the Colossians. Elias Andrews has suggested that the origins of the symbol are perhaps Stoicism, Paul's sacramental view of reality, or even the concept of the Roman Empire as a body.[4] The important emphasis, however, remains on unity and mutual responsibility. This lengthy passage is worth quoting because it is fundamental to an understanding of Paul's message. Paul writes of the various talents of the people in the young church and how they all are assumed under the Spirit:

For as the body is one, and hath many members, and all the members of that one body, being many, are one body: so also is Christ.

For by one Spirit are we all baptized into one body, whether we be Jews or Gentiles, whether we be bond or free; and have been all made to drink into one Spirit.

For the body is not one member, but many.

If the foot shall say, Because I am not the head, I am not of the body; is it therefore not of the body?

And if the ear shall say, Because I am not the eye, I am not of the body; is it therefore not of the body?

If the whole body were an eye, where were the

hearing? If the whole were hearing, where were
the smelling?

But now hath God set the members every one of
them in the body, as it hath pleased him.

And if they were all one member, where were the
body?

But now are they many members, yet but one body.

And the eye cannot say unto the hand, I have no
need of thee: nor again the head to the feet, I
have no need of you.

Nay, much more those members of the body, which
seem to be more feeble, are necessary:

And those members of the body, which we think to
be less honourable, upon these we bestow more
abundant honour; and our uncomely parts have more
abundant comeliness.

That there should be no schism in the body; but
that the members should have the same care one for
another.

And whether one member suffer, all the members
suffer with it; or one member be honoured, all
the members rejoice with it.

Now ye are the body of Christ, and members in
particular. (I Cor. 12.12-27)

The earliest commentators on passages in the
Epistles such as the above write a vague and usually
brief gloss which associates Christ and man through
the crucified body of the Messiah. Irenaeus, amplify-
ing Colossians 1.14, relates the blood of Christ to
man as the members of the body who are nourished by
its blood, and he also sees a connection between the
prophets who prefigured Christ and the members and the
whole body.5 Irenaeus does not make a precise distinction between Christ as the head and the members of the
body. The term members (membra) assures ambiguity because, quite literally, the body is composed of a head,
a trunk, or torso, and several members. Basil is content merely to quote Romans 12.4-5 in his explanation
of the importance and necessity of Baptism:

For as we have many members in one body, and

all have not the same office:

> So we, being many, are one body in Christ, and
> every one members one of another.

Augustine quotes almost the same lines and interprets
them as signifying that "This is the Christians' sacrifice. We are one body with Christ," and throughout
part of Chapter Twenty-Two of the second book of the
City of God, he quotes various passages in the Epistles
which describe the mystical body.[6] He is, however,
content to reproduce the passages without special ampli-
fication.

The essence of the doctrine is based on the
belief that Christ stands at the center of Christianity and that he is the source of grace and salvation.
Man can assent to the operation of grace and cooperate
with it, but nevertheless the source of salvation is
Christ. This means that Christ is the head of the
body, providing both spiritual life and moral direction
to the members. The basic statements of Paul relating
to the supreme importance of the head appear in his
letters to the Colossians:

> And he is the head of the body, the church:
> who is the beginning, the firstborn from the
> dead; that in all things he might have the pre-
> eminence. (1.18)

> . . . holding the Head, from which all the
> body by joints and bands having nourishment
> ministered, and knit together, increaseth with
> the increase of God. (2.19)

Irenaeus, maintaining his Pauline emphasis on Christ
crucified and risen, compares Christ to the head,
risen from the dead, and man to the body, which will
be risen, "blended together and strengthened through
means of joints and bands by the increase of God, each
of the members having its own proper and fit position
in the body." He refers to Ephesians 4.16 and relates
the mansions in heaven to the members of the body.[7]
Cyprian, writing on the proper dress for virgins,
reminds them that "your Master and Head is Christ."[8]
Chrysostom, explicating Colossians 2.19, warns his
readers of the consequence of relinquishing hold on
the head and grasping at the members of the church:

"Why then, letting go the Head, dost thou cling to
the members? If thou art fallen off from It, thou
art lost. From which all the body. Every one, be he
who he may, thence has not life only, but also even
connexion. All the Church, so long as she holds The
Head increaseth; because here is no more passion of
pride and vain-glory, nor invention of human fancy."9

Thomas Aquinas, taking as one might expect an
analytical approach to the head, isolates three of its
characteristics:

> so likewise Christ is called the Head of the
> Church from a likeness with the human head, in
> which we may consider three things, namely,
> order, perfection, and power, Order, because
> the head is the first part of man, beginning
> from the higher part; and . . . Perfection,
> because in the head dwell all the senses, both
> interior and exterior, whereas in the other
> members there is only touch . . . Power, because
> the power and movement of the other members,
> together with the direction of them in their
> acts, is from the head, by reason of the sensi-
> tive and moving power there ruling; . . .
> Now these three things belong spiritually to
> Christ.10

Irenaeus had emphasized the risen Christ in an imagi-
native manner, but Thomas was more interested in
dissecting the qualities that pertain to the human
head, despite the fact that he closes by reminding us
that the three qualities are possessed by Christ and
not by man.

In the Renaissance two Pauline commentators on
the Epistles of Paul were imaginatively attracted to
the symbol of the body of Christ. John Colet, in his
discussion of the Epistle to the Romans, is preoccupied
with an almost physiological orientation to the symbolism, and he elaborates it in great detail. Christ is
the head so that "as from a fountain, there might be
diffused life . . . through the members" so that every
man might be a member of the body. He asserts that
the apostles are "as angels and ministering spirits
between the head and the body," with each one having
a specific function depending on his closeness to the

source of life. The various members possess different colors and lights to convey a sense of beauty in the body.[11] Colet's preoccupation with the aesthetic facets of the body will be discussed later in their relation to its unity and harmony.

Calvin is particularly concerned with demonstrating the total role of Christ in the salvation of mankind, and he takes great pains to oppose the suggestion that anyone else can be the head of the church. In his commentary on Colossians, he glosses 1.18 through the metaphor of a "root, from which vital energy is diffused through all the members. Just like a root the head provides life for its members, and the members of the body should be made perfect like the head."[12] Just as Ignatius had depicted Christ as a "Captain," Calvin also relates the word caput or head to the concept of a captain and characterizes Christ as the captain who conforms the members to the head. Christ is the head to which the true (and not the false) church must attach itself. Not only must the false church not attach itself to the true head, but the false head must not be substituted for Christ--the Roman pontiff. Calvin is also sensitive to another alleged usurper of the headship of the body, Satan. Calvin explores the basic metaphor of Christianity of the struggling Christian and quotes Romans 16.20 on the prophecy of God crushing Satan beneath his feet. "In our Head," he continues, "indeed, this victory always fully existed, for the prince of the world had nothing in him."[13]

The orthodox Roman position stated that the pope was a "vicar" of God's on earth, but from the Protestant point of view he was supplanting Christ in a fashion similar to the way Mary was thought to be acting as a surrogate for Christ as the mediatrix of grace. Calvin attacks the position of the pope because Christ has given only limited roles to his members and not a supreme one as the pope claims. In the Epistle Dedicatory to his commentary on Hebrews, Calvin asserts that the papists have attempted even to separate the head, Christ, from the body, the church.[14] Other Reformers followed and exercised themselves on the same issue. For Paul Bayne the Roman church may as well

209

call the church the body of the pope, and Thomas Cartwright regards the Roman position as "a foolish thing"
because of the competition between the pope and Christ.[15]
The various possible meanings of the term head, including the metaphorical head of a body or the ecclesiastical head of an institution, were not at all regarded
as different phenomena, evidently, by either side or
sides in the controversy about the pope. The symbol
was too powerful.

Milton argued against the substitution of either
the pope or Satan for Christ as the true head of the
church. In the Reason of Church-Government, Milton
had argued strenuously against the tradition establishing the need for bishops in the church on the basis
of the necessity for a leader. For him the argument
leads inevitably to the establishment of the papacy,
but this approach represents a false view of the church,
for "take away the head Preist the rest are but a
carcasse."[16] One could similarly argue that the same
principle applies to the true church--take Christ away
and life desists, as Colet had implied. In Paradise
Lost the angel Gabriel, sounding very much like Calvin,
scolds Satan for apostasy from the true head and setting himself up as a false head:

> Army of fiends, fit body to fit head;
> Was this your discipline and faith engaged,
> Your military obedience, to dissolve
> Allegiance to th' acknowledged Power Supreme?
> (IV.953-956)

The symbol of the head of the body becomes allied
to other symbolic views of the Redemption. Paul Bayne
associates the head, Christ, with the head of the
human race, Adam, since Christ took on human flesh,
and so "as all who have descended, and shall descend,
from the first Adam, are a complete body natural under
Adam, the head and root of them . . . so the multitude
of those children are given to the second Adam . . . ,
they make up the whole body, whereof Christ, the second
Adam, is the head." Because Christ, as the second Adam,
is our head, he provides man with supernatural benefits.
Bayne likens the natural body to the mystical body in
that the hand will ward off a blow to the head, and
analogously Christians should "magnify God" as the

head.[17]

All, however, seemed to agree on the logic and
inevitability of the resurrection of the head, Christ,
which leads to the resurrection of the members of the
body, the faithful. For Calvin this truth provides a
consolation for the soul anxious for salvation "because
it is necessary that what has been accomplished in
Christ be accomplished in the members." He further
distinguishes between the ranks of the members who will
be resurrected on the Last Day, when Christ will "conform our lowly, inglorious body to his glorious body."[18]
Richard Hooker also regards Christ's body in the same
light since it is "the leader of the whole army of
bodies that shall rise again."[19] Thomas Jacomb con-
flates the two concepts of Christ as the head and as
the second Adam, as had Paul Bayne, in his iteration
that the resurrection of Christ produces the resurrection of the members, citing Augustine in support:
"Quod praecessit in capite, sequitur in corpore, as
Augustine speaks."[20] Thomas Cartwright maintains that
Christ not only provides life to the church as its
head but also that he causes the resurrection of the
members of the church.[21]

The life and nourishment of the body are supplied
either through the head Christ or through the Spirit,
which informs the body. For Philip Airay, Christ as
head provides vitality to those who grow with him.[22]
Juan Valdes had earlier noted the analogy between
those who by being baptized in Christ are "incorpo-
rated" (an etymological metaphor) into his body and
the various members of a natural body which are
"quickened" by the soul. In this connection the Spirit
of God, however interpreted, as a third person in a
Trinity or a facet of the Father, is compared to the
human soul which gives life to the body.[23] Paul Bayne
regards the life of the body as supplied by the Spirit
which informs both the members of Christ on earth but
also those in heaven.[24]

St. Paul employed the term πληρωμα in various
places in both Ephesians and Colossians to designate
the "fulness" of God which is achieved when the members
unite to the head. Chrysostom, who, unlike Aquinas, read

211

Paul in the Greek, defines the term pleroma as it appears in Colossians 2.9-10: "By fulness is meant 'the whole.' Then the word bodily, what does it intend to signify? 'As in a head.' But why does he [Paul] say the same thing over again? And ye are complete in Him. What then does it mean? That ye have nothing less than He. As it dwelt in Him, so also in you."25 This startling claim may mean nothing less than that the individual members of the body in some way possess divinity. Approximately a century earlier, some time in the third century, Clement of Alexandria, who, like Chrysostom, was reading the Epistles in the Greek, glossed Ephesians 4.13 in the context of the doctrine of Christ as the perfect man. His translation and explanation are rendered in The Instructor as follows: "And writing to the Ephesians, . . . 'Till we all attain to the unity of the faith, and of the knowledge of God, to a perfect man, to the measure of the stature of the fulness of Christ . . . ,' --saying these things in Christ, who is the head and man, the only one perfect in righteousness."26 The basis for the pleroma, according to Chrysostom, is that the Spirit permeates all the members of the body with his love, but elsewhere he claims that all must partake in the body to fill it all. His statement produces a certain degree of ambiguity.27 Either the fulness of Christ fills the body, or else it is dependent on some element outside Christ or God for complete fulfillment.

In the Reformation Calvin refers briefly to Ephesians 1.23, "the Church is his [Christ's] completion."28 John Colet, however, is quite taken with the notion of the fulness of God:

The soul of this body, and, if I may use the Greek term of Aristotle, its entelechy--that is, the perfection and completeness of its action, is God Himself, the Holy Trinity; and is present in full measure in the Head, for in Him dwelleth all the fulness of the Godhead bodily. [Col. 2.9] From the Head it is imparted to the several members in order, according to the will of God; who, as St. Paul writes, hath set the members every one of

212

them _in_ _the_ _body,_ _as_ _it_ _hath_ _pleased_ _him._
God imparts to them, I say, his own divinity,
that they may be with him in Christ; may be
wise, and good, and doers of something useful and godlike in the body; that so they may
be fellow-workers with God in this world, for
overcoming its evil ways.

He accepts the unusual assertion that God gives to the
members, to each man according to his will, "his own
divinity."[29] Richard Hooker assumes that the body's
fulness resides in Christ himself and not in the
membership of the church.[30] Paul Bayne appears ambiguous about the question of the body's fulness. He
first claims that the fulness depends upon the "university of true believers," defining this fulness as
that "which maketh full him who filleth all in all."
The faithful must abdicate their wills and obey the
head in order for the body to be fulfilled and for
them to receive fulness by an inward grace. This
fulness will be achieved when all the members of the
body achieve "glory," presumably in an eschatological
sense.[31] Thomas Jacomb fears that Christ would lose
his fulness if he lost any of his members.[32]

In the light of this discussion, it is noteworthy
that when Milton discusses Colossians 2.9 in _Of_ _Chris-_
tian _Doctrine,_ he transforms peculiarly the above
question and insists that the Son is not fully God:

"in him dwelleth all the fulness of the Godhead
bodily"; which passage I understand, not of the
divine nature of Christ, but of the entire virtue
of the Father, and the full completion of his
promises (for so I would interpret the word,
rather than "fulness"), dwelling in, not hypo-
statically united with, Christ's human nature;
and this "bodily," that is, not in ceremonies
and the rudiments of the world, but really and
substantially. . . .[33]

Milton thus goes far off the beaten track, ignoring
the traditional meaning of "fulness" and insisting
that the word refers to the providential plan and not
to the mystery of the body of Christ. Milton obviously
wanted to make his position quite definite, but the
basis for his assertion isn't clear.

The closest that Milton comes to manifesting the concept to the fulness of the body is in his discussion in <u>Of Reformation</u> of the need for wholeness in the church. He does, as indicated below, employ the image of the body in his first anti-episcopal pamphlet. (Strangely enough, he almost never either in his prose or poetry uses the terms <u>fulness, fill, fulfill, complete, completion,</u> or <u>wholeness.</u>) In his assault on the concept of ranks in the church, Milton regards them as inconsistent with the proper notion of a church as a whole: "Let no man cavill, but take the Church of <u>God</u> as meaning the whole consistence of Orders and Members, as S. <u>Pauls</u> Epistles express," (echoing I Corinthians 12.27).[34] He insists that in Cyprian's time (the third century) "then did the Spirit of unity and meeknesse inspire, and animate every joynt, and sinew of the mysticall body." Milton stops short of embracing Colet's Anglican position that divinity in some fashion pervades the members of the body. The independence of Milton's Protestantism did not allow him to accept this rather potent doctrine, despite the fact that he did not go to the other extreme and view man, as Luther did, as a creature more in opposition to God than in union with him. Luther agreed that man was saved totally by the grace and goodness of Christ, but that is not synonymous with saying that God imbues man with divinity.

The question of accepting a transfer of divinity from the head to the members is related to another difficulty--is the relationship between them metaphoric, symbolic in a deeper sense, or mystical in the sense of a true union with the Godhead? Very early in the history of the church, Justin Martyr (100-165 A.D.) had simply stated that the connection is an outright equation. Using the vehicle of the human body, he posits, "although it is made up of many members, it is called, and is, one body. So also in the case of the people and the Church: although they are many individuals, they form one body and are called by one common name."[35] Chrysostom is more explicit. For him the doctrine is meant to console the individual Christian. Thus, "all the members of that one body, being many, are one body." Christ is the head, and the church is the body, not in an analogical sense but in terms of a direct equation--the members

<u>are</u>, not <u>are like</u>, the body of Christ.[36] St. Paul
states the doctrine succinctly:

> For we are members of his body, of his flesh,
> and of his bones. . . .

> This is a great mystery; but I speak con-
> cerning Christ and the church. (Eph. 5.30, 32)

If indeed the doctrine of the body of Christ is
a mystery, then it is easy to associate it with the
doctrine of the Eucharist or the real presence of
Christ in the sacrament, a debatable point up to the
present day among Roman Catholic and Protestant theologians. If there is a presence in the host, is it
physical, real, symbolic, memorial, or mysterious?
The semantics are staggering. Luther assumes that
the basic sacrifice of Christ's body on the cross is
"perfect" but that the church can offer a "spiritual
sacrifice of His body," his church through the "mystical Passover," which apparently means escape from
the attractions of the world into a future state.[37]
In any case, the celebration of the Eucharist does
not seem to involve any real presence of Christ since
that would imply that the original sacrifice on the
cross was insufficient for the remission of sins.
Calvin agrees with Paul that the concept of the body
is indeed a mystery but refuses to accept the belief
that partaking in the Eucharist assumes the truth of
the doctrine of Transubstantiation,[38] in which the
substance of the bread and wine is changed into
Christ's body and blood, but the accidents or appear-
ances remain the same--bread and wine.

Protestants closer to the orthodox beliefs of the
Church of England like Colet and Hooker, however,
accept the doctrine of a real presence in the sacrament. Colet believes that in the Eucharist Christ as
the church "feeds on HIMSELF" as the body of the
church,[39] a rather interesting variation on the basic
theme combining the body concept with that of the
Eucharist, suggesting the emblem of the pelican who
devours her innards to feed her children. If the body
of Christ is the church and the Eucharist really contains the body, however, then Christ is, as it were,
feeding on himself. Richard Hooker is concerned with

both the real presence in the sacrament and also the
spiritual condition of the believer, but he insists
that there is a reality to the concept. He lists five
points of belief on the Eucharist to which all are
supposed to agree:

> first that this sacrament is a true and a real
> participation of Christ, who thereby imparteth
> himself even his whole entire Person as a mysti-
> cal Head unto every soul that receiveth him, and
> that every such receiver doth thereby incorporate
> or unite himself unto Christ as a mystical member
> of him, yea of them also whom he acknowledgeth to
> be his own; secondly, that to whom the person of
> Christ is thus communicated, to them he giveth
> by the same sacrament his Holy Spirit to sanctify
> them as it sanctifieth him which is their head;
> thirdly that what merit, force or virtue soever
> there is in his sacrificed body and blood, we
> freely fully and wholly have it by this sacra-
> ment; fourthly that the effect therof in us is
> a real transmutation of our souls and bodies
> from sin to righteousness, from death and cor-
> ruption to immortality and life; fifthly that
> because the sacrament being of itself but a
> corruptible and earthly creature must needs be
> thought an unlikely instrument to work so admi-
> rable effect in man, we are therefore to rest
> ourselves altogether upon the strength of his
> glorious power who is able and will bring to
> pass that the bread and cup which he giveth us
> shall be truly the thing he promiseth.[40]

Hooker is willing to admit that it is useless to ana-
lyze the nature of the sacrament and that "simplicity
of faith" is preferable to "knowledge," which cannot
plumb the mysteries of God.[41]

He focuses attention on the quality of the
receiver of the sacrament in order to improve the
spiritual state of the recipient. "The real presence"
is better sought in the person who receives the sacrament rather than in the sacrament itself. At one point
he disclaims interest in the question of Transubstantiation, but he does repeat that the presence is a
"true and a real participation of Christ." Each

receiver of the Eucharist then becomes a true member,
"a _mystical_ _member_" of the body. He explains the
relationship of the receiver's spiritual condition to
the participation in the body as that of instrumental
cause to effect.[42]

Those who see a connection between the Eucharist
and the doctrine of the body of Christ agree that the
relationship between the head and the members is
indeed mystical. To return to Richard Hooker, in his
usual fine prose he depicts the body as above comprehension:

That Church of Christ, which we properly term
his body mystical, can be but one; neither can
that one be sencibly [sic] discerned by any man,
inasmuch as the parts thereof are some in heaven
already with Christ, and the rest are on earth
(albeit their natural persons be visible) we do
not discern under this property, whereby they
are truly and infallibly of that body. Only
our minds by intellectual conceit are able to
apprehend, that such a real body there is, a
body collective, because it containeth an huge
multitude; a body mystical, because the mystery
of their conjunction is removed altogether from
sense. . . . love, mercy, and blessedness belong
to the mystical Church.

Later he defines the term mystical as meaning "as
though our very flesh and bones should be made con-
tinuate with his."[43] Those associated with the
established church of England like Hooker view the
concept of the mystical body as quite real. And so
Thomas Jacomb in various places in his sermons employs
various adjectives to characterize the union: "mystical," "intimous," "real," "spiritual," "total," and
"indissoluble," and he contradicts those who regard
the relationship as "notional, fantastic, or opinion-
ative, something that is merely a matter of fancy and
imagination." He grounds his belief in the union between Christ and his members on that between the
divinity and the humanity of Christ: "The hypostati-
cal union ascertains the mystical union."[44]

Although Milton was hardly on speaking terms with

the Church of England, he devoted a whole chapter in
Of Christian Doctrine to the "mystical or invisible
church." Although he does not define the word _mysti-
cal_ anywhere and even at times uses the word in a
derogatory sense, it is not to be confused with the
term _mysterious_, which denotes incomprehensibility to
the intellect but suggests a real union between the
head and the body. Whether this union produces some
degree of divinity in man cannot be precisely determined on the basis of Milton's use of the word. Since
he very concisely states his beliefs in this area,
direct quotation of the passages in question may be
simplest so that the reader can draw his own conclusions:

> This ⌊increase of the regenerate⌋ consists in
> our UNION and FELLOWSHIP with the Father through
> Christ the Son, and our glorification after the
> image of Christ. . . . The FELLOWSHIP arising
> from this union consists in a participation,
> through the Spirit, of the various gifts and
> merits of Christ. . . .

> From this our fellowship with Christ arises
> the mutual fellowship of the members of Christ's
> body among themselves, called in the Apostle's
> Creed THE COMMUNION OF SAINTS.

> Lastly, from this union and fellowship of the
> regenerate with the Father and Christ, and of
> the members of Christ's body among themselves,
> results the mystical body called THE INVISIBLE
> CHURCH, whereof Christ is the head. . . .

> Seeing then that the body of Christ is mysti-
> cally one, it follows that the fellowship of
> his members must also be mystical, and not
> confined to place or time, inasmuch as it is
> composed of individuals of widely separated
> countries, and of all ages from the foundation
> of the world.[45]

The implication of the last sentence hints that the
word _mystical_ means something like universal or tran-
scending time and place, but the entire chapter, quoting as it does Paul's references to the body of Christ,
suggests a deeper meaning. Paul called the relationship a mystery, and perhaps Milton was content to leave

it at that.

As Milton writes above, the body produces a "fellowship" between the members (the commutative symbol),
a fellowship which involves, as the tradition has it,
a mutual responsibility between the members to care for
each other in a Christian way through charity. No
member should cause another member suffering, and
should, in fact, alleviate the suffering of any other
member. St. Paul's perception of the relationship
between a man and other men is well summarized by the
Theological Dictionary:

> for Paul man can never be understood as a self-
> contained individual who can be considered in
> himself. He is always man related to God and
> his fellow-men, authentic only in this relation
> to them. In what he says about the community
> as the body of Christ . . . Paul adopts amongst
> other things a Greek mode of speach [sic] which
> views the body as a self-contained microcosm. . . .
> In the first instance, then, he finds in the body
> of Christ the community which is also self-
> contained . . . , though in him the accent is
> on mutual service . . . and this shatters the
> self-containment of the individual. If this
> service is still seen within the community,
> nevertheless at this point, too, the OT con-
> cept comes through strongly. In Col. and Eph.,
> however, the community is no longer a self-
> contained entity. As the body of Christ it
> grows in the world. It penetrates it, and in
> it Christ Himself penetrates the cosmos, ...
> Thus the ῥῶμα concept is reconstructed, and it
> is put in the service of Him who gave His body
> for the world, and who in His body, the Church,
> is still seeking the world.[46]

Paul uses the word soma in I Corinthians 12.27 to
designate a body which, in vv.14-25 needs all the
parts in order to form a totality. The community is
not merely like a body; it is one in Christ; thus the
concept moves beyond Greek formulations of the community as a body.[47]

In the early church, two contemporaries, Jerome

219

and Chrysostom, reflect an awareness of such
Christian responsibility. Jerome, combatting the
Pelagian heresy, wished to prove that Christ, the
perfect man, was necessary for salvation and that all
men are united to him through his body. "For," he
says, "if one of the members suffers, all of them
suffer with it and the entire body is tormented by
the pain of one of its members."[48] Chrysostom, moving from a discussion of the honor of the various
parts of the human body (a Pauline theme), exhorts
his readers to respect and care for others, and one
member must not "emulate" another "in order to de-
press him," that is, to put him in a lower position.
He asserts that each man must care for the other as
if the body were suffering from leprosy. The law of
charity, for Chrysostom, is based on membership in
the body, and concern for each member is essential to
maintain the beauty of the body.[49] There is no place
for social or spiritual independence in the body
according to St. Ambrose, who refers to I Corinthians
12.17 (quoted above) and comments, "So, then, we are
all one body, though with many members, all necessary
to the body. For no one member can say of another:
'I have no need of thee.' For those members which
seem to be more feeble are much more necessary and
require greater care and attention. And if one member
suffers, all the members suffer with it."[50] And so,
in the early years of the church, the theme of Christian charity, expounded especially in the thirteenth
chapter of First Corinthians, is wedded to the "fellowship" and the "communion of saints" of the body of
Christ.

John Colet's views of the body have already been
stated in their relationship to Christ as the head,
but they also apply to the mutual communion of the
members. He believes that the members may be strong
or weak, but this variety produces a sense of harmony:

all the parts have such coherence and sympathy,
and do so assiduously render mutual help to one
another, according to their means, by giving and
receiving aid, that in the whole body there is
presented, not a plurality of parts, but a united
whole composed of the several parts; with no private interest among them, no care for individual

advantage, but everywhere, and on the part of
all, through the silent teaching of instinct,
a singular desire for fellowship and unity and
the welfare of the whole body. In such a body
every member seems to own that it is then in
the best health when the whole body is health-
iest . . . .

To Colet every man should be willing even to die "if
need be, for the safety of the body."[51]

The Reformers did not disagree with the basic
stance adopted by Colet. Martin Bucer holds that the
members of the body should maintain their place and
be subjects to the head, and he feels that the Lord
wants "sacred assemblies" "because the Lord wants his
own to be closely connected with one another as members of a body, and support each other in the life of
God."[52] Philip Melanchthon, closely associated with
Luther and a major reformer in his own right, described
the need for a congregation of the Holy Supper and related to this need the corollary that because we share
the bread of the Eucharist, we must help one another
as members in Christ.[53]

Calvin's attitude toward the interrelationship
of the members is twofold. On the one hand, in his
commentaries on the Epistles, he is anxious to remind
his readers that they have a particular appointed
place in the body which they should maintain; on the
other, in the Institutes he regards the charitable
role of the members of some importance. In one gloss
on Ephesians 4.16, he stresses the supreme role of
Christ who is connected to the body by a "subservient
juncture," and in another gloss on I Corinthians 4.7,
he insists that each member should keep his proper
place.[54] He further admonishes his reader that the
members should be careful of "ambition or misdirected
emulation and envy" which might "lead one that occu-
pies an inferior station to grudge to afford his
services to those above him." He is convinced that
"equality interferes with the welfare of the body."
The rebellious member might be bold enough to "wage
war with God after the manner of the giants"[55]--
shades of Satan in Paradise Lost.

In the _Institutes_ Calvin is impressed by the
humility of Paul, who claims no special station in
the body, although he would have been entitled to a
high place. "And he does not make himself mediator
between the people and God, but he asks that all members are concerned for one another, and if one member
suffers, the rest suffer with it.' (I Cor. 12.25-26)
And thus the mutual prayers for one another of all
members yet laboring on earth rise to the Head, who
has gone before them into heaven, in whom 'is propi-
tiation for our sins' (I John 2.2)."[56] Elsewhere he
urges that the members who cling to Christ "must help
one another in our mutual tasks." Finally, he quotes
I Corinthians 13.4-5 in terms of self-renunciation as
a basis for loving and helping others. He refers to
Paul's image of the body of Christ:

> But Scripture goes even farther by comparing
> them to the powers with which the members of
> the human body are endowed (I Cor. 12.12 ff.).
> No member has this power for itself nor applies
> it to his own private use; but each pours it
> out to the fellow members. Nor does it take
> any profit from its power except what proceeds
> from the common advantage of the whole body.
> So, too, whatever a godly man can do he ought
> to be able to do for his brothers, providing
> for himself in no other way than to have his
> mind intent upon the common upbuilding of the
> church.[57]

Other reformers followed suit in advocating the
mutual responsibility of the members of the body for
each other. Michael Servetus iterates the role of
love in strengthening the body of Christ; once a member acknowledges by faith Christ as head, then the
member will love the other members of the body.[58]
Paul Bayne has a great deal to say on the subject of
the mutual responsibility of those in the communion of
the body. He sees the basic metaphor as "a great
motive to Christian concord," toward serving each
other, producing faith, forgiveness, and sanctification. Each part may, of itself, be perfect like the
head, but it should serve the other parts or members
in love and not be like "wens" or "hang-bys" which
may be cut off. Thus this symbolism produces an ethos

which includes diversity within unity:

> Again, we must, seeing in Christ our head we
> are joined as members of one and the same body,
> therefore we must be so affected each to other,
> as we see members are. They envy not one
> another; the foot envieth not the eye; they
> communicate each with other; the mouth taketh
> meat, the stomach digesteth, the liver maketh
> blood, the eye seeth, the hand handeth, all
> for the good of the whole: they will not
> revenge themselves. If going hastily one
> foot strike the other leg or foot, it will
> not strike again; they so bear the burden one
> of another, that their affection each to other
> is not diminished; as if the head ache, the body
> will not carry it and knock it here or there,
> but beareth the infirmity, doing it the ease
> it may, yea, being well affected to it no less
> than before.59

Philip Airay goes so far as to conclude that if any
member of the body suffers, then Christ himself, the
head is "touched."60

    In Of Christian Doctrine Milton fully agrees with
the tradition of the responsibility of the members of
the body for each other, especially when viewed from
the perspective of Christian charity as beautifully
defined in First Corinthians. He says, "BROTHERLY or
CHRISTIAN love is the strongest of all affections,
whereby believers mutually love and assist each other
as members of Christ, and are as far as possible of
one mind; bearing at the same time to the utmost of
their power with their weaker brethren, and with such
as are of a different opinion."61 Milton's belief in
this noble and altruistic vision of Christ's body was
violated in two areas of his experience--the ecclesiastical and the marital. We shall see below his
reaction to offenses against marital charity in the
comparison of the body of the church to the body of
marriage, but even earlier he had been upset by what
he considered sins against the members of the mystical and invisible church by its own leaders, the
bishops. Milton creates what he considers an accurate
picture of bishops who are over-dressed, worldly,

ignorant, cruel, and corrupt. Their desire for easy
living, their arrogant control over the members of
the body constitute a scandal; and their extortion of
tithes is "ignoble Hucsterage." The irate young Protestant rhetorically asks, "Were it such an incurable
mischiefe to make a little triall, what all this would
doe to the flourishing and growing of Christs mysticall body? As rather to use very poore shift, and if
that serve not, to threaten uproare and combustion,
and shake the brand of Civill Discord."62 In the
Reason of Church-Government he claims, on rather dubious grounds, that Pope Hyginus (154-158 A.D.) stole
the title of "clergy" from the people. As a result,
the prelates condemned the people to the condition of
laity and "separated from them by local partitions in
Churches, through their grosse ignorance and pride
imitating the old temple: and excluded the members of
Christ from the property of being members, the bearing
of orderly and fit offices in the ecclesiastical body,
as if they had meant to sow up that Jewish vail which
Christ by his death on the Crosse rent in sunder."63
In this charge Milton's tactic fuses the themes of the
body of Christ and opposition to the forcing of canon
and Mosaic law on Christians.

The story of Menenius Agrippa, told to troops
revolting from the authority of the Roman consuls,
provided Milton with an exotic fable to illustrate the
necessity for the members of the body to maintain their
relative position and function responsibly in relation
to all the other members. A monstrous wen claimed the
authority due to the head of the body, to the detriment of the rest of the body. After an assembly of
the members, a philosopher-surgeon is called in by an
assembly of the members, and he cuts off the excres-
cence.64 Calvin had found the story apropos of the
same point and warned that dissension in the body of
Christ could lead to the same situation. He points
out that "Menenius Agrippa, too, in ancient times,
when desirous to conciliate the Roman people, when at
variance with the senate, made use of an apologue, not
very unlike the doctrine of Paul here ⌊I Cor. 12.12⌋."
He makes a sharp distinction between the body as
politic and as mystical:

Among Christians, however, the case is very
different; for they do not constitute a mere
political body, but are the spiritual and
mystical body of Christ, as Paul himself
afterwards adds. (ver. 27) The meaning therefore is--"though the members of the body are
various, and have different functions, they
are, nevertheless, linked together in such
a manner that they coalesce in one. We,
accordingly, who are members of Christ, although we are endowed with various gifts,
ought, notwithstanding, to have an eye to
that connection which we have in Christ."[65]

And so both Milton and Calvin take advantage of a
classical apologue to illustrate the Christian symbolism of the need for unity in the body of Christ.

Similarly, Thomas Jacomb and Paul Bayne define
refusal to partake properly in the mutual responsibility of the members of the body as a deformity in
the body. After emphasizing the need for real and
active membership in the church, Jacomb asks, "What
is it for a man to be in Christ's mystical body only
as the wooden leg or eye of glass in the natural
body?"[66] Bayne insists that Christ is fulfilled by
"his true members," but also that he is disfigured by
false members: "as a wooden leg or glass doth to the
body of a man, or, at the most, as a bunching wen,
which is more inwardly continued, and hath a kind of
life, but is not quickened as a member of it, and
therefore it remaineth the more complete when such
are cut off from it."[67]

A pattern of image ancillary to the main motif of
the mutual responsibility of the members of the body
for each other is that of sinews or ligaments which
bind the body together, variously interpreted as
charity or faith. Chrysostom had compared charity to
the ligaments of the body keeping it together and
allowing it to function.[68] John Calvin insists that
discipline and order comprise the ligaments which
bind the church together. "Accordingly," he says, "as
the saving doctrine of Christ is the soul of the church,
so does discipline serve as its sinews, through which

225

the members of the body hold together, each in its
own place." This cohesion is effected by the "human
ministry" which governs the church at God's direction,
thus implying that the body can only be held together
by strict obedience to those (clergymen) in the ministry, to which St. Paul alluded in Ephesians 4.10-16.[69]
For Michael Servetus love keeps the members of the
body together.[70] For Thomas Jacomb the gift of faith
is the ligaments of the body,[71] and for Paul Bayne both
love and "doctrine," or faith, are the targets of Satan,
who seeks to cut them in order to destroy the church.[72]

An image analogous to that of the body is the grafting of trees, which Paul develops only in the eleventh
chapter of Romans. He alludes to the olive tree, common
in the Mediterranean area and especially in Italy. The
Romans he compares to a wild olive tree which is grafted
onto a domestic tree through the process of breaking
off branches so that the wild tree may grow with the
domestic variety: "And if some of the branches be broken off, and thou, being a wild olive tree, wert graf-
fed in among them, and with them partakest of the root
and fatness of the olive tree" (Rom 11.17). Paul warns
the Romans not to be proud that they have replaced some
of the natural branches since they were broken off because of unbelief, and so could the Romans if they are
guilty of disbelief. Nowhere, however, does he relate
this image to the body.

As far as this study has been able to ascertain,
in the Reformation Calvin was the first to associate
the grafting process to the image of the body and to
characterize it as producing charity and mutual responsibility. Baptism, for Calvin, provides the basis of
the engrafting of Christians into Christ's body. This
sacrament allows that the members, "being ingrafted
into Christ's body, are truly members one of another
. . . [and the result should be] mutual fellow-feeling,
mutual concern." This sympatheia is achieved through
the reception of Baptism and the Eucharist, which
eventually produces a perfect union with Christ in
heaven. The ultimate basis for the potency of the
sacraments is Christ himself, and the members must be
careful not to "disfigure" themselves "with any spot
or blemish."[73]

226

Other Christian thinkers thought in the same
symbolic manner of the union of the members to the
body. Richard Hooker, negatively, compares heretics
to "branches cut off from the body of the true Vine,
yet only so far forth cut off as their heresies are
extended."[74] Thomas Jacomb joins the metaphor of the
body with that of the branches, and Paul Bayne argues
that there will be life for the members if they are
properly grafted onto the stock. He likens the body
to a king and his nobles or the "master of a college,
with fellows and scholars."[75]

Milton continues this tradition in Of Christian
Doctrine, in one chapter entitled "OF BEING INGRAFTED
IN CHRIST, AND ITS EFFECTS," which represents the product not only of Romans eleven, Calvin, and other
traditions but also of various images in the gospels
suggesting the planting and nurturing of trees. Milton cites John 15.1, 2, for example: "I am the true
vine, and my Father is the husbandman: every branch
in me that beareth not fruit, he taketh away." The
effects of the "ingrafting" and "regeneration" are
"NEWNESS OF LIFE and INCREASE," which produce spiritual understanding (what one theologian calls "epig-
nosis")[76] and "love of holiness." For Milton "The
other effect is LOVE OR CHARITY, ARISING FROM A SENSE
OF THE DIVINE LOVE SHED ABROAD IN THE HEARTS OF THE
REGENERATE BY THE SPIRIT, WHEREBY THOSE WHO ARE IN-
GRAFTED IN CHRIST BEING INFLUENCED, BECOME DEAD TO SIN,
AND ALIVE AGAIN UNTO GOD, AND BRING FORTH GOOD WORKS
SPONTANEOUSLY AND FREELY. This is also called HOLI-
NESS. Eph. 1.4. 'that we should be holy and without
blame before him in love'." Milton defines this love
as something more than fraternal and ranks it after
faith and hope, citing Ephesians 3.17 ff. on the
regenerate being "rooted and grounded in love." The
spiritual increase is manifested in the regenerate
themselves, as members united with Christ, the head
(Eph. 4.15). The net effect of Milton's fusing of
various symbols to describe the community of Christians results in a wonderfully rich and organic metaphoric conception which illustrates man's growing in
Christ.[77]

Lucien Cerfaux has remarked on Ephesians 4.1-16

as an image "which illustrated the need for unity in an organism: such as the Body of Christ.[78] The need for unity in the church focuses on heresy and schism in due course, schism suggesting in Greek a literal tearing of the body. In an organism like a body, cutting or separating into parts is unthinkable, and so it has been argued in the church that unity is not only desirable but essential. This logical-imaginative process of equating or identifying one phenomenon with another was popular with Milton, especially for rhetorical purposes. The target of an argument is metaphorically identified as something undesirable, and through incremental repetition it then literally becomes that undesirable phenomenon. For example, if a bishop is a wolf (an image well grounded in Scripture), then he must possess all the unpleasant and dangerous characteristics of a wolf, such as tearing at the body. And so the body, to some theologians must maintain its unity or else be torn and die.

In the early church, St. Ambrose, although explicitly concerned about the need for the members of the human body to subordinate themselves under the unity of the Spirit, equates the process with that of the body of Christ and laments, "because the whole Church is the one body of Christ, we divide Christ as long as the human race disagrees."[79] Chrysostom was similarly concerned, and so he argues:

> For tell me, if the eye should bestow upon the hand the foresight which it has for the whole body, and withdrawing itself from the other members, should attend to that alone, would it not injure the whole? . . . For these things are not of love, but of division; schisms, and distracting rents. Since even if I separate and take a member from the whole man, the part separated indeed is united in itself, is continuous, and compacted together, but even so it is a separation, since it is not united to the rest of the body.

Chrysostom graphically compares the cutting off of members who had been restored to the worse evil of the piercing of Christ's body with the spear or the nailing of the body by the Jews.[80] Ultimately, to disagree

228

on a question within the church is not only like
tearing Christ's body--it is tearing Christ's body.

In the Reformation Calvin, translating the word
anakethalaiosis, in Ephesians 1.10, "he might gather
together in one all things in Christ," explains,
"Formed into one body, we are united to God, and
closely connected with each other. Without Christ,
on the other hand, the whole world is a shapeless
chaos and frightful confusion. We are brought into
actual unity by Christ above." Further emphasizing
the need for unity, Calvin notes that the name of
Christ refers to the whole body, although elsewhere
he insists that the basis for unity in the body is
the head, Christ, suggesting willy nilly some loose
metaphoric associations. Christ seems to be the head
one time and the whole body the other. He says, "For
we must be one body, if we would be kept together
under him as our head. If, on the other hand, we are
split asunder into different bodies, we start aside
from him also. Hence to glory in his name amidst
strifes and parties is to tear him in pieces: which
indeed is impossible, for never will he depart from
unity and concord, because 'He cannot deny himself'
(2 Tim. ii. 13.)."[81]

During this period other theologians besides Calvin remarked upon the importance of Christians working
together in the body in mutual responsibility and
charity, even though various members may possess different gifts.[82] John Colet provides a lengthy sketch
of the roles played by the parts of the body in a
spirit of unity and responsibility, the latter producing the former:

For all the parts of the holy society, which
Christ would collect together, must imitate a
whole and sound body and its members. For
although they be many, varied and diverse, both
in form, power and office, yet still, through
the harmonizing effect of the natural life, that
flows from the body's head to all the joints and
members, all the parts have such coherence and
sympathy, and do so assiduously render mutual
help to one another, according to their means,
by giving and receiving aid, that in the whole

body there is presented, not a plurality of
parts, but a united whole composed of the
several parts; with no private interest among
them, no care for individual advantage, but
everywhere, and on the part of all, through
the silent teaching of instinct, a singular
desire for fellowship and unity and the welfare of the whole body. In such a body every
member seems to own that it is then in the
best health when the whole body is health-
iest, ...[83]

Richard Hooker comments on the damage done when the
members do not take Colet's advice: "yea her schisms,
factions and such other evils whereunto the body of
the Church is subject, sound and sick remaining both
of the same body."[84]

If the body is unified and not torn by schism,
it then possesses a quality highly valued by the
Greeks as a result of the teaching of Pythagoras and
his followers--harmony, a concept which has been
assimilated into Christianity and is perhaps best
expressed in Dante's <u>Divine</u> <u>Comedy</u>. Very early in
the church, the Fathers became excited by the idea of
the harmony of the body of Christ, and not the body
of an athlete as the Greeks did. St. Basil, for
example, a Greek and the Bishop of Caesarea in Cap-
padocia, maintained that everyone in the community of
Christ must live "in accord with one another in the
charity of Christ, as are the members of the body."
As a bishop, Basil was concerned with harmony in more
than an aesthetic sense because he was laying down
rules for his flock. For him the head "exercises
dominion over and unites the members, each with the
other unto harmonious accord." Basil's practical
episcopal approach is reflected in this comment on
the harmony of the body: "If we are not joined
together by union in the Holy Spirit in the harmony
of one body, . . . we would not serve the common good
in the ministry according to God's good pleasure,
but would be satisfying our own passion for self-
gratification. How could we, divided and separated,
preserve the status and the mutual service of members
or our subordinate relationship to our Head which is
Christ?"[85]

The major interpreter of Paul's Epistles during
the early years of the church, St. John Chrysostom,
is certain that God "wishes us to withdraw from every
brother that walketh disorderly." Chrysostom, reflecting his Greek sense of proportion, assumes that the
mystical body ought to have the same harmony as human
nature, "the same concord of design."[86] The young
church was, of necessity, preoccupied with the problem of instituting a community which would function
together harmoniously to demonstrate to pagans that
the Christian way of life produced harmony and fellowship.

With the revived interest in the classical perspective in the Renaissance, educated men like John
Colet and John Calvin reintroduced into the concept
of the body the aesthetic sense of harmony in much
the same manner as it might be applied to a drawing
of the human body by Michaelangelo. However, this
sense of proportion appeared in Paul's Epistles themselves, probably as a result of his education in
Tarsus: "Now I beseech you, brethren, by the name of
our Lord Jesus Christ, that ye all speak the same
thing, and that there be no divisions among you; but
that ye be perfectly joined together in the same mind
and in the same judgment" (I Cor. 1.10). Calvin,
commenting on this passage, continues in the same
vein:

> for it is the main article of our religion that
> we be in harmony among ourselves; and farther,
> on such agreement the safety of the Church rests
> and is dependent. . . . Paul here makes use of
> a participle, which denotes things that are
> _fitly_ _and_ _suitably_ _joined_ _together_. For ΚαΤαρ-
> ΤιξΕσθαι itself . . . properly signifies,
> to be _fitted_ and _adjusted_, just as the members
> of the human body are connected together by a
> most admirable symmetry.[87]

Calvin attacks what he considers the deformity and
crookedness of the pope, who destroys the symmetry of
the church by refusing to be one of its members. No
man, he argues, should violate the just proportions of
the body by excessive claims. On the other hand, he

imagines that the members, through discord, might
tear Christ to pieces, but then he thinks more fully
about the possibility and denies it since "He cannot
deny himself (2 Tim. ii. 13)." The unity of the body,
he asserts, produces "a symmetry and fellow-feeling,
that what has been conferred on the members severally
contributes to the advantage of the whole body--and
hence love is the best directress in this matter."[88]
According to Ford Lewis Battles, who has translated
the Institutes, Calvin has joined together the concepts of natural law and charity, pointing to Seneca's
"recognition that we are born to help each other:
'Homo in adiutorum mutuum genitus est'."[89] The role
of love or charity in the body achieves prominence
because it forms the groundwork for the harmony in the
body.

John Colet, entranced by the image of the body,
liked to imagine the details of the image and the
particular functions of different members. For him
the senses determine "what was discordant and what
harmonious" in the body, and all the members together,
different though they may be, produce "equalization
and unity, arising from an equipoise of excellence."
Colet unites the practical functions of the body (of
such concern to Basil) with its beautiful qualities.
He speaks of the Spirit's influences of faith, wisdom,
knowledge, help, and miracles, and expatiates on their
results:

> so does the Spirit dispose and adapt the several
> members, even men, His instruments, in fitting
> proportion and harmonious order; that the result
> may be a beautiful utility and useful beauty in
> the Church in Himself; consisting, as it does,
> of men beautiful and useful in Him; in whom
> there is none that is not both beautiful and
> useful. . . . This concord and harmonious
> agreement of men in the Church, after the
> analogy of the human body, is finely described
> by St. Paul.[90]

Thus the aesthetic, the practical, and the charitable
unite in Colet's vision of the perfect and harmonious
body of Christ.

John Milton, in Of Christian Doctrine defends the

integrity of particular churches, citing Matthew
18.20 on the gathering of two or three people to worship as possessing a real presence of God. Any and
all churches or gatherings with a true presence "are
properly called churches," and therein all the elements
of worship may be performed, unlike the Jewish religion during the early days of the Christian church, when
Jews had to flock to Jerusalem to the Temple to worship.
Now there is no one particular church which can claim
to be the center of worship:

> whereas at present there is no national church,
> but a number of particular churches, each com-
> plete and perfect in itself, and all co-equal
> in divine right and power; which, like similar
> and homogeneous parts of the same body, con-
> nected by a bond of mutual equity, form in
> conjunction one catholic church: nor need any
> one church have recourse to another for a grace
> or privilege which it does not possess in its
> independent capacity.[91]

The bond of unity and harmony in the body of Christ,
to a thinker like Milton in the Reformation, allows
for unity in diversity, without the excessive con-
formity that Basil and later Calvin found essential.
Each church can function independently and equally as
members of the body, with no one church superior to
another. For Milton schism was not necessarily evil
but produced independent integrity, an argument and
an image developed beautifully in Areopagitica to
represent the body of truth which can endure a cutting
and yet survive.

Hitherto we have primarily been exploring the
positive qualities of the symbolic concept of the body
of Christ, its unity, harmony, and charity, but in
the Reformation enormous emphasis focused on the con-
verse--on the disease or illness of the body, which
needed curing.

It is very difficult to find any of the Church
Fathers emphasizing sickness in the body. St. Ambrose,
concerned with the role of bishop and its responsibility to cast out any member of the community found
unacceptable, describes this dilemma in terms of a
diseased limb:

Not without pain is a limb of the body cut off
which has become corrupt. It is treated for a
long time, to see if it can be cured with various
remedies. If it cannot be cured, then it is cut
off by a good physician. Thus it is a good
bishop's desire to wish to heal the weak, to
remove the spreading ulcers, to burn some parts
and not to cut them off; and lastly, when they
cannot be healed, to cut them off with a pain
to himself.[92]

Ambrose demonstrates a sensitivity to his episcopal
responsibilities, but to reform-minded thinkers of
the sixteenth century many bishops had not evinced
such a sense of duty and so had produced disease
(dis-ease almost literally) in the body of the church.
John Colet, for example, although he died before
Luther published his famous theses, was most concerned
over the state of the church but from a conservative
point of view. For him the illness was a product of
the members' not keeping both their faith and their
place in the body, and both faith and charity are the
means of curing the illness. God, he asserts, chooses
the members of the church for the reformation of the
individuals therein, but every member must maintain
his own place and form in moderation for the health
and beauty of the body. The body will remain healthy
so long as the members keep faith, but if they lose
faith and follow their own "disposition," the body
will suffer disease. It will lapse into "weakness and
private opinion" which generates "madness and folly"
in the soul--in opposition to faith, the basis for the
body's "fair and harmonious symmetry." Love should
impel the members to love each other, "even as Christ
loved the Church (Eph. 5.25)."[93]

Calvin begins with a somewhat jaundiced view of
man's nature when depicting the diseases of the body
of Christ, viewing man's body as "a mass, made up of
all vices." So it is simple for him to discover illness and disease throughout the body of the church.
In commenting on II Corinthians 13.1, he characterizes
Paul's harangue as devoted "to certain diseased and
half-rotten members" who have been guilty of sin.[94]
Calvin sees as the basis for contemporary problems in
the church the pope, who misdirects the members into

234

giving him allegiance and not Christ, producing "a
humpbacked body, and a confused mass that will fall
to pieces itself" since the kingdom of the pope is
swollen and monstrous (like the wen of Menenius
Agrippa alluded to by Calvin above, p. 224).[95] On
medical evidence from Galen and other physicians, he
distinguishes between a cancer and gangrene, and
dwells on the "eating" quality of gangrene, warning,
"Since, therefore, 'gangrene' is immediately followed
by (νεκρωσις   ) mortification, which rapidly
infects the rest of the members till it end in the
universal destruction of the body; to this moral con-
tagion Paul elegantly compares false doctrines; for,
if you once give entrance to them, they spread till
they have completed the destruction of the Church."
He then relates this disease metaphor to the loss of
the gospel among the Papists. He is concerned lest
a member who is ill will take offense at the other
members' attempt to help it to recover.[96]

Milton's use of imagery based on disease, illness, wounds, and medical phenomena in general has
been discussed effectively elsewhere, by Thomas
Kranidas and Kester Svendsen, but this imagery of
disease has not been placed properly in the context
of the body of Christ motif as prevalent in Milton's
tracts on prelaty and divorce. Svendsen explores
the medical and encyclopedic background of the medical and scientific allusions of Milton, and Kranidas
discusses the classical concept of decorum which
embraces the theme of wholeness or integrity as a
backdrop to Milton's imagery of disease which reflects
violations of that decorum.[97]

Milton's symbolic pattern of disease in the anti-
episcopal pamphlets is a syncretistic blend of the
classical, the scientific, and the Pauline symbol of
the body of the church. The pattern reflects two
facets, the positive picture of harmony and health
seen above and the negative motif of the sickness in
the body of Christ, as Calvin saw it. For Milton
reformation demands the cleansing and curing of a
sick body which has been poisoned and maltreated by
the bishops. Of Reformation reflects this concern
with restoring the body of the church to its proper

health. Don M. Wolfe and William Alfred have noted
in this pamphlet the importance of the image of the
body of Christ and the concomitant metaphor of disease:

> Notice . . . the governing image of the pamphlet,
> that of the members of the true church as members
> of the mystical body of Christ. It is in accord-
> ance with that image that the metaphors used when
> Episcopacy is treated tend to be metaphors of
> nausea, disease, and deformity.[98]

The pamphlet opens with Christ taking on flesh and the
Church being nurtured by the gospel, reaching "a
Spirituall height . . . that the body, with all the
circumstances of time and place, were purifi'd by the
affections of the regenerat Soule, and nothing left
impure, but sinne."[99]

Milton contrasts the _flesh_ and the _spirit_, and
this dichotomy may be confusing in this context of
exploring the body in a positive light. The definitions of the term _flesh_ were discussed in Chapter One,
but--briefly--for Milton the term signifies the attempt
to define religion and Christianity in terms of the
alleged self-sufficiency of the Law. In Paul's time
this was the Torah, but in Milton's, at least in this
controversy, it was canon law. In other words, those
who claim salvation through the fulfillment of either
kind of law are basing religion on legalisms binding
the flesh and not on the Spirit of God as visible in
Christ's Redemption. The spiritual manifestation of
Christ is in his body, which draws all men to salvation. A Platonic reading of the term _flesh_ is mistaken in almost all of Milton's prose and poetry, with
the most notable exception in _A_ _Mask_, as Sears Jayne
has ably proved.

In the anti-prelatical tracts, including _Of_
Reformation, the bishops and those dependent on them
are regarded as the cause of infection in the body,
and the description of the symptoms can be startling
in its detail. The motif extends so deeply that a
word like _infect_, appearing without any other medical
references, becomes a subtle metaphor of disease. The
targets of Milton's negative imagery are "episcopal
discipline, superstitious ceremony, the liturgy, and

his opponent's integrity."[100]

Milton seems to make a subtle distinction between the body of the church and the body of episcopacy, with the disease or sickness motif focusing on the latter. In _Of Reformation_ he asks, "But what doe wee suffer mis-shapen and enormous _Prelatisme_, as we do, thus to blanch and varnish her deformities with the faire colours, as before of _Martyrdome_, so now of _Episcopacie_?" Further on, in the same pamphlet, he accuses the bishops of the early church as suffering from "an universall rottennes, and gangrene in the whole _Function_." The editors of the Yale Prose Edition of the pamphlet note that the life of St. Martin of Tours "is a striking contradiction of this statement."[101] Milton reaches the level of the ridiculous with this depiction of the attempts during the time of Edward the Sixth to reform the church: "Then was the _Liturgie_ given to a number of moderate Divines, and Sir _Tho. Smith_ a Statesman to bee purg'd, and Physick't: And surely they were moderate _Divines_ indeed, neither hot nor cold."[102] One of Milton's primary complaints alleges that the bishops have looted the wealth of the church for their own ends and in the process have bled the nation: "What a Masse of Money is drawne from the Veines into the Ulcers of the Kingdome this way."[103] The most effective example of the illness of the body of the church, however, is the wen based on the story of Menenius Agrippa, which is cited above (pp. 224-225). Ultimately the work of reformation consists in curing the body.

In _Animadversions_ Milton portrays Cyprian as a bishop whose qualities set him off as a foil to bishops in contemporary England:

his personal excellence like an antidote over-came the malignity of that breeding corruption which was then a disease that lay hid for a while under shew of a full, and healthy constitution, as those hydropick humors not discernable at first from a fair and juicy fleshinesse of body, or that unwonted ruddy colour which seems gracefull to a cheek otherwise pale, and yet arises from evil causes, either of some inward

237

> obstruction, or inflammation, and might
> deceav the first Phisicians till they had
> learnt the sequell.[104]

Milton assumes that the corruption in the body of the
church has existed for centuries and that it is only
now, in his own time, obvious to all. (Milton refers
to the charge of heresies in the New Model Army in his
Second Defence, advising that they can best be removed,
not "by steel and scourges," as if from the body," but
by "sounder doctrine").[105] He thus can invert the
pattern by suggesting that heresy in the body of the
church, or in this case, the army, cannot be excised
in the same way it might be from the body of a particular human heretic.

In the Reason of Church-Government the body of
the church is collectively represented by the spiritually ill of all the parishes and the bishops by
physicians who are content only to speak to them from
a distance and not cure the sick souls with treatment
or medication. It is as if they stand in

> severall Pulpits of the City, and assembling all
> the diseased in every parish should begin a learn-
> ed Lecture of Pleurisies, Palsies, Lethargies,
> to which perhaps none there present were inclin'd,
> and so without so much as feeling one puls, or
> giving the least order to any skilfull Apothecary,
> should dismisse 'em from time to time, some
> groaning, some languishing, some expiring, with
> this only charge to look well to themselves,
> and do as they heare.

Milton concludes by pointing out Christ as the only
one who can cure these spiritually diseased people.[106]

As has been demonstrated, some of Milton's imagery
associated with the body of Christ symbol is largely
negative, emphasizing the unpleasant facets of human
bodies in general, but this emphasis results from the
polemical situation in which he found himself in the
anti-episcopal tracts.

Milton also exploits body symbolism in the area
of marriage, but so did St. Paul. To those interested

238

in the liberation of women, St. Paul has been regarded
as a sexist, as a male interested in keeping women in
a subservient position, and to some extent the charge
is true. His, and Milton's, position is the traditional one of regarding women as subordinate to man,
as suitable only for the lesser position in marriage.
On the other hand, both Paul and Milton were much
concerned with making this relationship between man
and woman elevated and in keeping with the belief
that Christ was born of woman and that he came of the
seed of woman as prophesied in Genesis. One of the
means that Paul employs to dignify the relationship
between man and woman in marriage is to represent it
in terms of the relationship between Christ and the
church, between the head and the body. The following
is the eloquent passage in Ephesians which sets forth
the analogy, or more accurately, the profound metaphor:

Wives, submit your selves unto your own husbands, as unto the Lord.
For the husband is the head of the wife, even
as Christ is the head of the church: and he is
the saviour of the body.
Therefore as the church is subject unto Christ,
so let the wives be to their own husbands in every
thing.
Husbands, love your wives, even as Christ also
loved the church, and gave himself for it;
That he might sanctify and cleanse it with the
washing of water by the word.
That he might present it to himself a glorious
church, not having spot, or wrinkle, or any such
thing; but that it should be holy and without
blemish.
So ought men to love their wives as their own
bodies. He that loveth his wife loveth himself.
For no man ever yet hateth his own flesh, and
of his bones.
For this cause shall a man leave his father
and mother, and shall be joined unto his wife,
and they two shall be one flesh.
This is a great mystery: but I speak concerning Christ and the church.
Nevertheless let every one of you in particular

239

so love his wife even as himself; and the wife
see that she reverence her husband. (5.22-33)

Paul culturally assumes that the husband is in command
and that the wife obeys, but that belief notwithstanding, the outline of the relationship elevates the position of the woman to the point of equal importance,
if not equal rights, in the marriage. The husband has
rather serious responsibilities to the wife in that
he must love her as much as he loves himself. Although
Paul makes a distinction between the relationship
between Christ and the church and the husband and the
wife in that the former is a mystery and the latter
apparently is not, nevertheless the very idea of viewing women in such a noble light must have constituted
a shock to Paul's contemporaries.

For the most part, two early commentators on the
Epistles seem content to echo Paul's sentiments, to
ignore the elevation of woman, or to belabor the duty
of wives to obey husbands and very little to point up
the duty of husbands toward their wives. Clement of
Alexandria emphasizes the espousal between the members of the church and Christ.[107] Chrysostom, glossing Titus 2.4, compares the husband to the head and
the wife to the rest of the body and urges the head
to rule the body. Writing on Ephesians 5, the passage
quoted above, he iterates the parallel and exhorts the
wife to obey the husband and the husband to love the
wife insofar as they obey them.[108] Thus the wife will
receive only so much love as she merits through her
obedience. At one point Chrysostom requests the husband not to despise the wife since she is a part of
his body. This approach seems to assume that the wife
is worthy of contempt under normal conditions--other
than vis á vis her function as the body in this Pauline metaphor. Chrysostom does point out that Adam
and Eve were from the same flesh and bone, but then
he insists that corruption (Eve) entered through his
side; and, conversely, life sprang from Christ's side.[109]
The inverse parallel here suggests that between Adam
and Christ, to be discussed in Chapter Six. But
enough insult to women readers; a final statement from
Chrysostom should end the indignity:

Thou art the head of the woman, let then the head

regulate the rest of the body. Dost thou not
see that it is not so much above the rest of
the body in situation, as in forethought,
directing like a steersman the whole of it?
For in the head are the eyes both of the body,
and of the soul. Hence flows to them both
the faculty of seeing, and the power of
directing. And the rest of the body is appointed for service, but this is set to command. . . . Seest thou not that it is
superior in foresight than in honour? So
let us rule the women, let us surpass them,
not by seeking greater honour from them, but
by their being more benefited by us.[110]

Both John Colet and John Calvin remain fairly
close to St. Paul's text in their comments on the
relationship between the husband as head and the wife
as body. Colet, explicating I Corinthians 11, portrays the man "as the head of the woman" and as such
has precedence over the woman, especially since he is
the image of God. On the other hand, he notes that
everyone in the church is female in that Christ is
the head and all are subject to him.[111] Calvin also
remarks on the pattern that the man is the head of
the woman and that the church is a bride of Christ.
He interprets I Corinthians 11.5, the veiling of
women, as symbolic of their "subjection" to men, and
the lack of covering as symbolic of "liberty." However, he maintains that the male should refrain from
having intercourse with a harlot because not only does
this represent adultery to the wife but also the man
as a member of the body of Christ "tears away a member
from Christ's body."[112] And so the wife is not to be
regarded as someone who might suffer from the impact
of infidelity in marriage. Adultery is therefore evil
for theological and not human reasons.

Associating the body and the members with the tree
and branches image, Richard Hooker carefully focuses
on the comparison between Adam and Christ and the
church: "The Church is in Christ as Eve was in Adam.
Yea by grace we are every of us in Christ and in his
Church, as by nature we are in those our first parents,
God made Eve of the rib of Adam. And his Church he

241

frameth out of the very flesh, the very wounded and
bleeding side of the Son of man . . . the words of
Adam may be fitly the words of Christ concerning his
Church, 'flesh of my flesh and bone of my bones,' a
true native extract out of mine own body."[113]

The distance between these Reformation attitudes
and modern theological opinions can be seen in a
statement by Lucien Cerfaux, who remarks that "Christian marriage symbolizes this union of Christ with
his Church."[114] To be specific, the modern theologian
regards what is considered Christian marriage (the
vehicle) as illustrating the mystery (as Paul depicted
it) of Christ and the body of the church (the term),
but Calvin explains the marital union (the term)
through the mystery of Christ's body (the vehicle),
as if that were more comprehensible than the marriage
relationship as Paul sees it--as noble and dignified.
C.M. Patrides regards Ephesians 5.22-25 as the basis
for a balanced view by Milton and his contemporaries
of marriage as seen through the symbol of the body of
Christ.[115] One would like to believe this of Milton
at least, but his references to the Pauline definition
of marriage don't seem to support Patrides' contention.
In Reason Milton makes only a passing allusion to the
symbolism of the body in that "through the mercy and
grace of the head and husband of his Church" will
England forego ranks in the church. Milton adheres to
the strict tradition in The Judgement of Martin Bucer
by translating Bucer's reproduction of I Corinthians
4.7 on the mutual sexual debt that wives and husbands
owe to each other and the subjection of the wife to
the husband in the manner of that of the church and
Christ.[116] Also in Judgement he does something very
strange with Bucer's text. He defines one of the four
properties of marriage: "That the husband beare himself as the head and preserver of his wife, instructing
her to all godlines and intigritie of life," but as
Arnold Williams observes, "Milton omits 'sicut CHRISTUS
se preaestat Ecclesiae, hoc est' (As Christ is the
other church, that is)."[117] What does this signify?
A meaningless omission or an unwillingness to associate
the problems of marriage and divorce with the sacred
relationship between Christ and his church?

In _Tetrachordon_, advocating a spiritual and not
a carnal (here sexual) view of marriage, that is, that
incompatibility is a better reason for divorce than is
the physical act of adultery, Milton develops a Pauline
reason for divorce. If spirituality and piety suffer
in a marriage, then divorce is permissible:

> Moreover, if man be the image of God, which con-
> sists in holines, and woman ought in the same
> respect to be the image and companion of man, in
> such wise to be lov'd, as the Church is belov'd
> of Christ, and if, as God is the head of Christ,
> and Christ the head of man, so man is the head
> of woman; I cannot see by this golden dependence
> of headship and subjection, but that Piety and
> Religion is the main tye of Christian Matrimony:
> So as if there be found between the pair a
> notorious disparity either of wickednes or
> heresie, the husband by all manner of right is
> disingag'd from a creature, not made and
> inflicted on him to the vexation of his right-
> eousness; the wife also, as her subjection is
> terminated in the Lord, being her self the
> redeem'd of Christ, is not still bound to be
> the vassal of him, who is the bondslave of
> Satan. . . .[118]

This "Pauline Privilege," although Milton does not call
it that, has been a traditionally accepted means of
dissolving the marriage contract for centuries in the
Roman church.[119] Further on in _Tetrachordon_ he develops
a similar line of reasoning, that the analogy between
marriage and Christ and his church was not meant to
force couples to remain together against their wills:
"Wee know that there was never a more spiritual mystery then this Gospel taught us under the terms of
body and flesh; yet nothing less intended then that wee
should stick there."[120] Milton is merely begging the
question; right or wrong in his conclusion, he feels
that divorce must be morally acceptable, and whatever
Scripture reads, he will find justification for his
position. I am not maintaining that he was doing this
cynically, but that under the pressure of his own marital experiences his perspective had solidified before
his examination of all the evidence. For, what are we
to make of this gloss on Ephesians 5 (focal chapter in

243

this whole area): "it cannot therefore be fitting
that a single member, and that not one of the most
important, [Adam's rib] should be independent of the
whole body, and even of the head." Milton, here
describing the duties of the wife, stresses the ultimate subjection of the woman in well nigh insulting
language, rejecting the notion of the nobility of the
members of the body in marriage (Works, XVII, 353).

Another facet of the image of the body of Christ
is worth examination. In the New Testament the term
temple, when not referring to the structure at Jerusalem, signifies either the temple of the body of
Christ "in which the fulness of the Godhead dwelt" or
the temple of the human body, as in some part of Paul's
Epistles. As the temple of Jerusalem, Paul was emphasizing the uniqueness of Judaism as opposed to the
multiplicity of heathen places of worship all over the
known world.[121] John 2.19-21 contains Christ's answer
to his questioners about the signs he would show them--
specifically that he would raise his body--the temple--
from destruction. The definition appears clear. Paul's
first definition of the body of man as a "temple of God"
is also lucid in its emphasis on the obligation of man
not to "defile" his own body since it belongs to God
(I Cor. 3.16-17). Paul warns that

> your bodies are the members of Christ? shall I then
> take the members of Christ and make them the mem-
> bers of an harlot? God forbid.
>
> What? know ye not that he which is joined to
> an harlot is one body? for two, saith he, shall
> be one flesh.
>
> . . . Flee fornication. Every sin that a man
> doeth is without the body; but he that commiteth
> fornication sinneth against his own body.
>
> What? know ye not that your body is the temple
> of the Holy Ghost which is in you, which ye have
> of God, and ye have of God, and ye are not your
> own?
>
> For ye are bought with a price: therefore
> glorify God in your body, and in your spirit,
> which are God's. (I Cor. 6.15-16, 18-20)

He further adds that God "will dwell in them" (II Cor. 6.16), and so Christians should not eat meat offered first to idols at a pagan temple--thus Paul's dichotomy between a piece of pagan architecture and a living body in which God dwells. St. Paul regards the body of man as a temple in which God dwells (in opposition to the temple of the Jews) since the body is also one of the members of Christ. The emphasis lies on sexual purity in the epistles to the Corinthians because this was one of their failings. Joining, then, with a harlot represents an insult and defilement to the body as a temple and as a member in Christ.

Attention in the early years of the church focuses on Paul's concern with the sin of lust. Cyprian quotes I Corinthians 6.19-20 and warns his virgin-readers that they need discipline for "Of these temples we are the keepers and the high priests."[122] According to Athanasius, because we are part of the temple, when the Spirit descended on Christ at the river Jordan, he descended on all, sharing the anointing.[123] Chrysostom reminds his readers that they "are members in Christ" and "the temple of the Spirit," associating the two symbols together firmly, and then warns them, "Become not then members of a harlot: for it is not your body which is insulted; since it is not your body at all, but Christ's." Thus Chrysostom takes the symbolic relationship two steps further and argues that the body now actually belongs to Christ and that it is a temple of the Spirit, not more generally God, as Paul had phrased it. He also takes the temple image to mean that the members of the church are unified through the temple in that each is a temple and all are, collectively a temple.[124] The word temple assumes a wholly new meaning in both the New Testament and the early years of the church. Augustine reenforces this Scriptural tradition in three places, and he stresses the unity of the church, its distinction from the old law, and not on the purity of the body.[125]

John Colet, in his discussions of the Epistles to the Corinthians, remarks on the various definitions of the body of Christ: "the name of Christ" is given to

the head, and the body is variously called "God's
Temple by the sacred writers, sometimes his Church,
sometimes his House, sometimes his City, sometimes his
Kingdom." Colet, with his strong disdain for the
appetites of the body, agrees that the sin of lust
defiles Christ's body and censures marriage as a neces-
say evil.[126] For Calvin the purpose of the body of
man being called a temple or a member of Christ is to
warn every man against falling into sin. Referring to
I Corinthians 6.16, he sees Paul as bringing "out more
fully the greatness of the injury that is done to Christ
by the man that has intercourse with an harlot; for he
becomes one body, and hence he tears away a member from
Christ's body." Calvin thereby remains close to Paul's
original injunction, and elsewhere in the same commentary, he notes the body-temple analogy and warns that
God will not dwell in either a profane temple or a
profane body. He further accepts Paul's warning against
the temple of the body to be defiled by association with
idols, in his view, Roman Catholic idols.[127] In the
Institutes he similarly admonishes that "Ever since the
Holy Spirit dedicated us as temples of God, we must
take care that God's glory shine through us, and must
not commit anything to defile ourselves with the filthiness of sin." He finally alludes to the temple image
to distinguish between the worship of God paid through
these bodily temples and that supposedly given in church
buildings.[128]

Milton is not so much concerned with the purity of
the body when he employs the temple-body image as he
is dedicated to formulating an inner awareness of worship instead of a concern with architectural complexity,
what someone has called "the edifice complex." In
Reason he admits that the temple in Jerusalem was part
of God's plan for the religion of the Jews in the Old
Testament. After the destruction of the temple (Ezekiel
40-48), God established a pattern to guide the Jews
away from the temple and the old law. He was more concerned with this new pattern than with the architectural
details of the old temple, and the design may best be
seen inwardly in man himself as the body of Christ:

should not he rather now by his owne prescribed
discipline have cast his line and levell upon the

246

soule of man which is his rationall temple,
and by the divine square and compasse thereof
forme and regenerate in us the lovely shapes of
vertues and graces, the sooner to edifie and
accomplish that immortall stature of Christs
body which is his Church, in all her glorious
lineaments and proportions.

The same motif is woven later in the same pamphlet
when Milton rebukes the prelates' "imitating the old
temple: and ⌊having⌋ excluded the members of Christ
from the property of being members, the bearing of
orderly and fit offices in the ecclesiastical body."[129]
Similarly, in Of Christian Doctrine, he interprets
Malachi 3.1, "the Lord whom ye seek shall suddenly come
to his temple, even the messenger of the covenant," as
referring to "the coming of the Lord into the flesh,
or into the temple of the body, as it is expressed in
John ii.21."[130] So Milton rejects the temple of the
Old Testament and the elaborate churches of his own
day: the true temple is the inward "temple of the
mind." It is no surprise that in Paradise Lost Satan
fails to understand such definitions and so has Pandemo-
nium built, a monument to his quintessential paganism:

Anon rose out of the earth a fabric huge
Rose like an exhalation, with the sound
Of dulcet symphonies and voices sweet,
Built like a temple, . . . (I.710-713)

NOTES: CHAPTER FOUR

[1]Milton and Science (Cambridge, Ma., 1956), and "Science and Structure in Milton's Doctrine of Divorce," PMLA, 67 (1952), 435-445. See also my The Function and Pattern of Imagery in Milton's Prose, 1642-1660, diss. New York University, 1967.

[2]A measure of Luther's antipathy to the symbol of the body is found when, writing on Romans 12.3-21, a key passage on the body of Christ, he does not at all refer to the body image, a lapse which can be expected because of his reaction against the symbolism of medieval Christianity.

[3]On I Corinthians, p. 8.

[4]Bultmann, Theology, I, 310; "soma," Theological Dictionary, pp. 1075-1076; Meaning, pp. 110, 110-111.

[5]Against Heresies, Bk.V, p. 528; Bk. IV, p. 509.

[6]City of God, I, 279 and II, 383-384. He cites Ephesians 4.10-16; I Corinthians 12.12-27; Colossians 1.24; I Corinthians 10.17; and Ephesians 1.22-23.

[7]Against Heresies, p. 449.

[8]"The Dress of Virgins," Saint Cyprian: Treatises, trans. & ed. Roy J. Defarrari (New York, 1958), p. 50.

[9]On Philippians & Colossians, p. 258.

[10]Summa Theologica, II, 757.

[11]On Romans, pp. 70, 77, 76-77.

[12]On Colossians, p. 152; On Galatians, p. 74; On Colossians, p. 166.

[13]Institutes, II, 1047, 1102-1103; I, 177.

[14]Institutes, II, 1110; On Hebrews, p. xxi.

[15]Commentary, p. 110; On Colossians, p. 41.

[16]YP, I, 782-783.

[17]Commentary, pp. 107, 109, 15-16, 17.

[18]On Corinthians II, p. 65; Institutes, II, 990-991.

[19]Laws, II, 217.

[20]Sermons, pp. 58, 272.

[21]On Colossians, pp. 429/19, 430/20.

[22]On Philippians, p. 116.

[23]Valdes, p. 221.

[24]Commentary, p. 65.

[25]On Philippians & Colossians, pp. 248-249.

[26]The Instructor, pp. 215, 216-217.

[27]On Ephesians, pp. 226-277, 128.

[28]Commentaries . . . Corinthians I, p. 405.

[29]On Corinthians, p. 123.

[30]Laws, Bk. V, II, 224.

[31]Commentary, pp. 107, 110, 111, 261.

[32]Sermons, p. 59.

[33]Works, XV, 261.

[34]YP, I, 542. See Thomas Kranidas, The Fierce Equation: A Study of Milton's Decorum (London, The Hague, 1965), pp. 52, 57-59.

[35]Dialogue with Trypho, p. 211.

[36] On Corinthians, Part Two, pp. 412, 413. The modern theologian, Gunther Bornkamm, comments that in I Corinthians Paul speaks of the body as a reality, not a simile (Paul, p. 194).

[37] On Hebrews, p. 220.

[38] Institutes, II, 1369-70, 1382.

[39] On Corinthians, p. 116.

[40] Laws, I, 324-325.

[41] Laws, II, 330.

[42] Laws, II, 322, 329.

[43] Laws, I, 284; II, 228.

[44] Sermons, pp. 37, 42, 43, 44, 271.

[45] Works, XVI, 57-65. The Latin is the same as the Engli

[46] "soma," Theological Dictionary, p. 1081.

[47] "soma," Theological Dictionary, pp. 1068-1069.

[48] Against the Pelagians, p. 258.

[49] On Corinthians, Part Two, pp. 433-435.

[50] Principal Works, p. 70.

[51] On Romans, pp. 79-80, 71.

[52] De Regno Christi, pp. 182-183. We should keep in mind that Milton sought the help of this treatise when he wished to find precedent for arguments favoring divorce, on the basis of Christian charity.

[53] Loci Communes, p. 219.

[54] On Hebrews, p. 80; On Corinthians I, p. 158.

[55] On Corinthians I, pp. 409, 410.

[56] Institutes, I, 878.

[57] Institutes, I, 800, 695.

[58] Righteousness, pp. 256-257, 260.

[59] Commentary, pp. 19, 242, 248, 66.

[60] On Philippians, p. 259.

[61] Works, XVII, 271.

[62] YP, I, 613.

[63] YP, I, 838-839. Ralph A. Haug, the editor of the pamphlet in the Yale Prose edition, points out the doubtful basis upon which Milton makes his accusation, p. 838, n. 61.

[64] See YP, I, 583-584, nn. 39, 41, for the story and for some useful annotation.

[65] Commentary . . . Corinthians I, pp. 407-408, 404, 405.

[66] Sermons, p. 46.

[67] Commentary, p. 110.

[68] On Philippians & Colossians, p. 274.

[69] Institutes, I, ixiii; II, 1230, 1055.

[70] Righteousness, pp. 256-257, 260.

[71] Sermons, p. 39.

[72] Commentary, pp. 256-257, 260.

[73] Commentary . . . Corinthians I, pp. 406, 412. See also p. 335, where he says that members are engrafted through the blood of Christ in a κοινωνια , a communion of blood.

[74] Laws, II, 339.

[75] Jacomb, Sermons, p. 54; Bayne, Commentary, pp. 270, 269.

[76] Lucien Cerfaux, Christian, p. 510.

[77] Works, XVI, 2-11.

[78] Cerfaux, The Christian, p. 504.

[79] Christian Faith, p. 305.

[80] On Philippians & Thessalonians, pp. 471-472.

[81] On Ephesians, p. 205; On Philippians & Colossians, p. 164; Commentary . . . Corinthians I, p. 67.

[82] See Juan Valdes, pp. 223-228.

[83] On Romans, p. 71.

[84] Laws, II, 338.

[85] "The Morals," p. 145; "A Discourse on Ascetical Disciplines," p. 41; "The Long Rules," p. 249 in Ascetical Works.

[86] On Philippians & Thessalonians, p. 509; On Corinthians, Part Two, p. 436.

[87] Commentary . . . Corinthians I, pp. 62-63.

[88] On Galatians & Ephesians, pp. 286-287, 288; Commentary . . . Corinthians I, pp. 67, 45.

[89] Institutes, I, 697-698.

[90] On Corinthians, pp. 134, 135; Jean Valdes, p. 26, deplores violations of decency and order in the church which produce "disorder, disturbance, and want of union."

[91] Works, XVI, 311.

[92] On the Duties, in Principal Works, p. 64.

[93]On Romans, pp. 80-85 passim.

[94]On Philippians & Colossians, pp. 198-199.

[95]On Philippians & Colossians, pp. 198-199.

[96]On II Timothy, pp. 223-224; Institutes, I, 697-698. Melanchthon's Loci Communes, p. 267, had depicted Paul's disciples in Corinth as "dead members of the Church."

[97]See Thomas Kranidas, The Fierce Equation, especially pp. 49-57, Kester Svendsen, Milton and Science, and "Science and Structure in Milton's Doctrine of Divorce, and my dissertation, all cited above (n. 1).

[98]YP, I, 519, n. 1.

[99]YP, I, 519.

[100]Function and Pattern, pp. 80, 83.

[101]YP, I, 537, 538, 538, n. 78.

[102]YP, I, 539.

[103]YP, I, 590-591.

[104]YP, I, 675-676.

[105]YP, IV, Pt. i., p. 649.

[106]YP, I, 756.

[107]The Instructor, p. 213.

[108]On II Timothy & Titus; On Ephesians, pp. 313-314.

[109]On Ephesians, pp. 318-319.

[110]On Philippians & II Thessalonians, p. 513.

[111]On Corinthians I, p. 113.

[112] *On Corinthians* I, p. 360; *Institutes*, II, 1024; *On Corinthians* I, pp. 355, 217, 219.

[113] *Laws*, II, 229.

[114] *Christian*, p. 319.

[115] *Milton and the Christian Tradition*, pp. 181-182.

[116] *YP*, II, 464. See also Paul Bayne, *Commentary*, pp. 338, 349, who takes the same traditional tack.

[117] *YP*, II, 466, 466, n. 2.

[118] *YP*, II, 591.

[119] See "Pauline Privilege," *New Catholic Encyclopedia*.

[120] *YP*, I, 606.

[121] *Cruden's Concordance*, and Gunther Bornkamm, *Paul*, p. 180.

[122] "The Dress of Virgins," p. 32.

[123] *Discourse*, I, p. 333.

[124] *On Corinthians*, Part One, p. 237; *On Ephesians*, p. 159.

[125] *City of God*, I, 276; II, 160, and "Enchiridion," p. 691.

[126] *On Corinthians* I, pp. 6, 217.

[127] *On Corinthians* I, p. 220; *On Corinthians* II, p. 260.

[128] *Institutes*, I, 687; II, 893.

[129] *YP*, I, 757-758, 838-839.

[130] *Works*, XIV, 241, 243. See also John Mulder, *The Temple of the Mind: Education and Literary Taste in Seventeenth Century England* (New York, 1969), pp. 142-150.

CHAPTER FIVE

THE FOOLISHNESS OF WISDOM
AND
THE STRENGTH OF WEAKNESS

In preaching the Crucifixion and Resurrection of
Christ as the basis of Christianity, St. Paul was
opposing the main intellectual and religious currents
of his time. Preaching in an area permeated by the
culture of the Greeks, he had to develop a strategy to
neutralize the high estimation in which wisdom was held
among the civilized men of his era. He chose to meet
the challenge head-on by directly opposing the death
of Christ to all Greek philosophy through the device of
irony. Lucien Cerfaux remarks on this paradoxical
tactic, "from the human point of view this is weak and
paradoxical; from the divine point of view it is full
of wisdom and power."[1] Paul deliberately defined
Christianity as foolishness contrary to the wisdom of
Greek philosophy and of the princes of the world. He
and Christian theologians after him castigated philosophy as vain and ridiculous because it did not lead to
the central truth for humanity, salvation through
Christ. This philosophy was merely bombast and empty
rhetoric which appeared convincing and attractive but
was hollow underneath. The Gospel had come to replace
it for all men, whether learned or ignorant, and only
the ignorant would reject its message. The kind of
knowledge opposed to Paul's was characterized as "carnal," as having its foundation in human reason, which,
without faith, could achieve no certainty. Only later,
with the Middle Ages and the Renaissance was there any
compromise so that some knowledge other than what led
to redemption was regarded as tolerable. A related
theme to Paul and the commentators on the Epistles was
that of love or charity which became the antidote to
the excessive vanity of earthly or fleshly knowledge.

An offshoot to the theme of the foolishness of
wisdom is the paradox of strength in weakness since
the wisdom of the Greek philosophers represented only
weakness and since, from a propagandistic perspective,
St. Paul was preaching to those who had no worldly

strength. This pattern is also directed against the
Jews who did not follow Christianity because they
believed in a Messiah of political power and who refused to accept one who died on a cross like a common
criminal.

Anyone familiar with Paradise Lost and Paradise
Regain'd recognizes these themes in Adam's desire to
learn more about how the world turns and the Son's
rejection of the temptation of worldly wisdom respectively. However, many readers have been somewhat
uneasy with the rather poor showing of science and
worldly knowledge in Milton's presentations. A
familiarity with the tradition of foolish wisdom may
make the Son's rejection more palatable to a twentieth-
century sensibility. The sub-theme of the strength of
weakness and the weakness of worldly strength may
receive a sympathetic hearing today in a world tired
of the wanton exercise of power.

Howard Schultz, in his Milton and Forbidden
Knowledge, has taken a different view of the question
of knowledge in his emphasis on the forbidden nature
of some of God's secret workings. Western civilization
has been fascinated by the notion of forbidden knowledge, especially as manifested in the Faustus legend,
but this attitude is distinctly un-Pauline in that
Paul would never give worldly knowledge or wisdom the
kind of power and attractiveness it receives at the
hands of a Marlowe or a Goethe.

At the beginning of his First Epistle to the
Corinthians, Paul announces the basic keryga or message of the gospel in terms of the cross of Christ:

For the preaching of the cross is to them that
perish foolishness; but unto us which are saved
it is the power of God.

For it is written, I will destroy the wisdom
of the wise, and will bring to nothing the understanding of the prudent.

Where is the wise? where is the scribe? where
is the disputer of this world? hath not God made
foolish the wisdom of this world?

256

For after that in the wisdom of God the world
by wisdom knew not God, it pleased God by the
foolishness of preaching to save them that believe.

For the Jews require a sign, and the Greeks seek
after wisdom:

But we preach Christ crucified, unto the Jews a
stumblingblock, and unto the Greeks foolishness;

But unto them which are called, both Jews and
Greeks, Christ the power of God, and the wisdom
of God. (18-24)

As Chrysostom perceives in the text above, Paul notes
carefully the two groups which he must conquer with
words: the Greeks and the Jews; the first must forego their vaunted wisdom and eloquence and the second
their reluctance to accept a shamefully crucified
Christ.[2]

Paul had been an educated man, versed in the Jewish religion as a student of Gamaliel; as his style
testifies, polished in rhetoric; and as the philosophic
tone of I Corinthians 13 witnesses, endowed with a
philosophic mind. However, for whatever reason,
whether his dramatic conversion on the road to Damascus or not, he reacted vigorously against the philosophy taught in the Greek schools. Paul's castigation
of human wisdom has precedent in Jeremiah's admonition,
"Let not the wise man glory in his wisdom, neither let
the mighty man glory in his might, let not the rich
man glory in his riches."[3]

Edward Gibbon perceived the growing antipathy of
Christianity to secular learning:

Even the study of philosophy was at length introduced among the Christians, but it was not always
productive of the most salutary effects; knowledge
was as often the parent of heresy as of devotion,
and the description which was designed for the
followers of Artemon may, with equal propriety, be
applied to the various sects that resisted the
successors of the apostles. 'They presume to alter
the holy Scriptures, to abandon the ancient rule
of faith, and to form their opinions according to
the subtile precepts of logic. The science of the

257

church is neglected for the study of geometry,
and they lose sight of heaven, while they are
employed in measuring the earth. Euclid is perpetually in their hands. Aristotle and Theophrastus
are the objects of their admiration; and they express
an uncommon reverence for the works of Galen. Their
errors are derived from the abuse of the arts and
sciences of the infidels, and they corrupt the simplicity of the Gospel'."[4]

St. Jerome explains the violent antipathy of Paul in
either one of two ways: "although the latter was
versed in Hebrew letters, and took instructions at the
feet of Gamaliel, whom he is not ashamed to call his
master, when he had already attained the dignity of
an apostle, nevertheless, he showed a contempt for
Greek eloquence, or, at any rate, he kept it a secret,
because of his humility, so that his preaching lay not
in the persuasiveness of his words, but rather in the
power of his signs."[5] John Calvin's positive Christocentric interpretation sets the negative tone of Paul's
stricture in balance: "For he overthrows all the wisdom of the world, that the preaching of the Cross may
alone be exalted."[6] Ultimately Paul established the
precedent of hostility to Greek philosophy and intel-
lectualism which was to last for over a thousand years.

As a polemicist, there was nothing subtle about
Paul, and so he directly attacked the wisdom of philosophy as ridiculous and foolish because it had no place
for the salvation of Christ. Early commentators on
Paul and other of the early Church Fathers, for the
most part, agreed with this outlook. Origen contrasts
the wisdom of the prophets and heroes of the Old Testament like Moses with the false wisdom of those who
seek profound truths and yet honor men and offer foolish sacrifices to idols. As long as philosophers offer
these sacrifices, they can hardly be taken seriously.[7]
Lactantius, basing his opposition to philosophy on
what he considered the nature of man, claims that men
should seek "religion and wisdom," but because men are
fooled by "reason," they either embrace religion at the
expense of wisdom or they pursue philosophy and disregard religion (undermining true philosophy in the process). Specifically he argues that philosophy cannot
achieve certainty of any kind: Socrates expressed doubt
about knowing anything; Zeno denied the value of

speculation; and Arcesilas "set up a new philosophy of not philosophizing."[8] Chrysostom, glossing the first chapter of First Corinthians, agrees with Paul that reasoning will not save man and makes two points in support of Paul's position: first, that some truths cannot be explained by language, and second, in answer to the question why Christ did not save himself on the Cross, Chrysostom maintains that Christ could have but did not wish to.[9]

Perhaps in reaction to the zeal with which many thinkers of the Renaissance embraced the wisdom of Greece and Rome, theologians gravitated to the same theme of condemning utterly the wisdom of classical civilization. John Colet exposes the pride of the Greeks in their "secular wisdom" and Paul's reaction against it since it comes from men and not from God, the true source of all things. He further argues that the Jews in Paul's day suffered from blindness in that their wills were depraved and that the Greeks suffered from depravity which resulted from ignorance. He concludes that "the very faculty by which the Greeks thought they could best see and discern the truth, was the one by which they were most blinded, so as not to perceive it. What they considered a help, was a hindrance to them; what was their strength among men, was their weakness before God."[10]

Luther, arguing against free will as advocated by Erasmus, wished to denigrate the achievements of classical and humanistic learning (as exemplified by Erasmus). He returns to the Epistles to the Romans and Corinthians for support on the futility of earthly wisdom:

Consider, moreover, whether Paul himself is not citing the most outstanding among the Greeks when he says it was the wiser among them who became fools and whose minds were darkened, or who became futile in their reasoning, that is, in their subtle disputations (Rom. 1:21f.). Tell me, does he not here touch the sublimest achievement of Greek humanity--their reasonings? For this means their best and loftiest ideas and opinions, which they regarded as solid wisdom. But his wisdom, which he elsewhere calls foolish (I Cor. 1:21),

259

he here calls futile, as having succeeded by
its many endeavors only in becoming worse, so
that at length, with darkened minds they worshipped idols and perpetuated the consequent
enormities which he records, if, therefore,
the noblest effort and achievement of the
noblest of the Gentiles is evil and ungodly,
what must we think of the rest, the common
herd or the lower orders (so to say) of the
Gentiles?[11]

Calvin insults even "the fortitude of philosophers" as little more than fanaticism. More important,
though, is the polemical use Calvin makes of Paul's
hostility towards wisdom. Just as Protestant theologians had associated the Old Law of the Jews with the
canon law of Roman Catholicism, Calvin relates the
wisdom of the Greeks to the medieval and Renaissance
theology of the Roman church. He accuses Rome of con-
juring up a phantasm in its own mind to worship rather
than the true God, a mistake which will lead to the
ruin of the church of Rome. As Calvin says, "Paul
eloquently notes this wickedness; 'Striving to be
wise, they make fools of themselves'." This stupid-
ity results from "vain curiosity" and "an inordinate
desire to know more than is fitting."[12] Glossing II
Corinthians 12.4, Calvin cites Dionysius the Areopa-
gite as an example of one who attempts to transgress
proper limits of inquiry by delineating the hierarchy
of heaven. A copy of his De Ecclesiastica et Coelesti
Hierarchia, de divinis nominibis was printed in Paris
in 1555.[13]

Richard Hooker associates both the Jews and the
Greeks as infatuated with their own wisdom and unable
to see the truth:

But there are that bear the title of wise men and
scribes and great disputers of the world, and are
nothing in deed less than what in show they most
appear. These being wholly addicted unto their
own wills, use their wit, their learning, and
all the wisdom they have to maintain that which
their obstinate hearts are delighted with, esteem-
ing in the frantic error of their minds the greatest madness in the world to be wisdom, and the

highest wisdom foolishness. Such were both Jews and Grecians, which professed the one sort legal, and the other secular skill, neither enduring to be taught the mystery of Christ: unto the glory of whose most blessed name, whose study to use both their reason and all other gifts, as well which nature as which grace hath endued them with. let them never doubt but that the same God who is to destroy and confound utterly that wisdom falsely so named in others, doth make reckoning of them as of true Scribes, Scribes by wisdom instructed to the kingdom of heaven, not Scribes against that kingdom hardned in a vain opinion of wisdom; which in the end being proved folly, must needs perish, true understanding, knowledge, judgement and reason continuing for evermore.[14]

Hooker assumes that pagans can see in the "works of nature" the wisdom of God revealed, but this wisdom cannot save them; only "the knowledge of the cross of Christ" has this capability. Hooker's broad humanity refuses to condemn utterly that sort of wisdom which cannot save the soul of man. It may be "vile" in contrast to the knowledge of salvation through Christ, but it can provide some light to the rational mind.[15]

Juan Valdes' commentary on First Corinthians adheres closely to the central symbol of the Cross as the antithesis of worldly wisdom. Those, he argues, who do not accept the wisdom of the Cross become "maddened" and so regard it as absurd and exaggerated.[16] On the contrary, he continues, "there is no wise man, no man of letters, no astrologer, or cosmographer, (natural philosopher), who is equal to the apprehension of this Christian doctrine. And he ⌊Paul⌋ says that God has thereby made the wisdom of the world foolish, for that He has set that before it, which is not attainable by science, but is only so by experience." Secondly, any person who absorbs through mind and heart the Cross, is superior in wisdom to those who pride themselves on external secular knowledge. Indicating how the minds of Reformation thinkers were preoccupied with the early church, Valdes characterizes those who attempt to understand the Cross through human knowledge as having what he calls "Gentile minds, and those who seek miracles and to whom the Cross is a

Pauline 'stumbling block' as having a Jewish mind."[17]

Related to the philosophical problems that Calvin
had with Scholastic thought are the methods of disputation and the rhetoric employed in the process of supposedly finding truth. St. Augustine had condemned
"vain and jangling philosophical disputation," a phrase
reminiscent of Paul's depiction of a lack of charity.
Calvin is unfavorably impressed by the mere show of
words and the endless wrangling that constitutes scholastic philosophy, all of which does not lead to God.
He describes this as Ματαλογια (vain talking),
which he contrasts with "useful and solid doctrine"--
the rest is "trivial and frivolous speculations, which
contain nothing but empty bombast."[18] St. Paul's
statement in Titus 1.10 had been concerned with the
Jews' teaching the circumcision, but Calvin finds it
convenient to substitute Scholasticism as the target.
As a result of his familiarity with and comprehension
of the Greek text, Calvin glosses the word Κενοφωνιας
as follows. He notes that the Vulgate had rendered it
as _Inanitas_ vocum, "vanities of voices," which depicts
"the high-sounding and verbose and bombastic style of
those who, not content with the simplicity of the gospel, turn it into profane philosophy. . . . that
swelling language . . . nothing underneath but 'empty'
jingle." Once again he applies this characterization
to theologians in the Roman church. Calvin finally
reduces philosophy to rhetoric itself, not just that
philosophy clothes itself in the garb of rhetoric but
that it is rhetoric and nothing else--in contrast to
the simple language of the Spirit.[19]

There had seemed to be an implication in I Corinthians 1.18 that the gospel was not intended for wise
men, but the tradition grew, nevertheless, that the
gospel was intended for all men indeed. Origen, for
example, makes this assertion and portrays wise men as
mistaken in that they neither thank nor glorify God
even when they know him in their ascent, in Platonic
terms, from the things of the senses to things invisible. On the basis of I Corinthians 2.6, he further
establishes a threefold division: (1) Of God, (2)
Of the World, and (3) Of Princes. The wisdom of God
was fully revealed after Christ; of the world as a

"training for a good or happy life"; of Princes as a
"secret and occult philosophy." The Princes, according to Origen, were actually spirits or powers who
wished to set a snare for Christ, "apostate and
refugee powers" who seek to possess man's mind, either
entirely or enough to turn it to evil.[20]

In the Reformation Luther observed that "The
proud, however, who trust in their merit and wisdom,
become angry and murmur when there is given to others
freely and without their merit that (salvation) after
which they sought with so much zeal." Calvin sees God
as manifested in nature to mankind but only after
illumination from within.[21] Milton firmly believed in
the openness and accessibility of the gospel to mankind, and he rebukes those (Anglicans and Roman Catholics) who would tailor doctrine to suit their own
image of God: "That which next declares the heavenly
power, and reveales the deep mistery of the Gospel,
is the pure simplicity of doctrine, accounted the
foolishness of this world, yet crossing and confounding the pride and wisdom of the flesh. And wherein
consists this fleshly wisdom and pride? . . . . in a
bold presumption of ordering the worship and service
of God after mans own will in traditions and ceremonies."[22]

If there is any validity in the wisdom-foolishness
equation as a tactical device for Paul to counter the
ridicule of the gospel by Greek intellectuals, then
one may wonder why Paul's definition of Christ's
redemption of mankind as "foolishness" became generally neglected in favor of typifying the wisdom of the
world as foolish. In other words, St. Paul was faced
with the problem of trying to explain a monumental
doctrine like the saving of all mankind on the basis
of the shameful, criminal death of an obscure carpenter's son in a Roman province that was proving more
of a nuisance than it was worth to the Roman authorities. He ironically termed the Crucifixion as foolish
in order to anticipate the arguments of his opponents
(Acts 17.15-34) that his message was ridiculous according to reason. In essence, the grounds of debate were
turned to faith, not reason, an area where Paul's
opponents stood on weaker ground. Not only must earthly

wisdom be foolish but apparent foolishness must be wisdom--both halves of the equation are necessary. Lactantius kept this double equation in mind two hundred or so years later: "Just as the wisdom of men is the height of foolishness with God, foolishness, as I explained, is the greatest wisdom, so he is lowly and despised with God who was conspicuous and lofty upon earth."23 St. Jerome's jaundiced view of man compares Paul's perception with that of Jeremiah 10.14, "Every man is brutish in his knowledge," because of offerings to pagan idols--which is hardly the same as the philosophic writings of Plato or Aristotle. Even so the religious habit was seized upon as proof that Greek philosophy was fraudulent.

Chrysostom employs both reason and emotion to convey his attitude on the subject. Analytically writing about the double equation of wisdom and foolishness, he says, "Since by this wisdom [about the earth and the heavens] the world was unwilling to acknowledge God, He employed what seemed to be foolishness, i.e. the Gospel, to persuade man; not by reasonings, but by faith. Reason can tell man that a powerful God created earth, but faith assumes control after that realization." However, he then thunders like Jerome: "The tenets of the Greeks indeed are rightly questioned. For they were of that nature, being but disputes, conflicts of reasonings, and doubts, and conclusions. But ours are far from all these. For human wisdom invented theirs, but ours were taught by the grace of the Spirit. Their doctrines are madness and folly, ours are true wisdom."24 This uncompromising attitude would have regarded Adam's questions to Raphael about the universe in Paradise Lost as an example of the spirit of Greek wisdom. Certitude becomes the touchstone of belief; all else is rejected since it is transmitted through man's reason. Thus reason cannot be the vehicle of a demonstration of God's revelation--only faith based on Scripture can.

By the time of the Renaissance the traditions of sceptically regarding human wisdom provided a counter-attack to the claims of the Humanists in their new discoveries in learning. This biblical scepticism

264

conveniently found a partner in classical scepticism as seen in Pyrrho and the other Sceptics. A perfect example of this union may be found in Montaigne's famous In Defense of Raymond Sebond, sometimes known as An Apology. . . . .(As Arthur H. Beattie notes, as of 1576, Sextus Empiricus' version of Pyrrho had a substantial effect on Montaigne's thinking.[25]) Montaigne affirmed that faith could provide man with the truth that reason could not, and the Defense illustrates the French philosopher's attitudes through allusions to both Scripture and the classics. Montaigne's trenchant description of man's foolish wisdom prepares the reader for Milton's portrait of the Son in Paradise Regain'd in the intensity of the dismissal of human questioning:

> Let us then consider for the moment man alone, without outside help, armed only with his own weapons, and stripped of grace and divine understanding, which are all his honor, his strength, and the foundation of his being. Let us see what kind of figure he cuts in such fine array. Let him make me understand by the effort of his reason upon what foundations he has built those great advantages which he thinks he has over all other creatures. What has convinced him that this admirable motion of the vault of heaven, the eternal light of those torches revolving so proudly above his head, the awe-inspiring movements of that infinite sea, were established and have continued for so many centuries for his convenience and in order to serve him? Is it possible to imagine anything so ridiculous as that wretched and puny creature, who is not even master of himself, exposed to offenses from all things, and who yet proclaims himself master and emperor of the universe, concerning which it is not within his power to know the slightest part, let alone govern it?[26]

Both John Colet and John Calvin see the situation in the same light. For Colet the problem resides not just in wisdom but in having trust, of the philosopher or thinker beginning to trust more in himself than in God, a familiar Renaissance theme. Man should "lay aside altogether every conceit of knowledge, and all trust in himself and in his own strength." Explicating the first chapter of First Corinthians, he invites men who had not been accounted wise to embrace the wisdom of God and then become both wise and powerful.[27] Calvin posits the conclusion that man should have learned wisdom from viewing the works of God, but because he did not, God called man "to the faith of Christ, which, because it appears foolish, the unbelievers despise." Keeping one eye on Scholasticism, he remarks that God traps the knowledgeable in their own knowledge and that God can more easily be discovered in his works than in man's airy speculations. Calvin also takes an extreme rhetorical position when he asserts that man's wisdom will "stink in its very foolishness."[28]

To reverse the chronology slightly, a look at the early history of the church may be in order so that some dissenters from a wholesale repudiation of human wisdom may stand out in relief.

Clement of Alexandria (c. 215) was reluctant to oppose or even forego the pursuit of knowledge or gnosis. With his Hellenistic leanings Clement refused to believe that Paul's rejection of worldly wisdom applied to all wisdom or knowledge pursued by all men. For him it was applied to sophistry and superficial learning. He clings to the gnostic idea that knowledge is a kind of mystery belonging only to a special elite. Those who have a habit of cynical criticism do not deserve the gnosis of the Christian redemption. When Paul ridicules the "wisdom of the wise," he is speaking of those "who devote their attention to empty words," these σοφούς, who "are skilled in words and arts." Clement insists that true philosophy offers a foundation for piety for the Greeks just as the Law was a preparation for the Jews.[29] Isaiah 40.13 and Wisdom had suggested the relationship between the Spirit (pneuma) and Intelligence (nous), which allowed a justification for a Christian desire for knowledge.[30] Philo of Alexandria had encouraged and taught a religion of the spirit, and similar Greek influences had stressed human intelligence as preparation for spiritual gifts.

At first glance it might appear that Clement is
setting up an antithesis between the wisdom of Scriptures and the wisdom of Greek philosophy and favoring
the latter, a stance explicitly conflicting with
Paul's statements on the subject--but not so. Clement
directs those extolling human knowledge to the Bible:
"But if human wisdom, as it remains to understand, is
the glorying in knowledge, hear the law of Scripture:
'Let not the wise man glory in his wisdom, and let
not the mighty man glory in his might; but let him
that glorieth glory in the Lord'. But we are God-
taught, and glory in the name of Christ."[31] For
Clement then the misuse of human wisdom lies in glorying in and opposing it to the wisdom of God, precisely
what Paul had vociferously condemned. He summarizes
this position succinctly: "we showed in the first
Miscellany that the philosophers of the Greeks are
called thieves, inasmuch as they have taken without
acknowledgement their principal dogmas from Moses and
the prophets." An echo of this belief is found in
the Son's rejection of Greek wisdom in Paradise
Regain'd (IV.336-342). Indeed Clement is angry that
the Greeks, according to him, have plagiarized from
the Hebrews, and he devotes a whole chapter to the
subject: "Greek Plagiarism from the Hebrews." Clement glosses the term "inflated" or "puffed up" from
I Corinthians 4.19 to characterize knowledge with the
argument that God "produces trust in the truth and
expansion of mind" through the study of Scripture,
contradicting knowledge which merely results in sin.[32]

One of the reasons that Clement's attitude did
not exert a significant influence on the later Church
Fathers is that he insisted on using the controversial
word gnostic to typify the man and the philosophy he
advocated.[33] St. Paul himself has been attacked as
a gnostic, as someone preaching a secret religion of
mystery for a special elite, but the simplest rebuttal
of that charge is Paul's continual emphasis on the
universality of Christ's redemption for all men:
"There is neither Jew nor Greek, there is neither bond
nor free, there is neither male nor female: for ye
are all one in Christ" (Gal. 3.28). Clement emphasizes the man who has become a Gnostic or "Perfect
Man," who has come to understand the gnosis of

Christianity, distinguishing him from the mass of
men. Those who reject the Redemption which opens
men's minds and teaches them, are simply fools.[34]
This perfect man is analogous to Chrysostom's "spiritual man" (I Cor. 2.14-16) whom Paul opposes to the
natural or carnal man. The spiritual man knows of
things present and of things to come, but Christ, not
Plato or Pythagoras, puts "His own things into our
mind."[35] (Significantly Paul, Clement, and Chrysostom
all were Hellenically oriented.) To place Clement in
clearer perspective, however, although he praises the
gnostic or perfect man, the gnosis that is essential
is the knowledge of Scripture, not of any occult
mystery which lies hidden from the natural or carnal
man. No matter how learned the gnostic may be in
Greek knowledge, he must ascend higher: "For Paul too,
in the Epistles, plainly does not disparage philosophy;
but deems it unworthy of the man who has attained to
the elevation of the Gnostic, any more to go back to
the Hellenic 'philosophy,' figuratively calling it
'the rudiments of this world'" [Col. 2.8]. Greek
philosophy was designed as a stepping stone to the
philosophy of Christ in contrast to the beliefs of
Epicurus, which are "voluptuous and selfish philosophy," more concerned with the things of the world than
with the spiritual.[36]

Central in Clement is this insistence on the
distinction between two kinds of philosophy or knowledge. That wisdom founded on faith in Christ is the
only true wisdom ultimately; and knowledge leading to
self-congratulation is foolish or that concerned with
things of the body (like the Stoic or Epicurean) is
sinful.[37] Philosophers are merely children unless
they are united with Christ. Nevertheless there is a
place for Greek philosophy which is not sophistic,
arrogant, or carnal, and Clement's adoption of this
attitude toward the heritage of Greece stands in sharp
contrast to the more central position of the church in
the Renaissance and even after, for Clement does admit
that "truth, and to some extent saving truth, was to
be found in Greek philosophy."[38] As we have seen
above, Calvin and many other Reformers could not accept
such a moderate compromise, and, as we shall see, Milton gave the extreme position to his protagonists or

268

spokesmen in <u>Paradise Regain'd</u> and <u>Paradise Lost</u>.   On
the other hand, his own life is a testimony to his
acceptance of the medial position of perceiving the
value of a Plato or an Aristotle, despite the tradition
of contempt for "foolish wisdom."

One of the problems in advancing the knowledge
of men, as Paul saw it, is the arrogance and lack of
charity that it sometimes produces. Thus he admonishes
his readers on that basis: "Knowledge puffeth up, but
charity edifieth"; and "this I pray, that your love may
abound yet more and more in knowledge and in all judgment" (I Cor. 8.1; Phil. 1.9). If the Acts offer a
reasonably accurate account of the reception that Paul
received in Athens, the ridicule of the Greek intellectual created in Paul a realization that charity
must accompany knowledge. Irenaeus cites several passages in Corinthians on the necessity for charity, and
he devotes a whole chapter to the thesis, "Knowledge
Puffeth Up, But Love Edifieth." He maintains "not
that he ⌊Paul⌋ meant to inveigh against a true knowledge of God, for in that case he would have accused
himself; but, because he knew that some, puffed up
by the pretence of knowledge, fall away from the love
of God, and imagine that they themselves are perfect."39
Chrysostom iterates this simple point as well; commenting on I Corinthians 8.1, he indicates that knowledge, "when it is without charity, it lifts men up to
absolute arrogance."40 When the advancement of the
ego or self (the sarx) constitutes the goal of knowledge, this is a sinful inflation of the self at the
expense of the divine. Augustine also reminded his
readers of the importance of two fit duties of the
Christian love and contemplation.41

In the Renaissance the same pair of qualities
received attention for the same reasons. John Colet
admits that knowledge is valid but on the condition
that it is accompanied by a love of God, which is
manifested through a love of others. Man must con-
fess his ignorance or else suffer the loss of divine
grace.42 Calvin paraphrases the key passage in Corinthians and adds his own comment: "Now that <u>knowledge</u>
of which you boast, O ye Corinthians, is altogether
opposed to <u>love</u>, for it <u>puffs up</u> with pride, and leads

to contempt of the brethren, while _love_ is concerned
for the welfare of brethren, and exhorts us to _edify_
them. . . . We must, therefore, lay it down as a
settled principle, that knowledge is good in itself;
but as piety is its only foundation, it becomes empty
and useless in 'wicked men'."[43] Both Calvin and Colet
agree that knowledge (outside of the purely religious)
is not intrinsically evil or foolish and that its
proper concomitant must be love, not only of God but
of men. Hardin Craig points out this concept in Hooker
and Bacon and in _Paradise Lost_: "Hooker's doctrine of
evil does not differ from that of Bacon as expressed
in 'Of Goodness and Goodness of Nature': 'Goodness
answers to the theological virtue of Charity, and admits
no excess, but error. The desire of power in excess
caused the angels to fall; the desire of knowledge in
excess caused man to fall: but in charity there is no
excess; neither can angel or man come in danger by it'."
This also Milton confirms in the third book of _Paradise
Lost_ in the speech of the Almighty on freedom to choose:

> The first sort by their own suggestion fell,
> Self-tempted, self-depraved . . . . (III.129-130)

Satan's atheism in the fifth book and elsewhere exem-
plifies the same conception of sin."[44]

One of the basic distinctions made by St. Paul
in his references to _gnosis_ or knowledge is that between
the spirit and the flesh. To the Romans he opposes two
states of mind:

> For they that are after the flesh
> do mind the things of the flesh; but
> they that are after the Spirit the
> things of the Spirit.
>
> For to be carnally minded is
> death; but to be spiritually minded
> is life and peace. (8.5-6)

To the Corinthians he contrasts the simplicity of the
worship of God with sophistication: "For our rejoicing
is this, the testimony of our conscience, that in simplicity and godly sincerity, not with fleshly wisdom,
but by the grace of God, we have had our conversation
in the world, and more abundantly to you-ward [sic]"
(II Cor. 1.12). And to the Colossians, he warns them

270

not to be upset by charges from intellectuals that
their belief in angels is naive: "Let no man beguile
you of your regard in a voluntary humility and worshipping of angels, intruding those things which he
hath not seen, vainly puffed up by his fleshly mind"
(2.18). In translations of Romans 8.6, the antithesis
between carnally minded and spiritually minded can be
variously rendered as psychic vs. pneumatic or animal
vs. spiritual.[45] Chapter One of this study discussed
the proper etymon for the term flesh as it appears in
the Epistles, but it is sufficient to note here that
the carnal, fleshly, or psychic refers to the manner in
which the world and not the Spirit views reality, the
world of "foolish wisdom." Origen, glossing I Corinthians 1.18 on the foolishness of wisdom, makes the
Pauline distinction between wisdom according to the
flesh (kata sarka) and according to the spirit, encour-
aging an ascent from the knowledge of things visible
to things invisible.[46]

The Reformers also noted the distinction between
the two kinds of knowledge and argued that the knowledge which men glorified in as their own was carnal
and opposed to the spirit. Luther, when speaking of
works as opposed to salvation by Christ and the Spirit,
links together "wisdom and works of the flesh" in that
both are products of the human ego and not of Christ.
Works do not provide a "new creation, a work of the
Holy Spirit, who implants a new intellect and will and
confers the power to curb the flesh and to flee the
righteousness and wisdom of the world."[47] Calvin remarks that Paul "gives the name of fleshly wisdom to
everything apart from Christ, that procures for us the
reputation of wisdom," and that in essence the "fleshly mind" of the Colossians means depending upon one's
own reason, "mere wind." And this is precisely what
the pseudo- or false apostles did in their struggle
against Paul.[48] Calvin reviews in detail the radical
but central view of Paul, that fleshly wisdom is empty
because it relies upon man and not God:

Nor is it without good reason that he inveighs so
vehemently against the wisdom of men, for it is
impossible to express how difficult a thing it is
to eradicate from men's minds a misdirected confidence

271

in the flesh, that they may not claim for themselves more than is reasonable. . . . a knowledge of all the sciences is mere smoke, where
the heavenly science of Christ is wanting; and
man, with all his acuteness, is as stupid for
obtaining of himself a knowledge of the mysteries
of God, as an ass is unqualified for understanding
musical harmonies.[49]

The basis for Calvin's jaundiced belief in human wisdom is his assumption that "nothing is more at variance with the grace of God than man's natural ability,
and so as to other things. Hence the only foundation
of Christ's kingdom is the abasement of men."[50]

Other commentators in the Reformation followed
Calvin's lead, and specifically Juan Valdes addresses
the problem in terms of man's wisdom being <u>carnal</u>:
"The carnally wise . . . who know that, which human
letters and human prudence teach. . . . they also see
the men, whom they hold to be ignorant, weak, vile
and contemptible, admitted to their enjoyment."[51]

Such a position as Calvin and Valdes take is
directly hostile to the kind of humanism represented
by an Erasmus or a More and indeed ignores the creation of man in Genesis as the image and likeness of
God. Milton refers to "this fleshly wisdom and pride,"
"the proud reasonings of the flesh," and "doctrine of
carnall might as Prelaty is" but in the context of
attacking the ceremonies and traditions of the bishops
and of Rome and not in general condemning humane
knowledge. He praises Wyclif's "example" and "his
reforming Spirit warring against human Principles and
carnall sense, the pride of flesh that still cry'd up
Antiquity, Custome, Canons, Councels and Lawes, and
cry'd down the truth for novelties, schisme, profane-
nesse, and Sacriledge" and rebukes the "fleshly
reasonings" of papacy and episcopacy.[52] And so Milton does not believe in "the abasement of men" as did
Calvin; indeed his portrait of Adam, whether before
the Fall or after, is hardly designed to abase him.

Milton's thesis on the foolishness of wisdom in
<u>Paradise Lost</u> focuses on the desire for this wisdom

272

as at least part of the basis for the fall of both
angels and men, although Adam himself falls out of
sentimental uxoriousness and not the search for
knowledge, as does Eve in partial measure. John M.
Steadman reminds us that, with reference to both of
Milton's epics, the heroism of the hero is partly produced by his realization of _sapientia_ and of his own
limited understanding. Samson, on the contrary, is
"heroically strong rather than heroically wise,"[53]
although he does advance in "heroic knowledge," to
use the phrase of Milton and Arnold Stein. In _Para-
dise Lost_, on the other hand, the reader encounters
creatures who assume the value of their secular knowledge. The first portrait of philosophers in the poem
ironically presents a group of the fallen angels in
Hell who, with nothing else to do, ponder serious
philosophic problems:

> Others apart sat on a hill retired,
> In thoughts more elevate, and reasoned high
> Of providence, foreknowledge, will, and fate,
> Fixed fate, free will, foreknowledge absolute,
> And found no end, in wand'ring mazes lost.
>
> (II.557-561)

Later Raphael tells Adam about the nature of angelic
knowledge, its intuitiveness, but the fallen angels
can intuit nothing but create various philosophical
categories, spinning cobwebs like the Scholasticism
that both Bacon and Calvin debunked. The absolute
irony in this passage rests on the basic fact of the
poem that they have been on the inside, to use a
slang expression, and have learned nothing from the
way that God the Father functions. They have fallen
because of their rejection of God's wisdom and power
and his demand of their obedience, but now they can
only philosophize "in wand'ring mazes lost" on the
outside.

The invocation to Book Seven immediately suggests
that the theme of proper vs. foolish wisdom will be
its concern since Urania is depicted as conversing
eternally with Wisdom before the Father (VII.9-12.
See Prov. 8.22-30 and Wisdom of Solomon 7-8). The
importance of the wisdom related in this book is that
it directly assists man in his pilgrimage toward God

273

by demonstrating his love through the Creation, in contradistinction to the sort of learning that Adam later requests in Book Eight. In Book Seven Adam makes his appeal for wisdom within the parameters of salvation:

> But since thou hast vouchsafed
> Gently for our instruction to impart
> Things above earthly thought, which yet concerned
> Our knowing, as to highest Wisdom seemed,
> Deign to descend now lower, and relate
> What may no less perhaps avail us known:
> How first began this heav'n which we behold.
>
> (80-86)

Raphael accedes to Adam's wish but first cautions him about the nature of wisdom, which must be designed "To glorify the Maker" and within lawful bounds; else an excessive desire leads to folly and flatulence (VII. 111-130). Book Seven also ends on this note. In the context of the Pauline tradition on the foolishness of earthly wisdom, this is a reasonable limitation for Adam. Much earlier, in Book Four, the narrator had praised the happiness of the wedded life of Adam and Eve, but, with a touch of poignancy, had interpolated the injunction, ". . . O yet happiest if ye seek/ No happier state, and know to know no more" (II.774-775).

Nevertheless, the impulse in Adam toward scientia and not just sapientia, toward earthly wisdom and not celestial wisdom, is too strong, and in Book Eight he continues his pursuit of knowledge.[54] Like a Rabelaisian character, Adam still has a great thirst for knowledge generated by the inductive nature of his thoughts about the superfluity of nature. In terms of the cultural patterns of seventeenth-century England, Eve retires before Raphael begins his explanation of astronomy, which proves to be less than enlightening. It is interesting that Adam asks all the theologically wrong questions, but Eve is later the one who succumbs to the temptation of foolish wisdom. Raphael does not blame Adam for asking his questions as long as it is put in the context of learning more about his creator's greatness and wisdom. Nevertheless, he is not very informative with his "What if . . .?" answers (11.122-166), speculating on instead of informing Adam

274

about the accuracy of the Ptolemaic or Copernican
systems. At the end of his questionable answers,
Raphael again warns Adam about asking the wrong questions:

> . . . . joy thou
> In what he gives to thee, this Paradise
> And thy fair Eve; heav'n is for thee too high
> To know what passes there; be lowly wise:
> Think only what concerns thee and thy being;
> Dream not of other worlds, what creatures there
> Live, in what state, condition, or degree,
> Contented that thus far hath been revealed
> Not of earth only but of highest heav'n.
>
> (11.170-178)

Adam totally agrees with the admonition of Raphael,
perhaps too readily, and the narrator describes him
as "cleared of doubt," although the less than reverent
modern reader may demur and insist that the teacher
never answered the student's question.

Although Eve did not ask any questions about the
workings of the heavens nor manifest any desire for
worldly wisdom, she later falls for the kind of empty
rhetoric that Augustine and Calvin had chastized as
foolishness. One is reminded, in looking at the
temptation of Eve, of the claims for expanded consciousness advanced by the drug culture in American
society. Satan as serpent avers that as a result of
eating the fruit he has experienced expanded consciousness, that his "capacious mind" draws in all on heaven
and earth, all that is good and beautiful, and that he
sees her as the epitome of both (IX.598-608). Eve,
in seeking after foolish wisdom, is intelligent enough
to be able to realize this is exaggerated flattery,
but during the seduction scene, it never occurs to
her that this serpent is the enemy she was warned
against and that the fruit he is extolling is the very
one that has been interdicted. When she sees that this
is indeed the forbidden apple, she informs the serpent
of the interdiction and adds, with the unconscious
irony of a naive humanist, that "our reason is our law"
(IX.654). If Eve is not wary of her adversary, the
narrator surely is, for he carefully relates Satan's
performance to an orator of Athens or Rome, the

sophisticated intellectuals who, in most cases,
ridiculed the foolishness of the wisdom of Christianity which St. Paul preached. Eve is unable to discern
the speciousness of Satan's rhetoric (a department of
foolish wisdom), especially when he boasts of the
"Life more perfect" that he now lives (IX.685-690)--
all this from a snake who is still a snake.

When Eve is about to eat the fruit, she first
manages, in a long passage of the sophistry warned
against by the Church Fathers and the Reformers, to
persuade herself to eat the apple. She shrewdly notes
that the fact of prohibition is enough to make the
fruit more enticing, that this enticement implies some
good unknown and therefore not bad, that this good
will make them wise, that the serpent is not dead but
alive and rational, that the serpent is a friend, and
that the fruit divine will make her wise (IX.745-789).
There are more unexamined assumptions and equivoca-
tions in this sorites than the casual reader might
see immediately, but this summary of them isolates and
set them in proper perspective. The intellectual and
moral dishonesty that ensues upon her fall are outside the range of the subject of the pursuit of earthly
wisdom and are so obvious as to need little or no comment here. Eve tells her tale of sorrow without
comprehending the full import of her actions, "with
count'nance blithe." Douglas Bush remarks that the
epithet is "One of the most telling of the many significant epithets in the stage directions of this drama;
Eve has no awareness of what she has done."55 Adam
at first responds by affirming the horror of Eve's
act, but then he begins the same pattern of rationali-
zation of the action of Eve and his own intended
action, to die with Eve, an archetypal pattern of the
first _liebestod_ in the providential history of man.
All of the warnings by Raphael in Books Seven and
Eight have failed because Eve, who should have listened to the affable archangel, chose to play the
role of the bourgeois housewife and allow the men to
have an after-dinner conversation by themselves (without the brandy and cigars). The target of Raphael's
admonitions, Adam, does not fall in a quest after
earthly wisdom but from sentimentalism.

At the end of Michael's summary of history in
Book Twelve, Adam acknowledges the lesson of St.
Paul's injunction about the foolishness of the earth-
ly wise:

> Greatly instructed I shall hence depart,
> Greatly in peace of thought, and have my fill
> Of knowledge, what this vessel can contain;
> Beyond which was my folly to aspire. (XII.557-560)

It is important to keep in mind that the element of
knowledge is defined as "folly" and not in terms of
the knowledge as necessarily forbidden. There is
nothing intrinsically evil in this scientia, but it
must be measured in a scale of hierarchical values
in which true sapientia has a higher place; that is,
the lower knowledge only becomes evil when it is set
above the higher. This is precisely what Eve did and
precisely why she fell. Adam continues in his epiphany to comprehend the providence of God in terms of
good over evil, weak over strong, meek over wise:

> Accomplishing great things, by things deemed weak
> Subverting worldly strong, and worldly wise
> By simply meek; . . . . (XII.567-569)

The poem concludes on the pairs of antitheses that St.
Paul had made famous: weakness over strength and
things "meek" (a meaningful substitution for "foolish")
over things "worldly wise."

This scale of intellectual values is reaffirmed
by the Son in the fourth book of Paradise Regain'd in
his rejection of the temptation of Athens. Throughout the respective temptations and rejections, the
narrator had carefully placed epithets at the beginning of each, and in this case, "our Saviour sagely
thus replied" (IV.285). He characterizes earthly wisdom (historically in line with St. Paul's concept) as
unnecessary in the context of "Light from above,"
although he admits that some of these doctrines may be
"granted true." He rejects this wisdom not on any
basis of sin or evil but on the grounds of its ten-
tative accuracy or inaccuracy. Next he turns the arguments of Socrates against Satan in that the former had
admitted that he only knew that he knew nothing, and
the remainder of the Son's rebuttal deals with the

277

self-centeredness and arrogance of intellectuals who
leave God out of their considerations or else depict
him as Fate. This rebuttal perfectly summarizes what
happened to the fallen angels and Eve, and the Son
makes the point that they are ignorant of "how man
fell" (IV.285-330). Paradoxically, man and angel fell
because of their desire for earthly wisdom, and the
earthly philosophers don't understand how man fell
precisely because their intellects have been clouded
as a result of the Fall. The more worldly knowledge
is sought in preference to God's wisdom, the less is
achieved.

The antidote to this search for the wisdom of
the world, in St. Paul's terms, is "Christ crucified,"
ironically termed "foolishness" by the apostle; but
in _Paradise Regain'd_'s time scheme, the Son has not
yet been crucified and does not know even that he is
the anointed one, the Christ. The terrible irony for
Satan here is that he is preaching earthly wisdom to
the _logos_ himself who will soon replace the wisdom of
the world as the source of truth. W. Wrede pointed
out that the devils are fooled by God's wisdom into
crucifying Christ, as is suggested by I Corinthians
2.6-8.[56] St. Basil had said, "But if the Prince of
this world, the supreme, consummate, and invisible
master of worldly wisdom, is caught in his own traps
and ends finally in ultimate folly, far more will his
followers and supporters be thus ensnared, even though
they devise a thousand wiles; 'professing themselves
to be wise, they became fools'."[57]

Milton's message in both poems, especially in
the latter, may appear strong or excessive to the modern mind, which is dedicated to _scientia,_ but this
knowledge must be arranged in proper perspective.
Although a humanist himself, Milton had read deeply
in the Church Fathers and in the Reformers and had
imbibed their distrust of human reason and the pursuit
of worldly wisdom. This side of him conflicted with
his own deep classical learning and his support of it in
Of Education and throughout his writings.[58] The sum
of his attitude may be found in _Of Christian Doctrine_:

To wisdom is opposed folly; which consists, first
and chiefly, in an ignorance of the will of God. . . .

> Secondly, in a false conceit of wisdom. . . .
>
> Thirdly, in a prying into hidden things, after the example of our first parents. . . .
>
> Fourthly, in human or carnal wisdom.[59]

This apparently anti-intellectual viewpoint was echoed, as we have seen, by others in the Renaissance, and one of the most eloquent statement is found in Montaigne's "In Defense of Raymond Sebond":

> What does truth preach to us when it instructs us to flee worldly philosophy, when it inculcates in us so often that its wisdom is only folly in the sight of God; that, of all vanities, the most vain is man; that the man who is proud of his knowledge does not yet know what knowledge is; and that man, who is nothing, is deluding and deceiving himself if he thinks he is something? These maxims of the Holy Spirit express so clearly and so precisely what I wish to maintain that I should need no other proof against people who would bow with complete submission and obedience to its authority.[60]

For whatever reasons, and one can only speculate, the corollary theme to that of foolish wisdom, the strength of weakness, did not receive as much attention among Christian thinkers (in the light of Christ's Redemption) as did the denigration of sophisticated learning. Jesus had indeed said that the meek would inherit the earth, but it may have been that Western Christianity ignored that prophecy or else regarded it as pertaining only to saints and not to all men. Certainly, to attack verbally universities or philosophers has never been a truly dangerous pastime; equally certainly to assault by words those in positions of military or political power holds the definite possibility of retort stronger than the philosophical or rhetorical. In any case, those commenting on St. Paul's Epistles did not notably amplify this theme, but Paulus Orosius, a theological historian, glorified the habit of God in choosing the weak "to confound the strong" in the context of the disintegration of the Roman Empire, an object lesson for those who put their faith in might. Like Augustine, who had asked Orosius to write the history, he denies that

Christians had anything to do with the fall of Rome.[61]
However, Orosius represents an exception to the pattern.
Those commenting on the Epistles of St. Paul did not
notably amplify this theme, and so Milton's strong
emphasis on it reflects his willingness to fly in the
face of established bases of power. The political-
religious treatises he wrote on the verge of the return of Charles II to England and power, A Treatise of
Civil Power, Considerations, and the Ready and Easy
Way, testify to his capacity to act on his principles
in the face of possible disaster.

Somewhat earlier, John Calvin, commenting on
First Corinthians, had exalted the levelling impact
of God's Providence, appearing to take pleasure in
demeaning those in positions of power and influence.
"God," he says, "therefore, by confounding the mighty,
and the wise, and the great, does not design to elate
with pride the weak, the illiterate, and the abject,
but brings down all of them together to one level."[62]
The closeness of John Colet's thoughts on the subject
to Milton's is remarkable in the former's foci: the
concept of the Christian warrior, the relation between
the virtue of patience, and the correlation between the
weak overcoming the strong and good overcoming evil.
Thus Colet remarks that "the Christian warrior's prowess is his patience, his action is suffering, and his
victory, a sure trust in God" and that "patience is
itself true fortitude."[63] Colet had observed that this
was Paul's advice to the Roman Christians living under
possibly hostile magistrates, but his interpretation
of Romans applies beautifully to a hero like Samson,
who needed the virtues of patience, trust, and fortitude in opposition to the strength he formerly had
depended upon.

Milton had consistently favored the paradox of
strength. William R. Parker pointed out that Christopher Arnold, a traveller from Europe, on November 19,
1651, had encouraged Milton to write in his album a
souvenir to remind him of their meeting. Milton
agreed and dictated to a secretary a Greek passage
from II Corinthians 12.9, "My strength is made perfect
in weakness," to which Milton signed his name.[64] John
M. Steadman's study of Renaissance heroism has pointed
out how deeply Milton was committed to this paradox.[65]

Of Reformation (1641) had associated the fate of the
Protestant martyrs with the paradox of strength in
weakness in the summary of the sufferings of the pre-
vious centuries, although, as Don M. Wolfe reminded
students of Milton, he did not mention the famous Acts
and Monuments of John Foxe which, like Milton, traced
the Reformation back to John Wycliff in the fourteenth
century. It is worth quoting Milton's grand description:

> Then was the Sacred BIBLE sought out of the
> dusty corners where prophane Falshood and
> Neglect had thrown it, the Schooles opened,
> Divine and Humane Learning rak't out of the
> embers of forgotten Tongues, the Princes and
> Cities trooping apace to the new erected
> Banner of Salvation; the Martyrs, with the
> unresistable might of Weaknesse, shaking the
> Powers of Darknesse, and scorning the fiery
> rage of the old red Dragon.

He confesses to some alleged confusion about whether
the bishops have joined together with the "prevalent
things of this world" to lord it over the weak things
through which Christ ministered.[66] Milton envisions
the power of the prelates as the strength of the
world, which has no true authority and is nothing but
"Christian censorship," noting that, in fact, the
prelates have embraced the side of worldly might and
not the side of divine weakness, in direct opposition
to the intention of Christ.[67]

On a personal level, in the Second Defence, Milton answers those who censure him for his blindness
by admitting that he is not ashamed to be categorized,
sightless as he is, with "the blind, the afflicted,
the suffering, and the weak," citing the teaching of
St. Paul on the path of weakness to strength.[68] If
St. Paul, when inverting the strong and the weak, had
in mind the secular powers of the world, John Milton,
in Reason, focused on the ecclesiastical power of the
prelates in opposition to the thrust of Christ's
teaching in the beatitudes and St. Paul's rejection of
might. He astutely equates the episcopal form of
government with the kind of worldly and military power
that the Son rejected in Paradise Regain'd:

> . . . yet God when he meant to subdue the world
> and hell at once, part of that to salvation, and
> this wholy to perdition, made chois of no other
> weapons, or auxiliaries then these whether to
> save, or to destroy. It had bin a small maistery
> for him to have drawn out his Legions into array,
> and flankt them with his thunder; therefore he
> sent Foolishness to confute Wisdom, Weaknes to
> bind Strength, Despisednes to vanquish Pride.
> And this is the great mistery of the Gospel made
> good in Christ himself, who as he testifies came
> not to be minister'd to, but to minister; and
> must be fulfil'd in all his ministers till his
> second comming. To goe against these principles
> S. Paul so fear'd, that if he should but affect
> the wisdom of words in his preaching, he thought
> it would be laid to his charge, that he had made
> the crosse of Christ to be of none effect.[69]

Next he identifies the Gospel with weakness and strength
with "mans reasoning," thus conflating the twin themes
of paradoxical foolishness and weakness as St. Paul had
done. The prelates have chosen to embroider the simplicity of the Gospel with the pomp of ceremonies, and in
doing so, they have run counter to the work of Christ.
Both the wisdom of tradition and the power of "fleshly
ceremony" have adulterated the pure doctrine of God.[70]

In his next chapter Milton attacks the juris-
dictional powers of the prelates in much the same manner as he had abused the historical origins of episcopacy and its ceremonies. With vigorous sarcasm Milton
lampoons the attempts of the prelates to impose religion through legal sanctions. He employs the dual
mirror image of the contrast of Jesus riding on a
humble ass being lionized with the endeavors of episcopacy to play the lion and instead be transformed
into an ass:

> But it is observable that so long as the Church
> in true imitation of Christ can be content to
> ride upon an Asse carrying her self and her
> government along in a mean and simple guise,
> she may be as he is, a Lion of the tribe of
> Juda, and in her humility all men with loud
> Hosanna's will confesse her greatnes.. But

when despising the mighty operation of the
spirit by the weak things of this world she
thinks to make her self bigger and more con-
siderable by using the way of civil force
and jurisdiction, as she sits upon this Lion
she changes into an Asse, and instead of
Hosanna's every man pelts her with stones and
dirt.[71]

Rather the church should, according to Milton, follow
the spiritual therapy of healing a man's sins with
gentle admonition in the spirit of II Corinthians
10.4-5 so that "ministeriall warfare, not carnal,"
will properly cure the inner diseases of man. Unfortunately the prelates have thrown in with the powers
of the world, the courts and legal authorities, to
function in hostility to the work of Christ, in essence
becoming his enemies, "smothering and extinguishing
the spirituall force of his bodily weaknesse in the
discipline of his Church with the boistrous and carnall tyranny of an undue, unlawful and ungospellike
jurisdiction."[72] This represents the distance that
prelacy has travelled from the original meaning of
Christianity.

The same Pauline theme reappears years later in
A Treatise of Civil power in Ecclesiastical causes, in
which Milton insists that the power of the magistrate
should not intrude into ecclesiastical matters.
Paul's paradox of God's weakness fits in neatly with
the central argument: "And since it is the councel
and set purpose of God in the gospel by spiritual
means which are counted weak, to overcom all power
which resists him; let them not go about to do that
by worldly strength which he hath decreed to do by
those means which the world counts weakness, least
they be again obnoxious to that saying which in another
place is also written of the Pharisee, Luke 7.30. that
they frustrated the councel of God." Milton goes on
to build on this fundamental concept the thesis that
if the church cannot follow weakness, then it should
at least not use force to compel in matters of faith.[73]

Paradise Lost dramatically and symbolically represents the paradox of strength in weakness over worldly
power, especially heroic power, as represented by Satan

and his legions. Satan does not understand the paradox and assumes that he must compete with God for power and that he can wrest power by means of military potency. The War in Heaven illustrates this misunderstanding, which is shared by Michael and the good angels, who do not realize that there is a limit to their military capacity. Only the Son has the means of driving the angelic forces of evil into hell. Satan never learns this lesson because, soon after his arrival in hell, he tells Beelzebub: "Fall'n Cherub, to be weak is miserable" (I.157). And so, in Book IV, when he is confronted by Gabriel and the host of good angels, he is humiliated by the knowledge that he is physically weak and unable to combat his foes, as the scales in heaven prove to him. His becoming physically weaker is not counterbalanced by any corresponding movement toward spiritual might, and so he suffers agonies. Adam, on the other hand, at the end of the epic, although he has lost earthly paradise and is therefore subject to the weakness of the human condition, with its concomitant disease and death, learns the manner of God's Providence, that God is

> Merciful over all his works, with good
> Still overcoming evil, and by small
> Accomplishing great things, by things deemed weak
> Subverting worldly strong, and worldly wise
> By simply meek; that suffering for truth's sake
> Is fortitude to highest victory,
> And to the faithful the gate of life.   (XII.565-571)

The Son, in _Paradise Regain'd_, is the very embodiment of the problem for the Jewish nation of seeking a Messiah who will deliver it from the Romans in a military or political fashion. Consequently the basis of the temptation of Parthian or Roman military power consists in the Pauline rejection of such might, a rejection a young Jew of the first century would find difficult. He would naturally be drawn toward fulfilling his mission in a dramatic way rather than being executed on a cross like a common criminal. The Father in heaven describes the planned temptation in the context of St. Paul's warfare of weakness and heroism of humility:

> There he shall first lay down the rudiments
> Of his great warfare, ere I send him forth

To conquer Sin and Death, the two grand foes,
By humiliation and strong sufferance:
His weakness shall o'ercome Satanic strength
And all the world, and mass of sinful flesh.
                                    (I.157-162)

When Satan offers the impressive panoply of war to the
Son, he is "unmoved" and rejects outright the ostenta-
tion of wars and battle, reminding Satan rather that
he does not need them and that, as Jesus said at the
wedding feast at Cana, his time "is not yet come."
For the Son the paraphernalia of war is just

                    . . . that cumbersome
Luggage of war there shown me, argument
Of human weakness rather than of strength.
                                    (III.400-402)

The Son stands in contrast to the Hebraic hero,
Samson, whose strength is basically physical, both in
the Book of Judges and in Milton's poem. Even though
Samson in the latter work learns that patience and
trust in God are necessary (as does the Son), yet it
is his physical prowess that tumbles down the Philis-
tine amphitheater and defeats the enemies of the god
of the tribe of Dan. The contrast between Samson and
the Son thus rests upon the Pauline inversion of
weakness and strength.

NOTES: CHAPTER FIVE

[1]Christian, p. 11.

[2]On Corinthians I, p. 40.

[3]Christian, p. 378.

[4]Edward Gibbon, The Decline and Fall of the Roman Empire (New York, 1963), pp. 262-263.

[5]Against Rufinus, p. 81.

[6]On Corinthians I, p. 41.

[7]Contra Celsum, pp. 340, 467.

[8]Divine Institutes, pp. 170, 187.

[9]On I Corinthians, pp. 36, 37.

[10]On Corinthians I, pp. 9, 11, 12, 26.

[11]On the Bondage of the Will, p. 296.

[12]On Corinthians II, p. 380; Institutes, pp. 47-48.

[13]On Corinthians II, pp. 370-371, 370, n.3.

[14]Laws, I, 315.

[15]Laws, II, 88-89, 22; I, 315.

[16]Valdes, p. 15.

[17]Valdes, pp. 17, 21.

[18]On Timothy & Titus, p. 297.

[19]On I Timothy & II Timothy, pp. 173-174; On Philippians & Colossians, pp. 180-181; and On Corinthians I, pp. 100, 114.

[20]Contra Celsum, p. 128.

[21] Luther, On Romans, p. 136; Calvin, Institutes, I, 68.

[22] YP, I, 826.

[23] Divine Institutes, p. 366. See also p. 170 for his condemnation of man's arrogant wisdom.

[24] On Timothy, Titus & Philemon, p. 9.

[25] Arthur H. Beattie, trans., In Defense of Raymond Sebond (New York, 1959), pp. vi-vii.

[26] Defense, pp. 17-18.

[27] On Romans, p. 44; On Corinthians, p. 17.

[28] Institutes, I, 341.

[29] The Stromata, or Miscellanies, pp. 303, 304, 305.

[30] Cerfaux, Christian , pp. 262, 265.

[31] The Instructor, pp. 218-219.

[32] Stromata, p. 446; Ch. XIV; p. 554.

[33] Editor's "Elucidations," Stromata, p. 557.

[34] Stromata, pp. 418, 433, 320.

[35] On Corinthians I, p. 89.

[36] Stromata, pp. 494, 495.

[37] Stromata, pp. 311, 312, and 358.

[38] Stromata, p. 324, n. 1.

[39] Against Heresies, p. 508 and Chapter XXVI.

[40] On Corinthians I, p. 262.

[41] City of God, II, 256-257.

[42]On Corinthians I, p. 100; On Romans, p. 45.

[43]On Corinthians I, p. 273.

[44]The Enchanted Glass: The Elizabethan Mind in Literature (Oxford, 1966), p. 26.

[45]A. Cleveland Cox, ed., Irenaeus Against Heresies, p. 324, n. 3.

[46]Contra Celsum, p. 129; Rudolph Bultmann, Theology, I, 241, defines the Hellenistic seeking after wisdom as, according to Paul, the knowledge after or according to the flesh.

[47]On Romans, p. 12; On Galatians, Vol. 27 (1535), pp. 139-140.

[48]On Corinthians II, p. 127; On Philippians & Colossians, pp. 197-198; On Corinthians I, p. 73.

[49]On Corinthians I, pp. 81-82.

[50]On Corinthians II, p. 323.

[51]Valdes, p. 24.

[52]Animadversions, YP, I, 704-705.

[53]Renaissance Hero, pp. 71-74.

[54]Dennis H. Burden, The Logical Epic: A Study of the Argument of Paradise Lost (Cambridge, Ma., 1967), pp. 119-121, regards this pursuit as futile because it is irrelevant and impracticable.

[55]Complete Poetical Works, p. 391, n. 886.

[56]Paul, p. 98.

[57]"Concerning Envy," Ascetical Works, p. 477.

[58]See Howard Schultz, Milton and Forbidden Knowledge (New York, 1955), pp. 192, 193, 207.

288

[59] Works, XVII, 31, 33, 35.

[60] Defense of Raymond Sebond, p. 17.

[61] The Seven Books of History Against the Pagans, trans. Roy J. Defarrari (Washington, D.C., 1964), p. 229.

[62] On Corinthians I, p. 90.

[63] On Romans, pp. 87, 90, 92, 98.

[64] William R. Parker, Milton: A Biography (Oxford, 1968), I, 388.

[65] Milton and the Renaissance Hero (Oxford, 1967), see especially p. 36.

[66] YP, I, 524-525, n. 24.

[67] YP, I, 830-831.

[68] YP, IV, p. 189.

[69] YP, I, 824.

[70] YP, I, 826-830.

[71] YP, I, 833.

[72] YP, I, 848, 849-850.

[73] Works, VI, 24, 33.

CHAPTER SIX

THE ADAM-CHRIST PARALLEL AND THE SEED OF EVE

One of the basic Pauline themes which lends itself to symbolic and dramatic expression is the inverted correspondence between Adam as sinner and Christ as savior, the one causing the death and corruption of mankind and the other renewing the soul of man both collectively and individually. John Mulder has remarked how popular was this notion since it was formulated in editions of Nowell's Catechism during the seventeenth century.[1] Anne Davidson Ferry sees the parallel as a "sacred metaphor" for reading Paradise Lost in that Adam represents mankind, and John M. Steadman states that "In basing the propositions of both epics [PR and PL] on the Pauline formulation of the parallel between Adam and Christ, Milton gives greater stress on the problem of merit and on the significant aspects of human nature--its subjection to original sin through Adam and its regeneration through the merits of Christ."[2] Indeed one of the major foci of the Reformation was the theological belief that Christ's death and resurrection, and not human works, were responsible for the justification of the human soul. For Calvin and Luther there was room for little else since man was such a despicable creature as to lie beyond the pale, but Milton did not go to such extremes, ever mindful of the place of reason and will, as well as faith in Christ, in the divine plan.

The nucleus of the Adam-Christ pattern appears in the fifth chapter of Romans:

For if by one man's offence death reigned by one; much more they which receive abundance of grace and of the gift of righteousness shall reign in life by one, Jesus Christ.

Therefore as by the offence of one judgment came upon all men to condemnation; even so by the righteousness of one the free gift came upon all men unto justification of life.

For as by one man's disobedience many were made sinners, so by the obedience of one shall many be made righteous. (17-19)

291

Paul was fond of antitheses like these to express the
mystery of Redemption because of the rhetorical training he more than likely received at Tarsus. Basically,
the parallel asserts that Christ compensates for the
sin of Adam by removing the effects of that sin and
restoring man and offering him a chance at salvation.
The concept is often formulated in terms of "the old
man" and "the new man," and the emphasis fixes on the
victory of life over death through resurrection achieved by the obedience of Christ, which negates the disobedience of Adam. Obedience represents one of the
main themes of both Paradise Lost and Paradise Regain'd,
as one might expect, but Milton further calls attention to two other elements. In the former poem love
is added to obedience, and in the latter the obedience
becomes an example for all men to emulate. This is
why in Of Christian Doctrine, as Maurice Kelley notices, Milton insists that Christ "should be very man"
and not just God in disguise.3 The addition of these
two elements distinguishes Milton from Reformers like
Calvin and Luther who strongly urge faith over love
and equally strongly discount the effects of man's
actions in achieving justification. Milton refuses
to abandon the humanistic concept of man as an image
of God, as portrayed in Genesis, no matter how tar-
nished.

Some of the early Church Fathers had noted the
relationship between the first man (Adam's name in
Hebrew connotes man) and Christ, who became man.
Irenaeus' Against Heresies explicitly states this
growing belief of his day:

> . . . but when He became incarnate, and was made
> man, He commenced afresh the long line of human
> beings, and furnished us, in a brief, comprehensive
> manner, with salvation; so that what we had lost
> in Adam--namely, to be according to the image and
> likeness of God--that we might recover in Christ
> Jesus. . . . it was not possible that the man
> who had once for all been conquered, and who had
> been destroyed himself through disobedience,
> could reform himself, and obtain the prize of
> victory.4

Irenaeus iterates the positive aspect of Christ's

292

contribution--that he brought salvation, but Athanasius, taking a more primitive view, defines the
destruction of sin and the serpent through the anointing of Christ. "For as when Adam had transgressed,
his sin reached unto all men, so, when the Lord had
become man and had overthrown the Serpent . . . that
the Lord . . . should be anointed and Himself sent,
that, He, being and remaining the same, by taking
this alterable flesh, 'might condemn sin in it'."[5]
Jerome accused the Pelagians of refusing to see "the
perfect man in Christ lest they be forced to accept
the sins of man in Him."[6] Cyprian observed that "the
Apostle declares that the first man is from the slime
of the earth but the second from heaven," and Chrysostom interpreted Paul's use of the term earthly to
describe Adam as "gross, nailed down to things present."[7] Tertullian, in keeping with his concept of
a corporeal soul, distinguished between the "soul-
informed body" of Adam and the spirit-informed body
of Christ since "the first Adam was made into a soul
and the last Adam into a spirit," so too man's body
follows the same pattern.[8] Whatever the perspective,
however, Christ was envisioned in his dual aspect as
God-man, the theanthropos, who somehow through his
being "very man," as Milton later put it, compensates
for the first man's sin. Augustine felt confident
that "as we fell into this misery by one man's sin, so
shall we ascend unto that glory by one divine Man's
righteousness," an assertion with which Chrysostom
agreed.[9]

There didn't seem to be much argument either in
the early church or in the Reformation on the question
of Christ's redeeming mankind. More debatable, however, was the question of the restoration of man while
still here on earth. Genesis had portrayed Adam as
being created in God's image, but Adam's Fall defaced
or destroyed that image entirely. What, then, was
the impact of Christ's death and resurrection on man
as the mirror of God?

Irenaeus believed that the Father's "hands formed
a living man in order that Adam might be created
(again) after the image and likeness of God."[10] In
the Reformation Calvin avers that God made man in his
image, "as in a mirror," but the image was "defaced by

sin," and for him the "new man" of the Epistles is
not Christ but the man regenerated by Christ. Calvin's view of regeneration and justification sees
those processes as beginning during man's lifetime
but not being consummated during his life. The only
purpose of Christ's taking on humanity was the freeing of man from sin.[11] Calvin's severe view is reflected in this statement in the Institutes:

> There is no doubt that Adam, when he fell from
> his state, was by this defection alienated from
> God. Therefore, even though we grant that God's
> image was not totally annihilated and destroyed
> in him, yet it was so corrupted that whatever
> remains is frightful deformity. Consequently,
> the beginning of our recovery of salvation is in
> that restoration which we obtain through Christ,
> who also is called the Second Adam for the reason
> that he restores us to true and complete integrity.
> For even though Paul, contrasting the lifegiving
> spirit that the believers receive from Christ
> with the living soul in which Adam was created
> (I Cor. 15:45), commends the richer measure of
> grace in regeneration, yet he does not remove
> that other principal point, that the end of
> regeneration is that Christ should reform us to
> God's image.

Glossing Hebrews 1.3, Calvin interprets the word heir
with reference to Christ as establishing a relationship
through which Christ can "restore" what Adam lost for
man.[12]

Milton's emphases in the Adam-Christ equation
depart from Luther's and Calvin's. In Tetrachordon,
arguing for divorce, he repeats the customary belief
that Christ had restored man, but he goes further and
includes in the restoration all that Adam had lost:
"Wisdom, Purity, Justice, and rule over all creatures,"
hardly Calvin's "frightful deformity." In Paradise
Lost Milton follows the Genesis story closely in the
creation of man in God's image. The Father speaks to
the Son about his intentions:

"Let us make now man in our image, man
In our similitude, and let them rule
Over the fish and fowl of sea and air." (VII. 519-
521)

The angels sing in praise of man created by God "in his image" (VII.627), and significantly for Milton the agent of Creation is the Son, portrayed by St. Paul as "being the brightness of his ⌊God's⌋ glory, and the express image of his person" (Heb. 1.3), and likewise by Milton as "The radiant image of his glory" (PL. III.63). Thus another pattern in the Adam-Christ motif emerges in that both man and the Son, later the Christ, are the image of God the Father. In Paradise Lost the Son created man in his Father's image while at the same time being God's image as well, and by the divine economy he is made man in order to restore mankind to the image of God and thus make man parallel to himself. Perfect Christians, as Juan Valdes points out, "proceed to lay aside the image of Adam, and to recover the image of Christ and the image of God."[13]

Another symbolic pattern within the Adam-Christ parallel is the life-death contrast between Adam and Christ which includes the resurrection as a facet of the lifegiving of Christ. Paul had expressed it succinctly: "For as in Adam all die, even so in Christ shall all be made alive" (I Cor. 15.22), and more subtly, "The first man Adam was made a living soul; the last Adam was made a quickening spirit" (I Cor. 15.45). The first Adam is made alive, but the second gives life. Irenaeus comments on the last passage: "As, then, he who was made a living soul forfeited life when he turned aside to what was evil, so, on the other hand, the same individual, when he reverts to what is good, and receives the quickening spirit shall find life." And so, for Irenaeus, "death is at the same time destroyed."[14] Ambrose, interpreting I Corinthians 15.22, adds the element of resurrection: "So, then, as the firstfruits of death were in Adam, so also the firstfruits of the resurrection are in Christ."[15] St. Augustine realizes that death had entered not only Adam but all men, but he also concludes that death is "made the ladder whereby to ascend to life."[16]

Calvin accepts the tradition of Christ's destruction of death and emphasizes the qualities of restoration and resurrection:

As, therefore, Adam did not die for himself alone, but for us all, it follows that Christ in like

manner, who is the antitype, did not rise for
himself alone; for he came, that he might restore
everything that had been ruined in Adam. . . .
The cause of death is Adam, and we die in him:
hence Christ, whose office it is to restore to
us what we lost in Adam, is the cause of life to
us; and his resurrection is the ground-work and
pledge of ours.17

Michael Servetus combined the motifs of captivity and
death and sin and hell in that Adam was responsible
for plunging man into all three states, but with the
Reformation's preoccupation with faith, Servetus visu-
alizes Christ as raising man out of his deplorable
condition and into heaven.18

In _Paradise Lost_ Satan, Sin, and Death are associated, and Satan in fact is the author of both Sin and
Death, but until the Fall of Man they are confined to
hell. It is Adam's responsibility that Sin and Death
are released on the world, and the connection between
these two is traditionally recognized in the phrasing
and conception of mortal sin, "mortal sin/Original"
(IX.1003). After she eats the apple, Eve is recognized
by Adam as being "Defaced, deflow'red, and now to death
devote!" (IX.901). Ironically, in order to seduce Adam
to follow her, she coaxes him with the senseless remark:

On my experience, Adam, freely taste,
And fear of death deliver to the winds. (IX.988-989)

The Father sends the son to Paradise to judge the
guilty pair and the serpent, "And th' instant stroke
of death, denounced that day" (X.210). Sin invites
Death along with her to earth after she scents the
change on earth:

Thou my shade
Inseparable must with me along;
For Death from Sin no power can separate. (X.249-
251)

Death replies that he is only too happy to invade the
earth and effect the destruction he enjoys so much,
and he is compared to a vulture who looks forward to
the carnage of a battlefield.

Book Twelve, in Michael's relation of events to

296

come, depicts the events of Christ's life and the con-
frontation between Satan and Christ, which Adam mis-
understands. Michael explains that the Saviour will
come to destroy Satan's works in man, but the evil one
will still have the power "to give thee thy death's
wound" which "thy Saviour shall recure" (XII.392-393).
Michael goes on to illuminate Adam:

> This Godlike act
> Annuls thy doom, the death thou shouldst have died,
> In sin for ever lost from life; this act
> Shall bruise the head of Satan, crush his strength,
> Defeating Sin and Death, his two main arms. (XII.
> 427-431)

Thus the victory of Christ-Adam over death is not to
be construed in a physical but in a spiritual sense--
the mortality of sin will be defeated--a new definition
of heroism.

The victory is executed through the proto-evangelium vehicle of Eve's seed which receives special powers
in Genesis. In speaking to the serpent, God announces:
"I will put enmity between thee and the woman, and
between thy seed and her seed; it shall bruise thy
head, and thou shalt bruise his heel" (3.15). Paul
succinctly comments: "And the God of peace shall
bruise Satan under your feet shortly" (Rom. 16.20).
The providential plan includes a chance for woman to
make recompense for her original sin, as Calvin sees
it. "Hence," he says, "it follows that Christ was
begotten of mankind, for in addressing Eve it was God's
intention to raise her hope that she should not be over-
whelmed with despair." He urges that the seed is literal and not metaphorical.[19] Michael Waddington
remarks how "the motif of death as the fruit of the
Fall . . . is balanced by the promise of deliverance
through the Seed of Woman."[20]

The seed, whether poetical in the epic or literal
in Calvin's theology, represents a major element in
the closing of Paradise Lost because it provides the
link between the fallen Adam and the eventually risen
Christ. Adam first thinks of it when discussing the
future with Eve after the Fall in the context of a
prayer he had uttered to the Father. He recalls "His

promise, that thy seed shall bruise our foe" (XI.155).
In Book Twelve Michael mentions the seed (XII.125-126)
in relation to the theme of the "one just man" of the
Old Testament who speaks out against evil, just as
Abdiel had done in Book Six. At this stage of Michael's
revelation, Adam, yet confused, needs more elucidation,
and Michael relates the story of Abraham:

> "This ponder, that all nations of the earth
> Shall in his seed be blessed; by that seed
> Is meant thy great Deliverer, who shall bruise
> The Serpent's head; whereof to thee anon
> Plainlier shall be revealed." (XII.147-151; see also
> XII.230-235)

Michael then informs Adam that the seed will become a
king of the house of David (XII.325-330), and finally
Adam comprehends the plan of salvation:

> "O prophet of glad tidings, finisher
> of utmost hope! now clear I understand
> What oft my steadiest thoughts have searched in
> vain,
> Why our great Expectation should be called
> The Seed of Woman: Virgin Mother, hail,
> High in the love of Heav'n, yet from my loins
> Thou shalt proceed, and from thy womb the Son
> Of God Most High; so God with man unites.
> Needs must the Serpent now his capital bruise
> Expect with mortal pain." (XII.375-384)

Milton, not content with the emphasis on the seed so
far mentioned, iterates its importance in the Last
Judgement, when the Saviour will "dissolve / Satan
with his perverted world" (XII.546-547). The providential plan of salvation is then not simply an
arbitrary fiat of a divine tyrant but a complex web
which involves man, even down to the smallest detail
of his seed. In Chapter One the symbol of the seed
was explored as a natural metaphor for the resurrection
of the body, another indication of the meticulousness
and economy of providence.

A further antithesis is developed in the Epistles,
that between the new man and the old man, and the
definition of this pair of terms varies with the commentator. Paul urges the Ephesians to "put on the new

man, which after God is created in righteousness and true holiness" (4.24), and the Colossians to "put on the new man, which is renewed in knowledge after the image of him that created him" (3.10). Ambiguities abound in the interpretation to be given to the old and the new man; generally the old man is Adam and the new Christ, or the old is man before justification and the new is the redeemed man. In either case, Christ stands at the center of salvation or conversion. For St. Jerome "the old Adam dies completely in the laver of baptism, and a new Adam arises with Christ in baptism; . . . the man of clay dies, and the super-celestial man is born."[21] John M. Steadman, distinguishing between the old man-new man contrast and the Adam-Christ contrast, sees Milton as focusing on the latter in his heroes, and it is indeed difficult to find in Milton's writings any references to the old man-new man concept.[22]

In the Reformation the old man is man who sins in Adam, and the new is redeemed through the grace of Christ. In one place Luther sees a correspondence between the old Adam and the new Christ in that the former is trapped by the Law and the latter is "delivered" by Christ. In another place the Reformer equates "the old Adam" with "the desires of the flesh,"[23] and such an equation is consistent because for Luther and most of his contemporaries the Law claimed that it could offer salvation through the works of the flesh, through all the devices that canon law (the old Mosaic law writ large for the Reformers) offered to justify man, such as pilgrimages, masses, indulgences, etc. But for Calvin and Luther these could no more justify man than the works of the Law during Paul's time. In his commentary on Galatians, Luther parallels "the flesh or the old man" and the Law and "the spirit of the new man [which] is joined to the promise and to grace."[24] For Calvin the second Adam becomes a "life-giving spirit" (I Cor. 15.45), and the process of regeneration is outlined by the metaphor of the old man-new man, which is the difference in this case between man's fallen condition and his regenerated self through Christ, "the image of God that had been disfigured and all but obliterated through Adam's transgression."[25] Paul Bayne repeats the idea of the

revitalization of man through the Second Adam. Bayne
also agrees with Calvin that Christ is the "medium of
grace" in the Augustinian tradition in opposition to
Adam who was the medium of guilt. Such a doctrine could
not brook the Counter-Reformation and medieval adula-
tion of Mary as the mediatrix of grace since this doctrine militated against the role assigned to Christ.[26]
Calvin extends the distinction between Adam as old and
Christ as new man, suggesting a kind of spiritual
schizophrenia: "In two persons, Adam and Christ, he
[Paul] describes what may be called two natures. As
we are first born of Adam, the depravity of nature
which we derive from him is called the Old man; and
as we are born again in Christ, the amendement [sic]
of this single nature is called the New man."[27] Thus
the terms old and new man take on a subtle yet profound meaning in the plan of Redemption.

For St. Paul Christ not only delivered man from
the sin of Adam, he also executed salvation through a
human virtue--obedience, to negate the disobedience of
the first man. In this way salvation was made possible,
and in this way each man can achieve his salvation by
imitating the obedience of Christ. As Paul says, "For
as by one man's disobedience many were made sinners,
so by the obedience of one shall many be made righteous" (Rom. 5.19), and "his servants ye are to whom
ye obey; whether of sin unto death, or of obedience
unto righteousness" (Rom. 6.16), and finally "And
being found in fashion as a man, he humbled himself,
and became obedient unto death, even the death of the
cross" (Phil. 2.8). Those who obey sin will find
death, as did Adam, and paradoxically Christ obeyed
his Father unto the death of the cross in order to
find life for mankind. Elias Andrewes contrasts the
motives of Adam and Christ in the Pauline formula in
that Adam's pride leads to his fall, while Christ's
humility leads to his sacrifice.[28] Thus Adam, total
man, in seeking to be God, disobeys, while the second
Adam, divine and human, in his humility obeys the
Father and accepts the role assigned to him, unlike
both Adam and Milton's Satan in Paradise Lost, who cannot accept their station.

300

The correlation between Christ's obedience and
his humility as opposed to Adam's disobedience and
self-interest appears in the Church Fathers and again
in the Reformation. St. Jerome employs the concept
as an argument against the Pelagians; speaking through
his persona, Atticus, he says that Christ, "though he
was by nature God, did not consider being equal to God
a thing to be clung to, but he emptied himself, taking the nature of a slave, becoming obedient unto
death, even to the death on a cross," an obvious para-
phrase of the kenosis of Philippians 2.8.[27] C.A.
Patrides explains how this focus on obedience in the
Adamic parallel led to one early theory of the atonement, the recapitulation theory, and notes how Justin
Martyr supported this theory.[29]

Calvin refers to the obedience of Christ frequently,[30] but his attention doesn't focus on the
example that Christ provides for man so that he can
exercise this virtue. Rather, he iterates the point
that it is Christ's obedience alone which saves mankind. Man is reconciled to God on the following condition:

> that man, who by his disobedience had become
> lost, should by way of remedy counter it with
> obedience, satisfy God's judgment, and pay the
> penalties for sin. Accordingly, our Lord came
> forth as true man and took the person and the
> name of Adam in order to take Adam's place in
> obeying the Father, to present our flesh as the
> price of satisfaction to God's righteous judge-
> ment, and, in the same flesh, to pay the penalty
> that we had deserved.[31]

John Colet suggests a different orientation in that
man is able to determine his own salvation (with the
help of Christ) through the virtue of obedience, which
was illustrated by Christ: "And hence, that the righteousness and obedience of Christ has far more power
to recall to God men who are to be recalled, than the
sin and disobedience of Adam had to call them away
from God. For without doubt virtue is a much more
life-giving thing than sin is deadening, and the Author
of virtue far more powerful than the cause of sin."[32]
Paul Bayne contrasted Adam's storing up of guilt as opposed to Christ's storing up obedience. Philip Airay

commented that Christ's obedience fulfilled the
demand of the Mosaic law: "For as in the disobedience of Adam there was transgressio legis unde facti
sumus peccatores, sic in obedientia Christi fuit
impletio legis, unde sumus justi, the transgression
of the law, whereby we are made sinners, so in the
obedience of Christ there was the fulfilling of the
law, whereby we are made sinners, so in the obedience
of Christ there was the fulfilling of the law, whereby we are made just."[32] For Philip Melanchthon, who
was preoccupied with the concept and habit of obedience, Redemption is based fundamentally on the obedience of Christ, although man is created for the purpose of obeying God nevertheless: "The Mediator's
entire obedience, from his Incarnation until the
Resurrection, is the true justification which is
pleasing to God, and is the merit for us."[34]

Milton views obedience as necessary for justification for man, and Christ's obedience provides a
model, as seen in Paradise Regain'd, for men to emulate. Moreover he is concerned with the interrelationship between obedience and love, as it is demonstrated
in Christ's obeying his Father and loving man in the
same act of Redemption in Paradise Lost. For Calvin
and some other Reformers, this connection, between
love and obedience, was not a primary feature of
their theology. C.A. Patrides claims that "Obedience
to God has traditionally been interpreted in the light
of the divine love revealed in and through Christ."[35]
This may be true in general, but an examination of
commentaries on the Pauline Epistles, from St. John
Chrysostom to Luther and Calvin, does not reveal this
tradition explicitly, particularly commentaries in the
Reformation. Whether the reason for this absence is
due to the Reformation's difficulties with Paul's concept of love which had been distorted by the Middle
Ages into a doctrine of works for their own sake is
difficult to determine. Certainly outside the commentaries on Paul the correlation between love and obedience is both suggested and stated. Augustine interpreted the man-for-man scheme of Redemption as a
result of God's "free pity" for man so that the sin
of the whole human race could be removed.[36] Richard
Hooker makes a humane and reassuring comment on why

302

God loves man in the context of Christ as second
Adam: "The sons of God have God's own natural Son as
a second Adam from heaven, whose race and progeny
they are by spiritual and heavenly birth. God therefore loving eternally his Son, he must needs eternally
in him have loved and preferred before all others them
which are spiritually sithence descended and sprung
out of him."[37] Milton states in <u>Of Christian Doctrine</u>
that "obedience and love are always the best guides
to knowledge," and he cites Romans 5.19 on the contrast between Adam's and Christ's obedience.[38]

In <u>Paradise Lost</u> and <u>Paradise Regain'd</u> the theological combination of love and obedience in Christ
are clearly and powerfully dramatized. The opening
lines of the former poem state explicitly the major
theme:

> OF MAN'S first disobedience, and the fruit
> Of that forbidden tree, whose mortal taste
> Brought death into the world, and all our woe,
> With loss of Eden, till one greater Man
> Restore us . . . .(I.1-5)

Milton, following both the ransom and satisfaction
theories of atonement, makes a distinction between
obedience and love in the Son in order to elevate
obedience over love in this particular context in
Book Three. Obedience to God is regarded as superior
to love for mortal men and not to be confused with
love of God. St. Augustine said that man can love God
and then do whatever he wants, but here the Son's
obedience to the Father is expressed through the vehicle of love for mankind:

> His words here ended, but his meek aspect
> Silent yet spake, and breathed immortal love
> To mortal men, above which only shone
> Filial obedience: as a sacrifice
> Glad to be offered, he attends the will
> Of his great Father. (III.266-271)

The Son offers himself as one man for another, the
second Adam for the first, but accordingly he must
assume human flesh. The Father tells the Son:

> Thou therefore, whom thou only canst redeem,
> Their nature also to thy nature join;

        And be thyself man among men on earth,
        Made flesh, when time shall be, of virgin seed,
        By wondrous birth; be thou in Adam's room
        The head of all mankind, though Adam's son.
        As in him perish all men, so in thee
        As from a second root shall be restored
        As many as are restored; without thee, none.   (III.
        281-289)

In this light, Paul Bayne remarks that Adam had a
"natural nativity" while Christ's was supernatural.[39]

        Adam and Eve had been amply warned by Raphael
about their responsibilites to their Creator, which at
one point are phrased as an equation of obedience and
love:

        Be strong, live happy, and love, but first of all
        Him whom to love is to obey, and keep
        His great command . . . . (VIII.633-635)

Loving God is identical with obeying God, but loving
man, or in Adam's case, loving woman, may sometimes
conflict with love of and obedience to God. When Adam
romantically and literally falls in love with Eve,
Eve defines it as a "glorious trial of exceeding love,"
a parody of the Son's love (III.410), as Douglas Bush
points out.[40] Michael Waddington beautifully summarizes the positive shift of Adam to Christ in Book
Twelve:

        The symbolic baptism ⌊from Michael's prophecy and
        his own tears⌋ which Adam has undergone implies
        purification by the death of his fallen nature,
        regeneration of the spirit, and movement toward
        union with Christ. The thematic division between
        first Adam and second Adam . . . dictates a shift
        . . . Adam must turn from this deadly fruit to
        the seed of new life growing within, to faith and
        love as he strives to recreate his spirit in the
        successive images of the "one greater man."[41]

        The obedience-disobedience theme appears again
and in explicit fashion with the opening of Paradise
Regain'd:

I WHO erewhile the happy garden sung,
By one man's disobedience lost, now sing
Recovered Paradise to all mankind,
By one man's firm obedience fully tried
Through all temptation, and the Tempter foiled
In all his wiles, defeated and repulsed,
And Eden raised in the waste wilderness. (I.1-7)

It is no wonder that this theme would receive sharp
prominence in the poem since the Son acts in his
human capacity, as a man who is in the process of
epiphany, of discovery that he is divine (though not
equal with the Father) and that his obedience will
redeem man and set a perfect example of perfect obedience by the perfect man. The Son is presented as
"th'exalted man". (I.36), and as Don Cameron Allen
observes, "We must, consequently, think of the
'exalted man' as forgetful of his divinity, of his
victory in Heaven, of his sacrificial offer, or its
foreordained fulfillment."42 Indeed we must, or else
both the dramatic interest of the poem and the validity of the example of his obedience are lost on the
human reader. The Son of _Paradise Regain'd_ is not
the same character as the Son of _Paradise Lost_.

One of Satan's weaknesses is his inability to
perceive the essential difference between tempting
Eve, thereby destroying the loyalty of Adam indirectly,
and seducing the Son. His confidence because of his
past success will prove to be mistaken:

I, when no other durst, sole undertook
The dismal expedition to find out
And ruin Adam, and the exploit performed
Successfully: a calmer voyage now
Will waft me; and the way found prosperous once
Induces best to hope of like success. (I.100-105)

His infernal companions commit the "enterprise" to his
care for the same reason. After tempting the Son with
bread, Satan undergoes an education similar to the
Son's in that he begins to be somewhat aware that the
parallel between Adam (and Eve) and the Son is not
precise:

I . . .
Have found him, viewed him, tasted him, but find

Far other labor to be undergone
Than when I dealt with Adam first of men,
Though Adam by his wife's allurement fell,
However to this man inferior far, . . .
Therefore I am returned, lest confidence
Of my success with Eve in Paradise
Deceive ye to persuasion over-sure
Of like succeeding here . . . .(II.129-143)

The comments of the narrator cheer on the Son as hero
and indicate that the dimensions of the temptation are
radically different from Satan's past experiences.
The bard looks back nostalgically to Eve's naivete and
forward hopefully to the discrimination of the new
protagonist:

Alas how simple, to these cates compared,
Was that crude apple that diverted Eve! (II.348-
349)

The crudeness and obviousness of the rhetoric that sway-
ed Eve (di-verted or turned her away from the true
path)   are contrasted with the persuasiveness that
Satan directs toward the seduction of the Son, and
the narrator's anti-feminist bias gets the better of
him. The rhetoric had

                        . . . won so much on Eve,
So little here, nay lost; but Eve was Eve,
This far his overmatch, who, self-deceived
And rash, beforehand had no better weighed
The strength he was to cope with, or his own.
                        (IV.6-9)

In Paradise Lost Eve had exuded a foolish self-
confidence and underestimated her enemy, but in Paradise Regain'd the Son has a mind like a steel trap,
able to intuit the giver and the purpose of the gift-
giving, none of which Eve could do. The reader never
knows what Adam's reaction might have been to Satan
because he was overcome with "female charm" and not
by reptilian cunning. It is a measure of the growth
of the hero in the later epic that he realizes how
monstrous is the idea of Satan tempting him when he
comprehends that he is the Son of God in more than a
metaphorical sense:

And dar'st thou to the Son of God propound
To worship thee accurst, now more accurst
For this attempt bolder than that on Eve,
And more blasphemous? Which expect to rue.
(IV.178-181)

Satan therefore fails because he is unable to fathom
and appreciate the difference between Adam and Christ.

Thomas Jacomb perhaps best summarizes the equation
of Adam and Christ in the perspective of the Reformation as he related this motif to the mystical body of
Christ which provides a kind of mechanism drawing man
to God in a regenerated state:

> There is the first Adam, and all the unregenerate
> seed are united to him as their head; and upon
> their union with this head, they derive nothing
> but guilt and wrath and condemnation. Then there
> is the second Adam, Christ Jesus, and all the
> regenerate seed are united to him as their head;
> and he, by virtue of union also, communicates
> pardon of sin, peace with God, justification,
> eternal life, &c. Both of these Adams and pub-
> lic heads proceed by the law, and upon the terms
> of union; for the first Adam could do us no hurt,
> were we not descended out of his loins, and in
> him as our common head; and so the second Adam
> can do us no good, unless we be made one with
> him and in him as our head also.[43]

NOTES: CHAPTER SIX

[1] _Temple of the Mind_, p. 122.

[2] _Renaissance Hero_, p. 191. Anne Davidson Ferry, _Milton's Voice: The Narrator in Paradise Lost_, (Cambridge, Ma., 1963), pp. 94-95.

[3] _This Great Argument_, p. 159.

[4] _Against Heresies_, p. 446.

[5] _Discourse I_, p. 336.

[6] _Against the Pelagians_, p. 262.

[7] Cyprian, p. 142.

[8] _Treatise_, pp. 159, 161.

[9] _City of God_, II, 337; Chrysostom, _On Romans_, pp. 150-151.

[10] _Against Heresies_, p. 527.

[11] _On Galatians & Ephesians_, p. 296; _Institutes_, p. 472.

[12] _Institutes_, I, 189; _On Hebrews_, p. 34.

[13] Juan Valdes, p. 37.

[14] _Against Heresies_, pp. 538, 457.

[15] _Belief in Resurrection_, p. 189.

[16] "Enchiridion," p. 673; _City of God_, I, 3.

[17] _Institutes_, I, 248; _Commentary . . . Corinthians_, p. 25.

[18] _Righteousness_, p. 256.

[19] _Institutes_, I, 478.

[20]"The Death of Adam: Vision and Voice in Books XI and XII of _Paradise Lost_," _MP_, 70 (1972), 12.

[21]_Against Rufinus_, p. 105.

[22]_Renaissance Hero_, p. 70.

[23]_On Romans_, p. 93; _On Galatians_, p. 84.

[24]_On Galatians_, p. 7.

[25]_Institutes_, I, 539, 600-601.

[26]_Commentary_, pp. 143, 50.

[27]_Meaning_, pp. 157-158.

[28]_Against the Pelagians_, p. 266.

[29]"Milton and the Protestant Theory of the Atonement," _PMLA_, 74 (1959), 7. Prof. Patrides in _Milton and the Christian Tradition_, p. 132, remarks how the obedience theme grows in Irenaeus, Justin Martyr, and Anselm.

[30]_Institutes_, I, 531, 735, 753.

[31]_Institutes_, I, 466.

[32]_On Romans_, p. 10.

[33]Bayne, _Commentary_, p. 50; Airay, _On Philippians_, p. 120.

[34]_Loci Communes_, pp. 181, 161.

[35]_Christian Tradition_, p. 161.

[36]"Enchiridion," p. 687.

[37]_Laws_, II, 228.

[38]_Works_, XIV, 25; XVI, 27. According to Burton O. Keith (_Milton and Christian Humanism_ [Hamden, Ct., 1966], p. 82), the Redemption was an act of mercy.

[39]Commentary, p. 30.

[40]Poetical Works, p. 392.

[41]Waddington, p. 21.

[42]Harmonious Vision, (Baltimore, 1954), p. 117.

[43]Sermons, p. 51.

CHAPTER SEVEN

THE PAULINE TRADITION IN PARADISE LOST

As we have seen, Milton's use of both Pauline concept and symbol establishes firmly the degree of influence which "that transcendent apostle" exercised on the poet. The multifarious associations of various themes and symbols reunite together in myriad combinations to form later religious and poetic vision. This study closes on the manner in which one such configuration of moral and religious virtues is symbolically represented. As yet no critic or scholar has demonstrated the profound effect on Paradise Lost of Paul's emphasis on the virtues of faith, love, and obedience and his imaging these virtues through metaphors of harmony.

The thirteenth chapter of First Corinthians, the nucleus of Paul's exaltation of charity, describes it in terms of harmony and its violation in terms of discord:

> Though I speak with the tongues of men and of angels, and have not charity, I am become as sounding brass, or a tinkling cymbal. (13.1)

> And so abideth faith, hope, charity, these three; but the greatest of these is charity. (13.13)

Paul further associates faith and charity together as essential to the performance of God's will. In Thessalonians 3.6 he compliments his flock by indicating that Timothy has just arrived with "good tidings of your faith and charity," and he advises Timothy elsewhere to "Flee also youthful lusts: but follow righteousness, faith, charity, peace, with them that call on the Lord out of a pure heart" (II Tim. 2.22). In another epistle to Timothy (I Tim. 1.5-6), he emphasizes the interrelationship of love or charity and faith and its metaphorical opposite, discord or noise: "Now the end of the commandment is charity out of a pure heart, and of a good conscience, and of faith unfeigned: From which some having swerved have turned aside unto vain jangling." St. John Chrysostom points up the "senseless and inanimate" nature of "sounding brass" and the phenomenon of chaos and disorder.[1]

311

Ultimately Paul provides an answer to those critics
like Waldock, Empson, and Peter who complain about
the Father's legalism in Paradise Lost since one of
the basic themes of the epic is that "Love worketh no
ill to his neighbour: therefore love is the fulfilling of the law" (Rom. 13.10). In the epic there is
no contradiction between the requirements of divine
justice and the generosity of divine love, for the
Son offers himself to fulfill the demands of both.

The Pauline equation appears in simple terms:
God's creatures must love him and have faith in him,
and they manifest this love through obedience to his
will; the antithesis of the love of God is hate, and
those who hate God have no faith in him and wilfully
disobey him. Paul consistently enjoins obedience and
takes a dim view of those who disobey God: "In flam-
ing fire taking vengeance on them that know not God,
and that obey not the gospel of our Lord Jesus Christ"
(II Thess. 1.8). Satan literally hates God, and the
poem demonstrates the fallen angel's motivation
repeatedly in these terms, and the "Adversary," Satan,
therefore suffers. God, the Father, the prototype of
man, loves his creatures and wants them to love him
without constraint. The Father defends himself on
the basis of the Pauline virtues:

> Not free, what proof could they have giv'n sincere
> Of true allegiance, constant faith or love,
> Where only what they needs must do, appear'd,
> Not what they would? What praise could they
> receive?
> When will and reason (reason also is choice)
> Useless and vain, of freedom both despoiled,
> Made passive both, had served necessity,
> Not me. (III.103-111)

One of Paul's primary theological axioms is that the
Redemption freed man from a strict adherence to the
letter of the Old Law, thus allowing man Christian
freedom: "for the letter killeth, but the spirit
giveth life" (II Cor. 3.6). The Doctor of the Gentiles further insists, "But now we are delivered from
the law, that being dead wherein we were held; that
we should serve in newness of spirit, and not in the
oldness of the letter" (Rom. 8.6).

Don Cameron Allen has remarked how Milton's concept of "the harmonious vision" of man living at peace
with himself and God is based upon the Pythagorean
notion of harmony which depends upon virtue. Man has
lost his virtue since the Golden Age and can only hear
the sound of celestial harmony when he possesses an
ethical wholeness. In Paradise Lost, Professor Allen
observes, Milton invests Eden with music to equate it
with the Golden Age. Sin destroys "nature's chime,"
but heaven represents the acme of harmony. "Sinless
vision, in Milton's mind, was the companion of sinless
music."[2] Herbert Agar also related the Platonic conception of order in the soul and order in the government to Milton's thinking.[3] Chrysostom had suggested
the fierce animosity between the power of evil and
charity: "For sooner would the grass endure the appli-
cation of fire, then the devil to the flame of charity."[4]
More precisely pertinent to Milton's epic than classical or Pythagorean conceptions is Paul's equating love
and harmony and sin and disharmony, respectively, in
the poem. In the context of the Creation, Nathaniel
Culverwell's vision of God's Creation and the disorder
of the Fall is worth noting: "When God first tun'd
the whole creation, every string, every creature
praised him; but man was the sweetest and loudest of
the rest, so that when that string apostatized, and
fell from its first tuning, it set the whole creation
a jarring."[5]

    Imagery of sound and music in Milton's poem pos-
sesses ethical nuances when depicting places, char-
acters, and situations; thus Chaos, hell, Satan, the
battle in heaven, Adam and Eve immediately after the
Fall, and man after the Fall (in Michael's prophecy)
are characterized by discord, while heaven, Eden
before the Fall, the Son, heaven, the creation, Adam
and Eve before the Fall and during their reconciliation
are typified by metaphoric harmony. The source of this
imagery may be both the Pythagoreans and Paul, in that
Paul may have been influenced by the Greek tradition
or that Milton was influenced by both. However, the
emphasis in Paradise Lost on the correlation between
faith, love, and obedience, and harmony suggests that
St. Paul is the dominant factor.

The transformation of the rebellious angels to
devils is revealed by the manner in which they lose
the sweetness and harmony they once possessed. Harmony involves balance and proportion, qualities which
gradually vanish from hell. As Thomas Kranidas perceived, "Hell, like Heaven, has light, motion, music--
'order.' But the unity in Hell is in process of dis-
persing, the energy is dissipating, the light is
wasting. The motion of Hell is out to dispersion,
not out to impregnation and return," and "The 'grasped
Arms / Clash'd on thir sounding Shields the din of war'
surely is loud, and it echoes."[6] The noise of hell is
loud indeed, with its "Sonorous metal blowing Martial
sounds" (I.540), but more subtle is the specious psy-
chological effect on the fallen angels of the Dorian
music played

> . . . to mitigate and swage
> With solemn touches, troubl'd thoughts, and chase
> Anguish and doubt and fear and sorrow and pain
> From mortal or immortal minds. (X.556-559)

Milton was so successful with this brazen music that
Isabel Gamble MacCaffrey had to warn readers that
"Noise, other than the sound of Dance or Song" (VIII.
243) is dominant in Books One, Two, and Six and that
this pattern is not typical of all of Milton's musical imagery.[7] These books depict the activities of
hell and the war in heaven.

Even the fallen angels' singing suggests their
moral debilitation: in heaven they had worshipped God
in concord with their singing, but in hell they begin
to lose their vocal talents along with their ethical
integrity. At first they retain their harmony:

> Their song was partial, but the harmony
> (What could it less when Spirits immortal sing?)
> Suspending Hell, and took with ravishment
> The thronging audience. In discourse more sweet
> (For eloquence the soul, song charms the sense).
> (II.552-556)

The reader, however, had been earlier warned about
the pleasant sounds in hell at the creation of Pande-
monium (now a synonym for disorderly noise):

314

> Anon out of the earth a fabric huge
> Rose like an exhalation, with the sound
> Of dulcet symphonies and voices sweet. (I.710-712)

Milton did not accidentally repeat "dulcet" and "sweet"
in the same line but was hinting at the excessive,
saccharine nature of the singing. The final sound the
bad angels utter is ugly hissing, their response to
the fall of man in Book Ten. In Book Two, after the
decision to seduce man, the announcement of the strategy is made with trumpets fashioned from alloys:

> Toward the four winds four speedy Cherubim
> Put to their mouths the sounding alchemy. (II.516-
> 517)

The phrase, "sounding alchemy," echoing Paul's
"sounding brass," seems apt since the horns were made
from the minerals scooped out of the bowels of hell,
an action which symbolizes the destructive disorder of
the hellions. Even their movements are dangerously
uncontrolled:

> A multitude, like which the populous North
> Poured never from her frozen loins, to pass
> Rhene or the Danaw, when her barbarous sons
> Came like a deluge on the South, and spread
> Beneath Gibraltar to the Libyan sands. (I.351-355)

They are "Poured" like barbarians, without control
over their own movement because they have abdicated
moral responsibility. They allow the debate, rigged
by Satan, to control their fate, and then ironically
they sing about predestination.

The fallen angels decide to follow their leader,
who, as one of God's creatures, should love him, but
instead chooses to hate and become "as sounding brass
or a tinkling cymbal." His motivation is hate, the
opposite of love or charity: the "study of revenge,
immortal hate" (I.107), as he puts it. Moloch, less
cautious, counsels "Desparate revenge, and battle
dangerous / To less than gods" (II.107-108). Beelzebub, as Satan's stooge, proposes a plan "devised /
By Satan," one which emanates from

> . . . the author of all ill,
> So deep a malice, to confound the race

Of mankind in one root. (II.379-380, 381-383)

As Paul said, "Love worketh no ill to his neighbour," but here Satan decides to destroy a neighbor who has done him no harm. On the basis of Revelation 9.11, Gilbert Murray, Isabelle MacCaffrey, Denis de Rougement, and Merritt Y. Hughes have all seen the appropriateness of the term, "the Destroyer," for Satan.[8] He, John S. Diekhoff, succinctly notes, "has come, not from love but from hate; not to exchange Hell for Paradise but to lay waste Paradise; not to taste pleasure but to destroy all pleasure save that only pleasure left for him the pleasure of destruction."[9] In the light of Professor Diekhoff's comment, it is interesting to speculate whether Milton considered having Satan entertain the thought of sexually deflowering Eve instead of seducing her through symbolic sexual overtones. That he did not lends support to the argument that Satan is indeed a destructive nihilist, who is interested more in ruin than in pleasure.

When, in Book Three, the Father views Satan raging on earth, he notices how there are no limits or controls on him, intimating how he is out of control like a madman:

"Only begotten Son, seest thou what rage
Transports our Adversary? Whom no bounds
Prescribed, no bars of hell, nor all the chains
Heaped on him there, nor yet the main abyss
Wide interrupt can hold; so bent he seems
On desperate revenge, that shall redound
Upon his own rebellious head." (III.80-86)

Satan's lack of psychic harmony, his confusion of values, becomes apparent when words and ideas become meaningless and chaotic, when he confuses love and hate. He asks himself,

Whom hast thou then or what to accuse,
But Heav'n's free love dealt equally to all?
Be then his love accurst, since love or hate,
To me alike, it deals with eternal woe. (IV.67-70)

Michael's words to Adam about man accurately portray what has happened to this almost demented angel:

Reason in man obscured, or not obeyed,
Immediately inordinate desires
And upstart passions catch the government
From reason, and to servitude reduce
Man till then free.   (XII.86-90)

Satan's intuitive reason is as disoriented as man's
discursive powers. Paul had warned the Galatians
throughout his fourth epistle about servitude to sin
under the Mosaic Law: "But now, after that ye have
known God, or rather are known of God, how turn ye
again to the weak and beggarly elements, whereunto ye
desire again to be in bondage?" (Gal. 4.9). Satan's
boastful freedom is, in reality, servitude to his
vicious impulses, although he creates his own law,
his own servitude.

A measure of the lack of harmony and the disorder
in Satan's mind is his perversion of the proper response to God's love and mercy. He loses faith in
himself as a redeemable soul:

For never can true reconcilement grow
Where wounds of deadly hate have pierced so deep;
Which would but lead me to a wors relapse
And heavier fall: so should I purchase dear
Short intermission bought with double smart.
                              (IV.98-102)

He allows himself the costly luxury of ingenious
rationalizations which obscure the cause of his agony:
his lack of faith in and love of God. He has explanations for everything "but faith which worketh by love"
(Gal. 7.6). Pride, which puffs up the fallen angels,
opposes love (I Cor. 13.4), and, as C.A. Patrides
observes, this distinction appears in Augustine's antithesis of <u>caritas</u> and <u>cupiditas</u>.[10] Satan fights the
impulse to love Adam and Eve after he is impressed by
their beauty:

Creatures of other mold, earth-born perhaps,
Not Spirits, yet to heav'nly Spirits bright
Little inferior; whom my thoughts pursue
With wonder, and could love, so lively shines
In them divine resemblance. . . .   (IV.360-364)

However, he perverts his potential love and decides
to destroy Adam and Eve. In his soliloquy before
seducing Eve, he candidly explains his motivation in

317

terms of hate, although he separates himself from his
thoughts, as if he were not responsible for them, an
indication that "inordinate desires" and "upstart
passions" have bewildered his thinking:

> Thoughts, whither have ye led me, with what sweet
> Compulsion thus transported to forget
> What hither brought us? Hate, not love, nor hope
> Of Paradise for hell, hope here to taste
> Of pleasure, but all pleasure to destroy,
> Save what is in destroying; other joy
> To me is lost. (IX.473-479)

In an examination of imagery of sexual perversion in
the poem, John T. Shawcross works on the assumption
that "love is . . . the theme of the poem" and traces
the perversion of Satan's relationship with Sin.[11]
Thus Satan's disruption of spiritual harmony, based
upon his refusal to love God, can be seen on several
levels. He does not understand God's motivation and
fails to see that

> . . . all his malice served but to bring forth
> Infinite goodness, grace and mercy shown
> On man by him seduced, but on himself
> Treble confusion, wrath and vengeance poured.
> (I.217-220)

Despite Satan's perversion of God's love to hate, he
becomes the unwilling occasion for more divine love.

It is no surprise that the War in Heaven represents the discord of hate on a political and military
level, and Milton's language conveys the chaos with
graphic concreteness:

> The adverse legions, nor less hideous joined
> The horrid shock. Now storming fury rose,
> And clamor such as heard in heav'n till now
> Was never; arms on armor clashing brayed
> Horrible discord, and the madding wheels
> Of brazen chariots raged; dire was the noise
> Of conflict; overhead the dismal hiss
> Of fiery darts in flaming volleys flew,
> And flying vaulted either host with fire.
> (VI.206-214)

The magnitude of the rupturing of "concord" in heaven
is indicated in the account of the battle between

318

Michael and Satan, which was

> . . . such commotion; such as (to set forth
> Great things by small) if, Nature's concord broke,
> Among the constellations war were sprung,
> Two planets rushing from aspect malign
> Of fiercest opposition in mid sky,
> Should combat, and their jarring spheres confound.
> (VI.310-315)

Through the device of prolepsis, the battle seemed an

> Infernal noise; war seemed a civil game
> To this uproar; horrid confusion heaped
> Upon confusion rose. And now all heav'n
> Had gone to wrack, with ruin overspread,
> [had not the Father intervened.] (VI.667-670)

Satan's forces attempt to turn heaven into hell, and
so it is just and necessary that the Son drive them
into hell.

Satan becomes the promoter of disorder, which
makes it fitting that Chaos, "the Anarch old," wishes
him well:

> "If that way be your walk, you have not far;
> So much the nearer danger; go and speed;
> Havoc and spoil and ruin are my gain." (II.1007-09)

To counterbalance the advancement of confusion and
disorder caused by the fall of the angels, the Father
performs the act of Creation, an act of divine love
opposing the act of angelic hate. The epic voice relates how

> I saw when at this word the formless mass,
> This world's material mold, came to a heap:
> Confusion heard his voice, and wild uproar
> Stood ruled, stood vast infinitude confines;
> Till at his second bidding darkness fled,
> Light shone, and order from disorder sprung.
> (III.708-713)

On the cosmic level, then, the drama between love--
order and hate -disorder is played. Northrop Frye
establishes the link between Creation and the harmonious worship of God by the loyal angels:

The activity of God, of which the central form
is creation, is regularly symbolized in Milton
by music, though music in Milton has its larger
Platonic meaning which includes poetry. We may
think of creation as the restraining of chaos by
order: this metaphor of 'harmony,' in the sense
of a stable relationship of parts to a whole.
There is 'harmony' in heaven, symbolized by the
songs of the angels, and when Christ moves into
chaos and creates order the angelic music accom-
panies the act. Creation itself takes the form
of spheres, harmoniously moving with a music
that Adam could hear before his fall.[12]

The one element in the Pauline equation lacking
here is obedience. The angels in heaven obey and
worship God through their harmonious singing, without tension between serving and loving God. As St.
Paul put it, "His servants ye are to whom ye obey;
whether of sin unto death, or of obedience unto
righteousness" (Rom. 6.16). We have seen what happens when Satan obeys the temptation to sin, but the
loyal angels express their harmony with God through
their song:

Then crowned again their golden harps they took,
Harps ever tuned, that glittering by their side
Like quivers hung, and with preamble sweet
Of charming symphony they introduce
Their sacred song, and waken raptures high;
No voice exempt, no voice but well could join
Melodious part, such concord is in heav'n.
(III.365-371)

Raphael explains to Adam this juxtaposition of
love and obedience which seems contradictory to Satan
because he hates God and cannot obey him. Raphael
relates the angelic posture toward God in order to
indicate to Adam how he must behave:

Myself and all the angelic host that stand
In sight of God enthroned, our happy state
Hold, as you yours, while our obedience holds;
On other surety none; freely we serve,
Because we freely love, as in our will
To love or not; in this we stand or fall.
(V.535-540)

320

God's creatures can obey him only if they love him and can only love him if they obey him. In Milton's view, the equation is just.

The Son provides the means of Redemption and a model for both angels and men to follow because he is divine love. C.A. Patrides has shown how Luther and the other Reformers tended to distinguish the Father as representing the demands of justice from the Son as symbolizing the offering of love. Milton's Son follows this tradition, for his face reflects "Divine compassion . . . / Love without end" (III.141-142).[13] Innumerable passages in Book Three, which might be called the Book of Love, validate this portrayal,[14] but one or two can demonstrate how intimately connected is obedience to love. When the Son offers himself to redeem mankind, he does so by joining obedience to his Father and love toward mankind:

> His words here ended, but his meek aspect
> Silent yet spake, and breathed immortal love
> To mortal men, above which only shone
> Filial obedience: as a sacrifice
> Glad to be offered, he attends the will
> Of his great Father. (III.266-271)

The Son's sacrifice results in the balancing of the scale of mercy and justice through the undoing of Satan's hate:

> So heav'nly love shall outdo hellish hate,
> Giving to death, and dying to redeem,
> So dearly to redeem what hellish hate
> So easily destroyed, and still destroys
> In those who, when they may, accept not grace.
>   (III.298-302)

The equation of obedience and love in the Redemption is iterated at the end of the poem when Michael tells of the future sacrifice:

> The law of God exact he shall fulfill
> Both by obedience and by love, though love
> Alone fulfill the law; thy punishment
> He shall endure by coming in the flesh
> To a reproachful life and curse death.
>   (XII.402-406)

321

Maurice Kelley cites _Of Christian Doctrine_ to clarify
why Christ must die for man. Milton there quotes St.
Paul: "there are reasons most distinctly assigned in
Scripture, why Christ should be very man. I Cor.
xv.21 'for since by man came death, by man came also
the resurrection of the dead.' . . . Finally, God
would not accept any other sacrifice as any other
would have been less worthy."[15]

Before the Fall of Man, Adam and Eve lived in
harmonious bliss because sin had not yet entered the
world. As Don Cameron Allen points out, there were
sounds of pleasant music in Paradise, a Miltonic addition to Hexaemeral tradition. Before Eve was created,
Adam had complained of a lack of proper harmony because he was alone, with only animals as his company.
He asked the Father:

> "Among unequals what society
> Can sort, what harmony or true delight?
> Which must be mutual, in proportion due
> Giv'n and received; but in disparity,
> The one intense, the other still remiss
> Cannot well suit with either, but soon prove
> Tedious alike." (VIII.383-389)

Douglas Bush notices how the words _intense_ and _remiss_
contain a musical metaphor which suggests Adam's
awareness of the lack of harmony in his situation.[16]
The Father is pleased that Adam can sense this dis-
proportion and so creates Eve. The love of the first
parents seems idyllic:

> Our two first parents, yet the only two
> Of mankind, in the happy garden placed,
> Reaping immortal fruits of joy and love,
> Uninterrupted joy, unrivaled love,
> In blissful solitude. (III.65-69)

As C.M. Bowra remarks, "The harmony of Adam and Eve
is the earthly counterpoint of the harmony that reigns
in Heaven; it is complete and satisfying because it is
based on love."[17] Adam, nevertheless, becomes intoxi-
cated by Eve's charms, and while appreciating her
beauty and grace, he reveals his weakness:

> "So much delights me as those graceful acts,
> Those thousand decencies that daily flow

From all her words and actions, mixed with love
and sweet compliance, which declare unfeigned
Union of mind, or in us both one soul;
Harmony to behold in wedded pair
More grateful than harmonious sound to the ear.
Yet these subject not." (VIII.600-607)

Adam claims that these attractions do not subject him,
but events prove otherwise. Raphael warns him about
this defect, and as the angel leaves the earthly pair,
he advises them in terms of the emphases of St. Paul:

"Be strong, live happy, and love, but first of all
Him whom to love is to obey, and keep
His great command; take heed lest passion sway
Thy judgment to do aught which else free will
Would not admit." (VIII.633-637)

John S. Diekhoff demonstrates how often the obligation
of the couple to obedience is mentioned in the poem.[18]

Isabelle MacCaffrey has called attention to the
imagery of storm and confusion which characterizes the
fallen Adam and Eve:[19]

They sat them down to weep; nor only tears
Rained at their eyes, but high winds worse within
Began to rise, high passions, anger, hate,
Mistrust, suspicion, discord, and shook sore
Their inward state of mind, calm region once
And full of peace, now tossed and turbulent;
For understanding ruled not, and the will
Heard not her lore, both in subjection now
To sensual appetite, who from beneath
Usurping over sovran reason claimed
Superior sway. (IX.1121-1131)

This storm imagery results from their loss of love for
God and for each other, a condition caused by their
disobedience:

Love was not in their looks, either to God
Or to each other, but apparent guilt,
And shame, and perturbation, and despair
Anger, and obstinacy, and hate, and guile.
(X.111-114)

Just as Satan becomes perverted through his abandon-
ment to hate, Adam and Eve pervert love. Eve begins

323

by claiming she will prove her love for him by condemning him to death:

> Confirmed then I resolve,
> Adam shall share with me in bliss or woe,
> So dear I love him, that with him all deaths
> I could endure, without him live no life.
> (IX.830-833)

Adam unconsciously parodies the Son's proof of love, (III.410) when he decides, in the true romantic tradition, to fall with Eve:

> So Adam and thus Eve to him replied:
> "O glorious trial of exceeding love,
> Illustrious evidence, example high!" (IX.960-962)

Eve goes on to extol Adam and his "happy trial of thy love," even telling him a lie in the process--that she would rather die than hurt him.

Their reconciliation occurs only through love, and Eve balances her specious love with true penitence to Adam and to God:

> "Forsake me not thus, Adam, witness Heav'n
> What love sincere and reverence in my heart
> I bear thee, and unweeting have offended
> Unhappily deceived; thy suppliant
> I beg, and clasp thy knees; bereave me not
> Whereon I live, thy gentle looks, thy aid,
> Thy counsel in this uttermost distress,
> My only strength and stay." (X.914-921)

Adam also realizes that only through love can they exist:

> But rise, let us no more contend, nor blame
> Each other, blamed enough elsewhere, but strive
> In offices of love, how we may light'n
> Each other's burden in our share of woe.
> (X.958-961)

Unfortunately for their posterity the harmony has been broken, and Michael's prophecy alludes to two incidents in history which prove the rupture, the Tower of Babel and Nimrod's rise to power. Nimrod will "quite dispossess / Concord and law of Nature from the earth" (XII.28-29), and at the Tower God causes

> . . . a jangling noise of words unknown
> Forthwith a hideous gabble rises loud
> Among the builders; each to other calls
> Not understood, till hoarse and all in rage,
> As mocked they storm; great laughter was in heav'n
> And looking down, to see the hubbub strange
> And hear the din; thus was the building left
> Ridiculous, and the work Confusion named.
> (XII.55-62)

The way back to happiness and harmony is through the paradigm offered by St. Paul's Epistles: that to love God is to obey him and have faith in his Providence. Adam comprehends this lesson finally and in response to Michael relates these Pauline injunctions to the major theme of the poem:

> Henceforth I learn that to obey is best,
> And love with fear the only God, to walk
> As in his presence, ever to observe
> His providence, and on him sole depend,
> Merciful over all his works, with good
> Still overcoming evil, and by small
> Accomplishing great things, by things deemed weak
> Subverting worldly strong, and worldly wise
> By simply meek; that suffering for truth's sake
> Is fortitude to highest victory,
> And to the faithful death the gate of life.
> (XII.561-571)

Milton's important theme of the weak overcoming the strong finds support in Paul (as we have seen): God's plan involves those virtues which the Apostle stressed over and over, virtues belonging to the weak. Michael tells Adam to

> ". . . add faith,
> Add virtue, patience, temperance, add love
> By name to come called charity, the soul
> Of all the rest; then wilt thou not be loth
> To leave this Paradise, but shalt possess
> A paradise within thee, happier far." (XII.582-587)

Thus charity, "the greatest of these," provides man a means of achieving "the harmonious vision" he lost at the Fall, a vision which will be internal and spiritual; in contrast to Satan's inner hell, which he has assidously cultivated by substituting hate, for love, its antithesis. Throughout _Paradise_ _Lost_ theme and imagery have been interwoven to demonstrate this dramatic opposition.

NOTES: CHAPTER SEVEN

[1] *On Corinthians, Part Two*, p. 442.

[2] *Harmonious Vision*, pp. xxv, xviii.   See also Leo Spitzer, "Classical and Christian Ideas of World Harmony," *Traditio*, 2 (1944), 409-464; 3 (1945), 307-364.   Spitzer's brilliant article mentions Paul only indirectly in the tradition of harmony and *consonantia*.

[3] *Milton and Plato* (Princeton, 1928), pp. 17-18. He states that Milton did not fully absorb the Platonic notion of harmony but that he was just "playing" with it.

[4] *On Corinthians, Part Two*, p. 455.

[5] Quoted in *Christian Tradition*, p. 109.

[6] *The Fierce Equation*, pp. 112, 115.

[7] *Paradise Lost as "Myth"* (Cambridge, Ma., 1959), p. 156.

[8] See Hughes, "Satan and the 'Myth' of the Tyrant," *Essays in English Literature from the Renaissance to the Victorian Age*, ed. Millar MacLure and F.W. Watt (Toronto, 1964), p. 127.

[9] *Milton's Paradise Lost: A Commentary on the Argument* (New York, 1958), p. 42.

[10] *Christian Tradition*, p. 171.

[11] "The Metaphor of Inspiration in *Paradise Lost*," *Th'Upright Heart and Pure: Essays on John Milton . . .*, ed. Amadeus P. Fiore, O.F.M. (Pittsburgh, 1967), pp. 79-80.

[12] "The Breaking of the Music," *The Return of Eden: Five Essays in Milton's Epics* (Toronto, 1965), p. 47.

[13] "Milton and the Protestant Theory of the Atonement," p. 10.

[14]See *PL*. III. 222-226 and 401-411.

[15]*This Great Argument*, p. 159.

[16]*Complete Poetical Works*, n. *PL*. VIII.383-389.

[17]Quoted in Patrides, *Christian Tradition*, p. 168.

[18]*Milton's Paradise Lost: A Commentary*, p. 51.

[19]*Paradise Lost as "Myth,"* pp. 140-141. She perceives that even Paradise is not completely ruled and is inordinate and that the word *rule* is important to appreciate in *PL* (pp. 142-143, 153-154).

BIBLIOGRAPHY

Agar, Herbert. <u>Milton</u> <u>and</u> <u>Plato</u>. Princeton, 1928.

Airay, Philip. <u>Lectures</u> <u>Upon</u> <u>the</u> <u>Whole</u> <u>Epistle</u> <u>of</u> <u>St</u>. <u>Paul</u> <u>to</u> <u>the</u> <u>Philippians</u>. Edinburgh, 1864.

Allen, Don Cameron. <u>The</u> <u>Harmonious</u> <u>Vision</u>. Baltimore, 1954.

Ambrose, St. <u>Some</u> <u>of</u> <u>the</u> <u>Principal</u> <u>Works</u>. Trans. Rev. H. DeRomestin. New York, 1896.

Andrewes, Elias. <u>The</u> <u>Meaning</u> <u>of</u> <u>Christ</u> <u>for</u> <u>Paul</u>. New York, 1949.

<u>Apologetical</u> <u>Works</u> <u>and</u> <u>Minucius</u> <u>Felix</u> <u>Octavius</u>. Trans. Rudolph Arbersmann et al. New York, 1950.

<u>The</u> <u>Apostolic</u> <u>Fathers</u> <u>with</u> <u>Justin</u> <u>Martyr</u> <u>and</u> <u>Irenaeus</u>. American Edition. Ed. A. Cleveland Cox. New York, 1885.

Aquinas, Thomas St. <u>Commentary</u> <u>on</u> <u>St</u>. <u>Paul's</u> <u>Epistle</u> <u>to</u> <u>the</u> <u>Galatians</u>. Trans. F.R. Larcher. Albany, 1966.

------------------. <u>The</u> <u>Summa</u> <u>Theologiae</u> <u>of</u> <u>St</u>. <u>Thomas</u> <u>Aquinas</u>. Trans. Fathers of the Dominican Province, rev. Daniel J. Sullivan. Chicago, 1952.

Aristotle. <u>The</u> <u>Works</u>. Trans. and Ed. W.D. Ross et al. 2 Vols. Oxford, 1931.

Augustine, St. <u>Basic</u> <u>Writings</u>. Ed. Whitney J. Oates. 2 Vols. New York, 1948.

-------------. <u>City</u> <u>of</u> <u>God</u>. Trans. John Healey. Ed. R.V.G. Trasker. 2 Vols. London, 1967.

-------------. <u>Concerning</u> <u>the</u> <u>Teacher</u> <u>and</u> <u>On</u> <u>the</u> <u>Immortality</u> <u>of</u> <u>the</u> <u>Soul</u>. Trans. George G. Leckie. New York, 1938.

Barker, Arthur. <u>Milton</u> <u>and</u> <u>the</u> <u>Puritan</u> <u>Dilemma</u> <u>1641-</u> <u>1660</u>. Toronto, 1942.

--------------, ed. <u>Milton</u>: <u>Modern</u> <u>Essays</u> <u>in</u> <u>Criticism</u>. New York, 1965.

Basil, St. <u>Ascetical</u> <u>Works</u>. Trans. Sister M. Monica
    Wagner, C.S.C. New York, 1950.

Bayne, Paul. <u>An</u> <u>Entire</u> <u>Commentary</u> <u>Upon</u> <u>the</u> <u>Whole</u>
    <u>Epistle</u> <u>of</u> <u>St</u>. <u>Paul</u> <u>to</u> <u>the</u> <u>Ephesians</u>. . . . Ed.
    Rev. Thomas Smith. Edinburgh, 1866.

Bolton, Samuel. <u>The</u> <u>True</u> <u>Bounds</u> <u>of</u> <u>Christian</u> <u>Freedom</u>.
    London, 1964.

Bultmann, Rudolf. <u>The</u> <u>Old</u> <u>and</u> <u>New</u> <u>Man</u> <u>in</u> <u>the</u> <u>Letters</u>
    <u>of</u> <u>Paul</u>. Trans. Keith R. Crim. Richmond, 1967.

---------------. <u>Theology</u> <u>of</u> <u>the</u> <u>New</u> <u>Testament</u>.
    Trans. Kendrick Grobel. 2 Vols. New York, 1951.

Burden, Dennis H. <u>The</u> <u>Logical</u> <u>Epic</u>: <u>A</u> <u>Study</u> <u>of</u> <u>the</u>
    <u>Argument</u> <u>of</u> <u>Paradise</u> <u>Lost</u>. Cambridge, Ma., 1967.

Burton, Ernest DeWitt. <u>Spirit</u>, <u>Soul</u> <u>and</u> <u>Flesh</u>.
    Chicago, 1918.

Bush, Douglas. <u>Paradise</u> <u>Lost</u> <u>in</u> <u>Our</u> <u>Time</u>. Ithaca,
    1945.

Calvin, John. <u>Commentaries</u> <u>on</u> <u>the</u> <u>Epistles</u> <u>to</u> <u>Timo-</u>
    <u>thy</u>, <u>Titus</u>, <u>and</u> <u>Philemon</u>. Trans. William Pringle.
    Grand Rapids, 1948.

------------. <u>Commentaries</u> <u>on</u> <u>the</u> <u>Epistles</u> <u>of</u> <u>Paul</u>
    <u>to</u> <u>the</u> <u>Galatians</u> <u>and</u> <u>Ephesians</u>. Trans. William
    Pringle. Grand Rapids, 1948.

------------. <u>Commentary</u> <u>on</u> <u>the</u> <u>Epistle</u> <u>of</u> <u>Paul</u> <u>the</u>
    <u>Apostle</u> <u>to</u> <u>the</u> <u>Hebrews</u>. Trans. and Ed. Rev.
    John Owen. Grand Rapids, 1948.

------------. <u>Commentaries</u> <u>on</u> <u>the</u> <u>Epistles</u> <u>of</u> <u>Paul</u>
    <u>the</u> <u>Apostle</u> <u>to</u> <u>the</u> <u>Philippians</u>, <u>Colossians</u>, <u>and</u>
    <u>Thessalonians</u>. Trans. John Pringle. Grand
    Rapids, 1948.

------------. <u>Commentary</u> <u>on</u> <u>the</u> <u>Epistle</u> <u>of</u> <u>Paul</u> <u>the</u>
    <u>Apostle</u> <u>to</u> <u>the</u> <u>Corinthians</u>. Trans. Rev. John
    Pringle. 2 Vols. Grand Rapids, 1948.

------------. <u>Institutes</u> <u>of</u> <u>the</u> <u>Christian</u> <u>Religion</u>.
    Ed. John T. McNeill and Trans. Ford Lewis Bat-
    tles. 2 Vols. Philadelphia, 1960.

Cartwright, Thomas. <u>A</u> <u>Commentary</u> <u>Upon</u> <u>the</u> <u>Epistles</u>
    <u>of</u> <u>St</u>. <u>Paul</u> <u>Written</u> <u>to</u> <u>the</u> <u>Colossians</u>. Edinburgh,
    1964.

Cassirer, Ernst et al. The Renaissance Philosophy of Man. Chicago, 1948.

Cerfaux, Lucien. The Christian in the Theology of St. Paul. London, 1967.

Chrysostom, John St. Commentary on the Epistle to the Galatians, and Homilies on the Epistle to Ephesians. Trans. J.H.N. Oxford, 1840.

--------------------. The Homilies of S. John Chryso-stom, Archbishop of Constantinople, on the First Epistle of St. Paul the Apostle to the Corinthians. Trans. J.K. Part I. Oxford, 1839.

--------------------. The Homilies of S. John Chryso-stom, Archbishop of Constantinople, on the Epistles of St. Paul the Apostle to the Philip-pians, Colossians, and Thessalonians. Trans. C.M. Oxford, 1843.

--------------------. The Homilies of S. John Chryso-stom, Archbishop of Constantinople, on the Epistles of St. Paul the Apostle to Timothy, Titus, and Philemon. Trans. C.M. Oxford, 1843.

--------------------. In Praise of Saint Paul. Trans. Rev. Thomas Halton. Washington, D.C., 1963.

--------------------. Stromata in Ante-Nicene Chris-tian Library: Translations of the Fathers. Ed. Rev. Alexander Roberts and James Donaldson. Edinburgh, 1868.

Cochrane, Charles Norris. Christianity and Classical Culture: A Study of Thought and Action from Augustus to Augustine. London, 1957.

Cohon, S.S. Judaism: A Way of Life, An Introduction to the Basic Ideas of Judaism. New York, 1948.

Colet, John. An Exposition of St. Paul's First Epis-tle to the Corinthians. Trans. J.H. Lupton. Ridgewood, N.J., 1965.

-----------. An Exposition of St. Paul's Epistle to the Romans. Trans. J.H. Lupton. Ridgewood, N.J., 1965.

Craig, Hardin. The Enchanted Glass: The Elizabethan Mind in Literature. Oxford, 1966.

Cruden's Complete Concordance of the Old and New Testaments. Ed. A.D. Adams, C.H. Irwin, and S.A. Waters. New York, 1949.

Cyprian, St. Treatises. Trans. and Ed. Roy J. Defarrari. New York, 1958.

Deissman, Adolph. Light From the Ancient East. Trans. Lionel R. Strachan. New York, 1910.

----------------. Paul: A Study in Social and Religious History. Trans. William E. Wilson. London, 1926.

Dictionary of the Bible, Revised Edition. 1963.

Diekhoff, John. Milton's Paradise Lost: A Commentary on the Argument. New York, 1958.

Ellis, E. Earle. Paul and His Recent Interpreters. Grand Rapids, 1961.

Encyclopedia Dictionary of the Bible. 2nd Revised Edition. New York, 1963.

Fiore, Amadeus P. ed. The 'Upright' Heart and Pure: Essays on John Milton . . . . Pittsburgh, 1967.

Fixler, Michael. Milton and the Kingdoms of God. Evanston, 1964.

Frye, Northrop. The Return of Eden: Five Essays in Milton's Epics. Toronto, 1965.

Gibbon, Edward. The Decline and Fall of the Roman Empire. New York, 1963.

Gregory Nazianzen, St. and St. Ambrose. Funeral Orations. Trans. Leo P. McCawley, S.J. et al. New York, 1953.

Gohn, Ernest S. "The Christian Ethic of Paradise Lost and Samson Agonistes." SN, 34 (1962), 243-268.

Hailperin, Herman, ed. Gentile Reaction to Jewish Ideals. New York, 1953.

Heninger, Jr., S.K. Touches of Sweet Harmony: Pythagorean Cosmology and Renaissance Poetics. San Marino, 1974.

Hooker, Richard. Of the Laws of Ecclesiastical Polity. Intro. Christopher Morris. 2 Vols. London, 1963.

<u>Interpreter's</u> <u>Dictionary</u> <u>of</u> <u>the</u> <u>Bible</u>. 4 Vols. 1962.

Jacomb, Thomas. <u>Sermons</u> <u>on</u> <u>the</u> <u>Eighth</u> <u>Chapter</u> <u>of</u> <u>the</u>
    <u>Epistle</u> <u>to</u> <u>the</u> <u>Romans</u> in <u>Nichols</u> <u>Series</u> <u>of</u> <u>Com-</u>
    <u>mentaries</u>. Edinburgh, 1868. Vol. 10.

Jerome, St. <u>Dogmatical</u> <u>and</u> <u>Polemical</u> <u>Works</u>. Trans.
    John N. Hritzu. Washington, D.C., 1965.

Justin Martyr, St. <u>Writings</u>. Ed. Thomas B. Falls.
    New York, 1948.

Keith, Burton O. <u>Milton</u> <u>and</u> <u>Christian</u> <u>Humanism</u>.
    Hamden, Ct., 1966.

Kelley, Maurice. <u>This</u> <u>Great</u> <u>Argument</u>: <u>A</u> <u>Study</u> <u>of</u>
    <u>Milton's</u> De Doctrina Christiana <u>as</u> <u>a</u> <u>Gloss</u> <u>upon</u>
    <u>Paradise</u> <u>Lost</u>. Gloucester, 1962.

Kranidas, Thomas. <u>The</u> <u>Fierce</u> <u>Equation</u>: <u>A</u> <u>Study</u> <u>of</u>
    <u>Milton's</u> <u>Decorum</u>. London, 1965.

Lactantius. <u>The</u> <u>Divine</u> <u>Institutes</u>. Trans. Mary
    Francis McDonald. Washington, D.C., 1964.

Lewis, C.S. <u>A</u> <u>Preface</u> <u>to</u> <u>Paradise</u> <u>Lost</u>. London, 1942.

Lightfoot, J.B. <u>Horae</u> <u>Hebraicae</u> <u>et</u> <u>Talmudicae</u>:
    <u>Hebrew</u> <u>and</u> <u>Talmudical</u> <u>Exercitations</u>. 4 Vols.
    Oxford, 1859.

Luther and Erasmus: <u>Free</u> <u>Will</u> <u>and</u> <u>Salvation</u>;
    Erasmus, <u>De</u> <u>Libero</u> <u>Arbitrio</u>. Trans. and Ed.
        E. Gordon Rupp and A.W. Marlowe; and
    Luther, <u>De</u> <u>Servio</u> <u>Arbitrio</u>. Trans. and Ed.
        Philip S. Watson and B. Drewery. Phila-
        delphia, 1969.

Luther, Martin. <u>Commentary</u> <u>on</u> <u>the</u> <u>Epistle</u> <u>to</u> <u>the</u>
    <u>Romans</u>. Trans. J. Theodore Mueller. Grand
    Rapids, 1954.

<u>Luther's</u> <u>Works</u>. Ed. Jaroslav Pelikan and Walter A.
    Hansen. 51 Vols. St. Louis, 1958.

MacCaffrey, Isabel Gamble. <u>Paradise</u> <u>Lost</u> <u>as</u> "<u>Myth</u>."
    Cambridge, Ma., 1959.

MacLure, Millar and F.W. Watt, eds. <u>Essays</u> <u>in</u> <u>English</u>
    <u>Literature</u> <u>from</u> <u>the</u> <u>Renaissance</u> <u>to</u> <u>the</u> <u>Victorian</u>
    <u>Age</u>. Toronto, 1964.

Meeks, Wayne. "Paul as Heretic." Yale Divinity School
    course, 1972.

Melanchthon and Bucer, De Regno Christi in The Library
    of Christian Classics. Ed. Wilhelm Pauch. Phila-
    delphia, 1969.

Melanchthon on Christian Doctrine: Loci Communes,
    1555. Trans. and Ed. Clyde L. Manschreck. New
    York, 1965.

The Complete Poetical Works of John Milton. Ed.
    Douglas Bush. Boston, 1965.

Complete Prose Works of John Milton. Ed. Don M.
    Wolfe et al. 8 Vols. New Haven, 1953--.

The Works of John Milton. Ed. Frank A. Patterson.
    18 Vols. New York, 1933.

Mohl, Ruth. Studies in Spenser, Milton, and the
    Theory of Monarchy. New York, 1949.

Montaigne, Michael. In Defense of Raymond Sebond.
    Trans. Arthur H. Beattie. New York, 1959.

Mulder, John. The Temple of the Mind: Education and
    Literary Taste in Seventeenth-Century England.
    New York, 1969.

New Catholic Encyclopedia: An International Work of
    Reference. Nashville, 1967.

O'Keeffe, Timothy. The Function and Pattern of
    Imagery in Milton's Prose. Diss. New York Uni-
    versity 1967.

Origen. The Writings. Trans. Rev. Frederick Crombie.
    2 Vols. Edinburgh, 1869.

Orosius, Paulus. The Seven Books of History Against
    the Pagans. Trans. Roy J. Defarrari. Washing-
    ton, D.C., 1964.

Parker, William R. Milton: A Biography. 2 Vols.
    Oxford, 1968.

Patrides, C.M. Milton and the Christian Tradition.
    Oxford, 1966.

--------------. "Milton and the Protestant Theory of
    the Atonement." PMLA, 74, (1959), 7-13.

The Dialogues of Plato. Trans. Benjamin Jowett. 5 Vols. New York, 1892.

Plotinus, Enneads. Trans. Stephen McKenna. Rev. B.S. Page. Second Edition. New York, n.d.

Samuel, Irene. Plato and Milton. Ithaca, 1965.

Schultz, Howard. Milton and Forbidden Knowledge. New York, 1955.

Schweitzer, Albert. Paul and His Interpreters. London, 1912.

Sencourt, Robert G. Saint Paul: Envoy of Grace. London, 1948.

Sensabaugh, George F. "The Milieu of Comus." SP, 41 (1944), 238-249.

Servetus, Michael. The Two Treatises of Servetus on the Trinity. Trans. Earl Morse Wilburn in Harvard Theological Studies, XVI. Cambridge, Ma., 1932.

Spitzer, Leo. "Classical and Christian Ideas of World Harmony." Traditio, 2, (1944), 409-464; 3, (1945), 307-364.

Steadman, John M. Milton and the Renaissance Hero. Oxford, 1967.

Stollman, Samuel S. "Milton's Dichotomy of 'Judaism' and 'Hebraism'." PMLA, 89, (1974), 105-112.

Letters of Sulpicius Severus in A Select Library of Nicene and Post-Nicene Fathers of the Christian Church. 2nd Series. Trans. Philip Schaff and Henry Wace. New York, 1894.

Svendsen, Kester. Milton and Science. Cambridge, Ma., 1956.

----------------. "Science and Structure in Milton's Doctrine of Divorce." PMLA, 67, (1952), 435-445.

Tertullian's Treatise on the Resurrection. Trans. Ernest Evans. London, 1960.

Theological Dictionary of the New Testament. Grand Rapids, 1971.

Valdez, Juan. _Commentary Upon St. Paul's First Epistle to the Church at Corinth._ Trans. John T. Betts. London, 1883.

Waddington, Michael. "The Death of Adam: Vision and Voice in Books XI and XII of _Paradise Lost._" MP, 70, (1972), 10-21.

Wittreich, Joseph. _Visionary Poetics: Milton's Tradition and His Legacy._ San Marino, 1979.

Wrede, W. _Paul._ Trans. Edward Lummis. London, 1907.

Mohl, Ruth, 13
Moloch, fallen angel, 315
Mulder, John, 42, 291
Murray, Gilbert, 316
Nimrod, 324-325
Ovid, 33
Parker, William R., 280
Patrides, C.A., 180, 182, 242, 301, 302, 317, 321
Pauline Epistles and Acts of the Apostles
    Acts of the Apostles, 1, 3, 7-8, 100, 263
    Colossians, 49-50, 113, 116, 117, 206, 207, 211,
        213, 270-271, 299
    Corinthians I and II, 38, 48-49, 56-57, 67, 69,
        72-73, 80, 105, 118, 122, 127, 128, 130, 133,
        141, 145-146, 151, 167, 172, 183, 184, 185,
        187, 192, 194, 214, 220, 222, 231, 234-235,
        241, 244, 245, 256-257, 259, 261-262, 266, 267,
        268, 269, 270, 271, 280, 283, 295, 299, 311,
        317
    Ephesians, 123, 180, 207, 211, 212, 215, 226, 227,
        229, 234, 239-240, 243-244, 298-299
    Galatians, 30, 60-61, 99-100, 115, 117, 118, 121,
        123, 125, 128, 134, 139, 142, 146, 168, 172,
        176, 184, 185, 192, 267
    Hebrews, 109, 114, 168, 171, 174, 176, 192, 209
    Philippians, 51, 119, 123, 146, 269, 300, 301
    Romans, 47-48, 56, 107, 108, 112, 118, 123, 125,
        127, 133, 134, 137, 141, 142, 143, 145, 167,
        168, 173, 174, 176, 180, 183, 192, 206, 209,
        226, 227, 259, 271, 291, 300, 303, 312
    Thessalonians, 311, 312
    Timothy, 121, 184, 229, 311
    Titus, 180, 240, 262
Pauline Privilege, 243
Peter, Apostle, 100
Pharisee (definition), 2
Philo Judaeus, 23-24, 57, 191
phoenix, 74-76
Platonism, Neoplatonism, 4, 11, 19, 20-23, 26, 28, 34,
    39, 40, 50-51, 54, 62-63, 64-66, 69, 71, 81-82,
    84-85, 124, 236
Plotinus, 24-26
Pythagoras, 230

Melanchthon, Philip, 12, 14, 19, 32, 102, 110, 128, 131, 136, 139, 143, 174, 193, 221, 302
Montaigne, Michael, 265, 279
Paraeus, David, 150
Servetus, Michael, 52-53, 106, 131, 140-141, 144-145, 178, 186-187, 222-223, 226, 296
Valdez, Juan, 58, 71, 75, 83, 187, 211, 261, 272, 295
Zanchius, Hieronymus, 149, 151
Samuel, Irene, 19
Satan, 32, 41-42, 79, 126, 170, 247, 275-276, 277, 283-284, 285, 296, 297, 300, 305-306, 307, 312, 313, 315-320, 323
Schultz, Howard, 256
Schweitzer, Albert, 1, 10, 15, 68
Sensabaugh, George F., 39
Shawcross, John T., 318
Son, character in _Paradise Lost_ and _Paradise Regain'd_, 126, 175, 190, 191, 267, 268-269, 281, 284-285, 294-295, 302, 303-304, 305, 306, 307, 312, 313, 321
Spenser, Edmund, 19, 39
Steadman, John M., 273, 280, 299
Stein, Arnold, 273
Stollman, Samuel, 165
Svendsen, Kester, 203, 235
Torah, 2, 5, 23, 51-52, 99-100, 104 (false etymology), 105
Waddington, Michael, 304
Williams, Arnold, 132-133, 242
Wittreich, Joseph, 16
Wolfe, Don M., and William Alfred (editor of anti-episcopal tracts), 236, 281
Woodhouse, A.S.P., 65
Wrede, W., 278
Wyclif, John, 272, 281

343